JN 1 '8	DATE DUE		
MAR 25 '80			
JAN 22 '81			
OCT 30 1982			
MAR 3 1983			
JUL 3 1 1985			
OCT 7 1986			
JAN 3			

RIO GRANDE

...to the PACIFIC!

Donated By

Sundance Publications

RIO GRANDE
...to the PACIFIC!

By Robert A. LeMassena

SUNDANCE *Limited*
100 KALAMATH STREET
DENVER, COLORADO 80223

FRONTISPIECE . . .

As a class, the 3600's outlasted all other steam locomotives on the D&RGW. All 20 were still running in the summer of 1955 when this photograph was taken. On this occasion the 3605 was leaving Burnham with freight for Pueblo. This handsome 2-8-8-2 had only recently emerged from the shops, and was unusually resplendent in shiny black and aluminum trim. The mighty locomotive was making one of its last great offerings of coal smoke to the gods of the Shining Mountains.

COVER SCENE . . .

The last regular usage of the D&RGW's huge Class L105 4-6-6-4's was in freight service between Denver and Pueblo. The cover scene shows Number 3710 leaving Burnham yard for Pueblo in 1952. Weighing-in at 641,700-pounds, the last five of the railroad's L105's — numbers 3710-3714 — were among the heaviest 4-6-6-4's ever built. Constructed by Baldwin in 1942, the 3710 served the D&RGW for only 13 years, a relatively brief period when compared with many of the railroad's other steam engines.

RIO GRANDE

...to the PACIFIC!

By Robert A. LeMassena

The complete saga of the spectacular Denver & Rio Grande Western System—graphically presented in one magnificent volume.

SUNDANCE LTD. STAFF MEMBERS RESPONSIBLE FOR THE CREATION OF THIS BOOK . . .

Editor-in-Chief — Russ Collman

Production Manager — Dell A. McCoy

Editorial Assistant — Paula R. Erickson

Color Director — Peter E. Voorheis

Copy Staff — Carol Garcia, Eva Van Vors

Business Manager — Viva A. McCoy

Editorial Consultant — Jackson C. Thode

SECOND EDITION — FIRST PRINTING

PRINTED IN THE U.S.A. BY SUNDANCE LIMITED / DENVER.

FIRST EDITION — SPECIAL LIMITED VERSION — PRINTED JUNE, 1974 — ISBN 0-913582-09-2. SECOND EDITION PRINTED OCT., 1974 — ISBN 0-913582-10-7.

PREFACE

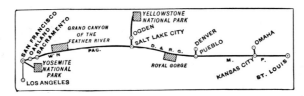

The "Rio Grande" railroad has been the subject of a great many publications, and deservedly so. It was no small enterprise. Whole volumes have been written about its financial affairs, corporate activities, construction, locomotives, trains, cars, traffic and scenery. The primary focus of most of this literature has been the Colorado company and its extensive and justly famous network of narrow-gauge track in the Rocky Mountains.

By comparison, the Utah lines have been neglected. Their origins, involving several independent narrow-gauge railroads, can be traced back to 1873, only two years after the Denver & Rio Grande commenced operating trains in Colorado. Furthermore, these small Utah companies were formed into a completely independent railroad company which retained its identity until absorbed by consolidation in 1908.

Even less appreciated is the Western Pacific Railroad (between Salt Lake City and the Pacific Coast), which was planned, financed and built by the Denver & Rio Grande, and included in its "system" by various corporate arrangements until 1947.

Should anyone entertain doubt that the Rio Grande system did indeed extend from Denver to the Pacific Ocean, he need only examine the Denver & Rio Grande public timetable for December, 1908. On the centerfold map the Western Pacific railroad is shown completed between Salt Lake City and Shafter, Nevada; tri-weekly passenger service had been inaugurated during the previous month. On the western end, WP rails extended northeastward from Oakland, California, into the mountains. The gap was scheduled for completion in 1909, but the first passenger train did not run over the entire line until August, 1910.

Subsequent timetables carried "Denver & Rio Grande—Western Pacific" on their covers, and the system map indicated both railroads were integrated into a single system. Schedules showed Denver - Oakland service, with two trains each way daily, bearing identical numbers on each line. Through sleeping cars were handled between Oakland and Denver, as well as St. Louis and Chicago. The unique and colorful "Descriptive Time Tables" issued in 1915 for the Panama - Pacific International Exposition in San Francisco, showed the two railroads united end-to-end, with a new train, the "Scenic Limited," running over their combined trackage.

By 1918 all that had changed. On the timetable route map the WP was indistinguishable from the Southern Pacific; it was only one more railroad in a long listing of through-car schedules. The D&RG had just been adroitly and completely looted of its tremendous investment and ownership in the WP, and the two lines were quite independent. Oddly, though, during the 1920's public timetables once again indicated that the WP and Denver & Rio Grande (Western) belonged to a common system, but the arrangement then was vastly different from the previous one. How the separation and reunion were accomplished is an intriguing episode in high finance.

Without its lines in Utah the original D&RG would have terminated in western Colorado, with survival wholly dependent on local traffic—truly a dubious prospect. Today the Utah lines are even more vital; branches originate enormous tonnages of coal and the main-line permits the railroad to operate as a high-speed bridge carrier across the Rocky Mountains. During the 1890's the Utah lines, which were then a rather independent corporation, came close to being divorced from the D&RG. How this trackage was acquired, rebuilt and finally merged into the Rio Grande system, heretofore treated only casually in other publications, now is delineated in detail.

Not only does this text include the most comprehensive account of the Western Pacific and Rio Grande Western railroad ever published, but it also presents material which has neither received mention in any previous history, nor even in the companies' annual reports. This concerns electrification—studies for which were commenced as early as 1906 and continued by either the railroad or outside organizations for five decades. Every imaginable reason was advanced for the electrification of certain trackage, the proposals ranging from the practical to the bizarre. An entire chapter is devoted to the several areas and schemes for electrification, none of which, (in the eyes of management) warranted the large expenditures which would have been required.

Unusual in the field of published railroad history is any detailed, coordinated examination of subsidiary companies; not infrequently they receive acknowledgment merely by name or are omitted entirely. The Rio Grande system embraced a great many such companies; 35 of them were of sufficient importance to be included here to show what they contributed to the final system. Some have been the subject of whole books, while others have not entered the public domain beyond recognition in ICC Valuation Reports. In addition, approximately 30 other railroad companies have been involved with the Rio Grande system in many different ways, ranging from disposition of a mile of track, to joint ownership and operation of an entire railroad facility. Mention of some of these companies can be found elsewhere, to be sure, but it is in this work that at last is incorporated a comprehensive exposition of their relationships.

This account of the Rio Grande system can be visualized in any of four different ways. It is a chronology of the development of the system's trackage—why it was built or bought, used, sold or abandoned. Motive power is traced in considerable detail, including the first complete compilation of RGW locomotives. The story of the railroad's activities can be read as one would read a novel, or the reader can discover how the system was assembled, company by company, each with its own peculiar contribution to the organization at the time.

However, to understand the system as it exists today, one must read the entire book. Again, it is no small enterprise.

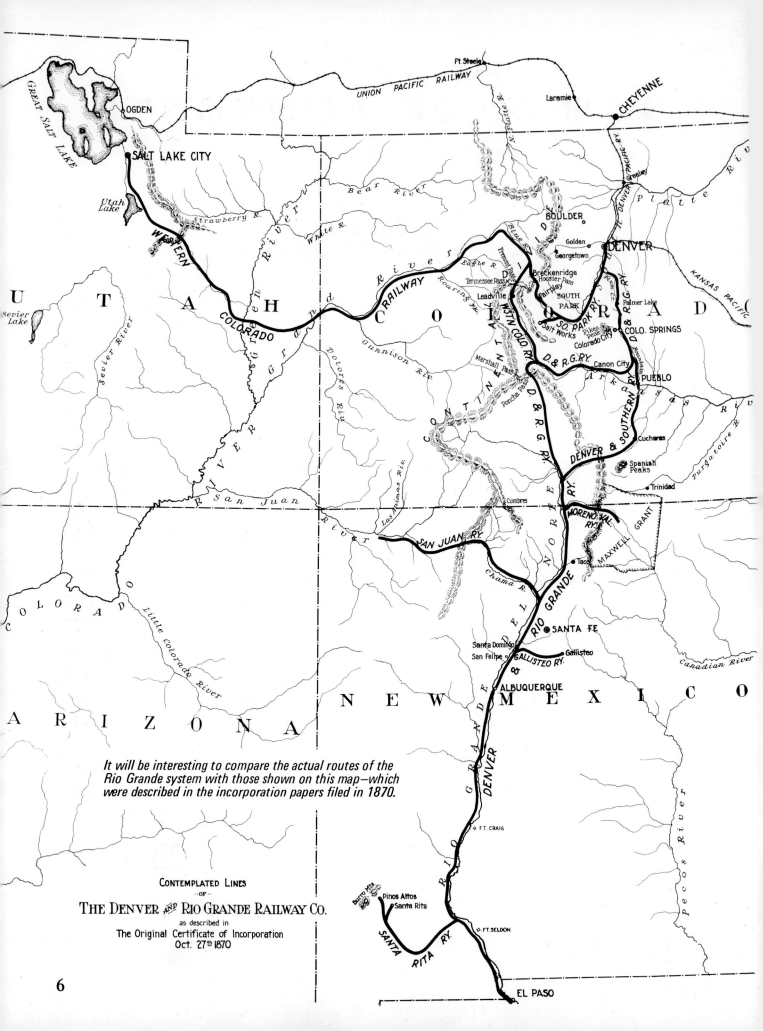

It will be interesting to compare the actual routes of the Rio Grande system with those shown on this map—which were described in the incorporation papers filed in 1870.

CONTEMPLATED LINES
··· OF ···
THE DENVER AND RIO GRANDE RAILWAY CO.
as described in
The Original Certificate of Incorporation
Oct. 27th 1870

6

TABLE OF CONTENTS

Acknowledgements

Although the author had no intention of producing a history such as this at the time, research upon which this publication is based began 25 years ago. Unemployed and 2,000 miles from home, he spent countless hours in the Denver Public Library compiling data on Colorado's railroads from Poor's and Moody's financial manuals. At the State Historical Society's Library he was fortunate in having been able to examine nearly every item comprising the Rio Grande archives, which had just been transferred from the railroad company. This casual interest over the following years expanded and intensified, culminating in a five-volume cyclopedia entitled "Colorado's Mountain Railroads," privately published in the mid-1960's.

It was evident that the Rio Grande system was extensive; half of the material in those little books was devoted to it. Yet it was also obvious that much more research on the Rio Grande Western was needed, and the Western Pacific should have been included as part of the system. Bringing the entire work up to date was out of the question; so it was decided to produce a new book on the Rio Grande system utilizing the information in Volumes 1-5 as a base. The present volume is the result of the decision.

Over this long period of time a great many persons, living and otherwise, have assisted the author in some way or other with this project. Their residences ranged from coast-to-coast and border-to-border, and a complete tabulation of their names would read like a "Who's Who." For example, the efforts of eight individuals were required to trace the origin of a single RGW locomotive, while a ninth produced a photograph of it. This is but one of numerous such incidents which swelled the list of "assistants" far beyond any accurate recollection. The author is indebted to all of them for their individual contributions, and he is very grateful for their help. One name, Jackson C. Thode, does stand out, however. His locomotive listings, chronology of passenger trains, timetable and annual report collections, profile sheets, maps, and access to obscure data have added immeasurably to the scope and accuracy of the finished product. Special thanks is extended to him for his unique assistance.

The author and publisher anticipate that human imperfections may be detected by others in this book. The author will appreciate hearing from their discoverers at their convenience, especially errors of fact, for which he alone is inescapably responsible.

Every reasonable attempt has been made to give credit for photographs to the proper sources. The publisher will appreciate being informed of any discrepancies in this respect.

Editor's Note

In the writing and editing of RIO GRANDE . . . to the PACIFIC! the author and editors have attempted to follow as consistent a style and format as possible. The reader will note that numerous railroad terms and abbreviations have been used throughout this book. In addition, standard D&RGW classification symbols have been used to designate each individual locomotive class.

Examples of style and abbreviations are shown below with appropriate explanations.

The major portions of this book have been divided into sections representing the chronological development of the Rio Grande system, its subsidiaries and associated lines. The history of the system has been shown in year-by-year compilations as follows: (1) date, (2) the most important events of the year, (3) construction and disposition information, and (4) a listing of locomotives acquired or rebuilt during the year.

CONSTRUCTION example:

Denver to Colorado Springs—76m N-G.

This shows that a line between Denver and Colorado Springs was constructed, consisting of 76 miles of narrow-gauge trackage.

The "76m" indicates mileage between points.

Other construction and disposition abbreviations are:

N-G = narrow-gauge.
S-G = standard-gauge.
3-R = three-rail (dual-gauge).

MOTIVE POWER example:

1, 4, 6, 7
Baldwin Locomotive   2-4-0   25N

The digits, 1, 4, 6, 7, are the locomotive road numbers. Road numbers are always shown on a line by themselves. The builder's name, steam locomotive wheel arrangement or diesel model number and railroad classification are shown on the following line.

The original railroad classification scheme worked in the following manner: 25N indicated that the locomotive weighed 25,000-pounds and was (N) narrow-gauge.

N = narrow-gauge.   S = standard-gauge.

Beginning in 1924 the railroad established a new locomotive classification scheme. New class symbols designated wheel arrangements by letters and tractive efforts by numerals, i.e., a C-16 was a Consolidation type (2-8-0) with 16,000-pounds tractive effort.

Letter designations were as follows:

C = Consolidation (2-8-0 and 0-8-0).
F = Santa Fe (2-10-2).
G = Mogul (2-6-0).
K = Mikado (2-8-2).
L = Mallet (2-6-6-0, 2-6-6-2, 4-6-6-4, 2-8-8-2).
M = Mountain or Northern (4-8-2 and 4-8-4).
P = Pacific (4-6-2).
S = Switcher (0-6-0).
T = Ten-wheeler (4-6-0).
Y = Shay geared-type.

SECTION ONE

UP THE RIO GRANDE.

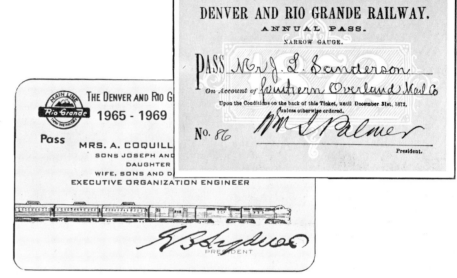

INTRODUCTION

Today's Denver & Rio Grande Western Railroad is a vastly different proposition from that conceived by its original incorporators. The product of numerous ancestors, combined with periodic financial failures, the railroad is now an east-west bridge carrier between Denver-Pueblo and Salt Lake City-Ogden, rather than the north-south trunk-line connecting Denver with Mexico City. It began its century as a narrow gauge steam-powered hauler of coal, ores and lumber; now (excepting the isolated Silverton branch) it is a standard gauge, diesel-electric-powered transporter of manufactures, coal, lumber and food. Passenger service of standard gauge variety spanned the years 1887 - 1974, though what remains of the narrow gauge operations is enjoying unprecedented popularity.

The Rio Grande system once embraced a 1670-mile network of narrow-gauge trackage (1888), 360-miles of 3-rail route (1902) and 1840-miles of standard-gauge line (1963). Today only 45 miles of narrow-gauge trackage remain, the mixed-gauge has just vanished and the standard-gauge mileage stands at 1829. The railroad has been so rebuilt and relocated that, excepting the Silverton line, and perhaps portions of the route between Denver and Pueblo, General William Jackson Palmer wouldn't recognize his "baby railroad."

During its past 100 years the railroad property has managed its own destiny during only 47 of them. Two other railroads controlled it for 18 years, one of them continuing for another 11 years jointly with a holding company. Five receiverships account for eight years, two of which were involved with the United States Railroad Administration. One trusteeship lasted 11 years; Jay Gould dictated policies for about a year; and the previously mentioned holding company ran things by itself for two years. A new holding company has owned the railroad for the past few years. It is intriguing to observe that transportation has not been always the primary function of the Rio Grande. During its formative years it was used primarily to enhance the value of raw land owned by its officials and their associates. In the early 1900's its resources and revenues were appropriated for the construction of the Western Pacific. Twice, later, the railroad was utilized in shameful stock and bond manipulations. Today, it is the cornerstone of a growing conglomerate industrial-financial enterprise.

COLORADO'S RAILROADS

An Historical Outline

With some justification, Colorado's 100-year railroad history can be called, "General Palmer and the Rio Grande vs. Jay Gould and the Union Pacific vs. James Hill and the Burlington." These three men and their railroads have dominated Colorado's rail transportation era ever since its very beginning. Perhaps a hundred other railroads have come and gone over the span of years, but these three have surmounted every obstruction: competition, panic, depression, failure, rivalry, floods, world wars, and industrial upheaval. Yet, in another sense, the history of Colorado's many railroads is identical with the history of the state, its cities and its people. Their development has been coincident and interdependent to a surprising degree.

Colorado's first railroads were those which built westward from cities along the Missouri River to embryonic settlements at the eastern foot of the Rocky Mountains. They were quite different from Eastern lines which built from town to town a few miles at a time; Denver and Omaha or Kansas City were almost 500 miles apart, with nothing between them except a vast empty prairie, herds of buffalo and innumerable Indians. The first rails within the state's boundaries were those of the Union Pacific, which sacrificed Denver's traffic to the interest of haste during its construction westward to an ultimate junction with the eastbound Central Pacific at Promontory, Utah, in 1869. The UP began laying track at Omaha in 1865, reaching Colorado's northeast corner in 1867, where nine miles of track following the South Platte River dipped into the territory. Julesburg (then Weir) thus became the first Colorado city to be blessed with railroad service and it was the only city to be so distinguished for another two years. Two decades later fourteen other railroad companies, now integrated into six systems operating today, had completed the construction of every trans-prairie route as they presently exist and only the Atchison, Topeka & Santa Fe, and the Chicago, Burlington & Quincy systems have made substantial additions to this pioneer trackage. In fact, the AT&SF's lines southeast of La Junta, built in 1937, were the last major new railroad projects within the state.

Jay Gould entered the scene when he bought control of the UP in 1873. By 1879, through personal ownership of stocks and bonds, he controlled every railroad in the state except one, the AT&SF, and he constrained it by threats of parallel construction and rate wars. In this period Gould had manipulated the securities and traffic of the Union Pacific, Denver Pacific, Kansas Pacific, Colorado Central and some lesser companies, giving the UP a near-monopoly of the state's railroad business. Only General Palmer's Denver & Rio Grande was able to escape Gould's financial depredations, and it did so by expanding so fast and issuing so much stock that Gould was obliged to accept defeat trying to maintain control. After fostering the merger of the DP and KP with the UP in 1880, Gould disposed of his holdings at an immense profit, adding to the

already enormous amounts which he had previously extracted from the UP's treasury by his manipulations. Leaving the UP's domain, Gould extended his Missouri Pacific into Colorado in 1887, touching off a financial battle which was not to end until 60 years later.

W. J. Palmer had built his narrow gauge D&RG south from Denver, starting in 1871, soon after the arrival there of the CC, DP and KP (1870), then ran into trouble with the AT&SF in 1878 over rights-of-way near Trinidad and Cañon City. After courts failed to produce a settlement, Gould dictated a peace treaty which kept the AT&SF out of Colorado's mountains and deterred the D&RG from continuing southward. This made the D&RG's north-south line the western boundary of the prairie railroads' empires. At this time Colorado's silver boom was in full fervor, and the D&RG built into every possible mining camp, competing only with the Denver, South Park & Pacific, a narrow gauge line which Gould had obtained for the UP. This tremendous mining activity attracted the Chicago, Burlington & Quincy which built into Denver in 1882, providing competition for the UP as well as the AT&SF. The subsequent arrival of the Missouri Pacific and Chicago, Rock Island & Pacific systems from the east added two new elements to the battle for traffic, and ended further plans for trans-prairie extensions by other Eastern railroads.

Overlapping the last half of the two-decade period during which the plains lines reached the mountains was the beginning of a 40-year interval characterized by railroad construction in the mountain regions. More than half of 35 new railroads tapped sources of precious metals, the others having served coal mines. The coal lines were among the first to be built because coal was used almost universally for smelting, ores, stationary steam engines, locomotive fuel, building heating and as the principal ingredient in the manufacture of illuminating gas. Though most of the mountain railroads were built immediately after the initial phases of the silver boom, some of them did not begin operating until after the silver panic of 1892 - 1893. Throughout this long period, branches and a few short lines were built to stone quarries, but some of them were so late in their efforts that stone for buildings had gone out of style meanwhile. Toward the end of the period a number of small railroads were constructed primarily for agricultural service, the AT&SF making substantial additions to its system along the lower Arkansas River for this purpose.

During the 25 years characterized by hasty railroad expansion in mining areas, Colorado's timber was cut, finished and consumed almost within sight of the forest. Though the first lumber railroad had been built in 1880, it was not until 1895 that a second one was constructed for the specific purpose of hauling logs and lumber. Seven such lines were built during the next two decades, a period which includes the early years of this entirely new industry for the state. The same era also saw the beginning of the interurban railroad whose steam or electrically propelled cars were filled with local citizens or less-than-carload merchandise. Half of the six companies in this category terminated in Denver.

During Jay Gould's absence from Colorado (1881-1887) the UP had indulged in expansion north of Cheyenne, Wyoming, and had given financial assistance to railroads which were busily assembling a through-line between Denver and central Texas. The burden of this latest venture, together with its other activities, had overtaxed the UP's resources, and no sooner had Jay Gould returned to Colorado with his MP than his peculiar financial abilities were requisitioned to put the UP's corporate house in order. Consequently, the long north-south line was separated from the UP's east-west main line, and was reorganized in 1890 as a new subsidiary, the Union Pacific, Denver & Gulf Railway. Gould died in 1892, before completing his work and the UP went into receivership the following year. Meanwhile, Palmer had left the D&RG before its financial reorganization in 1886, also leaving it without the exceptional leadership of its earlier years. Both systems were thus vulnerable to outside control, which was not long in appearing.

The stage had been set by the D&RG in 1890 when it gained standard gauge entry to Salt Lake City and Ogden, over the tracks of the Rio Grande Western in Utah. Not to be outdone, the AT&SF bought the Colorado Midland in the same year and then reached these two cities also via the RGW. This gambit was unsuccessful, however; the AT&SF failed during the silver panic and lost the CM in the resulting reorganization, eliminating itself as a major factor in subsequent maneuvers for control of Colorado's railroads. The next episode disclosed the UP being reorganized by the New York banking house of Kuhn, Loeb & Company, with E. H. Harriman as representative. The most noticeable result of their work was the return of the UP to its original role as an east-west carrier, its north-south subsidiary being combined with the former DSP&P narrow-gauge lines in 1898 to produce an independent railroad, the Colorado & Southern Railway.

Overnight, the UP's influence in Colorado had been greatly diminished in one area, but this did not prevent its attempt to regain an even stronger position elsewhere by trying to purchase the CB&Q, which was being sought currently by J. J. Hill and his two railroads, the Great Northern and the Northern Pacific. Harriman and his bankers failed to add the Burlington to the UP dynasty, the two Hill lines acquiring the CB&Q in 1901. Then, eyeing what the UP had discarded, the CB&Q in 1908 bought C&S, as well as control of its Texas subsidiary. This acquisition included a 50-percent interest in the Colorado Springs & Cripple Creek District, and Gilpin railroads. Though Harriman died in 1909, the UP's bankers continued their efforts to make their railroad the most powerful in the nation.

While all these titanic events were transpiring, the Missouri Pacific, under the guidance of Jay Gould's first son, George, had been purchasing D&RG stocks and bonds, obtaining control in 1901. Unlike his father who amassed wealth by devious methods purely for personal pleasure involved, George and his sister Helen aspired to a transcontinental system which would include the MP and the D&RG. Unable to effect a friendly connection west of Ogden or Salt Lake City, Gould was forced to build his own railroad, using funds derived from an initial bond issue and MP and D&RG revenues, an arrangement which caused severe deterioration of these two railroads. Though Gould completed the Western Pacific Railway to the Pacific Coast, he lost control of the MP and the D&RG in 1914, having sold their securities meanwhile, possibly anticipating their unfortunate fate. Exit George Gould and enter Kuhn, Loeb & Company, the UP's bankers, with working control of the MP and the D&RG. Gould's defeat was also the UP's victory, since it now had indirect control of its nearest east-west competitor, a situation which lasted until control of the MP was acquired by the Alleghany Corporation in 1930.

Over the half-century from 1867 to 1917, Colorado's railroad network had grown from one company with nine miles of track in the state to 50 companies operating almost 6000 miles of main-line and branches. But growth had ceased; the next half-century would see a reduction of trackage to 4000 miles by 1967.

Nevertheless, there had been noteworthy progress in other sectors. The Moffat Tunnel was opened to traffic in 1928, giving the state its lowest main-line crossing of the Continental Divide. Six years later the Dotsero Cutoff—linking the Denver & Salt Lake west of the Moffat Tunnel and the Denver & Rio Grande Western west of Tennessee Pass—shaved 175 miles from the circuitous D&RGW line between Denver and Salt Lake City, creating a new transcontinental route first used for a special coast-to-coast run by a new streamlined, diesel-electric train.

The D&RGW's extensive narrow gauge system suffered considerable attrition in the 1940's and 1950's, only the Alamosa to Silverton and Farmington line remaining in 1967—still operated by steam power more than 40 years old—the biggest such operation in the nation. Jet aircraft, the Interstate Highway System and the trucking of mail decimated passenger schedules in the 1950's and 1960's.

At the very end of the 1950-decade three new developments appeared on Colorado's railroad scene. The AT&SF, D&RGW and UP railroads were absorbed by newly-created industrial corporations, which could engage in any kind of business, and the CB&Q was combined with other out-of-state railroads to form the Burlington Northern, a similar company. Control of the MP was acquired by a non-railroad company, and the CRI&P became involved in a complicated abandonment-merger-dismemberment proceeding which is far from resolution as of the date of this printing.

Today, Colorado's railroad mileage is operated by six principal systems, of which only one, the Burlington Northern/C&S, has escaped financial catastrophe. The other five—Atchison, Topeka & Santa Fe; Chicago, Rock Island & Pacific; Denver & Rio Grande Western; Missouri Pacific; and Union Pacific—have been financially reorganized at least once apiece.

UTAH'S RAILROADS
An Historical Outline

Ever since 1869, when westward-building Union Pacific and eastward-building Central Pacific joined their rails at Promontory Summit — thus completing the Pacific Railway — rail transport in Utah has been dominated by the Union Pacific and its corporate allies. A distant second place has been occupied by today's Denver & Rio Grande Western and its accumulated ancestors. The only other major element in the state was a unique electric interurban transit system which rose to prominence between 1900 and 1920, then faded without trace forty years later. Unlike Colorado, whose rail-borne traffic had been principally of originating/terminating variety, Utah remains a hub of rail routes with transcontinental dimensions. Upon the present basic network are superimposed numerous short lines and branches which handle the state's mineral and agricultural bounty.

Utah's first railroads were the well-known UP and CP which, in their competitive haste to complete a line between the Missouri and Sacramento rivers, by-passed Salt Lake City, the territory's largest settlement. Though disappointed, the town's Mormon population, endowed with considerable railroad construction (UP) and freighting experience, promptly built their own line (Utah Central) from Ogden, and added a branch to a salt works (Ogden & Syracuse). During the 1870's the Mormons built more railroads with their own resources: Utah Northern from Ogden to Preston, Idaho; Utah & Northern from Cache Junction toward Butte, Montana; Utah Western from Salt Lake City to Terminus; Utah Southern from Salt Lake City to Provo; Utah Southern Extension from Provo to Juab; Summit County from Echo southward to a coal mine; and Echo & Park City, an extension to the mining town east of Salt Lake City. This extraordinary activity must have disturbed UP management; within the span of a few years all these railroads had been reorganized and brought under UP control.

The Mormons were not alone in their efforts, however. Other groups built railroads to precious metal and coal mines from points on the newly completed lines: Bingham Canon & Camp Floyd from Sandy to Bingham; Wasatch & Jordan Valley from Sandy to Alta; Utah & Pleasant Valley from Springville to Scofield; and American Fork from American Fork to Deer Creek. The last mentioned company was perhaps the most notable; its 42-inch track gauge matched neither narrow- nor standard-gauge connections; its only locomotive was the first USA-built example with all axles in pivoted trucks; and the whole enterprise lasted only two years, an unbeaten record for the state.

The decade of the Eighties exhibited none of the frenzied expansion into the mountains, nor the trunk-line race across the prairies, which had characterized that period in Colorado. Instead, new trackage was of modest proportions. The Salt Lake & Western connected the mines at Silver City with the Utah Southern's main-line at Cutler, while the reorganized Utah Central constructed a long extension from Juab to mines at Frisco. The Salt Lake &

Fort Douglas went up to quarries just east of Salt Lake City, and the Salt Lake & Eastern surmounted the Wasatch Range to reach silver mines at Park City. Colorado's Denver & Rio Grande performed a remarkable coup by organizing the Denver & Rio Grande Western, which absorbed the BC&CF, U&PV and W&JV railroads, and connected them with new trackage between Salt Lake City and Springville. Then, in quick succession it abandoned the U&PV's switchbacks over the mountains, replacing that line with a new one over Soldier Summit; raced eastward to Desert Siding where, in 1883, opposing construction forces completed a second (narrow gauge) rail route between Denver and Salt Lake City; and built northward to Ogden. Down in the San Pitch Valley country the San Pete Valley Railroad had taken over the moribund California Short Line and had completed a line from Nephi to coal mines at Wales. At the end of the decade the UN/U&N was rebuilt to standard gauge.

Following an interlude of managerial strife between the D&RGW and D&RG companies, the former was reorganized simply as the Rio Grande Western, and, co-operating with the latter, changed its system to standard gauge during 1890. This conversion necessitated the relocation of much roadbed east of Soldier Summit and the construction of an entirely new line between Crevasse, Colorado, and White House. Contrasting with almost no activity in the Union Pacific's domain, the RGW added a dozen branches to stone quarries, coal mines and silver mines. Some of these were quite long: Provo to Heber, Springville to Silver City, and Thistle to Belknap. Toward the end of the decade the SL&E and SL&FtD were absorbed by the RGW, giving it undisputed possession of Utah's eastern half, while the UP dominated the western and northern portions. Hardly noticed among all this activity were the beginnings of Utah's interurban systems—steam-powered lines to amusement areas close to Ogden and Salt Lake City.

The Twentieth Century began with Jay Gould's heirs buying control of the D&RG, whose trackage lay in Colorado. The Goulds possessed transcontinental-system aspirations and conceived a new routing far south of Salt Lake City (Farnham to Salina to Milford), anticipating a conjunction with the San Pedro, Los Angeles & Salt Lake Railroad then extending eastward through California. Other than surveys and some useless track between Salina and Nioche the scheme came to naught; the Union Pacific won the race. Its Oregon Short Line subsidiary had built southwest from Milford, and had joined the SPLA& SL out in the Nevada desert, thus creating another UP-controlled trunk-line from Utah to the ocean. This route was improved by the addition of two links in Utah: Terminus to Balfour on the Silver City Branch, and from Tintic on that branch to Lynndyl on the Provo-Milford line. Though these moves bottled up Gould's D&RG in Utah, he began to build his own railroad to the coast—the

Western Pacific — completed in the remarkable interval of three years. To better compete with this unwelcome rival the CP constructed a new line directly across the Great Salt Lake between Ogden and the Nevada border.

Of local and far greater importance was the discovery of immense copper deposits at Bingham, an event which initiated considerable railroad construction. The RGW built a branch from Welby to smelters at Garfield, and added a low-grade line around Bingham Canyon. The Copper Belt was constructed to connect mining spurs with RGW trackage, and the Bingham Consolidated Mining & Smelting Company built a branch from its mine and mill at Lark to RGW rails at Dalton. Overshadowed by all these momentous happenings, the expansion of the interurban railroads around Salt Lake City and Ogden was scarcely noticed. However, two of them—Emigration Canyon, and Ogden & Northwestern—were the state's first electric-powered railroads other than urban streetcar lines.

The copper boom continued into the 'teens. The WP added a branch from Burmester to a smelter at International, whence the Tooele Valley was constructed to copper mines across the range from Bingham. A few miles to the south the St. John & Ophir tapped more mines, though the Salt Lake & Mercur, built from Fairfield in the 1890's, was abandoned almost simultaneously. Copper mining and refining companies financed the Bingham & Garfield which provided a shorter haul than did the D&RG between mines and smelters. But all this was only the direct effect of copper mining; an indirect result was the great expansion of coal mining, predominantly in D&RG territory east of Soldier Summit. The easternmost mines were at Sego which was connected with the Denver & Rio Grande by the uncertain rails of the Ballard & Thompson railroad. Next, to the west, was the D&RG's Sunnyside branch built from Mounds in 1899. The greatest concentration, however, was located between Price and Castle Gate. The Southern Utah and Castle Valley railroads laid joint track from Price westward to Castle Junction, thence diverged to mines at Hiawatha and Mohrland, respectively. The Kenilworth & Helper ascended a steep gradient from Independent Junction to the seams at Kenilworth. Initially, these railroads were operated by the D&RG, but later the Utah railway built south from Castle Gate to Castle Junction, took over CV and SU mine trackage, and removed the track to Price. The Utah owned two subsidiaries — Helper & Western and Utah Terminal — and operated the National Coal Company's railroad, all these being branches to coal mines. The Utah then added its own track alongside the D&RG between Provo and Thistle, and after negotiating reciprocal trackage rights with the D&RG, operated its coal trains from the mines directly into Provo where interchange was made with the Union Pacific system. (Later, the UP obtained a financial interest in this railroad.)

Lastly, but by no means least, an extensive electric-powered interurban system flowered into full bloom. The interstate Ogden, Logan & Idaho was operated between Ogden and Preston, Idaho; Ogden and Salt Lake City were connected by the Salt Lake & Ogden; the Salt Lake, Garfield & Western (formerly Salt Lake & Los Angeles) went out to Saltair from Salt Lake City; and the Salt Lake & Utah extended west to Magna and south to Payson. There was nothing like this elsewhere within 500 miles of Salt Lake City.

During the prosperous years following World War I, changes in Utah's railroad structure were of minor magnitude, the Union Pacific accounting for most of them. It added some short branches in the agricultural northern area, removed useless trackage in the Tintic mining district, and built two long branches, Delta to Fillmore and Lund to Cedar City. The latter town was the base for UP tours to the scenic wonders of southern Utah; Fillmore was developing into an important livestock and agricultural community. Until the 1920's, removals of track had involved only trivial mileage, generally that related to exhausted mines or quarries. This trend continued into the following decade when almost no new trackage was laid in the state. Utah's last narrow-gauge railroad vanished in 1939 when the Uintah pulled up its rails to the gilsonite mines just west of the Colorado boundary. Nevertheless, there was offsetting compensation in a new UP branch to a mountain of iron ore near Cedar City.

World War II had negligible effect on Utah's railroad structure, only the Carbon County Railway being built from Columbia Junction to nearby coal deposits, and the SP track around Great Salt Lake being removed. The war's aftermath, however, brought about the complete dismantling of the SL&U and Utah-Idaho Central (formerly OL&I) electric interurban lines. The D&RGW's Park City Branch was removed as was most of its former SPV Branch. The B&G was also removed, having been replaced by the copper company's own electrified line, a short distance away. In the 1950's minor abandonments were predominant, the major events having been the demise of the Bamberger Electric line (formerly SL&O) and the elimination of the UP's branch to Five Mile Pass. In contrast, the next ten years showed virtually no changes of any kind anywhere in the state, the D&RGW's new branch from Crescent south to a potash deposit near Moab being the outstanding exception. In the early 1970's the D&RGW's branch to Heber was sold to a private group for operation as a scenic railroad.

Utah's railroads became involved in two major changes at the end of the 1960-decade. All four of its trunk-lines (D&RGW, SP, UP, WP) were absorbed by newly-incorporated companies which were empowered to undertake other varieties of business, some of which had formerly been subsidiaries of the railroad companies. After the rearrangement the railroad was a subsidiary company, conducting its business "in competition" with non-railroad enterprises. Then in mid-1971, Amtrak assumed responsibility for operation of the nation's passenger trains. Overnight, with two exceptions, passenger service in the state was terminated; the non-Amtrak D&RGW continued an every-other-day run between Salt Lake City and Denver, while the Chicago-Oakland Amtrak route passed through Ogden via UP and SP lines.

Compared to that of Colorado, Utah's rail network has exhibited remarkable stability. All of the main-lines are intact, though two have been relocated—Southern Pacific, completely; D&RGW, partially. The electrified interurban lines have come and gone, just as they have in other areas. Otherwise, outright abandonments have consisted of minor trackage to points of exhausted traffic potential. Aside from the trunk-lines—UP, SP, WP and D&RGW—only six independent railroads remain today: Salt Lake, Garfield & Western; Tooele Valley; Kennecott Copper Company; Utah; Carbon County; and Wasatch Mountain; and all but the first and last are owned by an associated industry.

13

Prior to the erection of Denver's Union Station, the D&RG's main-line ran down Wynkoop Street (lower right), and Milepost 0 was located in the Denver Pacific - Kansas Pacific yards, to the left of the near-end of the freight house (upper center). This view is toward the east from the depot's high tower.

This survey group luncheon appears to have been a rather elegant affair. Two ladies, General Palmer (with black hat and bow tie) and half-a-dozen gentlemen were attired more appropriately for dinner at a Denver hostelry than a picnic in the woods.

"EARLY FINANCING OF THE D&RG RAILWAY"

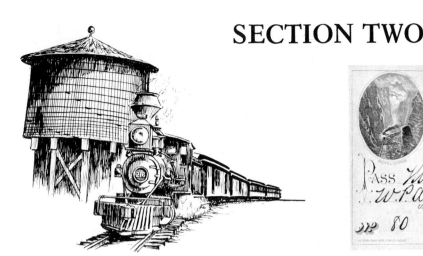

SECTION TWO

Denver & Rio Grande Railway
1870 - 1886

1870

The Denver & Rio Grande Railway Company filed its Articles of Incorporation in the Territories of Colorado and New Mexico on October 27. The proposed capitalization of $2½-million was to be used for building and equipping a main line from Denver to El Paso, Texas, with seven branches extending to Salt Lake City; the San Juan Mountains in southwestern Colorado; Santa Fé, New Mexico; and the silver mines in southwestern New Mexico.

There was no construction during the year, however; everyone was busy selling stocks and bonds to finance the project.

1871

The First Spike was driven on July 28, on the northwest side of the Denver Pacific and Kansas Pacific railroads' tracks opposite the original Denver Pacific station in Denver. (This location is about halfway between Nineteenth and Twentieth Streets, and in line with Wynkoop Street, next to the Union Pacific's present freight office.) The D&RG's first locomotive was steamed-up on August 1; the first passenger train was operated on August 14; and on September 7 the first revenue freight train pulled into Denver with a load of lumber from Plum (later Sedalia) a few miles to the south.

CONSTRUCTION

Denver to Colorado Springs—76m N-G.
    Leaving Denver, the track followed the South Platte River and Plum Creek to a high point at Divide (now Palmer Lake) and then followed Monument Creek down the other side.

MOTIVE POWER

1, 4, 6, 7
    Baldwin Locomotive   2-4-0   25N
    These were the only 2-4-0's to be ordered, and although they were much alike, they differed in several mechanical features. Their tenders had only four wheels.

2, 3, 5
    Baldwin Locomotive   2-6-0   35N
    These were the first freight locomotives to be ordered. No. 3 was built prior to the other two, and was slightly different from them in its mechanical details. Like the 2-4-0's, the tenders had only four wheels.

1872

Although General William J. Palmer, the railroad's President, was directing its rails toward Santa Fé, he authorized a long branch running west from South Pueblo to obtain some revenue-producing coal traffic. Unfortunately, however, the D&RG did not have sufficient funds to reimburse the contractor for the last few miles; hence they were built as a separate company.

The D&RG scored an important "first" in American railroading by purchasing six sets of straight air-brake equipment from Westinghouse for its freight locomotives, the first application of air-brakes to freight trains in the nation.

A depot was erected at Sixth and Larimer Streets in what was then called West Denver.

CONSTRUCTION

Colorado Springs to South Pueblo—43m N-G.
    This trackage paralleled Fountain Creek to its mouth on the Arkansas River.
South Pueblo to Coal Branch Junction—33m N-G.
    The line was built upstream along the banks of the Arkansas River.
Coal Branch Junction to Coal Banks—3m N-G.
    This "branch" was called the Canon Coal Railway, and ran south up Coal Creek to the mines.

MOTIVE POWER

8, 9, 10
    Baldwin Locomotive   2-6-0   35N

"EARLY FINANCING OF THE D&RG RAILWAY"

The D&RG's shops and terminal facilities were situated at Burnham, two miles south of the passenger and freight station in downtown Denver. By 1873 the shop buildings included a five-stall roundhouse (far right), erecting shop (center), blacksmith shop (between the two), car shop and storehouse (far left).

This group of locomotives had longer fireboxes and wheel-bases than the previous 2-6-0's, and the tenders had six wheels, the front pair being in rigid pedestals, the others being in a pivoted, four-wheel truck.

11

Baldwin Locomotive	2-6-0	35N

Although otherwise like the previous three locomotives, this one had its throttle in a second steam-dome, just behind the stack.

1873

The D&RG prospered during the first eight months, but the financial panic which began in September reduced traffic considerably. General Palmer proclaimed that the survival of his railroad was due to the economy of its three-foot gauge, whereas 77 wider-gauge lines had failed during the crisis. Nonetheless, with sources of capital dried up, further construction came to a halt.

A much larger locomotive was ordered from Baldwin for hauling coal trains up the grade between South Pueblo and Divide, but no record appears of it having been delivered; most likely, the D&RG was not able to pay for it.

MOTIVE POWER

12

Baldwin Locomotive	2-6-0	35N

This locomotive was identical with No. 11.

101

Vulcan (England)	0-4-4-0 T	No Class

This was Colorado's first articulated locomotive, of four-cylinder, simple-Fairlie design. At first, it was used to haul coal trains between South Pueblo and Divide. Later it was used as a road engine, then as a helper on the east side of the Veta Pass line. Oddly enough, it was the railroad's only narrow-gauge articulated locomotive.

1874

The financial distress of the previous year continuing, only a short branch was constructed. The new Denver, South Park & Pacific railroad began to use the D&RG's depot.

The D&RG's first locomotive was a tiny machine, the top of its boiler having been only six feet above the rails, and its total wheelbase only 26-and-one-half-feet in length.

Ready for service, with loaded tender, it weighed less than 20-tons.

BROADBELT COLLECTION

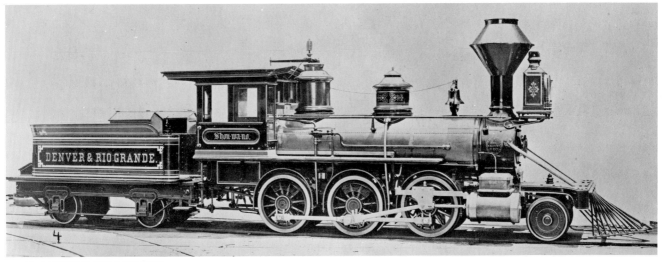

The railroad's first freight engine was only slightly larger than the 2-4-0's used on passenger trains, and it weighed only five tons more. The first two 2-6-0's and the first 2-4-0 were shipped to Denver from Philadelphia aboard flat-cars belonging to the Baldwin Locomotive Works.

Colorado's Governor, Alexander C. Hunt, attired in top hat and cutaway coat, posed with some of his immediate family, somewhat apart from the other assorted personages who frequented the primitive depot and lunch-room at Colorado Springs.

The D&RG's 11-stall roundhouse dominates this panorama of South Pueblo in 1879. A D&RG passenger train is seen between the roundhouse and Union Station (center), while on the other side of the depot is a passenger consist of the AT&SF.

17

Engines 8 - 12 were distinguished by their larger tenders riding on a forward rigid axle and a two-axle swivel truck at the rear. Numbers 11 and 12 were unique in having a second steam-dome placed next to the stack. The size of the crew provides an interesting comparison with the size of the locomotive.

The three known photographs of the D&RG's 0-4-4-0T, built by the Vulcan Foundry in England, show the locomotive after it had been modified. This view of it shows the engine before it was shipped from the builder's plant.

One of the D&RG's first 4-4-0's (Numbers 16-18) and one of the first few 2-8-0's (Numbers 32-34) sit beside the Cañon City depot in this photograph taken about 1879.

The structure in the foreground is the Kansas Pacific - Denver Pacific depot and office building situated between 21st and 22nd Streets in Denver. The freight house and passenger station of the D&RG, which stood between 19th and 20th Streets, can be seen in-line with the stairway.

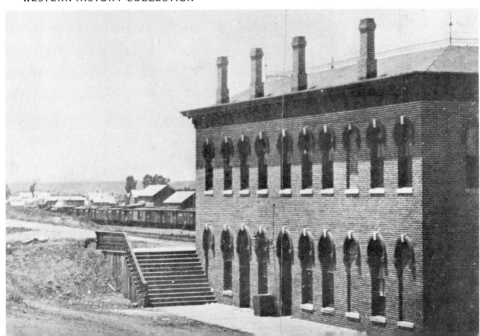

En route to the Camp

Brakemen man the brakes on each car as 2-6-0 Number 13 cautiously descends the four-percent grade around the Muleshoe Curve on the eastern side of Veta Pass; apparently, air-brakes had not yet been applied to passenger rolling stock.

The D&RG's first three 4-4-0's were constructed with the steam-dome directly behind the stack, a most unusual loca- *tion. This one is Number 17 with the daily passenger train at Del Norte.*

CONSTRUCTION

Coal Branch Junction to Cañon City—8m N-G.
> This extension of the line up the Arkansas River was built primarily to pacify the indignant citizens of the town, who were in a position to cause the railroad some locating difficulties later.

1875

Still in the grip of the money panic, though it was alleviating, the railroad could do nothing more than try to make as much money as was possible under the circumstances.

1876

The financial storm, which had involved Eastern and European sources of capital much more than those in Colorado, had abated, and Palmer was now able to raise money for further expansion, still toward the original goal of Santa Fé, but with the incidental idea of tapping the excellent coking-coal field around Trinidad.

CONSTRUCTION

South Pueblo to Cucharas (later Cuchara Junction) - 49m N-G.
> Heading south from South Pueblo, this line crossed the many local drainages with a succession of steep pitches and sharp curves.

Cucharas (later Cuchara Junction) to El Moro—40m N-G.
> Still building southward, the tracks wriggled in and out of each valley to avoid any heavy construction work.

Cucharas (later Cuchara Junction) to La Veta—22m N-G.
> This line was the beginning of a long extension into the San Luis Valley (an alternate route to Santa Fé) which lay beyond the Sangre de Cristo Mountains to the west. Its route followed Cucharas Creek upstream.

MOTIVE POWER

13-15, 19
Baldwin Locomotive   2-6-0   40N
> These 2-6-0's were slightly larger than the previous ones, and were the first D&RG locomotives to be equipped with eight-wheel, two-truck tenders.

16-18
Baldwin Locomotive   4-4-0   37N
> The original 2-4-0's were both too light and too unstable for passenger service; hence, these first 4-4-0's replaced them, the earlier locomotives being relegated to pay-car or special runs.

1877

Since the giant Atchison, Topeka & Santa Fé had rolled into Pueblo on 4'8½''-gauge rails in 1876, Palmer felt that the time had come to appraise the traffic prospects around the Leadville silver mines. The result of his survey was a decision to build there as soon as he could get the money to do so, hopefully in the following year.

CONSTRUCTION

La Veta to Garland City (later Mortimer)—29m N-G.
> Palmer, harboring his resources by building a shorter, though steeper, track across the mountains, had now reached the eastern edge of the San Luis Valley. This was the highest railroad in the country at the time, crossing Veta Pass at 9400 feet. On the east side the rails followed Cucharas Creek to its head; on the west side they went down Sangre de Cristo Creek.

El Moro (later Engleville Junction) to Engleville—6m N-G.
> This extension was built to reach coal mines southeast of Trinidad.

MOTIVE POWER

20, 21
Baldwin Locomotive   0-6-0 T   48N
> These were the first switchers to be acquired, both of them probably working at South Pueblo. They were of saddle-tank construction.

22
Baldwin Locomotive   2-8-0   60N
> This was the D&RG's first engine of this wheel arrangement, as well as its first one to have a wagon-top boiler. It replaced the Fairlie, No. 101, on the coal trains between South Pueblo and Divide. Although the 2-8-0 type was common in the Pennsylvania coal fields, this was its first use in Colorado.

Trinidad, at the northern foot of Fisher's Peak and Raton Pass, developed into an important coal-origination point served by the Union Pacific, D&RG, and Atchison, Topeka *& Santa Fe systems, an independent short line, an electrified interurban system, and numerous branches to the mines.*

23

Baldwin Locomotive	2-6-0	40N

This locomotive also had a wagon-top boiler.

24

Baldwin Locomotive	2-8-0	56N

This was a lighter version of No. 22, and it, too, had a wagon-top boiler. It was assigned to the South Pueblo - Divide coal traffic to compare its performance with that of No. 22. Both of them were tested on the Veta Pass grades also.

1878

When the D&RG, in extending southward from El Moro, began to grade over Raton Pass it found that the AT&SF had beaten it to the location, physically as well as legally. Retreating from defeat in that direction, Palmer's forces next began to grade westward from Cañon City up the Arkansas River toward Leadville, and here also the AT&SF, through its subsidiaries, the Cañon City & San Juan, and Pueblo & Arkansas Valley railroads, forced a halt to further progress. Blocked in both directions of expansion, and out of money for all practical purposes, Palmer chose to save the D&RG by leasing it to its deadly rival. This was on October 19, the formal transfer of the property taking place on December 13.

ACQUISITION

Cañon Coal Railway
   This was the branch from Labran to coal mines.

CONSTRUCTION

Garland City to Alamosa—29m N-G.
   This line ran across the flat country on the east side of the San Luis Valley, reaching Alamosa and the banks of the Rio Grande at the end of a 23-mile tangent, by far the longest stretch of straight track on the entire railroad.

MOTIVE POWER

25, 30-32

Baldwin Locomotive	2-8-0	56N

The Class 56 2-8-0 (No. 24), having been somewhat easier on the track than the heavier Class 60 locomotive (No. 22), was selected to be the "standard" freight locomotive for the next few years. Engines 30 and 31 had wagon-top boilers.

26

Baldwin Locomotive	4-4-0	38N

This locomotive was essentially identical with the Class 37 engines, the principal difference being its wagon-top boiler.

27-29

Baldwin Locomotive	2-6-0	40N

These were identical with No. 23, built in the previous year, and were the last to have wagon-top boilers for several years. Their arrival displaced the Class 35 2-6-0's to helper service on Veta Pass.

When D&RG track crews attained the crest of Veta Pass at 9,400-feet above the oceans, the railroad became the highest in the nation, and the approaches on both sides involved the steepest grades (four-percent) and sharpest curves (30°) encountered thus far on the railroad. Previous depots had been made of wood, but this one was of stone to resist the rigors of winter at high altitude.

COLLECTION OF DAVID S. DIGERNESS

Two of the D&RG's earliest 0-6-0T switchers lead two lines of derelict 4-4-0's awaiting dismantling at Burnham about 1890.

"SLOPES OF THE SANGRE DE CRISTO"

After the D&RG's track had surmounted Veta Pass, it descended quickly into the nearly level San Luis Valley, and ran past the southern end of the Sangre de Cristo Range on a 22-mile long tangent into Alamosa. Two well-dressed gentlemen try their hand at fishing while the photographer depicts the rails against the background of 14,000-foot peaks.

LE MASSENA COLLECTION

The line through the Grand Canyon of the Arkansas River (Royal Gorge) was constructed by a subsidiary of the Atchison, Topeka & Santa Fé, and it was purchased by the D&RG when the Royal Gorge - Raton Pass conflict was settled. Engine 32, one of the first 2-8-0's, pulls one of the first passenger trains into the defile—and just to be sure that the train will return safely—a second engine headed the other way was coupled to the rear.

D&RGW ARCHIVES

DENVER WORKS OF UNION PUBLIC ORE SAMPLING CO.

Two of the 28-ton 2-8-0's (Numbers 30, 31), like Number 22, had wagon-top boilers, all others being fabricated with straight-tops. This scene on the Muleshoe Curve shows Number 30 on the fill across Cucharas Creek at the eastern foot of Veta Pass.

RONZIO COLLECTION

The four-percent grades over Veta Pass required locomotives heavier than the tiny 20-ton 2-6-0's which were adequate elsewhere. Number 22, seen here descending the east side at Muleshoe Curve, was the D&RG's first 2-8-0, weighing 30-tons.

The D&RG's line from Salida (distant background) ascended the valley of the Arkansas River, meeting the rails of the Denver, South Park & Pacific at Nathrop. The DSP&P's line came down Trout Creek, crossed the D&RG a short distance above Nathrop, then turned sharply at the station to follow Chalk Creek upstream to Alpine Tunnel.

1879

Immediately upon leasing the D&RG, the AT&SF halted all further expansion of the D&RG and began to manipulate rates over the D&RG in an attempt to win a traffic war with the Kansas Pacific, which connected with the D&RG at Denver. Since such tactics would destroy the D&RG's source of income, Palmer went to the courts to protect his railroad from financial ruin. During the ensuing legal battles, the Cañon City & San Juan was allowed to build a roadbed from Cañon City to Texas Creek, and after that company was merged into the Pueblo & Arkansas Valley, track was laid on the completed grade. Then, to the chagrin of the D&RG, the AT&SF's General Passenger Agent, Major Anderson, ran a special excursion from Denver to the end-of-track, just beyond the narrowest point in the Royal Gorge. This was the first train to operate through the Gorge; the date was May 7.

One result of Palmer's appeal to the courts was to have the D&RG placed in the hands of a Receiver, Hanson A. Risley, who served only from June 11 until July 16, when the railroad was returned to the control of the AT&SF. However, the court felt that a receivership was desirable until the D&RG's motion that the lease be annulled could be decided. Consequently, on August 15, Louis C. Ellsworth, the new Receiver, took possession of the Denver & Rio Grande.

Meanwhile, Jay Gould, the very rascal who had personally caused the Panic of 1873, had begun to buy control of the D&RG with the thought of using it to punish the AT&SF for its rate actions against his Kansas Pacific! Now, regardless of the court's actions, Gould could dictate a peace, and he lost no time in doing so by threatening the AT&SF with parallel construction and ruinously low rates over the D&RG - Kansas Pacific route.

CONSTRUCTION

During the year the D&RG and the DSP&P were parties to a conference concerning a Denver Union Depot, one immediate result being the extension of each company's trackage into the Colorado Central station at Sixteenth and Delgany Streets from their Sixth and Larimer Streets depot in Denver.

MOTIVE POWER

33, 34, 37, 38
Baldwin Locomotive   2-8-0   56N
This group was essentially identical with previous Class 56 engines.

35, 36
Baldwin Locomotive   4-4-0   38N
These two locomotives, slightly heavier versions of the earlier Class 38 engine, plus Nos. 37 and 38, were part of an order, for two 4-4-0's and six 2-8-0's, which was placed by the AT&SF in late 1879. However, four 2-8-0's arrived in 1880, after the separation from the D&RG, and the AT&SF kept them even though it had no narrow-gauge track.

1880

Jay Gould, exercising his tremendous financial power at a meeting in Boston, set the terms for peace between the AT&SF and the D&RG, thus ending a conflict which had appeared hopeless of settlement in the courts. Among others, the terms were these: The D&RG was not to build south of Trinidad, Colorado, or Española, New Mexico, while the AT&SF was not to build into Denver or Leadville during the following ten years. The court actions were to be terminated and the Receiver discharged. The AT&SF was to give up its lease of the D&RG, and sell to it the completed trackage from Cañon City to Texas Creek.

On March 27 the D&RG was freed of its legal shackles, and was able to pursue its destinies as Palmer's ambitions and, now Gould's backing, might direct. Consequently, it embarked upon a fantastic expansion in every possible direction, racing for the rich revenues of Colorado's mining boom.

ACQUISITION

Cañon City to Texas Creek—22m N-G.
This trackage, purchased from the Pueblo & Arkansas Valley, ran the full length of the Grand Canyon of the Arkansas River, which was the key to the ore traffic of Leadville.

D&RG track reached the Continental Divide for the first time at Fremont Pass (11,330-feet) in November 1880. Just south of the summit the rails curled tightly inside the broader loop of the Denver, South Park & Pacific's *right-of-way. Both trains are headed downgrade toward Leadville. In the background the mountain wall of the Divide towers 2,000 - 3,000 feet above the valley floor.*

CONSTRUCTION

Texas Creek to Malta—89m N-G.
Continuing up the Arkansas River on a sustained grade with little relief, this line ended just below Leadville. Gould, in control of both the D&RG and the DSP&P, arranged for the DSP&P to run over D&RG track from Buena Vista to Leadville, in return for the reciprocal right for the D&RG to run over the DSP&P from Buena Vista into Gunnison. (The former right was used; the latter was not.)

Malta to Robinson—21m N-G.
The mines had been reached, at last, by building through Leadville to the head of the Arkansas River at Fremont Pass (11,330 feet), then going down Ten Mile Creek. This was the first railroad crossing of the Continental Divide in Colorado, and it was now the highest trackage in the nation, having displaced the DSP&P which had topped 9990 feet in 1879 at Kenosha Pass.

Eilers to Arkansas Valley Smelter—6m N-G.
The smelter being adjacent to the D&RG main-line into Leadville, this trackage consisted of what was necessary to serve the various parts of the extensive plant.

Malta to Crane's Park—10m N-G.
Charcoal, necessary for smelting precious metal ores, was produced by a battery of ovens in the forests near the head of Tennessee Creek.

Alamosa to Antonito—28m N-G.
Avoiding the canyon of the Rio Grande south of Alamosa, this route crossed tributary streams on long tangents. The railroad was now in a position to build southward to Española or westward to the San Juan mining region.

Antonito to Española—92m S-G.
Gould allowed Palmer to complete the line as far as possible toward Santa Fe. The track, staying well to the west of the canyon of the Rio Grande, wound in and out of the side canyons which led into it, but was forced to descend a steep grade to reach the river just north of Española.

Antonito to Chama—64m N-G.
This was a strange route. East of Cumbres Pass the track held to a constant 1.4% grade with 20° curvature, apparently wandering aimlessly in spaghetti-like convolutions over the barren country. In 28 miles the route crossed the Colorado-New Mexico state line ten times. On the west side of the pass the track dropped right down to Chama on a 4.0% grade with 20° curves.

27

No. 202. SALIDA FROM THE EAST. D. & R.G.R.R. MELLEN PHOTO.

COLLECTION OF DAVID S. DIGERNESS

Salida, situated on the triangle of level ground between the forks of the Arkansas River, became an important railroad center. The Marshall Pass line crossed the river (far right) and headed westward toward the Continental Divide. The other line followed the stream to the top of Tennessee Pass. Freight yards were to the right, locomotive terminal to the left, with the depot and hotel between them.

The original track of the D&RG climbed through Crane's Park to surmount Tennessee Pass (10,440-feet) the railroad's third crossing of the Continental Divide, in 1880-1881. This panorama toward the south from the pass over-

looks the site of the south portal of the tunnel bored 200-feet below during 1890. Railroad ties were piled along the track, and charcoal kilns can be seen in two places.

Locating engineers avoided the deep canyon of the Rio Grande, south of Alamosa, and maintained a one-percent gradient except for six miles of four-percent grade in Comanche Canyon between Barranca and Embudo at the *southern end of the Rio Grande's gorge. On this occasion 2-8-0 Number 77 was climbing the incline with a work or supply train.*

Colorado Springs to Manitou—5m N-G.
  This branch up Fountain Creek served a stone quarry and the plush spa around the mineral springs.
South Arkansas (later Salida) to Poncha Junction 2m N-G.
  This was the beginning of the Gunnison Extension.
Castle Rock to Girardot (later Hathaway) Quarry—2m N-G.
  This branch was built southeast from Castle Rock to obtain building stone for the new Union Station being erected in Denver.
Grape Creek Junction into Grape Creek Canyon—2m N-G.
  This was the beginning of the West Cliff Branch from Cañon City.
Coal Bank Branch Extension—1m N-G.
  This steep extension went to other coal mines south of Florence.

MOTIVE POWER

39, 40, 43-82, 84
  Baldwin Locomotive   2-8-0   56N
  This group of locomotives, like the previous ones in Class 56 except for a larger tender, were needed for the tremendous amount of construction and the flood of freight traffic which resulted from it.

41, 42
  Baldwin Locomotive   2-8-0   60N
  The Class 56 locomotives were proving to be too small for the 4% mountain grades; hence these heavier 2-8-0's were purchased. Almost identical otherwise, they had larger boilers than Class 56 engines.

85-88, 92-96
  Baldwin Locomotive   4-4-0   42N
  These were larger versions of the previous 4-4-0's.

89-91
  Baldwin Locomotive   4-4-0   38N
  These were identical with the earlier Class 38 locomotives.

97, 98
  Baldwin Locomotive   0-6-0 T   48N
  Like the previous switchers, these were saddle-tank engines.

1881

This was the D&RG's year of glory. Never before, or after, did it lay so much track. The through-line to Salt Lake City was started and the brand new Union Depot

Following the northern wall of the canyon carved by the Los Pinos River, the surveyors were obliged to advise the drilling of two short tunnels, one of which penetrated a promontory and emerged on the face of a sheer cliff hundreds of feet above the stream. A wooden trestle, built into the rocky face, carried the track from the mouth of Toltec Tunnel across the gap to less precarious ground beyond.

Although Cumbres Pass, at 10,020-feet, was not on the Continental Divide, its western approach involved nearly 15 miles of four-percent grade between Chama and the summit. Here a 4-4-0 crawls downhill past what was then called "White Rock Point."

31

Number 93, one of the several locomotives sold to the RGS in 1891, was used in pay-car service after having been displaced from passenger-train work. In this view it was posed next to the Mechanical Department building at Burnham. A corner of the storehouse can be seen at the right.

Engine 172, a 4-6-0, appears to have been brand-new in this panorama at the south end of the Denver's Union Station, prior to the addition of the long wings at each end of the building. The train was the "Pacific Express," due to depart at 7:30 a.m. for a 771-mile journey to Ogden.

The largest narrow-gauge 2-8-0's built for the D&RG were those numbered 400 - 411—intended for helper service. This one is the 402, stationed at Cimarron. This station was situated at the eastern foot of the four-percent-grade up to Cerro Summit.

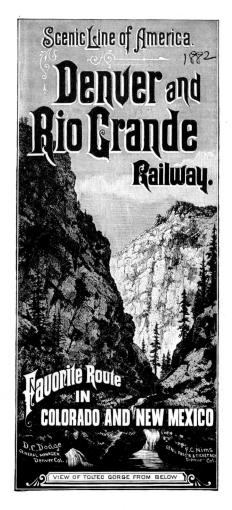

Scenic Line of America.

1882

Denver and Rio Grande Railway.

Favorite Route IN COLORADO AND NEW MEXICO

D. C. Dodge
GENERAL MANAGER,
Denver Col.

F. C. Nims
GEN'L PASS'R & TICKET AG'T,
Denver Col.

VIEW OF TOLTEC GORGE FROM BELOW

RONZIO COLLECTION

Durango, where the Rio de Las Animas River debounced
from the high mountains, was a natural railroad terminus.
The main-line from Alamosa came in from the south
(lower right), and the Silverton Branch skirted the town
(left), then followed the stream northward (background).
The RGS joined the D&RG from the west (lower left).
To the left of center can be seen the roundhouse and

depot, in front of which Durango's only streetcar waits
for a possible fare.

High up the eastern flank of Marshall Pass a track gang puts
finishing touches on new track—while on a lower level, two
2-8-0's bring up a supply train laden with ties, rail and
fastenings. The engine at the rear was headed downhill for
safety on the return trip down the four-percent-grade.

LE MASSENA COLLECTION

The mines in the Crested Butte area produced excellent coal which was delivered to smelters, mills and the mines which yielded ore for them. Slack coal too fine for shipment, was used to produce coke made in the ovens shown in this photograph.

" *The Scenic Line of the World* "

The silver ore mined near Silver Cliff was adequate inducement for the D&RG to build a branch through Grape Creek Canyon to West Cliff. It joined the main-line at the eastern end of the Royal Gorge, crossing the Arkansas River on a wooden through-truss bridge.

Engine 66, a 2-8-0, pulled the first passenger train into Gunnison. This scene shows it ready to depart for Salida on the following morning.

At Mears Junction the branch to the iron mines near Villa Grove diverged to the north, crossed over the Marshall Pass line, then climbed southward to the top of Poncha Pass. Locomotive 83, a 2-8-0, posed with its empty supply train atop the overpassing trestle.

"RIO GRANDE GREEN LIGHT"

Although the addition of a third rail permitted equipment of both gauges to be used in any combination of locomotives and cars, the arrangement was not without difficulties caused by intricate switchwork. In this scene at Burnham, the 538, a brand-new 4-6-0 southbound on a break-in trip with the local freight, strayed from the main track and came to an inglorious halt in the cinder pit.

Descending the north slope of Tennessee Pass, the track made a wide curve to the west in Mitchell Park, then circled eastward around Eagle Park, as shown here. A decade later this route was dismantled when a new standard-gauge line—somewhat steeper—was built along the rocky hillside in the background.

became the D&RG's Denver terminal. The conversion to standard gauge was begun, the decision being dictated by the economics of competition rather than by the economics of operation. The Chicago, Burlington & Quincy-backed Burlington & Colorado was preparing to join Denver with the Burlington & Missouri River Railroad in Nebraska, and restless John Evans was getting ready to build his standard gauge Denver & New Orleans from Denver through Pueblo and Trinidad to the Gulf of Mexico. Rather than have these new lines siphon off major portions of its traffic, the D&RG felt that it was only prudent to join the trend rather than to fight it. The decision was made in haste; narrow-gauge locomotives then on order were widened to 4'8½" in lieu of building standard-gauge ones from the rails up. Nor was there adequate time to prepare a wider roadbed; a third rail was simply spiked to longer ties inserted in the existing narrow-gauge track.

CONSTRUCTION

Chama to Durango—108m N-G.
This was the San Juan Extension which gave access to the silver-mining country north of Durango. Its profile was rough, crossing all of the local streams, and there was hardly any grade less than 1.4% nor curve less then 15°. The Continental Divide was crossed at only 7730 feet a few miles west of Chama.

Poncha Junction to Gunnison—69m N-G.
Enroute to Salt Lake City the D&RG vaulted the Continental Divide once more, at Marshall Pass (10,860 feet). On the eastern slope it followed Poncha Creek, while on the western side it descended the valley of Tomichi Creek.

Alamosa to South Fork—42m N-G.
This branch was built along the upper Rio Grande to tap the forests in the valley, and to handle the ore traffic originating near Creede.

Grape Creek Junction to West Cliff—32m N-G.
By adding 30 miles of track to the stub built in 1880, this branch reached another silver-mining area and a source of iron ore for the Palmer-backed Colorado Coal & Iron Company steel mill at Bessemer (later Minnequa). It followed Grape Creek for the entire distance.

Gunnison to Crested Butte—29m N-G.
The excellent coal mines near Crested Butte were served by this branch which ran up the broad valley of the Gunnison River.

Mears Junction to Iron Mine (later Orient)—28m N-G.
Iron ore for the infant Colorado Coal & Iron Company's smelter and steel mill at Bessemer originated on this line which went over Poncha Pass (9060 feet), dropping down to Villa Grove before reaching the mines on the west slope of the Sangre de Cristo Mountains.

Crane's Park to Red Cliff—21m N-G.
Crossing the Continental Divide once again at Tennessee Pass (10,430 feet), the D&RG dropped down Eagle River Canyon to reach some silver mines.

Durango to Rockwood—19m N-G.
Pushing toward Silverton, the trackage followed the Animas River, but deviated via Rockwood to avoid a narrow and deep canyon.

Robinson to Wheeler—8m N-G.
Silver mines were reached by this extension down Ten Mile Creek north of Leadville.

Poncha Junction to Maysville—7m N-G.
This branch, following the South Arkansas River, was headed for the gold and silver mines at Monarch.

Hecla Junction to Calumet—7m N-G.
Another Colorado Coal & Iron Company iron mine was served by this branch which ascended the steep ravine of Railroad Gulch north of Salida. The locomotives which ran on this line pushed the cars uphill, their fireboxes being raised several inches to maintain the proper water level in their boilers.

Madge Quarry Junction (later Douglas) to Madge Quarry—3m N-G.
Climbing the ridge between the Girardot Quarry and the D&RG's main line through Castle Rock, this branch reached another rock quarry.

Oak Creek Junction to Coal Mines—3m N-G.
This branch was extended southward from the stub built in 1880 east of Cañon City.

Chandler Creek Junction to Coal Mines—2m N-G.
Paralleling the branch up Oak Creek, this one also was extended from a stub built in 1880 east of Cañon City.

Placer (later Russell) to Trinchera Mines—2m N-G.
Still another CC&I Company iron mine was served by this branch, running north from the D&RG main line west of Veta Pass.

Leadville to Fryer Hill—2m N-G.
This trackage was a series of long spurs connecting the mines and mills east of Leadville.

Denver to Bessemer—121m N-G to 3-R.
This conversion was made to handle the output of the CC&I Company steel mill, as well as standard-gauge trains of the AT&SF, without disturbing the other (N-G) traffic on the Pueblo-Denver line.

Durango to San Juan Smelter—1m N-G.
This branch served the great smelter across the Animas River from the engine terminal.

MOTIVE POWER

1 (Second)
Renumbered from No. 4 temporarily.
No. 1 had been leased to the Denver, Utah & Pacific, and a "No. 1" was needed for the pay train.

83

Baldwin Locomotive	2-8-0	56N

This was the last Class 56 engine to be built.

99, 100, 101 (Second)

Baldwin Locomotive	4-4-0	42N

These were identical with earlier Class 42 locomotives.

102-106

Baldwin Locomotive	0-6-0 T	48N

Identical with previous engines in this class, they were the last tank-switchers to be purchased.

150-154

Baldwin Locomotive	2-6-0	45N

Having larger drivers, these last N-G 2-6-0's to be acquired replaced the lighter 4-4-0's in heavy passenger service.

155-156

Baldwin Locomotive	4-6-0	46S

These were the D&RG's first standard-gauge passenger locomotives, as well as its first 4-6-0's. They were nothing more than narrow-gauge 4-6-0's widened to standard-gauge, however.

200-221, 223

Grant Locomotive	2-8-0	60N

Although built by Grant, these locomotives were essentially identical with the previous Class 60 locomotives.

D&RG freight engines (2-6-0's and 2-8-0's) were given 36-inch drivers, while passenger power (4-4-0's and 4-6-0's) had 45-inch wheels, but one group of five 2-6-0's were equipped with 45-inch driving wheels, perhaps for mixed-train service. One of them, Number 150, after having borne the names of four intermediate owners, gravitated to the West Virginia Midland railroad, where it appeared for this portrait.

Like the D&RG's first standard-gauge freight engines, the first standard-gauge passenger locomotives were identical with narrow-gauge machines then being built. This relic was the first of three numbered 155 - 157. Renumbered 503, with a back-up pilot attached to its tender, it handled suburban local trains at Denver.

Baldwin wasn't at all disturbed when the D&RG ordered Numbers 412 - 416 built to standard-gauge. Representative of this group, identical otherwise with contemporary narrow-gauge engines, the 414 was one of the railroad's first standard-gauge freight locomotives.

The D&RG's earliest branches were built to sources of iron ore and coal for the steel mill established at Bessemer. One of them went over Poncha Pass to an iron ore deposit at Orient situated at the northern end of the Sangre de Cristo Mountains.

Although Baldwin built nearly all of the railroad's early locomotives, Grant produced a batch of 2-8-0's numbered 200 - 227. In this smoky interlude the 226 was charging upgrade at Lobato toward the summit of Cumbres Pass, towing double-deck stock cars crammed with bawling sheep.

Excepting the Vulcan 0-4-4-0T, they were the only non-Baldwin locomotives on the railroad up to the end of the century. Possibly Baldwin couldn't produce as many of this class as the D&RG had wanted, hence a supplementary order, using the same plans, was placed with Grant.

240-255
Baldwin Locomotive 2-8-0 60N

This group differed from the previous Class 60 engines by having extended smokeboxes and larger tenders.

400-411
Baldwin Locomotive 2-8-0 70N

This group of locomotives was assigned to helper service on the 4-percent grades over Veta, Marshall and Cumbres passes. They were larger versions of the Class 60 locomotives.

412-416
Baldwin Locomotive 2-8-0 75S

By widening N-G Class 70 locomotives to S-G, the builder was able to produce D&RG's first standard-gauge freight locomotives without undue delay.

1001 Renumbered from 101. 0-4-4-0T No Class
The Vulcan Fairlie, being an odd piece of machinery, was renumbered when conventional locomotives engulfed its original number.

1882

The frantic expansion of the past two years had weakened the D&RG's financial resources and had aroused some doubt concerning its ability to carry the ever-increasing load of debt. Consequently, further expansions were curtailed and practically all of the railroad's forces were concentrated upon completing the through line to Salt Lake City. On August 1 the Denver & Rio Grande Western Railway, which was building the line across Utah, was leased to the D&RG.

CONSTRUCTION

Gunnison to Grand Junction—133m N-G.
   Westward from Gunnison the track followed the Gunnison River into the upper part of Black Canyon as far as Crystal Creek, which was then followed to avoid extremely difficult construction which would have been required in the lower portion of the canyon. It crossed Cerro Summit (7970 feet) and descended to Montrose, on the Uncompahgre River, and followed this stream northward to Delta where it met the Gunnison again. The Gunnison was then followed to its meeting with the Grand (later Colorado) River at Grand Junction.

Grand Junction to State Line—37m N-G.
   West of Grand Junction the tracks followed the Grand River, but diverged to the northwest where the river headed southwestward into a long and deep canyon. The climb away from the river, across the local drainage, necessitated some steep grades and sharp curves. Once the Colorado-Utah state line was crossed, the trackage was part of the Denver & Rio Grande Western Railway, a Utah company formed by Palmer in 1881.

Rockwood to Silverton—26m N-G.
   The fabulous silver camp was reached by building up the Animas River, northward from the end of track at Rockwood.

Wheeler to Dillon—11m N-G.

By building down Ten Mile Creek to Dillon, on the Blue River, the D&RG was in position to go upstream to the gold-mining town of Breckenridge or downstream to the Grand River.

Crested Butte to Anthracite—4m N-G.
   This extension was built to reach coal mines north of Crested Butte.

Red Cliff to Rock Creek—3m N-G.
   This extension in Eagle River Canyon reached additional silver mines.

Girardot Quarry to O'Brien's Quarry—2m N-G.
   Another building-stone quarry was reached by this extension, which required two switchbacks to reach the quarry on top of a mesa southeast of Castle Rock.

Silverton to North Star Mill—1m N-G.
   This trackage went to a group of mines, mills and smelters.

MOTIVE POWER

157
Baldwin Locomotive 4-6-0 46S

This was the remaining engine from the 1881 order.

158-165
Baldwin Locomotive 4-6-0 45½N

Counterparts of Class 46S, these were the first N-G 4-6-0's, replacing 4-4-0's on passenger trains over Marshall Pass, and the unsuccessful high-wheeled 2-6-0's elsewhere.

222, 224-227
Grant Locomotive 2-8-0 60N

Remainders of the 1881 order, these were the last Grant locomotives to be built for the railroad.

256-291, 294-295
Baldwin Locomotive 2-8-0 60N

Last of Class 60 to be built, these were the remainders of the 1881 order.

1883

The D&RGW completed the through line to Salt Lake City on March 30, and dispatched the first passenger train from Salt Lake City on April 8. Palmer resigned as President of the D&RG shortly thereafter, since the new Board of Directors was composed primarily of Easterners who were hostile to Palmer's policy of expansion. However, he remained as President of D&RGW, while Frederick Lovejoy replaced him on the D&RG. As was to be expected, new construction came to a virtual stop, only revenue-producing lines being completed.

CONSTRUCTION

South Fork to Wagon Wheel Gap—14m N-G.
   A further extension along the Rio Grande toward Creede, this line was halted short of its destination by lack of funds.

Maysville to Monarch—9m N-G.
   This branch reached the gold mines at Monarch by means of a great double hairpin curve above Maysville, and a double switchback at Garfield.

Cannon (later Lehigh) Junction to Cannon (later Lehigh) Mine—5m N-G.
   A coal mine west of Sedalia was tapped by this branch along Cannon Creek.

Oro Junction to A.Y. & Minnie—3m N-G.
   This branch was built to a silver mine up California Gulch east of Leadville.

Wagon Wheel Gap was a deep narrow cleft in the mountains, through which the newborn waters of the Rio Grande flowed into the western end of the San Luis Valley. One of the D&RG's 4-4-0's—with the daily local to Creede— halts at the depot while a few passengers try for a quick catch in the stream.

Among the improvements executed after the financial reorganization in 1886 was the replacement of the original wooden-truss bridge across the Gunnison River at Roubideau. The new structure consisted of two steel spans totalling 370-feet in length, placed well above the level of the older bridge.

Silverton, cradled in an upland park, 9,300-feet above the sea, was surrounded by peaks towering 4,000-feet above the town. D&RG track came up the canyon of the Rio de

Las Animas (left) and terminated at the depot and freight-house (far left). A long spur went to the North Star Mill (center) at the foot of Sultan Mountain in the background.

Dillon to end-of-track—2m N-G.

This stub was the beginning of a never-to-be-completed extension down the Blue River.

MOTIVE POWER

2 Rebuilt from 2-6-0 Class 35N
by D&RG shops   0-6-0T   39N

This was the first of five such conversions to provide some needed switchers.

107-109
Baldwin Locomotive   4-4-0   42½N

Slightly heavier than previous 4-4-0's, these were the last of this type acquired.

110, 111	0-6-0	35N	Ex-D&RGW 2, 1
112, 113	0-6-0	40N	Ex-D&RGW 3, 4
114	4-4-0	40N	Ex-D&RGW 5
115, 117, 118	0-6-0	40N	Ex-D&RGW 6, 8, 9
116	2-6-0	40N	Ex-D&RGW 7

This group of locomotives represented the inclusion in the D&RG roster of the leased D&RGW's locomotives.

166-171
Baldwin Locomotive   4-6-0   47N

These were acquired for passenger service over Cumbres, Marshall and Veta Passes, and Cerro Summit.

Curecanti Needle, an isolated pinnacle rising from the bottom of the Gunnison River's Black Canyon, was the feature of the railroad's herald from the mid-1880's to the mid-1920's.

500, 501
Baldwin Locomotive   4-6-0   76S

These were the first standard-gauge locomotives designed as such, the previous ones having been modifications of narrow-gauge designs.

1884

Having begun operation of the through line to Salt Lake City and Ogden, Utah, and being unable to pay the interest upon the tremendous debt which had been incurred during the recent expansion, the D&RG went into receivership again. In a row with Palmer over management of the D&RGW, Lovejoy attempted to break the lease between them. Failing in this action, he ordered the tracks to be severed at State Line, an act which cost the D&RG the through business of the CB&Q and the B&MR. Receiver William S. Jackson took possession of the road on July 12. Also, the trackage-right contract with the DSP&P was terminated, since that line now had its own trackage into Leadville.

CONSTRUCTION

Bridgeport - A line change added a tunnel and shortened the line, eliminating a series of sharp curves adjacent to the Gunnison River and an old bridge at Roubideau, south of Grand Junction.

MOTIVE POWER

3, 8, 12
Rebuilt by D&RG shops from 2-6-0 Class 35N
         0-6-0T   39N

43

Number 162, posed at Durango, was typical of the D&RG's first narrow-gauge 4-6-0's which were assigned to the more difficult portions of the newly built lines, replacing 4-4-0's.

The line over Fremont Pass was extended northward to Dillon on the Blue River, with the intention of descending that stream to the Grand (Colorado) River, thence downstream to Grand Junction—but the track never went beyond Dillon. Traffic was not substantial, and a 2-8-0 with a single box-car and combination car handled the business. This scene shows engine 262 at Kokomo.

To reach Silverton, 45 miles up the Rio de Las Animas from Durango, the railroad was forced to carve a shelf high above the river in a narrow gorge north of Rockwood. Even though most of the branch was on a steady two-and-one-half-percent grade, this short segment was inclined slightly downward. In this colored lithograph, the southbound train—pulled by a 2-8-0 and a 4-4-0—was going uphill along the west wall.

West of Antonito the gradient was maintained the same as that (one-and-a-half-percent) between Denver and Pueblo and along the Arkansas River. The result was an alignment which was characterized by an incredible succession of hair- *pin-curves. In this view at Big Horn, 4-4-0, Number 107—at the head of the daily Alamosa - Durango train—was facing east on the middle level of the great S-curve at that lonely spot.*

Excepting the minor mechanical differences of original construction, these were identical with the one rebuilt in 1883.

172-177
Baldwin Locomotive   4-6-0   47N
Identical to the previous Class 47, these were the last narrow-gauge 4-6-0's acquired.

1885

Early in the year David H. Moffat replaced the capricious Lovejoy, and he began to mend the damage wrought by his predecessor. Foreign investors, anxious over their holdings, inspected the property and concluded that part of the D&RG's difficulties could be attributed to Palmer's policies which had favored the D&RGW and the Colorado Coal & Iron Company, both of which had been organized by the General and his associates. Reorganization seemed to be the only solution to the D&RG's dilemma and negotiations were

begun to undertake this procedure.

MOTIVE POWER

11
Rebuilt from 2-6-0 Class 35N
by D&RG shops   0-6-0T   39N
This was the last of the "home-made" six-wheel switchers.

1886

Poverty-stricken and still in receivership, the D&RG was barely able to meet its payroll, to say nothing of extending its trackage or buying new locomotives. A "friendly" foreclosure and sale were undertaken, and Palmer's original Denver & Rio Grande Railway Company was sold, going out of existence on July 13. The purchasers were its own stock and bondholders, who had formed the Denver & Rio Grande Railroad Company to take over the railroad's property and equipment.

The D&RG's first standard-gauge passenger locomotives were otherwise identical to the narrow-gauge 4-6-0's, and were barely adequate for narrow-gauge consists operated on the three-rail track between Denver and Pueblo. Three much larger machines, like the 502, were procured to handle the heavier cars running on the standard-gauge rails.

Number 177, last of 20 narrow-gauge 4-6-0's, was awaiting the arrival of an unscheduled train in Salida when this portrait was made. All of these engines were subsequently rebuilt with wagon-top boilers, and the extension on the smokebox was removed, probably at the same time.

On the turntable at Monarch Colo. Aug 1ˢᵗ 1884 — Goodman Photo

RONZIO COLLECTION

LEMASSENA

When the branch was built into the mining camp of Monarch the D&RG decided not to exceed a 4½-percent gradient. This policy required the construction of a great double-horseshoe curve at Maysville and a double-switchback at Garfield—shown in this view of a narrow-gauge train negotiating it.

Engine 73, a 2-8-0, rides the above-ground truss-rod turntable at Monarch in 1884. A wye eventually replaced this primitive device—which must have been inoperable most of the year due to the deep snows in that area. At the upper left, Mount Ouray towers 4,000-feet above the rails.

49

The completion of the 104-mile extension to Aspen was celebrated in unprecedented fashion. Four special trains, comprised of 24 cars filled with railroad officials and other worthy personages, arrived on November 1, 1887, before the depot (lower right) had been erected.

The Ouray Branch terminated in a tiny park surrounded by towering peaks of breathtaking beauty. Silver, gold and lead ores—extracted from these same mountains—were concentrated at the mines, then shipped to smelters over the D&RG.

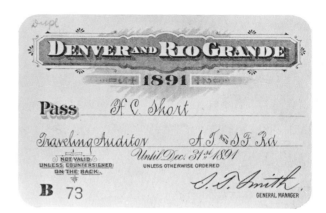

DENVER AND RIO GRANDE

1891

Pass *H. C. Short*

Traveling Auditor *A. T. and S. F. Rd.*

Until Dec. 31st 1891

NOT VALID
UNLESS COUNTERSIGNED
ON THE BACK.

UNLESS OTHERWISE ORDERED

B 73

C. T. Smith
GENERAL MANAGER

Denver & Rio Grande Railroad Company
1886 - 1908

1886

The D&RG Railroad Company was formed by the security holders of the D&RG Railway Company to take over its property and equipment, and to reorganize the old company. Instead of the railroad's financial obligations being reduced, however, they were increased by $28-million, all in preferred stock. The lease of the D&RGW was terminated on July 31, and in return for the elimination of the D&RG's guarantee of D&RGW bonds, considerable equipment, then in use on the D&RGW, was transferred to the latter company.

William S. Jackson, now President, apprehensive over the building of the standard-gauge Colorado Midland Railroad from Colorado Springs to the great silver camps of Leadville and Aspen, appealed to D&RG security holders for an immediate extension to Aspen. But this Jackson was denied, most probably because he sounded like Palmer, who had spent all of the railroad's earnings on new construction and equipment, with scant consideration for those who had expected a lucrative return upon their investments.

MOTIVE POWER

71-81
Sold. Became D&RGW 71-81.

108, 109
Sold. Became D&RGW 108, 109.

110-116
Returned. Became D&RGW 2, 1, 3, 4, 5, 6, 7, 8, 9. These nine locomotives had come from the D&RGW originally.

257, 275, 277, 279, 287-291, 294, 295
Sold. Became D&RGW 257, 275, 277, 279, 287-291, 295.

1887

David H. Moffat succeeded Jackson as President, and the former's personal interest in mining, combined with the rapid advance of the Colorado Midland across the Rocky Mountains, was now sufficient to prod the Directors into authorizing the extension into Aspen. Furthermore, they even approved another branch to an additional source of silver-ore traffic. Another competitor for the Denver-Pueblo traffic appeared when the AT&SF built a parallel track between the two cities, in open violation of the 1880 agreement.

CONSTRUCTION

Rock Creek to Glenwood Springs—63m N-G.
This part of the Aspen extension followed the Eagle River to its confluence with the Grand River at Dotsero. From this point the tracks went down Glenwood Canyon, emerging at Glenwood Springs. The construction of this latter portion was very difficult since the roadbed had to be blasted out of the canyon's sheer walls.

Glenwood Springs to Aspen—41m N-G.
This segment ran up the valley of the Roaring Fork River to reach the fabulous silver mines of Aspen.

Montrose to Ouray—36m N-G.
This branch, following the Uncompahgre River, was built to serve the silver mines around Ouray.

Engleville Junction to Trinidad—4m N-G.
This short extension up the Purgatoire River, built by a subsidiary company, the Trinidad & Denver Railroad, enabled the D&RG to compete for Trinidad coal traffic.

Leadville to Leadville Junction—3m N-G.
This cutoff was built to allow ore and coal trains from the Aspen Extension to reach the smelters at Leadville without having to go down to Malta, thence uphill to their destinations.

Minnequa to Cucharas (Cuchara Junction)—
47m N-G to 3-R.

South Pueblo to Coal Mines (via Coal Branch Junction)—
37m N-G to 3-R.
Six years had elapsed since the last previous conversion to dual-gauge track. These three-rail conversions, the

GRAND RIVER CANYON, COLORADO,

FRED JUKES

The final group of new narrow-gauge 2-8-0's, numbered 417 - 422, were different from previous ones, as can be seen in this photograph of Numbers 419 and 411—smoking their way toward Cumbres Pass from Chama. Their steam pressure was lower and the main rod was connected to the third axle. The high cars in the middle of the train were some of the D&RG's 100 bottom-dump gondolas used for hauling coke.

first in a long series, were necessitated, however, by the arrival of massive standard-gauge competition. The AT&SF had built into both Denver and the Cañon City coal fields. The Missouri Pacific had laid track almost into Pueblo, while the Chicago, Rock Island & Pacific (in the form of the Chicago, Kansas & Nebraska) had reached Colorado Springs. Furthermore, the Denver, Texas & Ft. Worth began operations southward from Trinidad, and its associate, the Denver, Texas & Gulf, was most anxious to connect its Denver-Pueblo trackage with that of the DT&FtW. As if this were not enough, the Colorado Midland was operating between Leadville

and Colorado Springs, and was hard at work on its extension into Aspen.

MOTIVE POWER

417-422
Baldwin Locomotive   2-8-0   70N
These, the last N-G 2-8-0's built for the railroad, were much like those in the earlier Class 70, although they weighed 4000 lbs. more on their drivers. Also, they were sprung differently, and the main rod was connected to the third instead of the second axle.

502
Baldwin Locomotive   4-6-0   76S
This was identical with locomotives on the 1883 order.

503-505
Renumbered from 155-157.

550-554
Renumbered from 412-416.

The lure of Aspen's silver boom was irresistible, and to reach the city the D&RG extended its track down the Eagle River, and along the Grand (Colorado), then up the Roaring Fork. The 17-mile segment along the Grand River required the boring of three tunnels, one of which is shown in this color lithograph of the rapids at Shoshone.

LE MASSENA COLLECTION

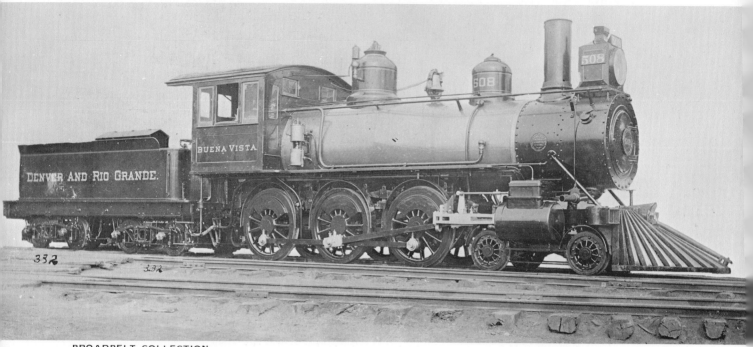

The next step in the progression of 4-6-0's was represented by the 508, 33 of which were delivered between 1887 and 1891.

The great expansion of the railroad's standard-gauge network at the very end of the 1880's required the acquisition of many new locomotives, including 75 identical 2-8-0's for freight duties. Next-to-last in this group, the 628 was being used for a special "Colorado College Potato Institute Train" on this occasion.

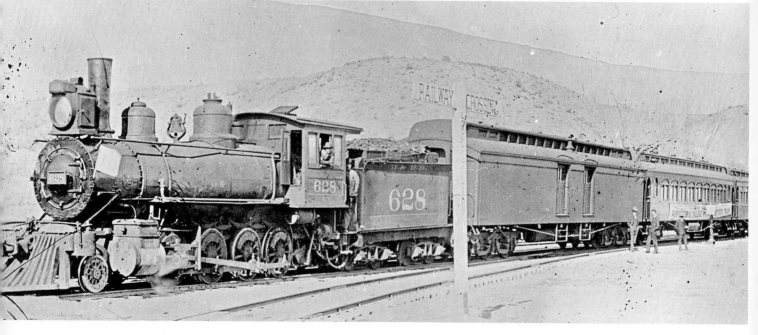

In need of switchers at Denver in 1888, the D&RG converted five of the 400 - 411 group of narrow-gauge 2-8-0's to standard-gauge for that purpose; 12 years later they were restored, but did not regain their original numbers. The 801 had been 410 originally; after its temporary metamorphosis it became 411.

These two renumberings moved the S-G locomotives out of the N-G number series.

506-508

Baldwin Locomotive	4-6-0	106S

These new 4-6-0's now were the heaviest locomotives on the railroad.

1888

Although this year was one of modest expansion to sources of immediate revenue, and of further extension of standard-gauge operations, it was also one in which the D&RG struggled to stay afloat in a flood of standard gauge competition. In an effort to co-operate with the more worthwhile of these newcomers, the railroad granted trackage rights to the CK&N from Colorado Springs to both Denver and Pueblo. DT&FtW trains were granted rights over D&RG rails between Trinidad and Pueblo, while the MP could run into Denver from Pueblo.

During this period the three-rail line between Denver and Pueblo must have presented an interesting panorama of mixed-gauge operations, with two MP, four CRI&P and eight D&RG passenger trains (four of each gauge) trying to make scheduled time in spite of several freight trains which lumbered along behind motive power of both gauges. No wonder the D&RG felt it essential to add considerable second track.

CONSTRUCTION

Chama to Chama Lumber Mill—3m N-G.
This was the first branch to be built to serve the new lumber industry.

Stewart's Junction to Stewart's Mill—2m N-G.
This branch went to a lumber mill west of Tres Piedras on the line to Española.

Aspen to Ore Bins—2m N-G.
This extension, around the town, served additional silver mines.

Cuchara Junction to Trinidad—45m N-G to 3-R.

Cuchara Junction to Loma Junction (later Walsenburg)— 6m N-G to 3-R.

Engleville Junction to Engleville—6m N-G to 3-R.

Coal Junction to Cañon City—8m N-G to 3-R.

Colorado Springs to Manitou Springs—5m N-G to 3-R.
These conversions were made primarily for handling coal in the larger S-G cars.

Leadville to Eilers—3m N-G to 3-R.
This conversion allowed entry of S-G Colorado Midland cars into the Arkansas Valley Smelter.

Denver to Pueblo—27m 3-R, second track.
This extra trackage in various places facilitated the movement of heavy coal trains from Pueblo to Denver.

Rouse Junction to Rouse (later Old Rouse)—5m S-G.

Santa Clara Junction to Santa Clara (later Rouse)— 6m S-G.

Loma Junction (later Walsenburg) to Pictou—5m S-G.

Chicosa Junction to Forbes Junction—1m S-G.
All of these branches were built to reach coal mines. Although they appear to have been the first S-G trackage constructed by the D&RG, that honor truly belongs to a tiny 0.2-mile connection between the D&RG and the Denver, Texas & Ft. Worth railroad at Trinidad.

MOTIVE POWER

509-511

Baldwin Locomotive	4-6-0	106S

These were identical with the previous Class 106 engines.

555-568

Baldwin Locomotive	2-8-0	113S

These were the D&RG's first standard-gauge freight locomotives designed as such, rather than as narrow-gauge conversions.

800-802

Converted to S-G by D&RG shops from 402, 410, 411 (Class 70N) and renumbered.	2-8-0	74S

Equipped with slope-back tenders, these locomotives were designed for yard switching.

55

A Denver-bound passenger train, headed by a diminutive 4-4-0 of the AT&SF, awaits its noon-time departure from Pueblo's Union Station. The D&RG freight yards with three-rail track are in the foreground where two new RGW 2-8-0's are seen en route to their owner. The narrow-gauge yards were situated at the far right against the embankment, but the engine terminal is obscured by the highway bridge over the tracks.

The circuitous narrow-gauge line over Tennessee Pass was unsuitable for standard-gauge operations; hence, a tunnel was bored beneath the Continental Divide, 200-feet lower, and a new line (temporarily narrow-gauge) was built between Pando on the west and Leadville Junction on the east. Locomotive 246, according to the inscription on this Kodak bulls-eye photograph, was the first one to enter the tunnel.

1889

This was a year of adversity for the D&RG. Palmer's D&RGW was converting its entire main line across Utah to standard-gauge, while the standard-gauge Colorado Midland was threatening to connect with it, or to build its own line into Salt Lake City. Then, to make matters worse, a flood in Grape Creek washed out most of the West Cliff Branch.

CONSTRUCTION

Lake Junction to Lake City—36m N-G.
  This branch to the silver-producing area around Lake City was built on a roadbed which had been constructed along the Lake Fork of the Gunnison River eight years previously.

Glenwood Springs to Rifle Creek—27m N-G.
  To forestall the possible construction of Colorado Midland tracks down the Grand River toward a connection with the D&RGW, the D&RG was forced to build this extension.

Aberdeen Junction to Aberdeen Quarry—4m N-G.
  Erection of the new Colorado State Capitol in Denver required construction of this branch to obtain the necessary granite.

Military Junction to Military Post (later Fort Logan)— 3m 3-R.
  A subsidiary company, the Denver, Clear Creek & Western, constructed this branch to a military post southwest of Denver.

Cuchara Junction to Trinidad—45m 3-R to S-G.

Engleville Junction to Engleville—6m 3-R to S-G.
  There being no N-G service on these two lines, the inside third rail was removed.

DISPOSITION

Grape Creek Junction to West Cliff—Removed.
> Most of this branch had been destroyed by flood and it was not rebuilt.

MOTIVE POWER

512-514
> Baldwin Locomotive   4-6-0   106S
> These were duplicates of earlier Class 106 locomotives.

569-581
> Baldwin Locomotive   2-8-0   113S
> These also were duplicates of previous ones in the same class.

803, 804
> Converted to S-G by D&RG shops from 401, 405 (Class 70N), and renumbered.   2-8-0   74S
> These were the last of the N-G to S-G conversions.

1890

In contrast to 1889, 1890 was a year of achivement. Although hardly comparable with the great expansion of 1881, completion of new standard-gauge trackage between Denver and Grand Junction via Tennessee Pass brought forth inauguration of a new transcontinental route in conjunction with the Rio Grande Western (the reorganized D&RGW) via Ogden, Utah. This was completed on November 14 at Grand Junction when track from Rifle Creek reached the city. A further improvement was the commencement of operation at the new Union Depot at Pueblo.

The fruits of these latest accomplishments were not to be enjoyed entirely by the D&RG, however; the Colorado Midland was a 50% partner in owning the final link between New Castle and Grand Junction, and it, too, could offer through service over the RGW in connection with its own line to Colorado Springs. An additional disappointment to the D&RG was the fact that its old rival of 1878-1879, the AT&SF, had bought the CM.

CONSTRUCTION

Villa Grove to Alamosa—54m N-G.
> Removing the third rail between Walsenburg and Minnequa isolated the N-G lines from La Veta to Silverton; hence this link was needed for connection with the rest of the N-G trackage. Having no curves for 53 miles north of Alamosa, it was the fifth-longest tangent in the nation, and was almost level.

Leadville Junction to Pando—15m S-G.
> This segment, replacing the previous line over the divide at Tennessee Pass, was built N-G temporarily, even though it was to become a part of the new S-G route between Denver and Grand Junction. It went under the summit through a tunnel at 10,240 feet, and thence through a shorter tunnel at Deen.

Minnequa to Walsenburg (via Cuchara Junction)—
> 53m 3-R to S-G.

Walsenburg to La Veta—15m N-G to S-G.

Cañon City to Malta—111m N-G to 3-R.

Oak Creek Junction to Oak Creek Mines—3m N-G to S-G.

Chandler Creek Junction to Chandler Mines—4m S-G.

Malta to Eilers—2m N-G to 3-R.

Oro Junction to A.Y. & Minnie—3m N-G to S-G.

Leadville to Leadville Junction—4m N-G to S-G.

Leadville Junction to Pando—15m N-G to S-G.

LE MASSENA COLLECTION

During 1890 the narrow-gauge track along the Arkansas River beyond Cañon City was converted to three-rail and narrow-gauge trains were usually handled by standard-gauge motive power. In this view 2-8-0 Number 592 threads the Royal Gorge with an assortment of narrow-gauge freight cars.

Pando to Red Cliff—5m N-G to S-G.

Red Cliff to Rifle Creek—93m N-G to S-G.

Glenwood Springs to Aspen Mines—43m N-G to S-G.

Rifle Creek to Grand Junction—63m S-G.
> This final link in the standard-gauge line between Denver and Salt Lake City was owned (and operated) as the Rio Grande Junction Railway, which, in turn, was owned equally by the D&RG and the CM. Its track followed the Grand River down to Grand Junction, joining there the west end of the D&RG's narrow-gauge main line over Marshall Pass.

Grand Junction to Crevasse—17m N-G to S-G.
> Before conversion this track was leased to the Rio Grande Western, which then was able to operate its trains into the terminal at Grand Junction.

57

Salida was the principal junction point between the D&RG's narrow-gauge and standard-gauge systems, and it was the only location having two roundhouses—one with 20 stalls,

the other with 26. The larger of these housed standard-gauge passenger power (4-6-0's) and a variety of 2-8-0's used for narrow-gauge consists, and mixed-gauge switching.

Grand Junction to Crevasse—leased to RGW Railway.

The several conversions and new construction listed above produced a standard-gauge main-line from Denver to Grand Junction, Aspen, Leadville, Trinidad and La Veta. Superimposed upon this network was a narrow-gauge line between Denver and Leadville. Beyond Leadville, Salida and La Veta the trackage was entirely narrow gauge, while beyond Malta there was nothing but standard gauge.

DISPOSITIONS

Malta to Pando—removed.

This was the original N-G line over the summit of Tennessee Pass, now no longer needed.

Lehigh Junction to Lehigh Coal Mine—removed.

As a result of this mine being worked out the branch was no longer needed.

Crevasse to State Line—removed.

This narrow-gauge line—connecting with the D&RGW's original main-line—had been replaced by the new RGW standard-gauge track through Ruby Canyon.

MOTIVE POWER

242, 244, 256—sold. Became Rio Grande Southern 1, 4, 2.

515-527

Baldwin Locomotive   4-6-0   106S

582-609

Baldwin Locomotive   2-8-0   113S

The vast expansion of S-G trackage required the acquisition of several more passenger and freight locomotives.

805-811

Baldwin Locomotive   2-6-0   100S

Together with the Class 74 engines, these first S-G 2-6-0's, with slope-back tenders, performed freight switching at Denver, Pueblo and Salida.

1891

During 1890 and 1891 the railroad had been financing the construction of another Colorado subsidiary,

In anticipation of imminent conversion, the rails of the narrow-gauge Aspen extension had been spiked to standard-gauge ties, the changeover having been made in 1890 when the standard-gauge line was completed between Leadville Junction and Grand Junction. As shown in this picture, an open-top observation car was added to trains traversing spectacular Glenwood Canyon during daylight hours.

D&RGW COLLECTION – COURTESY JACKSON THODE

Situated at the western end of Glenwood Canyon, Glenwood Springs with its hot springs and pool, and the great Colorado Hotel (lower right) became a resort community. The engine-terminal for the Aspen Branch and main-line helper engines was placed at Funston, across the Grand (Colorado) River from the town. Colorado Midland track—coming down the Roaring Fork River—swept around the base of the mountain (left), then followed the Grand to New Castle.

The trestle which carried the Lake City Branch across the Lake Fork of the Gunnison River was a wondrous wooden structure, a classic example of the bridge builder's art. At the head of the three-car train was one of the rare large-driver 2-6-0's, recognizable by the bell mounted atop its sand dome.

Bridge over Lake Fork

D&RGW COLLECTION -- COURTESY JACKSON THODE

Still another canyon of the Grand River was encountered between DeBeque and Palisade on the Rio Grande Junction railroad—which was owned by the D&RG and Colorado Midland. It was distinguished by substantial thicknesses of solid reddish sandstone.

Rather than purchase new 0-6-0 switchers, the D&RG preferred to utilize more potent standard-gauge 2-6-0's or outmoded 2-8-0's. This antique machine, originally the 606 built in 1890, had been given a slope-back tender from a 2-6-0, and was still at work half-a-century after delivery.

VOLLRATH COLLECTION

If this scene portrays structural confusion, the reason is due to the presence of three bridges across the Arkansas River at Pueblo, the one in the background having carried a highway across the stream. The nearest one was an unusual skew-truss bridge used by the Atchison, Topeka & Santa Fé; the one next to it was a similar one belonging to the D&RG. Number 805, a 2-6-0, was using it while switching at the north end of the freight yard (right).

Upon completion of the standard-gauge main-line via Glenwood Springs, the trackage at Grand Junction was converted to three-rail operation, but for some reason the location of the third-rail was on the opposite side of the track's centerline from its position elsewhere on the system. This view is toward the west, from the east end of the yard.

One could hardly devise a picture of an early mining town better than this one of Creede, situated in a narrow steep-walled canyon. Freight of every sort was piled on the platform awaiting transport elsewhere, and many varieties of mining personages had assembled at the depot to meet the daily train from Alamosa.

Acquired in 1891, the group of 4-6-0's numbered 528 - 538 were the last of the smaller engines of that type; later ones would be half again as heavy. This one was the 533, at the head of the "Denver Express," halted at Palmer Lake—the high point of the Denver - Pueblo main-line.

THODE COLLECTION

The later engines of the large group numbered 555 - 629, were somewhat different from those erected earlier, the sand dome immediately ahead of the cab having been one feature. This relic, awaiting final disposition at Salida in 1939, had been delivered as the 613 in 1891.

DON E. A. ROGERS

BROADBELT COLLECTION

Each successive order for new locomotives was for larger, heavier and more powerful machines to handle the increasingly longer trains. The dozen 4-6-0's numbered 700 - 711 were a third larger than their predecessors and they were the first engines to carry 200-psi steam pressure. This view of Number 700 was posed at the Baldwin plant in the city of Philadelphia before departing for Colorado during 1896.

One source of excellent coal was at Floresta, west of Crested Butte, on the far side of the mountain range. To reach this mine, the railroad built a branch over Kebler Pass in 1893, thence down to the mine.

The Santa Fé Southern railroad, connecting Española with Santa Fé, was added to the system in 1895. Engine 100, a 4-4-0, with two official cars occupied by executives, pauses for a portrait on the Rio Grande bridge at San Ildefonso.

The shops at Burnham were capable of repairing any of the railroad's engines, and in 1897—after the first two 700's had arrived—two complete duplicates (702, 703) were fabricated there, the only examples of entirely home-made motive power attempted by the D&RG. The 702 was posed at Burnham for this picture.

the Rio Grande Southern, and this drain upon its revenues, together with the cost of the S-G line between Denver and Grand Junction had necessitated the omission of an expected dividend. This caused the security holders once again to accuse the Officers and Directors of operating the railroad primarily for the benefit of Colorado and Denver, rather than for its owners. Angered by this opposition to his plans, Moffat resigned, and was replaced by Edward T. Jeffery, a man who was dedicated to maintaining the status-quo unless forced to do otherwise. Construction halted abruptly, and Moffat was even obliged to finance an extension to handle the traffic from his own mines in the Creede area. Also, during this year, S-G locomotives began to handle N-G trains between Denver and Leadville over the three-rail trackage.

CONSTRUCTION

Wagon Wheel Gap to North Creede—10m N-G.
This extension up the Rio Grande, to serve the silver mines, was built by the Rio Grande Gunnison Railroad, which was financed by Moffat. It marked a new type of financing-construction tactic; the shipper paid for the construction of a new line which was primarily for his benefit. He received a refund, based upon the tonnage handled, and when the line was paid for he transferred title to the railroad.

MOTIVE POWER

29 - Sold. Became Rio Grande Southern 11.

93 - Sold. Became Rio Grande Southern 36.

105 - Sold. Became Rio Grande Southern 14.

243, 245-255, 258-261 - Sold. Became Rio Grande Southern 3, 5-10, 12, 13, 15-21.

528-538			
Baldwin Locomotive	4-6-0	106S	
610-629			
Baldwin Locomotive	2-8-0	113S	

These two groups were the last of the smaller 4-6-0's and 2-8-0's.

812-826			
Baldwin Locomotive	2-6-0	100S	

These were the last 2-6-0's to be built for the D&RG.

1892

Jeffery, pursuing his policy of minimum expenditure, allowed only one short branch to be built, and no motive power was acquired.

CONSTRUCTION

Chama Lumber Mill to Brazos—10m N-G.
This extension, named Tierra Amarilla Southern Railroad, served lumber mills, and was operated separately.

1893

The financial panic resulting from the discontinuance of silver purchases by the mints of India and the United States in 1892, reached its peak during this year. Sixty-five railroads went into bankruptcy, including those mighty rivals of the D&RG, the Union Pacific and the AT&SF. The D&RG, although hurt badly by the loss of silver ore traffic, survived upon substantial volumes of coal, coke, lumber and agricultural products. Still, it must be admitted that Jeffery's penny-pinching practices were a major factor in the railroad's narrow escape from another failure. It is entirely possible that the success of such policies led to their continuation during more prosperous times, ultimately resulting in severe deterioration of the railroad's property, equipment and reputation.

CONSTRUCTION

Fremont Junction to Fremont Mine—2m S-G.
This branch was built from a point on the Chandler Branch to a coal mine.

It would have been logical for the D&RG to have converted its tiny standard-gauge 2-8-0's (412 - 416) to narrow-gauge.

Instead, these engines were rebuilt as 0-8-0T switchers in 1898, after having been renumbered 550 - 554 in 1887.

Crested Butte to Floresta—11m N-G.
This extension, which went over Kebler Pass to a coal mine owned by the Colorado Fuel & Iron Company (formerly Colorado Coal & Iron Company) was built at the insistence of the railroad's biggest single shipper.

1894

Although traffic began to recover somewhat during the year, the gains in revenue were offset by a great flood in the Arkansas River Valley which destroyed considerable trackage.

MOTIVE POWER

22, 41—Renumbered to 228, 229

24—Renumbered to 41 (second)
This renumbering placed these odd locomotives with others of the same class.

1895

Though the D&RG had weathered the financial storm by not expending revenues, its track and equipment had suffered from under-maintenance. Even as the situation was becoming dangerous, management did little to remedy it; in fact, the railroad now became the subject of "milking" accusations.

The Union Pacific, Denver & Gulf (a UP-dominated consolidation, which included the Denver, Texas & Ft. Worth in 1890) built its own line from Walsenburg to Trinidad, thus eliminating joint operation over D&RG rails between these two points.

ACQUISITION

Española to Santa Fé—34m N-G.
This line, the Santa Fé Southern—formerly the Texas, Santa Fé & Northern—was acquired by the D&RG in exchange for some RGS bonds, and re-incorporated as a D&RG subsidiary, the Rio Grande & Santa Fé.

MOTIVE POWER

24, 25 (second)
| Ex-Santa Fé Southern 4, 5 | 2-6-0 | 40N |

25 (first)—Renumbered 42 (second)

71 (second)
| Ex Santa Fé Southern 3 | 2-8-0 | 56N |

1896

Continuance by management of its cash conservation policy was resulting in public condemnations of poor service and accidents; still nothing was done to alleviate the situation.

CONSTRUCTION

Brazos to Tierra Amarilla—3m N-G.
This extension of the TAS went farther into the forests.
Pictou to Maitland—1m S-G.
This was an extension to another coal mine north of Walsenburg.

DISPOSITION

Stewart's Junction to Stewart's Mill—Removed.
The lumber mill on this branch had ceased operations.

MOTIVE POWER

700, 701
| Baldwin Locomotive | 4-6-0 | 150S |

Once again a 4-6-0 became the heaviest locomotive on the railroad.

1897

Failure of the sprawling AT&SF system also caused the collapse of its Colorado subsidiary, the Colorado Midland. During this year the CM was reorganized and was free to run its own railroad once more, competing with the D&RG for trans-mountain traffic. By comparison, however,

Silver mines at Ibex—above Leadville—lured D&RG rails to their greatest altitude in 1898, 11,520-feet at the depot. However, switchbacks to one shaft (foreground) went beyond to 11,600-feet. Snow remained on the ground most of the year, and snowsheds were erected over sections of track where drifting snow would have covered them.

The four-percent grade and 30⁰ curves of the original narrow-gauge line over La Veta Pass became an intolerable operation. This was improved considerably by the construction of a new standard-gauge line to the south of *the original one in 1899. From La Veta to Wagon Creek Junction the new line was 27-miles long—with three tunnels and several convolutions on the east side. This scene shows 2-8-8-2 Number 3615 crossing the summit of the pass.*

the D&RG was considerably more profitable—so much so, in fact, that there was public conjecture of its being bled to death for the benefit of its owners.

MOTIVE POWER

702, 703

D&RG Shops   4-6-0   150S

Close copies of the two Baldwin engines in Class 150, these were the only locomotives ever built entirely by the railroad's shops at Burnham.

1898

The collapse of the Union Pacific's empire caused, among other things, the failure of two of its Colorado subsidiaries, the Union Pacific, Denver & Gulf Railway and the Denver, Leadville & Gunnison Railroad. Both of these were competitors of the D&RG, the former running between Denver and Trinidad with extensions beyond both cities, and the latter having a narrow-gauge line between the points in its name. Toward the end of the year all of the DL&G trackage, plus most of the UPD&G track, was combined into a newly organized company, the Colorado & Southern, possessing a mixed-gauge system like that of

the D&RG. This railroad was to play a prominent part in the D&RG's future.

Although the Spanish-American War had increased the business and also profits, precious little of the D&RG's income went into maintaining roadbed and equipment; accidents were accepted as part of the daily routine.

CONSTRUCTION

Chrysolite Junction to Ibex—7m N-G.

Some rich silver mines east of Leadville made this branch worthwhile. (Ibex, at 11,520 feet, was the highest point ever attained by D&RG rails.)

Chandler Junction to Chandler Mines—3m S-G to 3-R.

This unusual conversion enabled mills on the N-G Florence & Cripple Creek Railroad to obtain coal without having to transfer it at Florence.

MOTIVE POWER

401, 402

Converted to N-G by D&RG shops from 800, 802 (Class 74S) and renumbered.

Apparently there was more need for these locomotives as N-G road engines than as S-G switch engines. Originally they had been N-G 402 and 411, respectively.

Narrow-gauge main-line operations were drawing to a close when the big Baldwin 2-8-0's numbered 901 - 916 arrived in 1900. To show the progress during three decades, the D&RG borrowed 2-6-0 Number 6—which had been sold to the Colorado Eastern railroad—and posed it alongside the 904 in Denver.

Purchased in 1899, the Brooks 4-6-0's were essentially identical in their principal dimensions to the earlier ones built by Baldwin. They differed mainly in external mechanical details: piston valves, driver spacing, cab structure and dome locations.

71

For 12 years after the branch up Grape Creek to the Silver Cliff - Westcliffe mining district had been destroyed by a flood, those communities had been without a rail connection. But in 1901 there was a local revival of silver mining, and the railroad built a new branch from Texas Creek to Westcliffe. In this view looking upgrade from Texas Creek a train was rounding the hill (upper left), descending toward a U-curve in the valley beyond the notch, thence across the wooden trestle over the Arkansas River to the main-line.

With the expectation of considerable mineral traffic, the D&RG built a branch in 1901 from Moffat to Cottonwood, site of a mine and mill. Passenger service went only as far as Crestone, where 2-8-0 Number 32 was resting, probably on a Sunday when the daily round-trip was not operated.

Westcliffe was situated in a broad and verdant valley, with the eastern slopes of the lofty Sangre de Cristo Mountains forming a most spectacular background. The silver mines were located northeast of the town—out of the picture to the left.

The growth of agriculture in the San Luis Valley required the conversion of the narrow-gauge line between Alamosa and Antonito, where the Santa Fé Branch diverged (left) from the line to Chama and Durango (right). Here again the position of the narrow-gauge third-rail differed from that of the main-line.

73

COLLECTION OF DAVID S. DIGERNESS

When the D&RG built up the North Fork of the Gunnison to Somerset in 1902 to reach a seam of coal, the rails passed through Paonia—where orchards were already well-established.

This line remained narrow-gauge only four years before being converted to standard-gauge.

550-554—Rebuilt by D&RG shops
    as saddle-tank switchers   0-8-0T   75S
    These locomotives were used as shop switchers, replacing the Class 48N 0-6-0T's which had been scrapped or sold.

704-711
    Baldwin Locomotive   4-6-0   150S
    After experimenting with the 702 and 703, the railroad must have decided it was cheaper to buy locomotives than to build them.

1899

Feeling, perhaps, that they had gone just about the limit in cutting expenses, the management now sought other means to the same end, even if a sizable capital expenditure was necessary. One such project was the relocation of the line over Veta Pass, combined with extension of S-G rails into the San Luis Valley.

CONSTRUCTION

Wagon Creek Junction (later Russell) to Alamosa—34m
N-G to S-G.
La Veta to Wagon Creek Junction—27m S-G.
    Avoiding steeper gradients by following a ridge to the south of Veta Pass, the new line crossed the range at La Veta Pass, then went down Wagon Creek on the west side of the hill. Its construction, plus the S-G conversion into Alamosa, enabled agricultural products from the San Luis Valley to move in S-G cars to points of consumption beyond the N-G trackage. On the other

hand, coal, ore and concentrates moved in N-G cars via Poncha Pass to the smelters and refining plants which were located at points served by both gauges. Hence, raw materials could move inbound on the N-G, while the finished product could move outbound via S-G to the ultimate destination. (The old N-G track over Veta Pass was not removed immediately since it served some coal mines just west of La Veta.)

ACQUISITION

Denver, Clear Creek & Western Railroad.
    This was the company under which the Fort Logan Branch had been built in 1889.

MOTIVE POWER

720-739
    Brooks Locomotive   4-6-0   170S
    These were the first non-Baldwin locomotives (and the first S-G non-Baldwins) built for the D&RG since the Grant N-G Consolidations of 1881-1882. The number-gap between 711 and 720 was provided to allow for future inclusion of the RGW's 4-6-0's.

1900

The beginning of a new century also marked the beginning of a new era in D&RG history. The late Jay Gould's eldest son, George, was attempting to piece together a transcontinental railroad system, and his Missouri Pacific had begun to buy up large amounts of D&RG stock. In turn, the D&RG began to acquire RGW stock, thus giving Gould control of a continuous line from

After the removal of the narrow-gauge third rail in 1902, the yards at Colorado Springs still utilized stub-switches. In this busy scene, a one-car Manitou Branch local and the train for Cripple Creek were exchanging passengers with the northbound express train from St. Louis—which had come in over the Missouri Pacific.

Despite the assemblage of seven persons at Creede, including the station agent, one more individual, the RPO clerk, was needed for this two-car consist awaiting its 4:20 p.m. departure time for Alamosa. There passengers could board the overnight train for Denver.

For the first run of its "Scenic Limited," which was operated for only three months in 1906, the D&RG selected the first of ten Vauclain-compound engines. In this picture the *short-lived train was rolling behind the 1001, southward from Littleton.*

St. Louis to Ogden. Also, the D&RG bought the Colorado Midland on a 50/50 basis with the Colorado & Southern. It is possible that these two acquisitions could have been the underlying cause for the tight-fisted policies of the previous few years.

CONSTRUCTION

Graham Park Junction to Wolftone Mine—2m N-G.
    This branch served silver mines above Leadville.
Alamosa to Monte Vista—17m N-G to 3-R.
    This conversion was made for the handling of agricultural products in S-G cars.
Pagosa Junction to Pagosa Springs—31m N-G.
    Built as the Rio Grande, Pagosa & Northern Railroad, this branch reached into a new lumbering area.

MOTIVE POWER

405, 410, 411
    Converted to N-G by D&RG shops from 803, 804, 801 (Class 74S) and renumbered. Originally these had been N-G 401, 405, 410, respectively.
901-915
    Baldwin Locomotive   2-8-0   185S
    Skipping the 600-series, which had been reserved for RGW 2-8-0's, these new engines were more than twice as big as the D&RG's first S-G freight locomotives.

1901

Now in complete control of the D&RG, George Gould became Chairman of its board, and having indirect control of the RGW also, he replaced Palmer with Jeffery as President of the latter road. The two companies were henceforth operated as one railroad, although they retained their individual names and equipment for a few more years.

CONSTRUCTION

Moffat to Cottonwood—17m N-G.
    This branch, incorporated as the Rio Grande, Sangre de Cristo Railroad, was built to reach an ore-reduction mill at the western foot of the Sangre de Cristo Mountains.
Alamosa to Antonito—29m N-G to 3-R.
Monte Vista to Del Norte, 14m N-G to 3-R.
    These two conversions also were for handling agricultural products in S-G cars.
Texas Creek to Westcliffe—17m S-G.
    Following Texas Creek, this branch, built by the Rio Grande Railroad Company, replaced—somewhat belatedly—the branch up Grape Creek which had been washed out in 1889.

1902

Gould found one possible route to the Pacific Coast blocked when the Union Pacific, eager to extend its influence westward, obtained control of the Central Pacific Railroad, the direct line between Ogden, Utah, and Oakland, California. Consequently, he was forced to consider alternatives, including the construction of his own railroad.

ACQUISITION

Tierra Amarilla Southern Railroad—Chama Lumber Mill to Tierra Amarilla—13m N-G.
    The D&RG had obtained stock control of this lumber branch, which was operated by a lumber company.
Rio Grande, Pagosa & Northern Railroad. This was the Pagosa Springs Branch built in 1900.

CONSTRUCTION

Delta to Somerset—43m N-G.

Companions to the 10 four-cylinder 4-6-0's were 30 2-8-0's, constructed with inverted Vauclain-compound cylinders, for freight service between Denver and Minturn. This one was the 1123, shown here awaiting its departure up the hill to Tennessee Pass. This engine's boiler, tender and some of its machinery survived when they were used to construct narrow-gauge locomotive 496.

The D&RG went all the way with the compounding concept, adding 15 narrow-gauge 2-8-2's to its collection. These were the first new narrow-gauge engines since 1887, and preceded by a decade standard-gauge 2-8-2's for the railroad. During their very long life these locomotives were modified in many ways, as other pictures will indicate.

Just above Austin, the branch to Somerset formed a great loop to the north, to cross Currant Creek. In this scene 2-8-0 Number 57 was pulling a 1902 construction train across the wooden trestle spanning the stream.

Coal was found in the rolling foothills northwest of Walsenburg. Maitland was typical of the small mining towns along the D&RG branch which served the mines of that area. This branch was extended from Maitland to Strong in 1904.

This branch, following the Gunnison River and its North Fork, ran through an agricultural region to reach some coal mines. Its N-G rails were laid on S-G ties in preparation for imminent conversion.

Zinc Junction to Blende—3m S-G.
　Named the Rio Grande, Pueblo & Southern Railroad, this branch served a zinc smelter southeast of Pueblo.
Overland Junction to Overland Park—1m S-G.
　This branch, replacing the Denver Circle railroad's facilities which had been removed a few years previously served a race track south of Denver.
Denver to Pueblo—119m 3-R S-G.
Castle Rock to O'Brien's Quarry—4m N-G to S-G.
Military Junction to Ft. Logan—2m 3-R to S-G.

Colorado Springs to Manitou—5m 3-R to S-G.
　These four conversions eliminated N-G operations between Denver and Pueblo.
Alamosa to Del Norte—31m 3-R to S-G.
Del Norte to North Creede—28m N-G to S-G.
　These two changes completed the standard-gauging of the Creede branch.
Arkansas Valley Smelter to A.Y. & Minnie—4m 3-R to S-G.

DISPOSITIONS

Douglas to Madge Quarry—Removed.
La Veta to Placer—Removed.
　(This had been the original N-G line over Veta Pass.)
Wagon Creek Junction to Trinchera Mines—
　Sold to Trinchera Estate Company.
　There was no further need for these three lines.

MOTIVE POWER

1001-1010
　Baldwin Locomotive　　4-6-0　　　179S
　(Four-cylinder Vauclain Compound)
　These locomotives, the railroad's first compounds, were assigned to passenger service between Denver and Salida.

1101-1130
　Baldwin Locomotive　　2-8-0　　　190S
　(Four-cylinder Vauclain Compound)
　As could have been anticipated, this new freight power was put to work hauling heavy freight trains between Denver and Salida.

1903

Determined to extend his railroad system to the West Coast, Gould committed himself and the financial resources of the two "Rio Grandes" to the construction of the Western Pacific Railway. Surveys were begun, and a $50-million loan guaranteed by the D&RG/RGW, was floated. This issue of bonds was to drastically affect every aspect of the D&RG's corporate life, ultimately causing its death. Only the most urgent expenditures were made on the

ED BONDS

Except for one 2-8-0, Number 584, small 4-6-0's of the 506 - 538 group were used between Durango and Farmington. This odd arrangement was discontinued in 1923 when the track was changed to narrow-gauge.

After having been served by three railroads for 15 years, Grand Junction was embellished with a substantial union depot in 1905. Of interest to locomotive experts is a D&RG 2-8-0, minus its pilot truck, headlight and road-number, but under steam and obviously working for somebody.

In 1906, when the narrow-gauge track from Grand Junction to Montrose (and also the branch from Delta to Somerset) was converted to standard-gauge, another portion of the D&RG's original main-line had been altered, leaving only the Montrose - Salida line undisturbed, and it was to remain so for nearly another half-century. This photograph shows the Gunnison River canyon near Dominquez.

Durango became a three-rail terminal in 1905 when the standard-gauge branch was built from Carbon Junction to Farmington. Not connected with other standard-gauge track, this isolated segment received its rolling stock in pieces which were re-assembled at Durango.

Influenced no doubt by the Missouri Pacific railroad, which had gained control of the D&RG, the railroad bought five 0-6-0 switchers—numbered 831 - 835 — for use in the Denver passenger terminal. Sixteen years later the 831 was found working in Salt Lake City.

D&RG, whose revenues flowed primarily into the WP's treasury.

The Colorado & Wyoming Railway contracted with the D&RG to operate its short branch to coal mines at Hezron.

CONSTRUCTION

Lumberton to El Vado—33m N-G.

This branch, known as the Rio Grande & Southwestern Railroad, used rail removed from the Tierra Amarilla Branch.

Howard's Quarry Junction (later Howard) to Howard's Quarry (later Calcite)—6m S-G.

A limestone quarry at the head of Howard Gulch southeast of Salida was reached by this branch.

Minturn to Rex—4m S-G second track.

The congestion on the west side of Tennessee Pass just outside the helper terminal at the foot of the grade necessitated this additional track.

DISPOSITION

Chama to Tierra Amarilla—Removed.

This had been the Tierra Amarilla Southern Railroad, operated by the lumber interests which had moved their operations to Lumberton, New Mexico.

MOTIVE POWER

450-464

Baldwin Locomotive	2-8-2	125N

(Four-cylinder Vauclain compound)

Not only were these the first 2-8-2's built for the D&RG,

but they were the only N-G compounds and the last Vauclain compounds.

512—Renumbered 536.

1904

All of Gould's activities were being concentrated on the embryonic Western Pacific, and except for the financial assistance extracted from the MP, D&RG and RGW, those three railroads were ignored and neglected.

CONSTRUCTION

Maitland to Strong—8m S-G.

Wandering cross-country to coal mines, this track was an extension of the branch running north from Walsenburg. It was owned by the Rio Grande Railroad Company, a separate corporation controlled by the D&RG.

DISPOSITIONS

Aberdeen Junction to Aberdeen—Removed.

Santa Clara Junction to Old Rouse—Removed.

There was no longer any activity on either of these branches.

1905

Construction of the Western Pacific was started despite the obstacles interposed by and opposition of the Union Pacific and its bankers.

CONSTRUCTION

Durango to Carbon Junction—2m N-G to 3-R.

Carbon Junction to Farmington—48m S-G.

This branch was built down the Animas River to serve the growing agricultural region of the lower valley. Perhaps in expectation of a connection with the AT&SF or the Southern Pacific in lower New Mexico, this line

After purchasing 30 compound 2-8-0's, the D&RG returned to less complicated machines, adding 10 2-8-0's—numbered 916 - 925—with slightly larger driving wheels. Some of them,

like the 922, which was assisting a Cripple Creek Short Line 2-8-0 at the time (during the great 1913 blizzard), were equipped with cylindrical tenders.

Missouri Pacific's domination of the D&RG brought motive power from American Locomotive Company, ending the

railroad's long patronage of Baldwin. Among the first arrivals were 20 large 2-8-0's in 1906—like the 1141 above.

was built as an isolated S-G segment, its locomotives and cars being dismantled at Alamosa and shipped piece-meal to Durango for reassembly.

DISPOSITION

Oak Creek Junction to Oak Creek Mines—Removed.
This track was no longer needed as the coal mines south of Florence had ceased operations.

MOTIVE POWER

916-925

Baldwin Locomotive	2-8-0	187S

These slightly larger versions of Class 185 2-8-0's were later equipped with cylindrical tenders.

1906

Westward across the empty Utah and Nevada deserts went Gould, the Western Pacific, and the D&RG's revenues, while the D&RG, itself, was all but coming apart at the joints from lack of maintenance. Not only were serious accidents increasing in frequency, but they were attracting more and more unfavorable notices in the public press. And it appeared to be cheaper to buy new motive power than to repair what they had, at least for the time being.

CONSTRUCTION

Longsdale to Cokedale—1m S-G.
This isolated piece of track served an American Smelting & Refining Company coking plant. To reach it the D&RG built a short connection with the AT&SF at Trinidad, operating over that line to Jansen, whence it traversed Colorado & Wyoming rails into Longsdale.
Grand Junction to Montrose—72m N-G to S-G.
Delta to Somerset—43m N-G to S-G.
Here, also, agricultural and coal traffic dictated the change from N-G to S-G.

MOTIVE POWER

831-835

Baldwin Locomotive	0-6-0	149S

These were the railroad's first S-G six-wheel switchers.

1131-1150

American Locomotive	2-8-0	220S

This was the beginning of a long series of orders from the American Locomotive Company, a change which was attributable to Gould's influence.

1907

The Western Pacific was proving to be considerably more expensive than Gould had anticipated. As fast as the two "Rio Grandes" made money Gould diverted it to the WP, allowing them to become even more run down.

CONSTRUCTION

Rex to Redcliff—4m S-G (second track).
This track was needed to reduce congestion on the west side of Tennessee Pass.
Strong to Big Four Mine—2m S-G.
This track was a further extension of the branch through the coal mining region northwest of Walsenburg. It was owned by the Rio Grande Railroad Company.
Tropic Junction to Tropic Mine—2m S-G.
This short branch served a coal mine west of La Veta.
C. B. Coal Company Junction to Bulkley Mine—1m N-G.
A coal mine south of Crested Butte was served by this branch.

MOTIVE POWER

839, 840

Baldwin Locomotive	0-6-0	149S

These were identical with previous engines in the same class.

In 1935 the Alamosa terminal was filled with unserviceable engines being cannibalized for parts, as illustrated by the 457 which has lost its valve stem, main rod and headlight. Delivered in 1903 as four-cylinder compounds, they remained

thus only three years before being changed to two-cylinder simple. Some of this group were modified a second time with piston-valves and Walschaerts valve-motion.

DON E. A. ROGERS

2446 CASTLE GATE - PRICE CAÑON - D.&R.G.Ry.

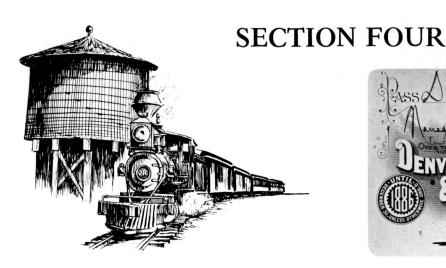

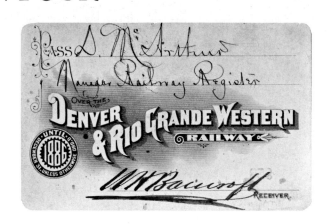

Denver & Rio Grande Western Railway

1881 - 1889

1881

The D&RGW Railway Company filed its Articles of Association in the Territory of Utah on July 21. Its proposed capitalization of $48-million was to be used for the construction of a narrow-gauge railroad from Salt Lake City to a connection with the Denver & Rio Grande Railway at the Utah-Colorado line, plus fifteen branches, totalling some 3,000 miles. Its first (and only) president was the indefatigable General William J. Palmer, who was also president of the D&RG.

Before building any track of its own, the D&RGW absorbed two existing and operating railroads which were located in the midst of a domain dominated by Union Pacific railroad interests. How this consolidation was accomplished was not revealed until a court case in 1916. The evidence showed that these two railroad companies had concocted a fraudulent combination in 1879 for the purpose of selling additional bonds, with the unannounced intention of defaulting upon their original ones. As was to be expected, the two companies were foreclosed and sold, Palmer and his associates purchasing them. The court records did not disclose who perpetrated this nefarious scheme, but it smacks of the crafty Jay Gould, who had obtained a controlling interest in Palmer's D&RG during 1878 and 1879.

ACQUISITIONS

Sandy Station to Bingham—18m N-G.
This had been the Bingham Canon & Camp Floyd Rail Road which hauled silver ore down to the smelters

THODE COLLECTION

This close-up view of the Price River bridge immediately west of Castle Gate shows the rough ties and uneven rails of the D&RGW's new track. Interestingly enough, the rail joints were opposite each other, rather than staggered, a practice which was not changed when the line was converted to standard-gauge.

on the Utah Southern railroad south of Salt Lake City.
Sandy Station to Alta—16m N-G.
This had been the Wasatch & Jordan Valley Railroad which also brought silver ores to the smelters. This unusual railroad was operated with locomotives only to the granite quarry at Wasatch, beyond which point mules pulled its tiny cars through eight miles of almost continuous snowshed to Alta.

MOTIVE POWER

The BC&CF had four locomotives, while the W&JV owned three. The available data about them does not indicate that they were immediately relettered "D&RGW Railway" or given new numbers.

1882

This was a busy year for the D&RGW. It picked up another railroad at a foreclosure sale and tied together its three pieces of acquired trackage. Then, it struck out eastward across the mountains and desert toward a connection with the D&RG at the Utah-Colorado border. On August 1, it leased its properties to the D&RG, which would operate them.

ACQUISITION

Provo to Scofield—60m N-G.
This had been the Utah & Pleasant Valley Railway, which brought coal into the Great Salt Lake Valley.

CONSTRUCTION

Salt Lake City to Provo—46m N-G.
Following the Jordan River and parelleling the Union Pacific's standard-gauge Utah Southern trackage, this line connected with BC&CF-W&JV trackage at Bingham Junction, two miles west of Sandy.
Clear Creek to Grassy Trail—70m N-G.
The track crossed the Wasatch mountains at Soldier Summit (7440-feet), whence the Price River was followed eastward.

Provo, situated on the eastern shore of Utah Lake, occupied a strategic site at the mouth of Timpanogos Creek and became a commercial center of considerable importance—due partly to its having been the northern terminus of the Utah & Pleasant Valley railroad. In this early view—looking toward the Wasatch Range—the "Pacific Express," which had left Denver the previous morning, was halted at Provo for a meal stop, since its passengers had not eaten since breakfast at Green River.

A train-load of coal, extracted from mines near Scofield, was awaiting its departure for P.V. Junction on the main-line when this portrait of the crew, motive power—2-8-0 Number 77—and local facilities was made. The former U&PV line climbed over the ridge in the background to reach Scofield, but it had been abandoned in favor of the longer route over Soldier Summit.

In 1883—when the D&RGW's track on the eastern slope of the Wasatch Range was new—it followed the Price River closely, but avoided its more difficult canyons. Even so, *floods washed away much of the roadbed in the lower canyon near Cedar, and a considerable stretch of track was relocated on higher ground, away from the stream.*

P. V. Junction (later Colton) to Scofield—15m N-G. This line up Fish Creek replaced the former U&PV track between Clear Creek and Scofield, which surmounted the Wasatch Range south of Soldier Summit.

DISPOSITION

Clear Creek to Scofield—Removed.
   This tortuous trackage, with two unusual switchbacks over the mountains, was unsuitable for a main-line.

MOTIVE POWER

The U&PV contributed two locomotives to the D&RGW's roster, bringing the total to nine, which were renumbered into a D&RGW number-sequence. After the lease of the D&RGW to the D&RG the latter road assigned them numbers in its own series.

D&RGW		D&RG				
(1st)	(2nd)					
1	1	111	0-6-0	Class 35N	Ex-W&JV	1
2	3	112	0-6-0	Class 40N	Ex-BC&CF	1
3	2	110	0-6-0	Class 35N	Ex-W&JV	2
4	4	113	0-6-0	Class 40N	Ex-BC&CF	2
5	5	114	4-4-0	Class 40N	Ex-W&JV	3
6	6	115	0-6-0	Class 40N	Ex-BC&CF	3
7	7	116	2-6-0	Class 40N	Ex-U&PV	7
8	8	117	0-6-0	Class 40N	Ex-BC&CF	4
9	9	118	0-6-0	Class 40N	Ex-U&PV	8

1883

In a frenzy of hasty construction the D&RGW built eastward, meeting the westbound trackage at Desert Switch on March 30. As soon as this trackage was completed the D&RG sent some of its own motive power to the D&RGW to serve in lieu of the latter's engines, which were hardly more than switchers.

CONSTRUCTION

Grassy Trail to Desert Switch—24m N-G.
   This segment left the Price River Valley at Lower Crossing and headed cross-country around the west toe of the Beckwith Plateau toward Green River. The new line had no more than commenced operations, however, when floods washed it out for a period of about two months. It was relocated several miles to the north, thus avoiding the treacherous canyon between Farnham and Cedar.
Desert Switch to State Line—97m N-G.
   This trackage was built by D&RG forces working for the D&RGW. Situated on the uplands on the north side of the Grand River, and crossing the local drainage to reach Green River, the line was a frightful combination of curves and roller-coaster grades.
Salt Lake City to Ogden—36m N-G.
   This final link, skirting the eastern shores of the Great Salt Lake, was completed on May 21, thus providing a new through-route from Denver, Colorado Springs and Pueblo, via Salida, Gunnison and Grand Junction, to Salt Lake City and Ogden.

1884

D&RG President Frederick Lovejoy became embroiled with D&RGW President Palmer over matters of rental payments and management of the leased Utah line, with the result that Lovejoy ordered the D&RGW-D&RG connection severed at State Line in July. Later in the month

85

RICHARD KINDIG

On March 30, 1883, the D&RG - D&RGW narrow-gauge line was completed between Denver and Salt Lake City. The last rails were laid at a lonely spot west of Green River, appropriately named Desert Switch, and except for the big 4-6-6-4—Number 3703—racing down the rails, the landscape had not changed over a period of six decades since the track was completed.

The vast emptiness of the arid desert in eastern Utah is well illustrated by this photograph of the D&RGW's original narrow-gauge line near Cisco. This difficult route was abandoned in 1889 when the standard-gauge line was constructed through Ruby Canyon of the Grand (Colorado) River.

DAVID DAVIDSON

When completed in 1883, the line from Salt Lake City formed a half-circle west of the UP-CP depot in Ogden and entered the yards from the north. In this panorama to the south, D&RGW narrow-gauge and three-rail track are visible at the left.

UTAH STATE HISTORCIAL SOCIETY

The D&RGW was leased to the D&RG as its Utah Lines and several D&RG locomotives were assigned to this latest addition to its system. When the lease was terminated in 1886

by the D&RG, it was required to give several engines to the D&RGW. Among them were 2-8-0's 71 - 81, all like the 74 shown in this picture.

he tried to break his company's lease of the D&RGW. Afterward, when the D&RG went into receivership, Palmer felt that it would be wise to do the same thing to protect the D&RGW. William H. Bancroft, a long-time operating man under Palmer on the D&RG, was appointed its receiver in July, and he immediately began to cooperate with Receiver William S. Jackson of the D&RG to restore the earning power of the two companies.

1885

The courts upheld the legality of the D&RG's lease of the D&RGW and found further that the D&RGW had been damaged by the D&RG's capricious conduct. Consequently, the D&RG reached the decision that it would be best to settle with Palmer on some mutually agreeable basis.

1886

The D&RG Railroad Company, which had acquired the property of the D&RG Railway Company, did not continue the lease of the D&RGW, which emerged from its period of receivership in August. The D&RGW received considerable equipment from the D&RG as compensation for damages incurred during operation by the latter company.

CONSTRUCTION

New trackage was nothing more than spurs to coal mines, totalling about six miles.

MOTIVE POWER

The nine D&RGW engines were removed from the D&RG's roster, regaining their D&RGW numbers.

71-81		
Ex-D&RG 71-81	2-8-0	56N
108, 109		
Ex-D&RG 108, 109	4-4-0	42½N
158, 159, 165		
Ex-D&RG 158, 159, 165	4-6-0	45½N
257, 275, 277, 279, 287-291, 294, 295		
Ex-D&RG 257, 275, 277, 279, 287-291, 294, 295	2-8-0	60N

These four groups were obtained from the D&RG in the settlement for damages.

1887

With a new spirit of independence, having been freed from all obligations to the D&RG, the D&RGW began to court the favor of the Colorado Midland, the new standard-gauge railroad which was racing the D&RG to the fabulous silver camp at Aspen and the territory toward Utah.

CONSTRUCTION

Lake Park Junction to Lake Park—2m N-G.
    This was a branch to a bathing and amusement park on the shore of the Great Salt Lake between Salt Lake City and Ogden.
Diamond Junction to Diamond Quarry—1m N-G.
    This spur served a stone quarry at the mouth of Diamond Creek, just west of Thistle.

1888

The obvious outcome of the D&RG-CM race across the Colorado mountains could only be the construction of a standard-gauge line between Glenwood Springs and Salt Lake City. Rather than have a S-G competitor alongside his D&RGW, Palmer decided to convert his N-G railroad to S-G to handle the traffic of both the D&RG and the CM. Consequently, conservation of financial resources in preparation for the formidable task of relocation and standard-gauging precluded any construction or motive power acquisition during the year.

1889

Changing the D&RGW to standard-gauge was no mere matter of moving one rail outward by 1-foot, 8½-inches; instead, it meant widening roadbeds, inserting numberless longer ties, and eliminating curves and undulations in alignment. About 100 miles of entirely new railroad had to be built where the D&RGW's trackage was inadequate.

Such an undertaking being beyond the D&RGW's financial resources, Palmer organized a new company, The Rio Grande Western Railway, to acquire the D&RGW and to construct all of the required trackage. So, on May 16, the D&RGW was absorbed into the RGW, and its colorful corporate career came to a close.

A pair of 4-4-0's—108, 109—were among the 27 D&RG locomotives transferred to the D&RGW in 1886, together with considerable other rolling stock. The 108, renumbered RGW 15, is shown in this photograph taken at the Lake Park pavilion north of Salt Lake City.

Three 4-6-0's, originally D&RG Numbers 158, 159 and 165, became the property of the D&RGW in 1886. The first of these, renumbered RGW 20, was near the end of its career in Utah, having been assigned to Lake Park excursion runs just prior to the change of track-gauge.

Rio Grande Western Railway
1889 - 1908

1889

The RGW Railway Company was formed on May 16, 1889, as a consolidation of the D&RGW Railway and the State Line & Denver Railway, filing its Articles of Incorporation in both Colorado and Utah on June 24. The D&RGW had been the "Utah Lines" of the D&RG, while the SL&D had been organized to acquire a right-of-way between the Utah-Colorado state line and Glenwood Springs, Colorado, terminus for both the D&RG and the Colorado Midland railroads.

Reconstruction and gauge-widening of the former D&RGW N-G line across eastern Utah began immediately at Salt Lake City. During the period of conversion the RGW continued main-line passenger and freight service, apparently transferring persons and merchandise from car to car at the various locations where the track gauge differed. (During the summer and fall S-G trains were composed of N-G cars mounted temporarily on S-G trucks, the locomotives having been N-G power hastily widened to S-G. This interesting expedient ended late in the year when new S-G equipment began to arrive.) In December the RGW leased 17 miles of D&RG track between Grand Junction and Crevasse, Colorado, the new junction point of RGW and D&RG trackage.

CONSTRUCTION

Ogden to Provo—82m N-G to S-G.
Lake Park Junction to Lake Park—2m N-G to S-G.

MOTIVE POWER

1-2			
Ex-D&RGW 1-2	0-6-0	35N	
3-4			
Ex-D&RGW 3-4	0-6-0	40N	
5			
Ex-D&RGW 5	4-4-0	40N	
6-9			
Ex-D&RGW 6-9	2-6-0	40N	

15, 16			
Ex-D&RGW 108, 109	4-4-0	42½N	
70-80			
Ex-D&RGW 81, 71-80	2-8-0	56N	
100-110			
Ex-D&RGW 257, 275, 277, 279, 287-291, 294, 295	2-8-0	60N	

All of the above locomotives were narrow-gauge, inherited from the D&RGW.

30, 31			
Ex-Denver Circle 5, 7	4-6-0	47N	

It is not known why these two locomotives were purchased from the defunct suburban line. Nevertheless, it is quite possible that they, together with engines 20-22, operated from Grand Junction over the N-G line to the eastward-moving point of gauge conversion.

33-36			
New York Locomotive	4-6-0	107S	
111-121, 127-130			
Baldwin Locomotive	2-8-0	113S	

These Class 107S and Class 113S engines, the first standard-gauge power acquired by the RGW, were immediately put into service between Ogden and the points of gauge conversion.

1890

In June the conversion to S-G was completed, and through service between Ogden and Denver was inaugurated in November when standard gauging of the D&RG and construction of the Rio Grande Junction railroad into Grand Junction from the east was accomplished.

CONSTRUCTION

Thistle to Manti—61m N-G.
This branch, built to tap the rich mineral and agricultural resources of the Sevier River Valley, climbed along Thistle Creek to a summit at Hill Top, then followed the San Pitch River downward into the new territory.

The narrow-gauge trackage at Salt Lake City was taken up and replaced with a standard-gauge layout, and the various structures embracing depots (left) and shops (right) were newly built to accommodate the much larger locomotives and cars used after the change of gauge in 1889.

Provo to White House—184m N-G to S-G.

With minor reconstruction, this line completed conversion of the usable N-G alignment, a new S-G main-line having been built eastward from White House into Colorado.

White House, Utah, to Crevasse, Colorado—51m S-G.

This entirely new S-G line, south of the original N-G route out on the desert, dropped down to the Grand River at Westwater and followed its spectacular red sandstone canyon to Ruby where it emerged, joining the original line at Crevasse. The new route was much easier to operate and actually shortened the rail

distance between Grand Junction and White House by 18 miles.

Diamond Junction to Diamond Quarry—1m N-G to S-G.
Bingham Junction to Bingham—16m N-G to S-G.
Bingham Junction to Wasatch—8m N-G to S-G.
Pleasant Valley Junction to Utah Mine—18m N-G to S-G.

The conversion of these branches completed the standard-gauging of the operated trackage, service on the remainder of the branch to Alta being continued intermittently for several years as a narrow-gauge tramway.

DISPOSITION

White House to State Line—Removed.

This former N-G main-line had been supplanted by the new S-G line through Ruby Canyon of the Grand River.

MOTIVE POWER

37, 38			
New York Locomotive	4-6-0	107S
51-54			
New York Locomotive	4-6-0	96½S

These locomotives were assigned to main-line passenger trains.

The RGW's new standard-gauge line followed the Grand (Colorado) River for 15-miles through a deep and beautiful canyon between Westwater and Ruby. In this spectacular stretch near the eastern end, a 2-8-0 was accompanying a single car over the newly-laid track for the benefit of an inspection party.

Eleven larger D&RG 2-8-0's, numbered in the upper-200 series, were acquired by the D&RGW as part of the cancelled-lease settlement in 1886. One of them, drifting downgrade through Castle Gate, was dwarfed by the towering wall of rock through which the Price River had eroded a narrow channel.

106-110—Converted by RGW shops
from Class 60N   2-8-0   60S

These widened locomotives were used on construction trains.

122-126, 131-135
Baldwin Locomotive   2-8-0   113S

These duplicates of the earlier Class 113 engines went into freight service.

1891

Having successfully survived the frenzy of reconstruction and re-equipping from N-G to S-G, the RGW promptly began expansion into new traffic-producing areas. Financing of the new construction was accomplished through the organization of subsidiary companies owned by the stockholders of the RGW, a strategem which put them beyond the possible claims of RGW bondholders.

CONSTRUCTION

Springville to Eureka—40m S-G.
This branch, organized as the Tintic Range Railway, was built to reach the productive silver mines close to its terminus. After crossing the flat Goshen Valley the line ascended the east slope of the Tintic Mountains on a difficult alignment which necessitated three tunnels and a loop with several long, high timber trestles.

Thistle to Manti—61m N-G to S-G.
This branch had been built temporarily as N-G.

Manti to Salina—26m S-G.
This southward extension along the Sevier River was built as the Sevier Railway.

Bingham to Upper Bingham—2m N-G.
This tram line served the silver mines at the upper end of Bingham Canyon, and was operated with horses and mules, the RGW having no N-G locomotive able to negotiate such grades and curves.

Scofield to Winter Quarters—2m S-G.
This extension from the end of the Pleasant Valley Branch tapped another coal mine.

MOTIVE POWER

20-22—Sold. Became Rio Grande Southern 22-24.

30—Converted by RGW shops
from Class 47N   4-6-0   47S

31—Sold. Became Rio Grande Southern 25.

39-42
New York Locomotive   4-6-0   107S

71-74, 76-80—Sold. Became Rio Grande Southern 27-35.

75—Converted by RGW shops
from Class 56N   2-8-0   56S

100, 103, 104—Converted by RGW shops
from Class 60N   2-8-0   60S

136-148
Baldwin Locomotive   2-8-0   113S

The rapidly developing coal traffic required more of these locomotives. Although the RGW no longer needed N-G locomotives, since it had no N-G track in operation, four such engines had been retained. The Rio Grande Southern had refused Number 70, while Numbers 101-102 and 105 were useful at Grand Junction, where D&RG narrow-gauge trains serving the Gunnison and Uncompahgre river valleys terminated.

In addition to purchasing new standard-gauge locomotives for both freight and passenger service, the RGW for some inexplicable reason acquired two 4-6-0's from the defunct Denver Circle railroad in Denver. Having been built by the New York Locomotive Works in 1884, the engines were in fine condition, and were given Numbers 30 and 31.

The RGW's first branch was a very long one—constructed in 1890 from Thistle to Manti in the Sevier River country— to provide a source of traffic other than coal and ore. Contrasting sharply with the desert in eastern Utah, this landscape near Manti reflects verdant farmlands.

The Rio Grande Western's first standard-gauge passenger locomotives were 4-6-0's numbered 33 - 36, from the New York Locomotive Works. Number 36—appearing as shiny as if it had just been delivered—had just coupled to the eastbound "Atlantic Mail" at Helper and was awaiting the conductor's signal for departure, C. 1889.

In this 1890 view, old and new roadbeds parallel each other east of Helper (center) at the foot of the steep grade through Price River Canyon (left) to Soldier Summit. The 14-stall roundhouse sheltered 4-6-0's and 2-8-0's used in pairs and triplets to hoist passenger and freight consists up the hill.

In this frigid portrayal of harvesting ice from Scofield Lake, one of the RGW's first new standard-gauge 2-8-0's provides warmth for the workmen. At the same time the locomotive served as an appropriate photographic background for a group portrait of the ice-train's crew. This trim little engine was purchased in 1889 from Baldwin.

Besides the 4-6-0's produced by the New York Locomotive Works for main-line passenger trains, the RGW bought four smaller ones the same year (1890) from the same builder. They were numbered 51 - 54 and were used for secondary service. On this occasion, Number 51 was stopped in Springville while head-end business was being transacted with the Thistle-Ogden local train.

Soldier Summit was a broad treeless saddle separating the headwaters of the Price River, on its eastern flank, from those of Soldier's Creek, on the west. Unrestrained wind-blown snow would fill the cut through the final ridge, necessitating the erection of a snowshed, a veritable rarity in Utah. RGW Number 114, a 2-8-0, has emerged from the shed and was ready to depart eastward.

The Bingham depot (center) was surrounded by a confusion of mine structures and railroad trackage in 1906. RGW track occupied the bottom of the canyon and the new low-grade line was perched high on the mountainside (right). Copper Belt tracks were at the far left and right, encircling the terminus.

Green River—named for the great river in the background—was an isolated community in the midst of Utah's eastern desert country. At this time (in 1890) its facilities included both passenger and freight stations, a six-stall roundhouse, a coal chute, and a capacious hotel.

THODE COLLECTION

*Thistle—at the western foot of the long ascent to Soldier Summit—was initially a helper station. It became a junction when the branch into the Sevier River valley was constructed. For only the first year—**1890**—its trackage had three rails, as shown in this superb Jackson photograph. The following year the branch was converted to standard-gauge. Barely visible at the left are seven narrow-gauge engines: two 4-4-0's, two small 2-8-0's and three larger 2-8-0's.*

*The branch from Thistle to Manti—61 miles long—was first built to narrow-gauge, probably because the RGW possessed a surplus of unneeded narrow-gauge equipment. Only a year later—in **1891**—the gauge was changed, and narrow-gauge cars and locomotives were likewise converted for use on the line, as shown in this scene near Hill Top.*

THODE COLLECTION

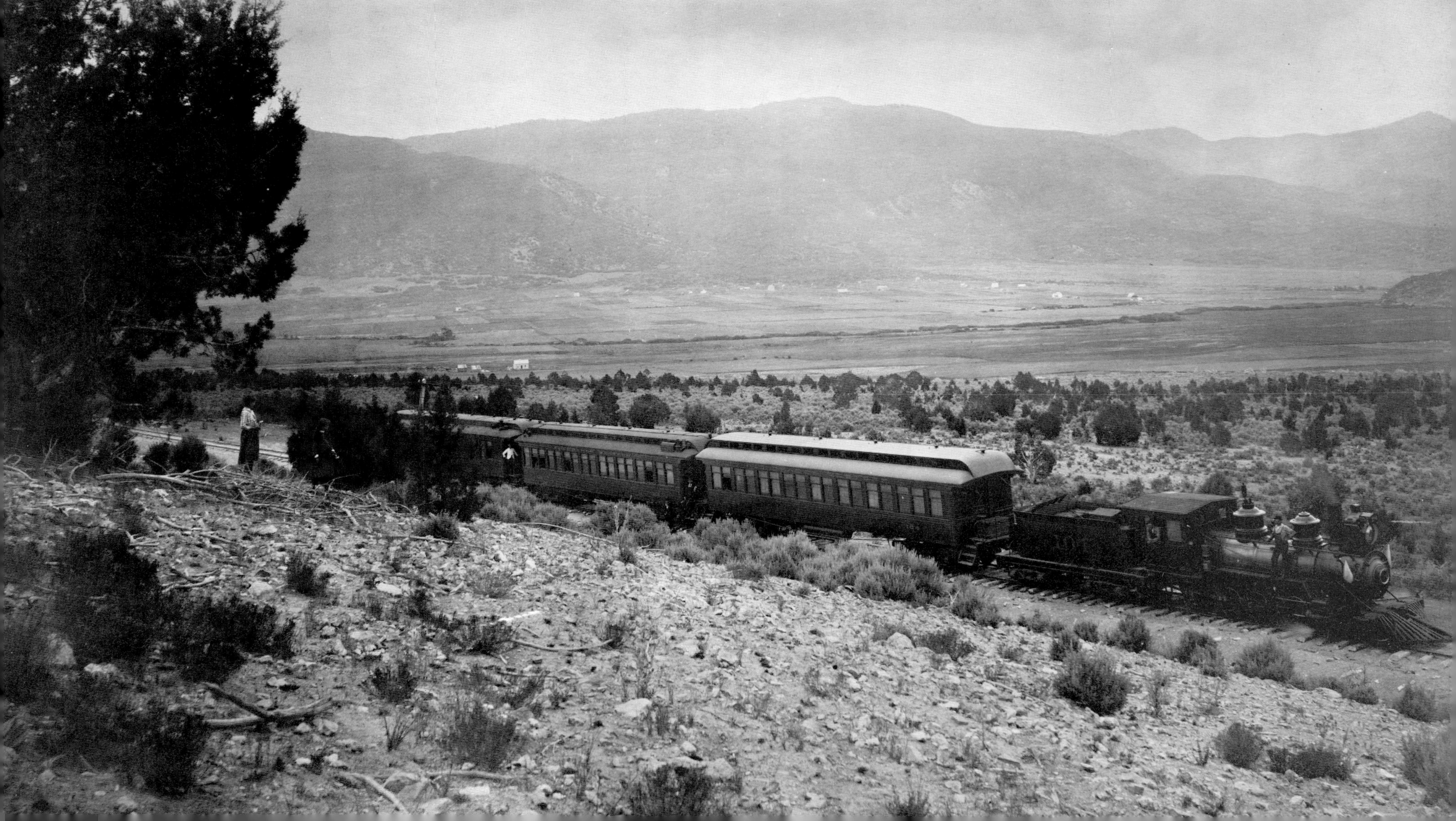

Having no further use for narrow-gauge locomotives after the change of gauge, the RGW scrapped its oldest ones, sold most of those remaining and converted some to fit the wider gauge. One of these converted engines was Number 106, a 2-8-0 obtained from the D&RG—shown in this view at Springville during the changeover there in 1890.

A second branch of the RGW took its tracks into a rugged, barren land southwest of Utah Lake—where rich silver ore lured both the RGW and Union Pacific. Silver City and Eureka—shown in this picture—situated on top of a high saddle, were focal points of mining activity.

1892

Having completed the conversion of its entire system from narrow-gauge to standard, the RGW built short branches to sources of new traffic.

CONSTRUCTION

Jennings Junction to Jennings Quarry—3m S-G.
    This branch was built to reach stone quarries east of P. V. Junction.
Eureka to Mammoth Junction—2m S-G.
    The large new ore mill at Mammoth was reached via this extension connecting to another mile of track owned jointly with the Oregon Short Line.
Stockyards Junction to Stockyards—1m S-G.
    This also was joint track with the Oregon Short Line, north of Salt Lake City.

MOTIVE POWER

Several early locomotives were renumbered: 30, 75, 100, 108, 103, 104, 106, 109, 107, 110, 101, 102, 105, 70, became 1-14.

61-66
    Baldwin Locomotive   4-6-0   134S
    This group of 4-6-0's was intended for heavy passenger service. Engines 61 and 62 had two simple cylinders; the others were four-cylinder Vauclain-compounds.
101—Converted by RGW shops
    from Class 60N   2-8-0   60S
149-153
    Baldwin Locomotive   2-8-0   113S
    The arrival of these 2-8-0's marked the end of new motive power acquisitions by the RGW for several years.

1893

The frightful Silver Panic did not plunge the RGW into the financial disaster which became the fate of many a larger carrier. While the Colorado Midland, the AT&SF and the Union Pacific fell as victims of over-expansion, combined with evil times, both the RGW and the D&RG managed to survive. The financial stringencies brought on by the panic caused new construction to be limited only to the most promising sources of traffic.

CONSTRUCTION

Mammoth Junction to Silver City—2m S-G.
    This trackage, plus seven miles of long spurs, served other silver mills in the precious-metal mining complex surrounding Eureka.
Copper Plant Junction to Copper Plant—1m S-G.
    This spur served the new smelter north of Salt Lake City.

1894

The continuing business depression brought a halt to all new activity.

1895

Although business began to show improvement in 1895, the RGW deemed it prudent to maintain the status-quo to preserve its solvency.

1896

Mining prospects around Marysvale seemed promising; consequently, the RGW raised funds for a further extension toward that area.

CONSTRUCTION

Salina to Belknap—40m S-G.
    This extension was an addition to the Sevier Railway, and followed the Sevier River upstream toward the gold-producing area to the south.

DISPOSITION

Silver City to end of track—Removed.
    This unneeded trackage consisted principally of spurs to idle mines and mills.

1897

Once again construction was at a standstill; funds for further extensions were not available.

MOTIVE POWER

12—Converted by RGW shops
    from Class 60N   2-8-0   60S

1898

With the resumption of more favorable business conditions the steadily increasing coal traffic over Soldier Summit resulted in congestion on the four-percent grade on the west side of the hill. Although it would have been desirable to reduce the grade with a new low-grade line, RGW funds could finance only a second main track up the steepest section.

The trackage of the Utah Central Railway (and its affiliated Salt Lake & Fort Douglas and Salt Lake & Eastern railways) was added to the RGW system. A new RGW subsidiary, the Utah Central Railroad, was organized to acquire these companies in return for the RGW's guarantee to pay their bond interest. The RGW dismantled some of the acquired trackage which it did not need, and added the equipment to its own roster.

ACQUISITION

Salt Lake City to Fort Douglas, Red Butte Quarry, Emigration and Mill Creek—11m N-G.
    This trackage, consisting of short three-rail spurs east and south of Salt Lake City, had been the former Salt Lake & Fort Douglas Railway.
Mill Creek to Park City—29m N-G.
    This line had been the former Salt Lake & Eastern Railway.
Mill Creek to Wilford—1m 3-R.
    The Utah Central Railway had owned this track.

CONSTRUCTION

Tucker to Soldier Summit—8m S-G second track.

DISPOSITION

Lincoln Park Junction to Emigration, Fort Douglas and Red Butte—Removed.
    These short branches of the Utah Central were no longer needed.

In order to handle its ever-increasing passenger traffic, the RGW bought six Baldwin 4-6-0's in 1892, the first two of which had single-expansion cylinders, while the other engines were built as compounds with four cylinders. This busy station scene at Price shows Number 62 at the head of the eastbound "Atlantic Mail."

Although equally as exciting as the Colorado Central's famous narrow-gauge "Georgetown Loop," the RGW's standard-gauge equivalent at Laguna on the Eureka Branch was almost unknown. Despite this spectacular stratagem to gain elevation, the gradient was still a frightful three-percent.

The last four 4-6-0's delivered in 1892 were of four-cylinder compound design, a popular arrangement at the time. As shown in this smoky scene at Castle Gate, they were capable of taking five cars unassisted up the two-and-one-half-percent-grade from Castle Gate to Kyune.

In 1892 the RGW renumbered the remaining ex-D&RGW engines 1 - 14, nearly all of which had been changed to standard-gauge. Numbers 2 and 14—originally D&RG 75 and 81—were assigned to passenger service on the new branch into the Sevier River country. Number 2 received the honor of bringing the first train into Richfield in 1896, as recorded in this photo of civic jubilation.

Number 9, prior to 1892, had been RGW 107, D&RGW 290 and also D&RG 290. It had been converted to standard-gauge in 1890, and thereafter worked principally on the branches to Manti and Silver City.

When RGW rails reached Belknap in 1896, twice-daily passenger service in both directions was inaugurated—using three standard-gauge cars and tiny locomotives which previously had run on narrow-gauge track. On this particular trip it appears that the consist had two patrons, though they seemed to possess the outward characteristics of those who travel without paying fares.

Despite the conversion of narrow-gauge 2-8-0's to standard-gauge, the RGW needed still more locomotives to handle its growing traffic. The 144, shown here at Thistle, was one of 13 new 2-8-0's added in 1891.

The D&RG had used 2-6-0's for switching chores, while the RGW acquired four locomotives of that wheel arrangement in 1898 with large driving wheels for fast-freight service between Salt Lake City and Thistle. This photograph shows one of these husky 2-6-0's—Number 201—posing for a group portrait at Thistle.

The RGW's third new extension went up Timpanogos Creek in 1899—through a beautiful and spectacular canyon to Heber City. In this noontime portrait of commerce, the entire crew of the local freight train posed beside its motive power, one of the railroad's oldest and smallest 2-8-0's.

As passenger traffic increased and trains grew longer, RGW's existing 4-6-0's were hard-pressed to maintain schedules. As a result, four slightly larger engines—numbered 70 - 73— were purchased in 1898 to handle the business. Outwardly, their appearance was remarkably like that of D&RG 4-6-0's bought from the same builder (Baldwin) at the same time.

Apparently satisfied with the cross-compound conversion of its Vauclain-compound 4-6-0's, the RGW ordered four new machines of that type from the Schenectady Locomotive Works in 1901. More powerful than earlier engines, the 80 - 83 were the last 4-6-0's acquired by the railroad.

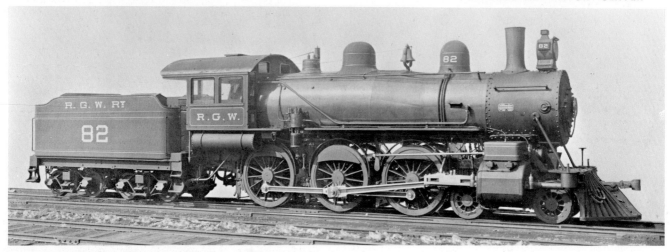

Locomotives 63, 64, 66 must have presented an enigma to onlookers; they carried Baldwin builder's plates, but "Richmond" was cast into their cylinders. Built as four-cylinder compounds, the engines had been sent to the Richmond Locomotive Works in 1900 where they were changed to two-cylinder compound arrangement.

MOTIVE POWER

At this time the RGW reclassified its locomotives by cylinder size.

Number 14 was converted by RGW shops		
from Class 60N	2-8-0	15S
33-42	4-6-0	18S
51-54	4-6-0	17S
61-62	4-6-0	19S
63-66	4-6-0	24S
70-73		
Baldwin Locomotive	4-6-0	21S

These new locomotives, acquired for handling the main-line expresses, were the heaviest locomotives on the RGW at the time.

111-153	2-8-0	20S
200-203		
Baldwin Locomotive	2-6-0	26S

These 2-6-0's, heavier than any of the 2-8-0's, were used in merchandise service in the Salt Lake Valley west of Thistle.

01		
Ex-UC 1	2-8-0	16N
02		
Ex-UC 2	2-8-0	15N
03		
Ex-UC 3	2-8-0	16N

1899

Since agriculture had become an important industry, the RGW built a new branch into one productive area, and to further develop its coal traffic it expanded into the coal fields on the east slope of the Wasatch range. As before, subsidiary companies were used to finance the construction.

CONSTRUCTION

Provo to Upper Falls—11m S-G.
This portion of a new branch following the Provo River was built by the RGW.

Upper Falls to Heber City—15m S-G.
This part of the line was owned by the Utah Eastern Railway, a subsidiary.

Utah Mine to Clear Creek Number 2—5m S-G.

Mounds to Sunnyside—17m S-G.
Both of these extensions—the latter being built up Grassy Trail Creek east of Helper— were owned by the Carbon County Railway, another RGW subsidiary.

Ogden Sugar Junction to Ogden Sugar Works—2m S-G.
This branch to a sugar factory was owned jointly with the Oregon Short Line.

Grand Junction to Sugar Works—1m S-G.
This branch to Colorado's first beet sugar factory was owned jointly by the RGW, the D&RG and the CM.

1900

In July the RGW and the recently-formed Colorado & Southern railroad bought the Colorado Midland. This strategy assured the RGW of a controlled route into eastern Colorado, and of almost equal importance, a friendly connection northward into Wyoming and southward into Texas. The RGW was now in a formidable

R. H. CARLSON COLLECTION

Until the arrival of three 0-6-0 switchers in 1900, the railroad had used its gauge-widened ex-D&RG 2-8-0's for switching work at Grand Junction, Salt Lake City and Ogden. The new engines were assigned to the shunting of passenger cars at Salt Lake City, thus releasing the older locomotives for branch-line service. D&RG 805 was originally RGW 21.

The water tank at Barclay was located at the foot of a four-mile grade of six-percent to the top of the ridge at Altus. Though not needed after the relocation in 1900, the structure remained until operations on the Park City Branch were discontinued in 1946.

DON E. A. ROGERS

Six 2-6-0's, numbered 500 - 505, rolled out of Schenectady's shops just ahead of the 4-6-0's numbered 80 - 83, and like the 4-6-0's the fast-freight engines were two-cylinder compounds also.

Baldwin counterparts of the 600-series 2-8-0's were four-cylinder compounds numbered 700 - 704 delivered in 1901. They were much like D&RG 2-8-0's constructed in the following year.

The RGW's final locomotives ordered to its own specifications were two groups of compound 2-8-0's. The 600 - 604 were two-cylinder compounds, built by Richmond, with an enormous 36-inch diameter right-side cylinder, plainly visible in this builder's photograph of 1901.

The long branch projecting southward from Thistle to Marysvale in the midst of a new gold-producing district was completed during 1900. From the end-of-track in this vista—

looking toward the uninhabited land to the south—it was nearly 250 miles to the next railroad. The line between Manti and Marysvale was built as the Sevier Railway.

position, and its stockholders used this advantage to advance the price of RGW stock whenever the D&RG tried to negotiate for acquisition of the RGW. The situation was not to last much longer, however, for it interfered with the ambitions of George Gould (Jay Gould's eldest son) to assemble a transcontinental railroad system.

Putting his grandiose plan into action, Gould had the Missouri Pacific railroad acquire substantial blocks of D&RG stock, and the latter company, in turn, began to purchase the available stock of the RGW.

CONSTRUCTION

Belknap to Marysvale—6m S-G.
   This last segment of track into the gold-producing area was another part of the Sevier Railway.
Jennings to Potters—2m S-G.
   Another stone quarry was served by this extension.
Springville to Sugar Factory—1m S-G.
   The construction of this spur marked the beginning of the RGW's association with a new Utah industry, sugar-beet growing and beet-sugar refining.
Roper to Sugar House (Mill Creek)—2m S-G.
   This cutoff, owned by the Utah Central, eliminated the original line through Salt Lake City over which Park City Branch trains had been operated.
Sugar House to Park City—29m N-G to S-G.
   When the branch to Park City was converted to S-G, the nine miles between Barclay and Gorgoza were relocated on a new alignment, reducing the grade from 6.3-percent to 4.2-percent.
Park City to Ontario Tunnel—2m S-G.

This was joint track with the Union Pacific to reach a new precious metal mine.

DISPOSITION

Barclay to Gorgoza—Removed.
Salt Lake City to Sugar House—Removed.
   Both pieces of track were replaced by other trackage in a different location.
Diamond Quarry Branch—Removed.
   The stone quarry on this stub had gone out of business.

MOTIVE POWER

21-23
   Schenectady Locomotive   0-6-0   22S
   The receipt of these switchers made more of the smaller 2-8-0's available for branch-line service.

63—Rebuilt by Richmond from four-cylinder Vauclain-compound to two-cylinder
   cross-compound   4-6-0   24S

300-303
   Richmond Locomotive   2-8-0   28S

400-403
   Richmond Locomotive   2-8-0   28S
   The first group of 2-8-0's, with larger drivers, was intended for merchandise service between Helper and Grand Junction, while the second group worked over Soldier Summit between Helper and Thistle. They were the last RGW locomotives to be equipped with link-and-pin couplers.

The second group of Richmond 2-8-0's built in 1900 had smaller driving wheels, like the previous Baldwin engines, but they were much heavier. D&RGW 970 in 1936 had begun its career as RGW 400.

The RGW had three locomotives numbered 1—and all of them had been built for other railroads. The first had been Wasatch & Jordan Valley 1; the second had been built for the Denver Circle as its Number 5. The third, shown in this picture at Heber City, was originally Utah Central 1.

04
    Ex-Rio Grande Southern 30 2-8-0   15N

08—Converted by RGW shops
    from Number 8, Class 15S 2-8-0   15N
    This was a temporary conversion for use during re-
    building and widening the gauge of the Park City
    Branch.

1901

Fully aware by now that Palmer and the RGW had the upper hand, and that they were blocking his scheme for a transcontinental system, George Gould came to terms. He arranged for his D&RG to acquire the RGW by floating a new issue of stock, using the cash proceeds to buy the controlling interest from Palmer and his associates. The D&RG management took over on July 1, with D&RG President Edward T. Jeffery replacing Palmer as President of the RGW. The Colorado Midland was not included in these negotiations since it was not essential to Gould's plan.

Taking a respite from additional construction, the new management reclassified all of the RGW's motive power to correspond with the system used by the D&RG.

CONSTRUCTION

Bingham to Old Jordan and Commercial Mines—3m S-G.
    This trackage, some of which had been N-G and operated by animal power, was at first leased to the Copper Belt Railroad, which purchased Shay locomotives to negotiate its steep grades and sharp curves. Later, in 1905, the Copper Belt was given title to this trackage when it issued its stock to the D&RG.
Keystone Junction (Summit) to Keystone Mine—1m S-G.
Metropolitan Junction to Metropolitan Quarry—1m S-G.
Stockyards to North Salt Lake Elevator—1m S-G.
    These short branches were built to serve specific industries.

MOTIVE POWER

1, 13 (second)—Converted by RGW shops from N-G
    numbers 03, 01.   2-8-0   77S
    These engines were equipped with steam-heat connections for branch-line passenger service at this time.
2, 14   2-8-0   64S
3-12   2-8-0   65S
    (08 had been re-converted to S-G Number 8.)
21, 22 (second), 23   0-6-0   96S
33-42   4-6-0   115S
51-54   4-6-0   104S
61, 62, 66   4-6-0   124S
    Number 66 had been rebuilt by RGW shops from four-cylinder Vauclain-compound to single expansion.
63, 64   4-6-0   130S
    Number 64 also was rebuilt by Richmond from four-cylinder Vauclain-compound to two-cylinder cross-compound.
65   4-6-0   130S
70-73   4-6-0   145S
111-153   2-8-0   120S
200-203   2-6-0   141S
300-303   2-8-0   183S
400-403   2-8-0   180S

To this roster of locomotives the RGW (now dominated

by the D&RG) added several cross-compound locomotives and some more Vauclain-compounds, attracted, no doubt, by their economy in the consumption of coal and water.
80-83
    Schenectady Locomotive   4-6-0   161S
500-505
    Schenectady Locomotive   2-6-0   154S
600-604
    Richmond Locomotive   2-8-0   186S
    All of these locomotives were two-cylinder cross-compounds.
700-704
    Baldwin Locomotive   2-8-0   199S
    These locomotives were four-cylinder Vauclain-compounds.

1902

The D&RG, now owner of 99.8-percent of the RGW's stock, consolidated the management and operation of the latter company into its own. Though legally alive, the RGW ceased to function as a separate organization; its equipment, however, continued to bear its name, mute evidence that a corporate merger had not yet been effected.

The Continental Mines & Smelter Corporation, owners of some mining properties at Alta, approached the RGW regarding their leasing the unused Alta Branch, with the intent of operating it electrically.

CONSTRUCTION

Scofield to UP Coal Mine—1m S-G.
    This was another branch into the coal fields near the end of the Pleasant Valley Branch.

1903

Following two years of relative inactivity, the RGW now began to add trackage to new sources of business. It also initiated construction on a short-cut from its main-line, near Farnham, to Milford, Utah, on the San Pedro, Los Angeles & Salt Lake railroad. In mid-year, however, the SPLA&SL came under Union Pacific control, thus thwarting the possibility of Gould extending a transcontinental line in this direction.

CONSTRUCTION

Salina to Nioche—20m S-G.
    This line up Salina Creek involved great difficulty of construction, four tunnels being required in the steep canyon. It was incorporated as the Castle Valley Railway.
Salt Lake City to Bingham Junction—10m S-G second track.
    This additional track was needed to handle the copper ore from mines at Bingham to the copper smelters located along the main-line south of Salt Lake City. This expansion in trackage between Bingham and the copper smelters and refinery near Salt Lake City marked the beginning of a new era for the region—the mining and processing of non-ferrous ores.

ACQUISITION

Dalton to Lark—4m S-G.
    This branch to a copper mine at Lark was purchased from the Bingham Consolidated Mining & Smelting Company.

Richmond delivered two groups of four 2-8-0's in 1900, differing principally in their driving-wheel diameters, both about 50-percent heavier than 44 Baldwin engines which preceded them. Those with larger wheels were used on passenger trains between Helper and Thistle—as shown in this picture—or on freight trains between Helper and Grand Junction.

The gigantic copper mill (center) and smelter (left) at Garfield were supplied with ore from the workings at Bingham by the RGW. Trainloads of ore were brought down the track at the right, then shoved onto the three unloading tracks (center). This branch was built in 1905.

The four-percent grade on the west side of Soldier Summit exacted a tremendous toll of motive power, five locomotives having been needed to haul 11 passenger cars up the hill when this photograph was taken in 1911. The first and rear engines were new 2-8-0's in the 1180 - 1199 series and a 70 -73 series 4-6-0 was coupled immediately ahead of the first car. In the middle was a pair of 2-6-0's which had been recently converted from cross-compound to single expansion.

None of the three varieties of compound expansion locomotives lasted very many years, the economy of fuel and water not having justified their mechanical complexity, and all were modified to single expansion. This one—with a south-bound passenger train awaiting departure at Salt Lake City—was Denver & Rio Grande engine Number 843, originally Rio Grande Western Number 81. This engine was one of the 80-83 series built in 1901.

GERALD BEST

Disenchanted with the performance of the lopsided cross-compound locomotives built by Richmond, the RGW converted them to single expansion after a very few years of service. The 940, bearing D&RGW heraldry in 1935, was once RGW 600.

Like the 2-8-0's numbered 1180 - 1190, three 0-6-0 switchers received by the RGW in 1907 were numbered in the D&RG's series. D&RG 838 originally had the same number on the RGW and is shown here working at the passenger station in Salt Lake City.

R. H. CARLSON COLLECTION

DON E. A. ROGERS

Although the Baldwin 2-8-0's numbered 700 - 704 worked only six years as Vauclain-compounds, they lasted four decades after having been changed to single expansion in

1907. The 934 (D&RGW), shown here at Alamosa, was the last "RGW" locomotive, all succeeding ones having been constructed to D&RG specifications.

1904

The "short-cut" branch to Nioche was washed out completely in several places without ever having a revenue train run over it; it was to remain thus for several years.

1905

Copper mining, smelting and refining had mushroomed to gigantic proportions and the D&RG/RGW management was quick to recognize this potential source of substantial revenues. First, the D&RG acquired the stock of the Copper Belt railroad in exchange for its trackage previously leased from the RGW. Then, to participate in the tremendous volume of copper-ore traffic, the RGW built a branch down to the gigantic new Garfield smelter at the south end of the Great Salt Lake.

CONSTRUCTION

Garfield Junction (Welby) to Garfield—16m S-G.
  This branch was built to handle copper ore between the Bingham mines and the Garfield smelter.
Hooper Junction (Roy) to Hooper—5m S-G.
  This branch served canning factories south of Ogden.

1906

Operating congestion due to the vast tonnages of coal and copper ore was hampering the RGW once again; hence, additional second track was built to relieve the situation.

The Continental Mines & Smelting Corporation leased and agreed to reconstruct the Alta branch to transport silver ores from the mines to the smelters in the Salt Lake Valley. Steam locomotives were to be used, however, rather than electric ones as proposed previously. During the negotiations it was revealed that the N-G portion of the branch (Wasatch to Alta) had been used spasmodically by outside parties for several years.

CONSTRUCTION

Loline Junction to Copper Belt Junction—12m S-G.
  Bingham Canyon was so narrow that another track could not be laid along its course; consequently this new low-grade route was built high on the south wall of the gorge, connecting with the original track via the CB railroad above Bingham.
Colton to Soldier Summit—7m S-G second track.
  This additional track aided the handling of heavy west-bound coal trains.
Bingham to Copper Belt Junction—2m N-G to S-G.
  This conversion connected the end of the Bingham Branch and the Copper Belt railroad with the new low-grade line.

MOTIVE POWER

80-83—Rebuilt by RGW shops.	4-6-0	161S

These engines were converted from two-cylinder cross-compound to single expansion. Although using less coal and water, compounds cost more to maintain than locomotives with single-expansion cylinders.

1180-1199			
American Locomotive	2-8-0	220S

These truly big locomotives were needed to handle heavy coal trains over Soldier Summit, and they were given numbers in the D&RG's numerical series.

1907

Another acquisition by the D&RG/RGW was the San Pete Valley Railway which connected Manti on RGW's Marysvale Branch with Nephi on the SPLA&SL railroad. It appears that this coal and stone hauler was added more for protection purposes and its asset value than for any inherent ability to produce revenue. The eventual merger of the RGW into the D&RG was now being perfected, and the RGW's days were numbered.

Continental M&S failed to undertake reconstruction of the Alta Branch, and the RGW cancelled its lease, thus ending any immediate hopes for placing the line back in operation.

MOTIVE POWER

63-64—Rebuilt by RGW shops.	4-6-0	130S
65—Rebuilt by RGW shops.	4-6-0	130S
500-505—Rebuilt by RGW shops.	2-6-0	154S
600-604—Rebuilt by RGW shops.	2-8-0	186S
700-704—Rebuilt by RGW shops.	2-8-0	199S

During this year the above group of engines was converted from compound to single expansion. Worn beyond economical repair, the compounds were converted as rapidly as the shops could handle them.

836-838		
Baldwin Locomotive	0-6-0	149S

These switchers were the last locomotives built for the RGW. Like the Class 220 locomotives received in 1906, they were given D&RG numbers.

1908

On August 1, all subsidiaries of the D&RG (excepting the Rio Grande Southern), the D&RG itself, and the RGW and all of its subsidiaries were merged into a single consolidated company called the D&RG Railroad Consolidated. At the time, the RGW owned half of the Colorado Midland, a competitor of the D&RG, while the C&S owned the other half. The CM, in turn, owned half of the Rio Grande Junction Railway, the D&RG owning the other half. Neither of these partly-owned companies were merged into the new D&RG Railroad, however.

The reason for this great consolidation was not to be found in more efficient operations or management; instead, it was perpetrated with the thought of floating a gigantic issue of bonds, the proceeds of which would be used incidentally to retire earlier bonds and, primarily, to yield several million dollars extra, enabling Gould to continue financing the construction of his Western Pacific railroad, the extension of the Rio Grande system to the Pacific.

The new low-grade line along the south wall of Bingham Canyon was constructed in 1906. It gained elevation by means of a great loop to the south of the line previously built in the gorge. This panorama looks across the loop toward Salt Lake City and the Wasatch Range.

Previously built branches of the RGW had penetrated agricultural and mineral-ore regions; the new one to Sunnyside went to a deposit of coal situated far to the east of other mines served by the railroad. Subsequent development opened up a field extending all along the eastern flank of the Wasatch Mountains, providing the railroad with additional tonnage.

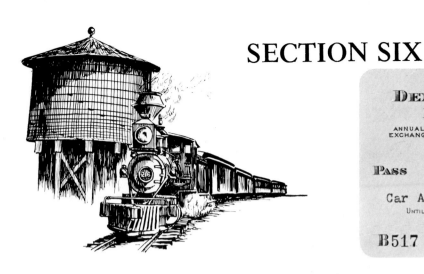

SECTION SIX

Denver & Rio Grande Railroad Company (Consolidated)
1908 - 1921

1908

On July 31 the Rio Grande Western was merged with the D&RG, and on the following day this successor company acquired the following subsidiaries: Carbon County Railroad; Castle Valley Railway; Copper Belt Railroad; Rio Grande Railroad; Rio Grande Gunnison Railway; Rio Grande, Pagosa & Northern Railroad; Rio Grande, Pueblo & Southern Railroad; Rio Grande, Sangre de Cristo Railroad; Rio Grande & Santa Fé Railroad; San Pete Valley Railway; Sevier Railway; Tintic Range Railway; Utah Central Railroad, and Utah Eastern Railway. All but three of these companies (see acquisitions below) were non-operating subsidiaries of the D&RG or RGW.

Though Gould had maneuvered the D&RG into a precarious financial situation, there was every expectation that completion of the WP, with its superior route across the desert and through the Sierra Nevada Mountains, would extricate everybody. Correct as this anticipation may have been, it did not take into account the merger of the Bowling Green Trust Company into the Equitable Trust Company. Edwin Gould, George's brother, together with D&RG President Jeffery, were Trustees of Equitable, but so were E. H. Harriman of the Union Pacific and Otto Kahn of Kuhn, Loeb & Company (the UP's banker), men violently opposed to building the Western Pacific.

Now the key to the D&RG's financial fate, the Western Pacific's First Mortage, was unquestionably in enemy hands, and they had a noose around the D&RG's corporate neck in the form of its guarantee to pay the interest and principal on those WP bonds, no matter what this might mean ultimately to the D&RG.

ACQUISITIONS

Bingham to Copper Mines—4m S-G.
This track had formed the Copper Belt Railroad.
Salt Lake City to Park City—32m S-G.
This had been the Utah Central Railroad's line.
Nephi to Sterling—48m S-G.
This had been the San Pete Valley's track.

CONSTRUCTION

Louviers to Powder Plant—1m S-G.
This branch was constructed to a dynamite factory south of Denver.

MOTIVE POWER

31, 50, 58, 64, 65
By D&RG shops.   0-8-0   56N
Converted from 2-8-0, Class 56N
These switchers were probably assigned to the three-rail yards at Pueblo and Salida.

760-774
American Locomotive   4-6-0   184S
These 4-6-0's were needed to handle the heavier passenger trains, but half of those ordered (744-759) were delivered to the WP.

1101-1130
Rebuilt from compound to simple
by D&RG shops.   2-8-0   190S

1151-1178
American Locomotive   2-8-0   220S
Essentially identical to earlier Class 220 locomotives, these were equipped with Walschaerts valve gear, and were the last 2-8-0's built for the D&RG.

During the following two years all RGW locomotives were renumbered into the D&RG series, some D&RG engines being renumbered to provide space for the RGW locomotives.

PREVIOUS ROAD AND NUMBERS		NEW D&RG NUMBERS AND CLASS	
Copper Belt	1-5	1-5	Shay-S
D&RG	Same	30, 34, 83	56N
D&RG	Same	31, 50, 58, 64, 65	56N
D&RG	Same	160-164	45½N
D&RG	Same	166-177	47N

The 64 was one of five older narrow-gauge 2-8-0 switchers converted to 0-8-0's by the removal of their pilot trucks. Footboards and a headlight had been added to the rear of the tender, and the three-pocket couplers had been installed on both engine and tender.

The new D&RG - WP station in Salt Lake City was officially opened with the departure of the WP's first train destined for Oakland, California, on August 20, 1910. This photograph, taken on that same day, shows D&RG 4-6-0 Number 774 at the head of the "San Francisco & Chicago Limited" ready to depart at 8:10 a.m. for Denver.

When the D&RG consolidated with the RGW, several subsidiary railroad companies were merged into the corporate structure. Among these was the Copper Belt, which employed five three-truck Shay locomotives on its steep trackage to copper deposits around Bingham. Retaining their original numbers, 1 - 5, these engines first became part of the D&RG's motive power roster, afterward going to the D&RGW in 1921.

Machinists are setting the valves on 2-8-0 Number 1127, which has just come out of the Burnham Shops after having been converted from four-cylinder compound to two-cylinder simple. This was accomplished in 1908.

Here is 2-8-0 Number 1167 running on the three-rail line between Alamosa and Antonito, towing two idler cars and a narrow-gauge caboose. At La Jara it will pick up several standard-gauge cars loaded with potatoes and return to Alamosa.

Three 4-6-0's of assorted vintages assail the two-percent-grade at Castle Gate (obscured by the smoke), hauling the westbound "Pacific Coast Limited." This photograph was taken in 1910, as the train was heading uphill toward Soldier Summit.

Although 15 switchers like the 843 had been ordered in 1909, only three were delivered to the D&RG—the other 12 having gone to the Western Pacific railroad, the Pacific Extension of the D&RG. These three worked around Salt Lake City.

DON E. A. ROGERS

The *750* and *754*, lacking headlights, window glass and minor parts, were stored at Salida in *1935* awaiting dismantling. Originally these had been four-cylinder locomotives, numbered *1010* and *1004*, delivered in *1902*, and converted to two-cylinder simple in *1909*.

One of the Brooks 4-6-0's is seen in this picture, blasting its way up the new three-percent-grade line in Eagle Canyon. The slightly steeper original line is at the right and the town of Gilman is perched atop the sandstone cliffs rising almost vertically above the track.

D&RGW COLLECTION -- COURTESY JACKSON THODE

The D&RG's first standard-gauge articulateds were purchased to replace paired 2-8-0 helpers on steeply graded lines. Here, the 1055, a 2-6-6-2, was assembling a train of copper ore at Bingham in 1915. The new low-gradient uphill line appears atop the high fill in the background.

Marnel was little more than an isolated station on the new double-track line between Southern Junction and Walsenburg. The D&RG and Colorado & Southern each owned one track, and operated their trains over them regardless of ownership.

The two standard-gauge 2-8-0's of the San Pete Valley were so small that the D&RGW gave them numbers (287, 288) in the narrow-gauge series. This picture shows them struggling past the plaster mill in Nephi.

D&RG	Same	200-227	60N
D&RG	Same	228, 229	60N
D&RG	Same	240, 241 262, 263 265-274 276, 278 280-286	60N
D&RG	Same	400-411	70N
D&RG	Same	417-422	70N
D&RG	Same	450-464	125N
D&RG	Same	500-502	76S
RGW	51-54	503-506	104S
D&RG	507-511, 506, 513-538	507-538	106S
RGW	33-42	540-549	115S
RGW	61, 62, 66	550-552	124S
RGW	11	553	65S
RGW	1, 13	554, 555	77S
D&RG	Same	556-580	113S
D&RG	555	581 (2nd)	113S
D&RG	Same	582-629	113S
RGW	111-153	630-672	120S
SPV	50, 52	680, 681	80S
D&RG	Same	700-711	150S
RGW	63-65	712-714	130S
RGW	70-73	715-718	145S
D&RG	Same	720-739	170S
RGW	80-83	740-743	161S
D&RG	1001-1010	750-759	175S
D&RG	550-554	800-804	75S
RGW	21-23	805-807	96S
D&RG	Same	808-826	100S
D&RG	805-807	827-829	100S
D&RG	Same	831-835	149S
RGW	Same	836-838	149S
D&RG	Same	839-843	149S
D&RG	Same	901-915	185S
D&RG	Same	916-925	187S
RGW	200-203	940-943	141S
RGW	500-505	950-955	154S
RGW	300-303	960-963	183S
RGW	400-403	970-973	180S
RGW	600-604	980-984	186S
RGW	700-704	990-994	199S
D&RG	Same	1101-1130	190S
D&RG	Same	1131-1178	220S
RGW	Same	1180-1199	220S

1909

Although the D&RG system was being bled to death by Gould to complete the Western Pacific, some improvements were necessary to prevent traffic stagnation.

CONSTRUCTION

Red Cliff to Pando—5m S-G second track.
Helper to Castle Gate—4m S-G second track.
Kyune to Colton—5m S-G second track.
  These three sections of second track relieved the congestion of freight trains and returning helper engines on the Tennessee Pass and Soldier Summit grades.
DuPont Junction DuPont—1m S-G.
  This branch went to a dynamite factory north of Trinidad.
Sugar Junction to Sugar Factory—1m S-G.
  This branch served a sugar factory near Monte Vista.

Sigurd to J&K Mills—1m S-G.
  This branch went to a sugar mill south of Salina, Utah.
Summit to E&BB Mine—1m S-G.
  This branch was built to a silver mine north of Eureka, Utah.

MOTIVE POWER

750-759
  Rebuilt from compound Class 179S to simple by D&RG
  shops   4-6-0   175S
775-793
  American Locomotive   4-6-0   184S
  These were the last 4-6-0's built for the railroad.
841-843
  American Locomotive   0-6-0   149S
  These were the last switchers to be delivered.

1910

Even though through passenger service was inaugurated over the Western Pacific during this year, it was hardly the cause of universal joy, particularly on the part of the D&RG, which was obliged to make up the WP's operating deficits. And of considerably greater import was the fact that the D&RG had guaranteed to pay the interest and sinking-fund payments upon that $50-million WP bond issue. The D&RG and WP built a Union Station in Salt Lake City since the Union Pacific and its associates did not care to have them in their depot. The tunnel under Tennessee Pass caved in forcing the D&RG to detour its trains over the difficult profile of the Colorado Midland between Snowden (near Malta) and New Castle for a short time.

The Southern Utah and Castle Valley railroads (southwest of Helper and Price) were leased and operated by the D&RG, using SU and CV equipment, however.

CONSTRUCTION

Welby to Loline Junction—3m S-G second track.
  This additional track eased the congestion resulting from the enormous tonnage of copper ore coming out of Bingham.
Pando to Deen—3m S-G second track.
  This trackage further relieved the congestion on the west side of Tennessee Pass.

MOTIVE POWER

1050-1057
  American Locomotive   2-6-6-2   340S
  These — the railroad's first standard-gauge articulated locomotives — were assigned to helper service on the western sides of Tennessee Pass and Soldier Summit, eliminating the spectacular five-engine trains.

1911

The financial strain of the WP was now beginning to show in another place: the D&RG preferred-stock dividend was used to pay the interest on the WP bonds. Then another blow fell. Copper ore, in tremendous tonnages, which had been routed from Bingham through Welby to Garfield, dwindled to but a fraction of the former quantities. The reason was simple enough: the copper company wanted more reliable service. The D&RG ignored this request, with the result that the copper company eliminated the D&RG completely by building the Bingham &

At Thistle, eastbound passenger trains added one or more helpers for the long climb up the two-percent grade to Soldier Summit. Having replenished its fuel supply, 4-6-0 Number 763 takes water while 2-8-2 Number 1211 couples to its pilot.

Numbered 1060 - 1075, 16 monstrous 2-8-8-2's with 40-inch low-pressure cylinders, were acquired to displace double-headed 2-8-0's on the Tennessee Pass grades. In this photograph, the last one has just been pulled from the erecting shop of the American Locomotive Company in Schenectady, New York, and will soon be on its way to Pueblo.

Garfield railroad. In spite of this setback, the D&RG found money to build a new double-track joint-line with the Colorado & Southern, eliminating the former tortuous track between Minnequa and Walsenburg.

Service on the line over Fremont Pass between Leadville and Dillon was discontinued, all traffic being handled by the C&S, which operated a parallel line. In return, the D&RG operated the C&S trackage from Quartz through Gunnison to Baldwin, since this segment had been isolated by the collapse of the tunnel under Alpine Pass. Floods destroyed much N-G trackage in southwestern Colorado; no trains ran west of Chama for about a month, and the Silverton branch was out of service for more than two months.

CONSTRUCTION

Southern Junction to Walsenburg—52m S-G double-track.
  The D&RG owned the south-bound track while the C&S owned the north-bound, the line being operated as a joint double-track. This more direct route across rough country necessitated considerable heavy construction.
Pueblo to Cleora—93m 3-R to S-G.
  This change was made because the smelters at Pueblo had closed permanently, operations being shifted to the Arkansas Valley Smelter at Leadville.

1912

Now that the Western Pacific was in successful operation, the anti-Gould forces felt the time had come to undertake the destruction of his Western railroad empire. They began to buy large blocks of Missouri Pacific and D&RG stock, soon dominating the two Boards of Directors. They elected Benjamin F. Bush as President of the MP, and the D&RG as well, and ousted Gould from the D&RG Board.

Though Bush was dismayed at the sadly deteriorated and even dangerous condition of the D&RG, his promises of corrective action proved to be worthless; the D&RG's and WP's bond interest was taking almost all of its net income. However, it did find funds to buy the Colorado Midland's share of the Rio Grande Junction Railway at 55 cents on the dollar, the result of some financial hocus-pocus by the Midland's bankers. The lease of the RGJ continued, however, since the RGJ was not absorbed by the D&RG.

CONSTRUCTION

Reliance Junction to Ojo—5m S-G.
  Built on the old N-G Veta Pass grade, this branch served a coal mine.
Thistle to Detour—6m S-G second track.
  This was the beginning of a line change to relieve the frightful congestion and grade against freight traffic on the west side of Soldier Summit.

MOTIVE POWER

1200-1213

Baldwin Locomotive	2-8-2	280S

These 2-8-2's replaced 2-8-0's in freight service between Pueblo and Denver.

1913

During this year the MP, the D&RG, the WP and the RGS were combined into a single operating system, with the thought of effecting economies. Still, Bush had to admit that most of the improvements to the D&RG

would have to be sacrificed to pay its own debt charges and to keep the WP going.

Operation of the Ballard & Thompson railroad was initiated under contract, and the San Luis Central, a new railroad, was given trackage rights from its terminal at Sugar Factory to Monte Vista. Though unused for several years, the track from Sandy to Wasatch was leased to the Salt Lake & Alta Railroad for reconstruction and operation.

ACQUISITION

Spring Canyon Junction to Storrs—4m S-G.
  This had been owned and operated by the Spring Canyon Coal Company.

CONSTRUCTION

Leadville to Graham Park Junction—3m N-G to 3-R.
Graham Park Junction to Wolftone Junction—
  1m N-G to S-G.
  These two conversions enabled S-G cars to be loaded at several mines east of Leadville.
Castle Gate to Kyune—9m S-G second track.
  Completion of this segment gave the D&RG a double track line up the sharply curved grade east of Soldier Summit.
Detour to Soldier Summit—14m S-G double track.
  This longer line eliminated seven miles of four-percent double track, a bottleneck on the west side of Soldier Summit.
Salina to Nioche—20m S-G.
  Reconstruction of this branch, washed out in 1904, was begun.

MOTIVE POWER

958
Ex-Spring Canyon

Coal Company.	2-8-0	172S

This locomotive was acquired with the Spring Canyon Coal Company property.

1001-1006

Baldwin Locomotive	4-6-2	261S

The D&RG's only 4-6-2's, these new locomotives were assigned to the Atlantic and Pacific Limiteds between Denver and Grand Junction.

1060-1075

American Locomotive	2-8-8-2	458S

At first these big Mallets were used as road engines between Denver and Grand Junction, later being assigned to helper service on the east side of Soldier Summit and the west side of Tennessee Pass, where four-engine trains ceased to be a common sight.

1914

Having advanced roughly $50-million to the Western Pacific at terrible sacrifice to itself, and with its credit also destroyed on behalf of the WP, the D&RG was now in an exhausted condition, financially and physically. Its Board expressed the opinion that the WP's obligations should be readjusted to bearable proportions. Consequently, the Eastern bankers were approached late in the year to begin negotiations for financial rearrangements.

The coal-hauling Utah Railway built a track adjacent to that of the D&RG between Provo and Thistle and agreed to operate this new line with the D&RG providing joint double-track operation over the entire distance between Provo and Helper, with trackage rights over the D&RG

ONE MILE

Stretching diagonally across the center of this picture is the abandoned roadbed of the four-percent gradient from Detour to Soldier Summit—which had been replaced in 1913 by a new double-track two-percent-grade line. In this scene, a mile from the bottom, two 2-8-0's, one of which was cut into the train, ascend the lower level of the great double-horseshoe-shaped route.

For their times the D&RG's six 4-6-2's for the "Atlantic Coast Limited" and "Pacific Coast Limited" were rather small locomotives—like those of the New York Central system. In this morning scene, Number 1001 was departing Denver Union Station for Pueblo.

When the D&RG took over the railroad belonging to the Spring Canyon Coal Company, a new 2-8-0 came with the property. It was renumbered from 958 to 915 in 1924, and by 1931 it had lost some essential parts and was stored in Salt Lake City, never to run again.

Northwest of La Madera was a vast pine forest which was being logged by the Hallack & Howard Lumber Company. Their mill was at La Madera to which the D&RG built a branch from Taos Junction. In this panorama the D&RG came in from the left, and H&H trackage went up the valley of the La Madera (upper right).

Short of narrow-gauge power during World War I, the D&RG purchased three engines from the defunct Crystal River railroad, the only outside-frame 2-8-0's on the system. This is the 431, showing minor modifications to conform with D&RG mechanical standards.

128

between Thistle and Helper. The D&RG was to operate the Utah Railway for its owners, however.

Another short coal line, the Kenilworth & Helper, successfully negotiated a lease of its railroad, complete with Shay locomotives, to the D&RG, and this operation was assumed during the year.

CONSTRUCTION

Taos Junction to La Madera—16m N-G.
   This branch connected with a lumber railroad running west from La Madera.
Oro Junction to A. V. Sampler—1m 3-R to S-G.
   N-G operations had ceased on this branch.
Florence to Fremont Mine—5m 3-R to S-G.
   Since the narrow-gauge Florence & Cripple Creek had abandoned operations into Florence, N-G access to this coal mine was no longer needed.

1915

Events of this year were entirely financial, most of them transpiring in locations far removed from D&RG rails. For one thing, the Missouri Pacific, which owned 30 per cent of the D&RG's common and preferred stock, went into receivership. Gould regained temporary control of the D&RG Board, fired President Bush, and replaced him with Henry U. Mudge. Then the Interstate Commerce Commission upheld the Union Pacific's right to charge local rates on through shipments which moved via D&RG track between Ogden and Denver.

But the most important item was the failure of the D&RG negotiations with the Eastern bankers concerning the WP's debt obligations. The scheme to wreck Gould's transcontinental system now became apparent: the bankers wanted the WP to go into receivership, followed by a foreclosure sale at which the Trustee (Equitable Trust Company) of the WP's first-mortgage bonds would buy the property, thus eliminating completely the D&RG's investment in the WP. Furthermore, this Trustee announced its intention to hold the D&RG liable for the difference between the $50-million WP bond issue and whatever price was bid for the WP at the foreclosure sale. In retrospect, at least, the trap was quite obvious; yet the D&RG's Board (on which sat three Goulds) agreed to the bankers' propositions. The Board withheld the March payment of interest on the WP first-mortgage bonds, tripping the WP immediately into receivership as planned. So far, so good, but now the Equitable Trust Company re-entered the picture and asked the courts to substantiate its proposed claim against the D&RG in the event of a foreclosure sale of the WP for less than $50-million.

Operation of the Southern Utah Railroad was terminated.

1916

The D&RG's Board appears to have been rather unconcerned over the proceedings relative to the Western Pacific. They acted as though there was no doubt that the WP would bring far more than $50-million at a foreclosure sale; after all, it was a brand-new railroad and had cost about $80-million to build. Furthermore, they seemed to feel that such a sale would relieve the D&RG of the burden of the WP's debt. This strange behavior becomes clear, however, when it is known that Kuhn, Loeb & Company, who were reorganizing the Missouri Pacific, controlled its Board and thus also controlled the D&RG's

Board. Having a major interest in the Equitable Trust Company as well, obviously it would be allowed to do whatever it wished with the WP and D&RG; hence, the WP could be neatly severed from the D&RG, at the same time insuring the D&RG's subsequent failure, primarily for the benefit of the bankers.

In July the WP was sold to the first-mortgage Bondholders Protective Committee for its bid of only $16-million, which didn't appear to bother the D&RG in the least, even though the sale meant the complete loss of its entire $50-million investment in the WP. Then the Committee instituted legal action to obtain an additional $38-million judgment against the D&RG, this being the difference between its bid of $16-million and the $50-million bond issue, plus roughly $4-million more in unpaid interest. At one point it even offered to sell the WP back to the D&RG for a mere $55-million!

CONSTRUCTION

Gunnison to Gunnison Sugar Mills—1m S-G.
   This branch served a sugar mill south of Manti, Utah.

DISPOSITION

Detour to Soldier Summit—Removed.
   This was the old four-percent-grade line, now replaced by the new lower-grade line up the west slope of the Wasatch Range.

MOTIVE POWER

402—Sold. Became RGS 40.

409—Sold. Became RGS 41.

420—Sold. Became RGS 42.

430, 431
   Ex-Crystal River 101, 102   2-8-0   93N
432
   Ex-Crystal River 103   2-8-0   112N
   These locomotives were obtained to replace the three Class 70N locomotives which had been sold to the RGS.

1250-1259
   American Locomotive   2-10-2   429S
   The only 2-10-2 type on the D&RG, these were the world's largest two-cylinder locomotives at the time. At first these engines were used as helpers on the west side of Tennessee Pass, and on coal trains between Pueblo and Denver. However, with their tremendous power they were more suitable for moving the high volume coal traffic in Utah, and they were reassigned to the east side of Soldier Summit. All were built with cylindrical "Vanderbilt" tenders.

1917

In the early fall the courts affirmed the $38-million claim of the Western Pacific Railroad Corporation (a holding company to which ownership of the WP railroad and the $38-million claim had been transferred) against the D&RG, and the bankers began to plot the extraction of this huge sum from the railroad's assets. Kuhn, Loeb & Company were now in complete control of the D&RG, Edward L. Brown of the MP having replaced Mudge as President of the D&RG. The USRA took over operating control of the railroad in December, a move which helped the railroad somewhat, although it wreaked havoc with most others.

Operation of the Utah Railway was discontinued. The Little Cottonwood Transportation Company leased the

Originally, the 375 (previously numbered 432) resembled the 431, also from the Crystal River railroad. By 1924, when this photo was taken of it at Alamosa, its cab, headlight, smokebox and pilot had been greatly altered.

D&RG's ponderous 2-10-2's weighed only 30,000 pounds less than the new 2-8-8-2's and 90,000 pounds more than the older 2-6-6-2's. The 1254 is shown here in Denver during 1916, shortly after the railroad had taken delivery from American Locomotive Company's Brooks works.

When the ex-Florence & Cripple Creek 2-8-0's first arrived on D&RG rails in 1917, they looked like Number 424, shown here at Gunnison.

long unused and almost disintegrated N-G tramway from Wasatch to Alta, and began its reconstruction. The D&RG took over operation of the branch to Wasatch, terminating operation by the Salt Lake & Alta Railroad.

Seven miles of S-G track from Cokedale to Bon Carbo was paid for by American Smelting & Refining Company to obtain additional coal for their coke ovens at Cokedale. The D&RG leased the track and operated freight trains over it. In 1920, AS&R leased a D&RG locomotive and coaches to haul miners from the end of the electric line at Cokedale to the mine.

ACQUISITION

Storrs to Standardville—1m S-G.
  This extension of the Spring Canyon Branch west of Helper, Utah, was purchased from the Standard Coal Company, which had paid for its construction.

CONSTRUCTION

Leadville to Graham Park Junction—3m 3-R to S-G.
Graham Park Junction to Ibex—6m N-G to S-G.
  These two conversions completed the S-G trackage serving the Leadville mining district.
Kingsville Junction to Kingsville—2m S-G.
Hooper to Cox—1m S-G.
  These two branches served canneries and sugar factories south of Ogden.

DISPOSITIONS

Manti to Sterling—Removed.
Kyune to Potter's Quarry—Removed.
  The Utah rock quarries served by these branches were no longer operating.

MOTIVE POWER

425-429
  Ex-Florence & Cripple Creek
  3, 11, 5, 8, 9   2-8-0   72N
  Compared to D&RG power these second-hand engines were in good condition.
821   2-6-0T   100S
  Rebuilt from 2-6-0 by D&RG shops.

1918

Since the Colorado Midland possessed the shorter route between Colorado Springs and Grand Jct., the USRA diverted D&RG traffic to the shorter carrier. The Midland, however, was in no physical condition to handle such an enormous volume and, shortly, all business reverted to the D&RG. Thus starved, the Midland failed and the D&RG lost its investment in that railroad a few years later.

The USRA gave the D&RG $3-million to improve its facilities, and guaranteed it an annual income. At the same time, the WP RR. Corp. was busily engaged in attaching the D&RG's assets. Hence, in a somewhat surprising move, the D&RG Board sought court protection by going into receivership on January 25, with Brown and Alexander R. Baldwin as co-Receivers.

CONSTRUCTION

El Vado to Gallinas—7m N-G.
  This extension of the RG&SW was built by the New Mexico Lumber Company, which operated the line, the

D&RG acquiring it later.
Pueblo to Bragdon—11m second track.
  This new trackage, together with construction of connections at grade around AT&SF overhead crossings at Sedalia, Palmer Lake and Fountain, and a new connection at Bragdon, permitted operation of the lines between Denver and Pueblo as joint double-track by both the AT&SF and D&RG, with operating agreements to the C&S and CRI&P.

MOTIVE POWER

554, 555
  Converted to N-G by D&RG shops
  from Class 77S.   2-8-0   71N

1919

With its property being operated under the direction of the USRA, and its finances being administered by the courts, the D&RG could do little more than endure the agony of this dual leadership, knowing further that its release from this "protection" would deliver it again into clutches of the rapacious WP Railroad Corporation.

Owners of the Goshen Valley railroad contracted with the D&RG for operation of their railroad in Utah.

ACQUISITION

Standardville to Rains—2m S-G.
  This extension of the Spring Canyon Branch was purchased from the Carbon Fuel Company.

1920

After its release from Federal control on March 1, the D&RG was in such weakened condition, physically and financially, that its principal creditor, the WP Railroad Corporation, urged an immediate foreclosure sale. The sale was held on November 20, the WP Railroad Corporation buying the D&RG for a trival $5-million bid. Now the WP Railroad Corporation owned both the WP Railroad and D&RG, subject only to court approval of the sale and about $120-million in bonded debt.

MOTIVE POWER

424
  Ex-Cripple Creek & Colorado Springs 35.
                           2-8-0   72N

1921

Dismissing all opposition, the courts confirmed sale of the D&RG to the WP Railroad Corporation on July 27, the very last day of the fiftieth year following the driving of the First Spike. Its founders and builders had vanished from the scene; its property and equipment were in an advanced state of deterioration, and it was now no more than a pawn in a struggle between financial giants who had little interest in it as an operating railroad.

CONSTRUCTION

Cañon City to Pueblo—41m S-G.
  This line was rebuilt due to destruction by flooding of the Arkansas River.

Quite unlike Tennessee and Marshall passes in Colorado, Soldier Summit in Utah is a broad, open saddle. For 11 years —1920 - 1930—it was a division point with a large yard and a nine-track rectangular engine-house. The arrangement was impractical and the terminal was dismantled and moved to Helper.

The Salt Lake City shops had always maintained an independent attitude toward motive power design, as is indicated by this 2-6-0T shop switcher, fabricated from an 1890 2-6-0, Number 821.

Unlike the D&RG, whose track occupied a favorable location east of Plum Creek, the AT&SF laid its rails on the west side and crossed the stream on a four-span bridge at Larkspur. After 1918 both railroads used this track for southbound movements.

The 306—awaiting dismantling at Durango in 1933—was an unique locomotive. Built in 1895 as Utah Central Number 1, it became RGW 01, then RGW 1 after conversion to standard-gauge in 1901. The D&RG numbered it 554 when it absorbed the RGW in 1908, and changed the engine back to narrow-gauge in 1918. It was renumbered 306 in 1924.

133

The Arkansas River flood of 1921, in addition to the havoc wrought at Pueblo, washed away long stretches of roadbed between that city and Cañon City.

For two decades the railroad had not bought a new narrow-gauge locomotive. In 1923 10 outside-frame 2-8-2's, numbered 470 - 479, replaced ancient 4-6-0's on passenger trains operated between Salida and Gunnison, and between Alamosa and Durango. The first one is seen here taking water at Chama.

134

Denver & Rio Grande Western Railroad
1921 - 1946

1921

The D&RGW Railroad Company was incorporated in Delaware (primarily) and Colorado (secondarily) in November, 1920, by the banking interests which owned the Western Pacific Railroad Corporation, in anticipation of their acquiring the property and assets of the D&RG Railroad. The D&RGW, with Joseph H. Young as its first President, took over the D&RG Railroad on August 1, 1921, regardless of concerted opposition to such action and an ICC investigation into WP Railroad Corporation and D&RG relationships.

CONSTRUCTION

Salina to Nioche—20m S-G.
Reconstruction of this "short-cut" across southern Utah, discontinued in 1914, was begun once again.

1922

A business depression, the greatly deteriorated condition of the entire railroad, and even natural catastrophes, combined to reduce the D&RGW's income to the point of defaulting upon its bonds, and on July 21 it was back in receivership, with Young as its Receiver. The railroad's credit had sunk so low that Young sold Receiver's Certificates to obtain money for track improvement and new locomotives.

For a short time, until all Colorado Midland trackage was removed, D&RG ran its trains from Wild Horse to the Newett quarry, and from Glenwood Springs to the Spring Gulch coal mines.

CONSTRUCTION

Salida to Malta—56m 3-R
This twisting line along the upper Arkansas River was rebuilt in several places to reduce its severe curvature, obliterating portions of the CM's recently abandoned grade.

Salina to Nioche.
Reconstruction continued, although this did seem to be a waste of money.

DISPOSITION

Grand Junction to Sugar Works—Removed.
This joint track with the Colorado Midland was no longer needed.

MOTIVE POWER

1501-1510

American Locomotive	4-8-2		377S

Among the heaviest 4-8-2 types ever built, these locomotives eliminated the double-heading of 4-6-0's on heavy passenger trains, and of 2-8-0's on freight trains between Denver and Salida. They were the first of this type on the railroad, as well as its first engines to have twelve-wheeled tenders.

1923

While the bankers, the courts, the WP Railroad Corporation, the MP Railroad, the ICC and local business leaders wrangled over the ultimate fate of the railroad, Receiver/President Young resigned late in the year in favor of Thomas H. Beacom. Apart from all this, track gangs and train crews fought an almost hopeless battle to revive the badly battered railroad.

CONSTRUCTION

Durango to Carbon Junction—2m 3-R to N-G.
Carbon Junction to Farmington—48m S-G to N-G.
These conversions eliminated this isolated S-G branch in otherwise N-G territory.
Big Four to Alamo—3m S-G.
This extension reached new coal mines for the AS&R coke plant at Cokedale.
Salina to Nioche.
Reconstruction was continued.

The D&RGW's standard-gauge Farmington Branch—isolated by narrow-gauge trackage from the rest of the system—was changed to narrow-gauge in 1923. Number 463, a twice-rebuilt 2-8-2, has just brought a string of empty tank cars to Farmington for reloading.

By increasing the boiler pressure slightly, the American Locomotive Company was able to construct a 2-8-8-2 with 39-inch low-pressure cylinders, and the firm's Richmond, Virginia, works produced 10 of them. This one is Number 3506, posed for a portrait during steam tests before shipment to the D&RGW in 1923.

D&RGW COLLECTION -- COURTESY JACKSON THODE

In 1922 the first 10 of 30 gigantic 4-8-2's arrived to replace 2-8-2's, 4-6-2's and double-headed 4-6-0's on passenger trains. Appearing brand-new, the 1510 may have been making its first trip over the D&RGW, handling an unscheduled passenger train near Denver.

An improvement program—undertaken in 1922—eliminated a great many severe curves along the Arkansas River near Granite. In this scene one of the D&RGW's 2-6-6-2's hauls a train of ballast across a new fill which covers the recently abandoned roadbed of the Colorado Midland railroad.

D&RGW COLLECTION -- COURTESY JACKSON THODE

The second group of huge 4-8-2's was equipped with trailing-truck boosters, and bore numbers 1511 - 1520. This photograph shows the 1511 hauling the 13-car "Scenic Limited" unassisted up the one-and-a-half-percent-grade in the Arkansas River canyon near Princeton. The well-manicured track hardly resembles that of only a few years previous.

The 760—one of two 4-6-0's rebuilt in 1924 with smaller driving wheels for branch-line mixed-train service—pauses at the Woody Creek tank for water, while en route to Aspen with the daily one-car local from Glenwood Springs.

LE MASSENA

DISPOSITION

Hecla Junction to Calumet—Removed.

    This branch had been out of service for almost twenty-five years.

MOTIVE POWER

470-479

American Locomotive   2-8-2   140N

These were the first new N-G locomotives received since 1903. They were assigned to passenger service on the Marshall Pass and Cumbres Pass lines.

1511-1520

American Locomotive   4-8-2   383S

The only booster-equipped (trailer-truck) locomotives on the railroad, these engines were assigned to passenger and freight trains between Salt Lake City and Grand Junction; later, they worked between Salida and Minturn.

1521-1530

American Locomotive   4-8-2   378S

These duplicates of the Class 377 4-8-2's worked in passenger and freight service between Salida and Grand Junction.

3500-3509

American Locomotive   2-8-8-2   532S

Copies of the USRA standard design, these Mallets hauled coal trains over Soldier Summit.

1924

The Receivership was ended on October 29, when the Equitable Trust Company and Kuhn, Loeb & Company, representing bondholders, bought the railroad for $18-million at the foreclosure sale. Owned equally by the Missouri Pacific Railroad and Western Pacific Railroad Corporation, the D&RGW was reorganized financially, but it was saddled with such a staggering debt that its failure again in the future was virtually a foregone conclusion. J. Samuel Pyeatt, from the New Orleans, Texas & Mexico Railway, a subsidiary of the MP, became the new President, and his policies were hardly expected to be of primary benefit to the D&RGW and/or Colorado and Utah.

CONSTRUCTION

Mustang to Larimer—1m S-G.

    This was a connection between the segmented original main-line and the new one between Pueblo and Walsenburg.

DISPOSITIONS

Castle Rock to O'Brien's Quarry—Removed.

    This was an unused quarry branch south of Denver.

Coal Junction to Coal Banks—Removed.

    This branch south of Florence was no longer needed.

Capers to Graneros—Removed.

Lascar to Larimer—Removed.

    These were unused portions of the original main-line south of Pueblo.

Leadville to Dillon—Removed.

    All of the traffic along this branch was being handled by the Colorado & Southern over its own trackage.

Durango to City Mine—Removed.

    This branch was no longer needed.

Copper Belt Junction to Bingham—Removed.

Bingham to Yampa Smelter—Removed.

    The advance of open-pit copper mines devoured these roadbeds.

Beginning in December, 1923, all locomotives were given new class symbols which designated wheel arrangement by a letter (C=2-8-0), and tractive efforts by a numeral, (16= 16,000 lbs.). Then they were regrouped by the new classification symbol, and renumbered as shown below:

NARROW GAUGE

OLD NUMBERS AND CLASSES		NEW NUMBERS AND CLASSES	
166-177	47	166-177	T12
200-227	60	200-227	C16
228, 229, 240, 241		228, 229, 240, 241	
262, 263, 265-274, 276		262, 263, 265-274, 276	
278, 280-286	60	278, 280-286	C16
427, 421, 422, 418, 419	70	300-304	C17
555, 554	71	305, 306	C17
425-429, 424	72	315-320	C18
400, 401, 411, 403-408, 410	70	340-349	C19
430, 431	93	360, 361	C21
432	112	375	C25
450-464	125	450-464	K27
470-479	148	470-479	K28

STANDARD GAUGE

OLD NUMBERS AND CLASSES		NEW NUMBERS AND CLASSES	
1-5	Shay	1	Y21
		2	Y25
		3	Y32
		4, 5	Y33
800	75	10	S19
805-807	96	20-22	S23
831-840	149	50-59	S33
841-843	149	60-62	S33
680, 681	80	287, 288	C16
553	65	290	C14
545, 548	115	500, 501	T17
512, 524, 533, 528, 509, 510,		505-515	T18
508, 530, 534, 529, 537	106		
712, 713	130	521, 520	T19
718, 715-717	145	525-528	T19
740-743	161	530-533	T24
705-709, 700-704, 710, 711	150	535-546	T26
821, 826, 822, 828, 819	100	575-579	G20
940, 942	141	590, 591	G28
952-955, 950, 951	154	592-597	G28
630, 631, 652, 647, 634-637,		600-626	C26
650, 649, 640-642, 646, 654-			
660, 670, 672, 663, 664, 639,			
662	120		
570-574, 566, 556-562, 569,		630-691	C28
564, 565, 606, 607, 592, 609-			
616, 593, 618-620, 601, 622-			
627, 595, 629, 600, 594, 602-			
605, 576-587, 596, 589-591	113		
720-739	170	720-739	T28
750-759	175	750-759	T31
763, 777	184	760, 761	T29
762, 764-776, 778-793	184	762, 764-776, 778-793	T29
760, 761	184	763, 777	T31
1006, 1001-1005	261	800-805	P44
960-963	183	900-903	C38
958	172	915	C39
916-925	187	916-925	C39
990-994	199	930-934	C40
980-984	186	940-944	C40
915, 901-914	185	950-964	C41
970-973	180	970-973	C42
1130, 1101-1129	190	1000-1029	C41
1131-1178, 1180-1199	220	1131-1178, 1180-1199	C48
1200-1213	280	1200-1213	K59
1250-1259	429	1400-1409	F81
1501-1510	377	1501-1510	M67
1511-1520	383	1511-1520	M78
1521-1530	378	1521-1530	M67
1050-1057	340	3300-3307	L62
1060-1075	458	3400-3415	L96
3500-3509	532	3500-3509	L107

Note: Locomotives bearing old numbers were lettered "D&RG", while those with new numbers were lettered "D&RGW".

LE MASSENA

Number 464 was one of a few 2-8-2's in the 450 - 464 series whose machinery had been changed twice, first from four-cylinder compound to two-cylinder simple, then in 1924 from slide valves and Stephenson motion to piston valves and Walschaerts motion. In this 1962 photograph, taken just before retirement, the engine was switching the consist of the popular "Silverton" summer tourist train at Durango.

OTTO PERRY

Two of the last ten new narrow-gauge 2-8-2's, 482 and 485, head south from Alamosa on a crisp fall morning in 1949, towing an endless string of empty stock and tank cars over the straight and level three-rail track to Antonito.

140

ROBERT HANFT

There weren't any 4-8-2's heavier than the 1600 - 1609 three-cylinder group delivered from Baldwin in 1926. The 1605, resting at Salt Lake City, was one of five equipped with an Elesco feedwater heater.

Initially coal from the mine at Kenilworth moved over the steep Kenilworth & Helper railroad to the D&RG. In 1926 the D&RGW built its own track on a lesser gradient, and used 2-6-6-2's instead of the two K&H three-truck Shay locomotives.

D&RGW ARCHIVES

D&RGW COLLECTION – COURTESY JACKSON THODE

The 3606 was practically a new locomotive when it was photographed at Castle Rock leading a solid train of Western Pacific box cars loaded with lumber destined for Denver.

R. H. CARLSON COLLECTION

Hidden beneath the embellishments added since it was built in 1881 was the D&RG's first standard-gauge freight engine, Number 412. Five such locomotives were renumbered to 550 - 554 in 1887, and were converted to 0-8-0T engines in 1898. The 412/550 was given Number 800 in 1908, and in 1924, having lasted a decade beyond its companions, was renumbered 10. It was scrapped in 1927.

RALPH HALLOCK

The last narrow-gauge locomotives—numbered 490 - 499—were constructed from standard-gauge 2-8-0's which had been built as four-cylinder compounds in 1902. The 494, shown at Sargent in 1948, was derived from original 1120 which had been renumbered 1020 in 1924.

More suited to freight service than passenger, the 30 two-cylinder 4-8-2's were replaced after a few years by much faster 4-8-4's like the 1710, which is seen accelerating the "Royal Gorge" southward out of Littleton in 1950.

ROBERT ANDREWS

143

D&RGW COLLECTION – COURTESY JACKSON THODE

The *592* was propelled by a pair of gasoline engines mounted beneath the carbody, driving the inner axle of each truck.

After about three years of use on branch-line runs it was set aside, and later restored to its previous configuration.

OTTO PERRY

A third-rail was added to the southern end of the Valley Line —between Alamosa and Hooper—to allow the movement of standard-gauge cars in narrow-gauge trains. Four such cars

are spliced between an idler-car at their rear, and an auxiliary tender coupled behind the *481*. The Valley Line ran through the heart of the arid San Luis Valley in southern Colorado.

144

760, 761—Rebuilt by D&RGW shops from 763, 777
and renumbered   4-6-0   T31S
763, 777—Renumbered from
760, 761   4-6-0   T29S

1925

Although the general prosperity of the times had been yielding about $33-million in revenues, maintenance (much of which had been deferred from previous years) and fixed charges had been consuming roughly two-thirds of the total. By drastically reducing maintenance expenditures, the otherwise net-deficit was made to appear as a very profitable one in 1925.

The Little Cottonwood Transportation Company terminated operation of the N-G trackage between Wasatch and Alta. Private parties, however, operated it occasionally during the next few years.

CONSTRUCTION

Hale to Scofield—6m S-G.
   This portion of the Pleasant Valley Branch south of Soldier Summit was relocated to bypass a new reservoir.
Salida to Eilers—58m 3-R to S-G.
   Coal, coke and ores for Leadville's Arkansas Valley Smelter were no longer coming from points on N-G trackage, hence this N-G third-rail was not needed.

DISPOSITION

Minnequa to Graneros—Removed.
   There was no longer any need for this original mainline track south of Pueblo.
Ephraim to Manti—Removed.
   This former San Pete Valley Railroad track paralleling the Marysvale Branch had not been used for several years.
Lake Park Junction to Lake Park—Removed.
   The resort at Lake Park having been abandoned, this branch was not needed.
Salina to Nioche.
   Reconstruction of the southern Utah "cut-off" was begun once again.

MOTIVE POWER

480-489
   Baldwin Locomotive   2-8-2   K36N
   These locomotives were the first to be purchased from Baldwin since 1913, and they were the last new N-G engines to be acquired by the D&RGW.

1926

Assisted by heavy traffic, new equipment and deferred interest on obligations, the D&RGW managed to post a net profit for the year.

CONSTRUCTION

Kenilworth Junction to Kenilworth—5m S-G.
   This branch replaced the Kenilworth & Helper Railroad trackage which had been leased and operated by the D&RGW.
Salina to Nioche.
   Reconstruction work was continued.

MOTIVE POWER

1600-1609
   Baldwin Locomotive   4-8-2   M75S
   The D&RGW's only three-cylinder locomotives, these were the last 4-8-2's built for it. Initially they worked in passenger and freight service between Denver and Salida, replacing M67 4-8-2's. Later, they replaced the M78 engines between Grand Junction and Salt Lake City.

1927

Increases in the operating and maintenance expenses cut the D&RGW's precarious profit position considerably, but prosperity on a national scale provided sufficient traffic to yield a small profit.

ACQUISITION

Pearl to Dividend—7m S-G.
Flora to Iron King—2m S-G.
   The Goshen Valley Railroad, connecting the Tintic Branch east of Eureka, was purchased from its owners, but was not merged into the D&RGW until several years later.

CONSTRUCTION

Pictou to New Pacific Mine—2m S-G.
   This branch was built to a coal mine north of Walsenburg.

MOTIVE POWER

3600-3609
   American Locomotive   2-8-8-2   L125S
                                           (later L131S)
   The world's largest locomotives at the time, these were the D&RGW's first S-G simple-articulateds. They replaced combinations of 2-8-0, 2-8-2 and 4-8-2 locomotives in freight service between Salida and Grand Junction.

Motor Car 592 - unclassified - railroad shops
   The D&RGW's only self-propelled car was fashioned from an existing car by the installation of two gasoline engines and mechanical transmissions.

1928

This being another boom year, with freight traffic density greater than ever before, the D&RGW continued to bask in the comparative luxury of its temporary prosperity. Traffic over Tennessee Pass had once again reached the stagnation point, due to the single track through the tunnels at the summit and at Deen. To relieve this situation, the entire trackage from the east portal at the top to the end of double track west of Deen was put under Centralized Traffic Control operation—the first such installation west of the Mississippi River, and one of the first in the United States. The CRI&P's use of D&RGW trackage between Denver and Pueblo was terminated.

CONSTRUCTION

East Mitchell to West Mitchell—3m S-G, second track.
   This completed double tracking of the three-percent grade on the west side of Tennessee Pass.

DISPOSITION

Lumberton to Gallinas—Removed.
   This was the RG&SW Railroad, operated by the New Mexico Lumber Company. It had logged out the area, moving its operation to Dolores, Colorado.

WILLIAM MOEDINGER

Prior to discontinuance of passenger service on the Pagosa Springs Branch in the early 1930's, the line's passenger train was an operating anachronism. Number 317—built in 1895—had seen 20 years of duty on the Florence & Cripple Creek, and the 1880-vintage combination car had been given a cupola for mixed-consist work.

Another product of the imaginative shops in Salt Lake City was this conversion of 2-8-0 Number 955 to a shop switcher in 1937.

LE MASSENA COLLECTION

DON E. A. ROGERS

Not content to use "standard" 2-8-0's as switchers, the Salt Lake City shops converted the 1013 into an unduplicated 0-8-0 by removing its pilot truck. In 1938 it was working in Ogden, where it was caught crossing the Southern Pacific's trackage.

MOTIVE POWER

490-495—Converted to N-G by D&RGW shops from 1014, 1026, 1021, 1005, 1020, 1004 (Class C41S) and renumbered   2-8-2   K37N

578—Rebuilt from 2-6-0 by D&RGW shops.   2-6-0T   G20S

1929

Although revenues had soared to all-time heights, and transportation and maintenance expenses had been cut substantially, net income was only a little higher than that of 1928. Fixed charges, deferred in previous years, now became due, and more than 20-percent of the D&RGW's income went for this item. The prospects of another inevitable financial doom were ominous indeed, at a time when most other railroads in the nation were enjoying unprecedented prosperity.

ACQUISITION

At Cokedale—1m S-G.
The D&RGW bought the AS&R Company trackage through the yards and continued to operate coal trains to the mine at Bon Carbo.

CONSTRUCTION

Upper Junction to Midas—4m S-G.
At various times between 1924 and 1928, segments of the low-grade line of the Bingham Branch between Loline Junction and Cuprum had been removed due to the encroachment of strip mining. This portion of the line was rebuilt on an adjacent grade to serve a copper mill.
Somerset to Oliver—2m S-G.
This extension was built to tap a coal mine.
Salina to Crystal—18m S-G.
Reconstruction was completed to a coal mine.

DISPOSITION

Crested Butte to Floresta—Removed.
The CF&I Company coal mine had closed down, and this track was no longer needed.
Moffat to Cottonwood—Removed.
This branch was dismantled because the mine and mill at its end had been idle for about 15 years.

MOTIVE POWER

1700-1713
Baldwin Locomotive   4-8-4   M64S
These first 4-8-4's for the D&RGW replaced the three-cylinder 4-8-2's in passenger service, and operated without change between Denver and Salt Lake City.

1930

The D&RGW, in spite of a few years of prosperity, was now in another financial predicament, as had been prophesied. The decline of business activity, following the Stock Market Crash of 1929, cut the railroad's net income in half, and worse, fixed charges had climbed to 25-percent of the railroad's gross income. Furthermore, to protect itself against the possibility of ruinous competition through the Moffat Tunnel (via the Denver & Salt Lake Railway, thence by a new line along the Colorado River connecting the D&SL with the D&RGW), the D&RGW began to buy the stock of the D&SL. In so doing, it realized

that it might itself become obligated to build this connecting link, adding further to its financial distress.

CONSTRUCTION

Alamosa to Hooper—19m N-G to 3-R.
This conversion was made for agricultural and livestock shipments consigned to points beyond N-G trackage.

DISPOSITION

Engleville Junction to Engleville—Removed.
This coal mine branch had not been used for more than 15 years.

MOTIVE POWER

496-499—Converted to N-G by D&RGW shops from 1023, 1003, 1009, 1025 (Class C41S)
and renumbered   2-8-2   K37N
These were the last N-G locomotives to go into service.

3610-3619
American Locomotive   2-8-8-2   L127S
    (Later L132S)
Almost identical to the Class L125S engines, these were the last of this type to be built for the D&RGW.

1931

The D&RGW reached agreement with the Denver & Salt Lake Railway by which it would be given trackage rights over that line, as well as over the proposed connection between Bond and the D&RGW main-line.

Having been allowed by the Interstate Commerce Commission to acquire control of the D&SL, as well as its subsidiary Denver & Salt Lake Western Railroad (in which name the proposed connection, ultimately to be known as the Dotsero Cutoff, would be built and owned), the D&RGW bought the D&SLW's stock, agreed to purchase all privately-held D&SL stock, and reached agreement with the D&SL by which it would be given trackage rights over that line between Utah Junction and the future Cutoff, but neglected to arrange for such rights over the D&SL's subsidiary, Northwestern Terminal Railroad between Utah Junction and Denver, until the day prior to the opening of the Cutoff.

DISPOSITION

Upper Junction to Midas—Removed.
The advancing open-pit copper mine necessitated the removal of this track.

1932

The D&RGW was now in the unfortunate position of being unable to finance the Dotsero Cutoff, the 1932 deficit being $2.5-million. The Reconstruction Finance Corporation agreed to lend almost $4-million for the project, and construction was begun on behalf of the D&SLW as owner of the Cutoff.

DISPOSITION

Lascar to Cuchara Junction—Removed.
Part of the original main-line east of Walsenburg, this trackage was no longer needed.
Taos Junction to La Madera—Removed.
The lumber mill at La Madera had moved its operations to Glencoe on the Rio Grande Southern.

The five big new 4-8-4's obtained from Baldwin in 1937—numbered 1800 - 1804—made their break-in runs on fast-freight trains between Denver and Salt Lake City. Here is the 1803—resplendent in new paint—heading eastward out of Helper with a trainload of fruit. These were the last steam passenger engines purchased by the D&RGW.

The ceremonies incidental to the opening of the Dotsero Cutoff route in 1934 required three special trains to carry participants to the site. This was the first one running north of Denver, powered by 2-8-0 Number 1161 and 4-6-2 Number 801. Both locomotives have been specially painted and polished to perfection for the occasion.

1933

Things looked somewhat brighter for the D&RGW; its loss was only $2.1-million for the year. But construction of the Dotsero Cutoff progressed very slowly.

Operation of the Colorado & Wyoming's Hezron Branch ceased. Control of the Rio Grande Southern was restored when the WP Railroad Corporation transferred its RGS securities to the D&RGW.

DISPOSITION

Scofield to UP Mine—Removed.
Scofield to Winter Quarters—Removed.
These spurs from the Pleasant Valley Branch were removed because the coal mines had stopped production.
Lake Junction to Lake City—Sold.
Traffic on this line had decreased to almost nothing, and the trackage was purchased by the San Cristobal Railroad.

1934

Any joy occasioned by initiation of through operations via the Dotsero Cutoff was nullified by deepening losses, which totalled $3-million by year-end. To compound the gloom, the D&RGW was called upon to pay for the remainder of the D&SL stock which it had agreed to purchase, and this it was unable to do. To resolve the situation, the Reconstruction Finance Corporation loaned the necessary funds to the D&SLW (which the D&RGW owned) and the D&SLW purchased the D&SL stock, depositing it as collateral with the RFC. Now, having received other D&SL stock as collateral for a loan to build the Cutoff, the RFC had full control of the D&SL.

Operation of the branch to Quartz, for the Colorado & Southern, was discontinued. Trackage rights over Northwestern Terminal track between Denver and Utah Junction were negotiated so that D&RGW trains could reach D&SL track.

CONSTRUCTION

Dotsero to Orestod—38m S-G.
This connection, following the Colorado River, reduced the D&RGW's rail distance between Denver and Salt Lake City by 175 miles. As the Dotsero Cutoff, it was leased by the D&RGW, which used it exclusively, while the D&SL continued to operate only between Denver and Craig.

DISPOSITION

Sand Pit to Alta—Removed.
There was no further need for this trackage.

1935

With a net loss of $3-million for the year, and unable to obtain further funds to meet its mounting debt payments, the financially stricken D&RGW sought refuge in the courts on November 1. However, instead of the appointment of Eastern bankers as Receivers, two local men, Henry Swan and Wilson McCarthy, were appointed Trustees. This date marked the end of almost 60 years of absentee/banker control, an era in which the railroad had been used to enrich a handful of men while ruining thousands of others. The thought of its becoming a prosperous common carrier benefiting Colorado and Utah had never been more than a casual consideration. During

those 60 years it had been milked dry more than once. Its equipment and track had been allowed to deteriorate to a frightful condition; it had been hopelessly debt-ridden; and its general reputation was likened to that of the Erie.

The Trustees faced the enormous task of rebuilding and reviving a railroad which had been bled financially by the Goulds and their enemies, and which was all but dead.

DISPOSITION

Tropic Junction to Tropic Mine—Removed.
The coal mine had closed, eliminating the need for this trackage west of La Veta.

1936

Regardless of vociferous, skillful and unrelenting opposition by Eastern trust and insurance companies representing bondholders, the Trustees, with the full backing of the court, borrowed and otherwise produced money from every possible source and transformed it into the elements of reconstruction. Main-line track received heavier rail, tie plates, creosoted ties and slag ballast. Antiquated cars and engines went to the scrap heap in wholesale lots and everything remaining made a trip through the repair shops. The net loss soared beyond $4-million, but the Trustees were not to be deterred from their program of reconstruction.

By mid-year the D&RGW's Board of Directors (still dominated by outside interests) had put together a plan of reorganization, including among other items the merger of the Denver & Salt Lake (which was controlled by the dissenting RFC). Later the Board opposed an insurance company plan to distribute the ownership of the D&RGW among the MP, WP, CB&Q and CRI&P in equal amounts. Although the MP, and WP Railroad Corporation were striving mightily to retain control of the D&RGW, U. S. District Judge J. Foster Symes, while courteously considering their supplications, based his decisions upon the unique premise that the welfare of Colorado, Utah, their citizens and their railroad, merited precedence over other considerations.

DISPOSITIONS

Chicosa Junction to Forbes Junction—Removed.
Cuchara Junction to Trinidad—Removed.
There being no need for two railroads between these points, the D&RGW dismantled this long stretch of its original trackage and operated over the Colorado & Southern from Walsenburg to Trinidad.
Du Pont Junction to Powder Works—Removed.
Rouse Junction to Mayne—Removed.
The D&RGW was now using C&S trackage to reach coal mines previously served by its original main-line.
Gato to Pagosa Springs—Removed.
Lumber traffic in this area of southwestern Colorado had dwindled to the point where this line was no longer needed.
Howard to Calcite—Removed.
The CF&I Company limestone quarry was closed, operations being transferred to Monarch.
Crystal to Nioche—Removed.
This was the part of the Castle Valley Branch in Utah which had been idle since its construction.
Denver to Littleton, Pikeview to Kelker. Second track removed.
This track was not needed, while the rails and ties were usable elsewhere.

The 15 4-6-6-4's, purchased in 1938 and 1942, were among the heaviest and most powerful of their type. Originally they were assigned to fast-freight service between Salt Lake City and Grand Junction, where this photograph was taken. However, they were equipped for passenger service and were frequently so used.

1937

The Trustees had spent more than $18-million, yet the net loss went beyond $6-million, to the dismay of practically everyone except the court and its Trustees. Another plan of reorganization was revealed at mid-year, this one being formulated by the Institutional Bondholders' Committee. Now there were two rivals contesting for the slowly reviving D&RGW, but the court deferred both of them, encouraging the Trustees in their every effort of reconstruction and rehabilitation.

CONSTRUCTION

Kingsville to Farnsworth—3m S-G.
   This extension was built to serve sugar and canning works south of Ogden.

ACQUISITION

Gunnison to Baldwin—16m N-G.
   This line—operated by the D&RGW for the C&S since 1911—was finally discarded by its owner.

DISPOSITIONS

Cuchara Junction to Walsenburg—Removed.
   This stub of original main-line was no longer in use.
New Pacific Junction to New Pacific Mine—Removed.
   This mine had closed, eliminating the need for this track.

MOTIVE POWER

01
Converted by D&RGW shops from 955 (Class C41S)—and renumbered.   2-8-0T
   This was for use as shop switcher at Salt Lake City.
1013
Converted by D&RGW shops from 2-8-0.
                                                0-8-0   C41S
   This was an experiment which was not repeated.
1800-1804
Baldwin Locomotive   4-8-4   M68S
   These were not only the last steam passenger engines built for the D&RGW, but were also the last 4-8-4's as well as the last non-articulated locomotives to be built for it. Considerably larger than the earlier 4-8-4's, they handled passenger trains over the entire distance between Denver and Salt Lake City via both the Royal Gorge and Moffat Tunnel routes.

1938

Although a sharp business recession reduced gross revenues by some 13-percent from the preceding year, the D&RGW's greatly improved physical condition enabled it to reduce its net loss by about five-percent, marking the turning of the tide, at last, for the recovering railroad.

Still another reorganization plan was conceived; this time it was the ICC's turn. It provided for merger with the D&SL and elimination of the MP, and WP Railroad Corporation ownership, but turned the property over to the bondholders. Hardly anyone was in favor of the plan, but ICC hearings were begun. Also, during the year, the railroad issued an internal report upon the past and probable traffic potential of each of its branch-lines. Hardly any of them had enough current traffic to pay their minimal expenses and the possibilities of future traffic were remote indeed. The most hopeless were designated for abandonment whenever the spirit might so move.

A new kind of motive power, the multiple-unit diesel-electric locomotive, was tested on the D&RGW's severe grades to evaluate its performance. A four-unit FT model locomotive, General Motors Number 103, was used in the trials.

DISPOSITION

Texas Creek to Westcliffe—Removed.
   Traffic on this branch had decreased to practically nothing.

MOTIVE POWER

3700-3709
Baldwin Locomotive   4-6-6-4   L105S
   This new type of locomotive was put into fast-freight service between Grand Junction and Salt Lake City, allowing the modern 2-8-8-2's to be withdrawn for freight service on the Moffat Tunnel route.

1939

With traffic improving slightly, the deficit shrank to $4-million for the year, and still the Trustees were pouring all available funds into the reconstruction. Oddly enough, though, some of the bondholders' groups protested that the railroad was being overbuilt; the court however, did naught but listen to their pleas. Reorganization plans proliferated; the ICC approved its own plan, while the insurance companies submitted another, which the ICC turned down.

DISPOSITIONS

Zinc Junction to Blende—Removed.
   The zinc smelter near Pueblo had terminated its operations.
Colorado City to Manitou—Removed.
   There was no traffic on this branch.
Reliance Junction to Ojo—Removed.
   The coal mine on this branch had ceased operations.

MOTIVE POWER

455—Traded. Became Rio Grande Southern 455.

1940

The ICC modified its own plan of reorganization and approved it, readying it for presentation to the court. Revenues were up about $1-million and the deficit was down by the same amount. Still, the Trustees relaxed not one bit in the momentum of their rebuilding program.

CONSTRUCTION

Laguna to Canyon Siding—1m S-G.
   A short piece of four-percent grade eliminated the spectacular three-bridge loop on the Tintic Branch.
Leadville to Eilers—3m 3-R to S-G.
   The C&S N-G line from the east no longer handled shipments into the Arkansas Valley Smelter.

DISPOSITIONS

Leadville to Leadville Junction—Removed.
   The cutoff was taken up because passenger trains no longer ran via Leadville.
A.Y. & Minnie to A.V. Sampler—Removed.
   The two mines had shut down permanently.

D&RGW COLLECTION — COURTESY JACKSON THODE

The first "Prospector" was an overnight train, consisting of two self-powered cars, running each way between Denver and Salt Lake City. This picture of the M2 shows the "Bringham Young" and "Heber C. Kimball" on a trial daytime run in Glenwood Canyon.

Rolling northward near Santa Clara, the 470 heads for Antonito with the last passenger train on the Santa Fé Branch, on September 1, 1941. The line was dismantled in 1942.

OTTO PERRY

RICHARD KINDIG

After the Alpine Tunnel collapsed, the D&RG operated trains over Colorado & Southern track between Quartz and Baldwin; later, the D&RG acquired the Baldwin

Branch. Here, in 1940, the 223 and 278 at the age of 60 years, were found still working hard at Castleton.

152

For a period of three decades the D&RGW's 2-8-8-2's were their most formidable locomotives. They smoked copiously while working hard—as the 3614 was doing as she rolled through Salida's unique three-rail yard with an eastbound freight in 1945.

To commemorate its 75th-Anniversary, the D&RGW assembled a special train which was exhibited all over the system. This anniversary special was comprised of both standard-gauge and narrow-gauge equipment. Included in the consist was a sleek, modern dome-coach for the future "California Zephyr," historic narrow-gauge rolling stock and colorful Number 268, one of the tiny 2-8-0's built by Baldwin in 1882. Motive power for the train was the 548, a four-unit FT-model locomotive. In this scene—photographed in 1945—the special was heading east across the spacious Utah desert at Cisco.

Half-a-dozen of these little one-man B-B switchers replaced the various shop-switchers at Burnham, Alamosa and Salt Lake City. The 42 is shown in this picture at the Burnham roundhouse.

In the first years of its conversion to internal-combustion motive power the D&RGW purchased switchers from all five manufacturers. The 66 - 74 were examples of BLW's 660-hp unit.

The D&RGW's first diesel-electric locomotive was a GM-EMD NW-1 model switcher numbered 7000, delivered in 1941. Before the year was over, it was renumbered to 100.

The 119 was the last of 19 1000-hp B-B switchers delivered by ALCO between 1941 and 1944. Most of them worked in the Denver area.

The 3714, a 4-6-6-4 built in 1942, was the last new steam locomotive bought by the D&RGW, all subsequently acquired ones having been leased or second-hand. In

this 1947 scene, that engine was leaving Helper on the long trip across the desert to Grand Junction.

Mayne to Monson—Removed.
 This segment of the original Walsenburg-Trinidad mainline was no longer needed.

1941

The ICC's modified plan for reorganization was rejected by the court, and a substitute plan was offered immediately. Also, the RFC had some thoughts of its own and it, too, submitted a plan, while the insurance companies turned in another version of their ideas. The court, however, remained unaffected by all these suggestions, allowing the Trustees to continue their tremendous and thorough task. Otherwise, the year was notable for the last deficit, $2.3-million, and the first diesel-electric locomotives. Also, late in the year, two two-car self-propelled trains were placed in overnight service between Denver and Salt Lake City.

CONSTRUCTION

Vivian Park to Charleston—10m S-G.
 This portion of the branch to Heber was relocated to avoid a new reservoir.

DISPOSITIONS

Graham Park Junction to Wolftone—Removed.
Wolftone Junction to North Moyer—Removed.
 The mines on these Leadville branches had closed permanently.
Pryor to Mayne — Removed.
 C&S track was used in lieu of this short segment south of Walsenburg.

MOTIVE POWER

M1, M2
| Budd | Model-None | Unclassified |

 These were the numbers assigned to the two experimental 2-car self-propelled trains.

38
| General Electric | 44-ton | DE B-B 26 |

66-74
| Baldwin Locomotive | VO660 | DE B-B 60 |

100—Renumbered from 7000.

101-104
| American Locomotive | S2 | DE B-B 69 |

 These locomotives replaced steam switchers at major terminals.

7000
| General Motors | NW1 | DE B-B 61 |

 This was the first diesel-electric locomotive acquired by the D&RGW.

1942

War traffic boosted the D&RGW's net income into the black by a startling $11-million, and net ton-miles exceeded 1941's figure by 50-percent. Even though the first road-haul diesel-electric locomotives had gone into service, the D&RGW had to borrow heavy 2-8-2's from the Missouri Pacific, and 2-8-8-4's from the Duluth, Missabe & Iron Range, to handle the traffic. As somewhat of an afterthought, the ICC approved its own latest reorganization plan for the D&RGW.

The "Colorado Eagle" was owned by the Missouri Pacific, but operated with MP motive power by the D&RGW between Pueblo and Denver. In this 1943 view the 7002 *and 7002B were hauling the train southbound on AT&SF track near Tomah.*

CONSTRUCTION

Roper to Ordnance Plant—2m S-G.
As part of the Salt Lake City terminal, this was a joint track with the Western Pacific railroad.

DISPOSITION

Antonito to Santa Fé—Removed.
Traffic on this branch had decreased to essentially zero.
Salina to Crystal—Removed.
Unoperated since 1933, this line was considerably more useful as a source of rail and track material.
Villa Grove to Orient—Removed.
The San Luis Valley iron mines had been abandoned for many years.
Alamo to Calumet Mine—Removed.
Fremont Junction to Fremont Mine—Removed.
These branches were taken up due to the closing of coal mines.
Silverton to North Star Mill—Removed.
Durango to San Juan Smelter—Removed.
These tracks were no longer needed due to decreased mining activity.

MOTIVE POWER

39-42

| General Electric | 44-ton | DE B-B 26 |

These switchers were identical with the original one.

540-542

| General Motors | FT | DE 4 B-B 226 |

These were the railroad's first diesel-electric locomotives (four-units) for road service. They pulled freight trains between Denver and Salt Lake City via the Moffat Tunnel route.

3350-3351

| Ex-Norfolk & Western | 2-6-6-2 | L76S |
| 1453, 1457 | | |

These engines were needed for mine-run service out of Helper, Utah.

3710-3714

| Baldwin Locomotive | 4-6-6-4 | L105S |

Except for a change in feedwater heaters, these engines were identical with those of the same class ordered earlier, and were the last new steam locomotives purchased by the D&RGW. In addition to hauling freight across the Utah desert, they handled heavy passenger trains over Tennessee Pass as far as Pueblo.

1943

This year was a real record-breaker. Ton-miles were up another 25-percent; the number of passengers almost doubled; freight trains earned more than $10 per train mile for the first time; and the average freight train tonnage exceeded 1000 tons. And last, but hardly least, the court approved the fourth ICC plan for the financial reorganization of the railroad. Since this plan eliminated the stock held by the Missouri Pacific Railroad and Western Pacific Railroad Corporation, they rose in vehement protest, aided by the interested insurance and trust companies who also added their unanimous objections.

DISPOSITIONS

Eureka to Silver City—Removed.
Kubler to Castleton—Removed.
Sandy to Sand Pit—Removed.
The mines at the ends of these branches had closed down, eliminating the need for the trackage which served them.

During World War II the D&RGW bought four 4-8-2's, two 2-6-6-2's and 15 2-8-8-2's from the Norfolk & Western to handle the enormous increase in traffic. The 2-6-6-2's— numbered 3350 and 3351—joined the D&RGW's eight other 2-6-6-2's. These older articulated locomotives worked in mine-run service on branch-lines in Utah.

157

Though their machinery dimensions were alike, the four 4-8-2's bought from the Norfolk & Western in 1945 ranked in weight just midway between the D&RGW's 1500's and 1600's. Usually they were operated between Grand Junction and Helper across the Utah desert.

Wartime brought 15 Norfolk & Western 2-8-8-2's—built by Baldwin or the N&W's shops—to work as helpers on the D&RGW's steep grades. The 3558, seen here at Helper, was one of four built by the N&W, and all were much like the D&RGW's 3500 - 3509 group.

After having acquired a dozen GM-EMD FT-model four-unit diesel-electric locomotives for freight service, the D&RGW added three similar ones of the F3-model equipped for passenger duties. In this scene in Glenwood Canyon, just east of Glenwood Springs, the 553A, B, C, D was making a trial run with some of the "California Zephyr's" equipment.

DON E. A. ROGERS

When the D&RGW wanted more Baldwin 4-6-6-4's in 1943 the War Production Board leased to it six of that type which were then being built by ALCO for the Union Pacific. The 3805, sitting at Helper with 4-8-2 Number 1524, was the last new steam locomotive to bear the "Rio Grande" legend.

Overland Park to Overland Junction—Removed.
 There was no further need for this trackage.

MOTIVE POWER

43
 General Electric   44-ton   DE B-B 26
 This was the remaining engine of the 1942 order.

105-114
 American Locomotives   S2   DE B-B 69
 These switchers were identical with those ordered in 1941.

543-547
 General Motors   FT   DE 4 B-B 225
 These road units were essentially identical with earlier units.

3550-3557
 Ex-Norfolk and Western 1701, 1722, 1724, 1728, 1729, 1730, 1710, 1727   2-8-8-2   L109S
 These engines, much like those of Class L107, were obtained for freight service helpers between Denver and Tabernash, and between Minturn and Tennessee Pass.

3800-3805
 American Locomotive   4-6-6-4   L97S
 Although the D&RGW wanted more Baldwin-built L105's, the War Production Board assigned to it these locomotives being built on a current Union Pacific order. The D&RGW did not buy them, however, leasing them instead from the Defense Plant Corporation. They were the last new steam locomotives to go into service on the railroad.

1944

The very parties who had consistently opposed rehabili-tation of the D&RGW now tried to block execution of the Reorganization Plan, which was approved by the Court in Denver.

DISPOSITIONS

Leadville to Ibex—Removed.
Chrysolite Junction to Fryer Hill—Removed.
 Precious-metal mining was prohibited during World War II, and the rails of these branches were usable elsewhere.
Chandler Junction to Chandler—Removed.
 The coal mine on this branch had closed.

MOTIVE POWER

115-119
 American Locomotive   S2   DE B-B 69
 The arrival of these engines completed the conversion of major switching operations from steam to diesel-electric power.

548
 General Motors   FT   DE 4 B-B 228
 This four-unit locomotive was equipped with a steam generator for passenger service.

549-551
 General Motors   FT   DE 4 B-B 229
 These were slightly heavier versions of the previous FT locomotives, and the last of this model to be acquired.

1945

Influenced by the temporary prosperity generated by wartime traffic, as well as by the complaints of those opposed to the court-approved Reorganization Plan, and ignoring the fact that some of these very complainants had been responsible for the exhausted physical and financial condition of the railroad (and also that they had opposed its reconstruction), the United States Circuit Court overruled the lower courts's approval of the Reorganization Plan. Undaunted, the Trustees and the ICC appealed to the U. S. Supreme Court.

CONSTRUCTION

Tennessee Pass—A new and larger tunnel replaced the original bore.

MOTIVE POWER

M1, M2—Returned to builder. Although these two self-propelled trains were not satisfactory on the D&RGW's difficult profile, they were instrumental in the ultimate development of the successful Budd "RDC" equipment.

1550-1553
Ex-Norfolk & Western
206-209   4-8-2   M69S
Similar to the D&RGW's M67 engines, these were pooled with the railroad's other 4-8-2's.

3558-3564
Ex-Norfolk & Western 1706, 1709, 1713, 1714, 1719, 1725, 1726   2-8-8-2   L109S
These joined the other articulated compounds on the railroad's heavy main line grades, helping war-time freight and passenger trains.

1946

Although the U.S. Supreme Court upheld the Reorganization Plan, it was not immediately effective due to a final flurry of protests by organizations which opposed it. Transcontinental sleeping-car service between New York City and Oakland, California, was inaugurated on the "Exposition Flyer" via Chicago, Illinois, on the WP-D&RGW-CB&Q and NYC/PRR.

ACQUISITION

Provo Junction to Orem—6m S-G.
This branch was purchased from the abandoned Salt Lake & Utah electric interurban line.

DISPOSITIONS

Castleton to Baldwin—Removed.
This trackage was removed due to the closing of the coal mines around Baldwin.
Cement Quarry to Park City—Removed.
Although the branch did have a small amount of traffic, part of its right-of-way was needed for a multi-lane highway.

MOTIVE POWER

552-554
General Motors   F3   DE 4 B-B 232
The only F3 units delivered to the D&RGW, these engines were equipped for passenger service.

Number 1031, ex-Denver & Salt Lake 111, was equipped with a snow-flanger in place of its pilot, and it still retained its two original single-stage air compressors until it was dismantled. This 2-8-0 was a Schenectady product of 1908.

The D&RGW bought a pair of three-unit locomotives for the "California Zephyr," and repainted them in aluminum with orange noses in 1950 to match the cars—a scheme which lasted for only a few months. On this occasion the locomotive was the 6011 - 6012 - 6013 pulling the westbound train through Gore Canyon at Azure.

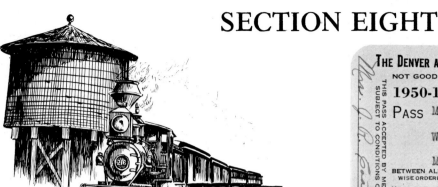

Denver & Rio Grande Western Railroad (Reorganized)
1947 - 1970

1947

Emancipation Day for the long troubled D&RGW came on April 11. The Trusteeship was terminated, McCarthy staying on as President of the reorganized company, which was now owned by its former bondholders. Although the ill-gotten stock interests of the Missouri Pacific Railroad and the Western Pacific Railroad Corporation had been eliminated, the railroad's new common and preferred stock was placed in escrow until 1955 to thwart any attempt by other railroads or companies to gain control of the new company. The Denver & Salt Lake, Denver & Salt Lake Western, Rio Grande Junction, and Goshen Valley railroads were merged into the D&RGW, but the Northwestern Terminal—which owned the D&SL's terminal property and trackage in Denver—was leased.

ACQUISITIONS

Denver to Utah Junction and Stockyards—8m S-G.
   This was NWT trackage.
Utah Junction to Craig—228m S-G.
   This trackage had been the Denver & Salt Lake Railway.

DISPOSITION

Crested Butte to Anthracite—Removed.
Bulkley Mine to C & B Coal Company Junction—Removed.
   The coal mines on these branches had closed.

MOTIVE POWER

600-601
   American Locomotive   P1   DE 3 A1A-A1A 147
   These two three-unit locomotives were intended for the "California Zephyr."

795-796
   Ex-D&SL 302, 303   4-6-0   T33S
1031-1039
   Ex-D&SL 111-113,
   118-123   2-8-0   C43S

1220-1229		
Ex-D&SL 400-409	2-8-2	K63S
3360-3375		
Ex-D&SL 200-209,		
211-216	2-6-6-0	L77S

1948

Now that the D&RGW had been rebuilt into a first-class competitive railroad and freed from financial oppression, its managers did not relax in their efforts to improve the property and to make its operation even more efficient. The magnitude of this task can be partly appreciated from the realization that the D&RGW possessed the two most difficult main-line crossings of the Continental Divide. The Moffat Tunnel route, climbing to 9240-feet at the Tunnel, ascended almost 50 miles of continuous 2.0-percent grade, passing through 31 tunnels in 17 miles west of Denver. The Royal Gorge route ascended 122 miles of unrelieved 1.4-percent grade to 10,240-feet at Tennessee Pass. Furthermore, curvature on the Moffat Tunnel route was so severe that train-speeds could exceed 30 mph in only a few locations.

The ensuing years were to see the gradual replacement of steam locomotives with diesel-electrics, discontinuance of unremunerative trains, removal of unprofitable branches, modernization of freight yards, extension of Centralized Traffic Control, acquisition of new rolling stock, and laying of stronger rail on a better roadbed.

DISPOSITION

Moroni to Gypsum Mill—Removed.
Gypsum Mill to Nephi—Sold to Union Pacific Railroad.
   Traffic on this trackage had decreased to essentially nothing.

MOTIVE POWER

120-122
   Fairbanks-Morse   H 10-44   DE B-B 72

Although the D&SL's locomotives had been acquired by the D&RGW in 1947, some of them were not relettered and renumbered until a year or two later. Consequently,

D&SL 302 bore "Rio Grande" 795 for only four months before it was scrapped. This 4-6-0 was built in 1907 by American Locomotive Company's Schenectady works.

After the D&RGW absorbed the D&SL, the 4-6-0's which had hauled passenger trains for four decades were replaced with some of the D&RGW's 35-year old 4-6-2's. This one

was the 800, shown leaving Denver Union Station with the usual two-car consist.

All of the engines built by Lima were acquired when other railroads were merged into the Rio Grande system—five Shays from the Copper Belt and eight 2-8-2's, renumbered 1220 - 1227, from the Denver & Salt Lake, like the 1225 stored at Burnham in 1947. The 1225 was originally Number 405 on the D&SL and was built in 1915.

The three F-M switchers with 1500-hp engines, numbered 150 - 152, worked at first on branches in Utah. Later, they were moved to the new yard at Grand Junction where they teamed with "slug" Number 25 for hump duties.

RALPH HALLOCK

The backbone of the D&SL's motive-power roster was the nation's largest group of the uncommon 2-6-0 type, 16 of them having gone to the D&RGW in the 1947 merger.

A year later, the 3363 (ex-203) and the 3367 (ex-207)—both of which had been built as 0-6-0's—trudge up the two-percent grade past Rollinsville at only 10 mph.

The D&RGW bought diesel-electric switchers from nearly every builder—six of them evenly divided between two models which were produced by Fairbanks-Morse. The 120-122, powered by 1000-hp engines, worked in the yards at Salt Lake City and Provo, the locale of this scene. This engine was obtained from F-M in 1948.

Although the GM GP9-model units were delivered in four-unit sets, they were soon separated and coupled in the middle of F7-model four-unit locomotives to form a combination having 7750-engine-horsepower. This group, standing at Grand Junction was comprised of the 5734 - 5731 and the 5943.

167

This intriguing combination of General Motors diesels—throbbing upgrade at Louviers—was a rolling catalog of models. In order, the models were: GP7 5106, F9 5762, GP9 5921, SD9 5309 and GP40 3085.

In 1949 the narrow-gauge line down the Black Canyon of the Gunnison and over Cerro Summit between Sapinero and Cedar Creek was removed. This segment—noted for its spectacular scenic beauty—was part of the original main-line between Denver and Grand Junction, and it was the first part of that route to be removed. The scene on the opposite page shows the last passenger train—pulled by 2-8-0 Number 361—in the depths of the canyon.

When four-unit diesel-electric locomotives were assigned to D&RGW freight trains, they replaced 2-8-8-2's on a one-for-one basis; however, steam helpers were still required on grades steeper than one-percent. This west-bound consist—moving uphill at Rocky—was assisted by 4-8-2 Number 1527, a 1923 product of American Locomotive's Brooks works. When this engine was new it was used in main-line service between Salida and Grand Junction.

169

The "San Juan Express" made its last trip between Alamosa and Durango in January, 1951, but due to legislative delay in New Mexico it continued to run through the lonely country between Chama and Dulce, 30 miles apart. Engine 473 and a single car provided more than adequate accommodations for a handful of passengers.

150-152
Fairbanks-Morse   H 15-44   DE B-B 72A
These switchers, the only F-M units purchased by the D&RGW, replaced steam 2-8-0's at Salt Lake City.

556
General Motors   F7   DE 4 B-B 235
This four-unit locomotive was the first of the F7 model.

1949

Released from a long era of financial serfdom, the D&RGW now took on a Goliath, in the form of the Union Pacific, by filing with the ICC a complaint that it should be allowed to participate in the non-discriminative routing of through freight via Ogden. This was the beginning of an attempt to open the Ogden Gateway, which Harriman had closed almost 50 years earlier.

During February the UP was blocked with snow, and it detoured almost all of its tremendous main-line traffic over the D&RGW between Denver and Ogden. UP diesel-electrics hauled passenger trains over the Moffat Tunnel route, while four of their 4-6-6-4's helped freight trains up the west side of Tennessee Pass.

A new deluxe train, the "California Zephyr"—running between Chicago, Illinois, and Oakland, California, over the CB&Q, D&RGW and WP railroads—replaced the "Exposition Flyer."

CONSTRUCTION

To eliminate terminal delays to freight moving via the Moffat Tunnel route, the former D&SL yards and shops at Utah Junction were replaced with entirely new facilities, called North Yard. The CRI&P, which previously had terminated at Burnham Yards, built a connection between the Union Pacific's Limon-Denver line (used by the CRI&P) and Northwestern Terminal track, then transferred its freight operations to the new yard.

DISPOSITIONS

Rouse to Pryor—Removed.
This branch was no longer needed to serve the coal mines.
Sapinero to Cedar Creek—Removed.
Dismantling of this trackage, which supported scant traffic, did three things: it broke the "N-G Circle," it isolated the N-G Ouray Branch, and it severed the original N-G through route between Denver and Ogden.

MOTIVE POWER

555, 557
General Motors   F7   DE4 B-B 235
Numbers 555-557 (four units) were equipped with steam generators for occasional use in passenger service.

558-564
General Motors   F7   DE4 B-B 241
The arrival of these four-unit freight-haulers expedited the transport of perishables between Salt Lake City and Denver.

1950

Hearings on the Ogden Gateway were held before the ICC all during the year, without clear-cut indication of the eventual outcome, although the D&RGW appeared to have a strong case of discrimination against it by the UP.

Contract operation of the Ballard & Thompson railroad, begun in 1913, was terminated. Operation of AS&R track to Bon Carbo was discontinued.

Two of the ALCO road-switchers, Numbers 5201 and 5200—assisted by a GM unit numbered 5102—roll south through Oak Creek in 1951, soon after their delivery. In the back-ground are the conveyor system and preparation facilities for the Edna coal mine. These RS3 units were obtained to replace steam locomotives in branch and local freight service.

MOTIVE POWER

461—Sold. Became Rio Grande Southern 461.

Early in the year all multiple-unit diesel-electric locomotives were renumbered to assign a specific number to each unit.

540-564—Renumbered 5401, 5402, 5403, 5404 - 5641, 5642, 5643, 5644

600, 601—Renumbered 6001, 6002, 6003 and 6011, 6012, 6013

5101-5104
General Motors   GP7   DE B-B 60
These—the first of the GP models—replaced steam locomotives in local and branch-line service.

5481—Rebuilt from
FT-model   F7   DE B-B 59

5651, 5652, 5653, 5654-5691, 5692, 5693, 5694
General Motors   F7   DE 4 B-B 237

1951

Narrow-gauge main-line passenger trains became a thing of the past when the Alamosa-Durango "San Juan" was discontinued. Only the "Silverton Mixed" remained. In this year revenues from freight traffic received from and delivered to connecting railroads exceeded all other freight revenues combined. Consequently, the D&RGW had became more of a "bridge carrier" than one which derived its principal revenues from originated or terminated traffic.

CONSTRUCTION

Alamosa to Hooper—19m 3-R to S-G

This conversion was part of the removal of unneeded N-G lines in the San Luis Valley.

DISPOSITION

Mears Junction to Hooper—Removed.
This dismantling of the "Valley Line," which was no longer needed, resulted in some interesting circumstances. It eliminated the nation's fifth-longest stretch of tangent track, and broke the N-G lines into three separate segments connected only by S-G trackage. The branch to Ouray could be reached, however, over Rio Grande Southern track between Durango and Ridgway.

MOTIVE POWER

5200-5204
American Locomotive   RS3   DE B-B 60
These units also replaced steam power in branch-line and local freight service.

1952

The summer of this year brought frustration to the D&RGW; the ICC ruled that the Ogden Gateway case should be completely re-argued since the Commission now had two new members. The Rio Grande Southern was sold at a foreclosure sale and dismantled, finally eliminating the D&RGW's long-time investment in that unfortunate carrier.

CONSTRUCTION

Rocky to Dow—4m S-G.
This branch was built to an isolated atomic-materials factory northwest of Denver.

LE MASSENA

The 1804 remained in service longer than its four companions, probably because it had been given a new boiler after the original one exploded in 1942. On this occasion it was pulling the eastbound "Royal Gorge" and had just replenished its coal and water supply at Salida. Mount Princeton, 20 miles distant, can be seen at the right.

LE MASSENA

Two veteran steam locomotives—resplendent in green boiler jackets—await disposition at Montrose in 1951. Narrow-gauge 340 had been delivered to the Denver & Rio Grande in 1881, while standard-gauge 605 was built for the Rio Grande Western in 1889, one of the first standard-gauge locomotives acquired for the RGW.

DISPOSITION

Hooper to Cox—Removed.
 Industries on this part of the branch south of Ogden no longer used the railroad.

MOTIVE POWER

5104-5113
 General Motors   GP7   DE B-B 60
 These were the last of the smaller diesel-electric road-switchers.

5701, 5702, 5703, 5704—5741, 5742, 5743, 5744
 General Motors   F7   DE 4 B-B 238

5751, 5752, 5754—5761, 5762, 5764
 General Motors   F7   DE 3 B-B 178
 The last two were three-unit locomotives intended for helper service on the west side of Soldier Summit.

1953

The ICC, finally, decided that the D&RGW did have a reasonable complaint and it ordered the UP to establish equitable freight rates, but only on a few commodities. Disagreeing with this piecemeal decision, the D&RGW promptly went to the Federal Court in hope of obtaining a more liberal ruling.

The railroad's first hump yard—named East Yard—for the classification of all freight cars at a centrally located point on the system was built on the east edge of Grand Junction.

The D&RGW became a part-owner of Associated Railroads, and began operating it, alternating with the Colorado & Southern.

CONSTRUCTION

Montrose to Ridgway—26m N-G to S-G.
 Dismantling of the Rio Grande Southern permitted this conversion.

DISPOSITION

Montrose to Cedar Creek—Removed.
Ridgway to Ouray—Removed.
 All available traffic on these two segments was now being handled by trucks.
Alamo Number 2 to Alamo Number 1—Removed.
 Closing of the coal mines on the branch north of Walsenburg caused this reduction in trackage.

MOTIVE POWER

25   Booster   Unclassified
 Rebuilt by D&RGW shops from 68 (Class DE B-B 60) and renumbered for use with F-M H 15-44 units in Grand Junction East Yard.

5300-5304
 General Motors   SD7   DE C-C 89
 These six-motor units were acquired for heavy branch-line service.

5401, 5402, 5403, 5404—5471, 5472, 5473, 5474—5491, 5492, 5493, 5494—5511, 5512, 5513, 5514
 Rebuilt by D&RGW shops from DE 4 B-B
 226, 225 and 229   FT   DE 4 B-B 239

These older locomotives were loaded with concrete ballast and regeared, allowing them to be used interchangeably with F3 or F7 units in slow-speed service.

1954

The Federal Court at Omaha (the UP's headquarters) decided that the ICC had gone too far, thus forcing the D&RGW to return to the court in Denver to ask again for what it had first sought back in 1949.

CONSTRUCTION

Snyder to Lark—3m S-G.
 This branch was rebuilt to avoid new mining and tailings areas in Bingham Canyon.

DISPOSITION

West of Pueblo—second track removed.
 This consisted of no longer needed portions of the double track.

1955

The court in Denver ordered the entire Ogden Gateway case reopened, which gave the D&RGW renewed hope for a more favorable ruling by the ICC. The capital stock was released from escrow and the railroad was now in the hands of its individual owners. During this year the N-G lines suffered their maximum attrition.

DISPOSITION

Gunnison to Castleton—Removed.
Gunnison to Crested Butte—Removed.
Poncha Junction to Sapinero—Removed.
 The coal mines at Crested Butte and Castleton had closed, and livestock from Sapinero and Gunnison was being shipped by truck. Hence, these lines, having insignificant other traffic, were dismantled.
Mustang to Capers—Removed.
 Again, the closing of old coal mines south of Pueblo eliminated the need for railroad trackage.

MOTIVE POWER

5762—Renumbered 5753, combined with 5751, 5752, 5754.

5762, 5763
 General Motors   F9   Unclassified
 These two new "B" units were combined with "A" units 5761, 5764. These two combinations converted the two DE 3 B-B 178 locomotives into DE 4 B-B 238 locomotives.

5771-5774
 General Motors   F9   DE 4 B-B 238
 These were the last cab-units ordered by the railroad.

5901, 5902, 5903, 5904-5921, 5922, 5923, 5924
 General Motors   GP9   DE B-B 60
 These locomotives were used as four-unit engines in main-line road service, replacing FT, F3 or F7 model units.

1956

The Denver court upheld the ICC's original order and the Union Pacific conceded the struggle, establishing through rates on certain commodities routed via the D&RGW. Not content, the D&RGW prepared for another attempt to obtain a more equitable division of freight traffic at Ogden.

President McCarthy died in office, being replaced by Gale B. Aydelott.

Standard-gauge steam operations came to an end on December 26 when Number 1151 made a round trip from Alamosa to South Fork. There appears to be no record of the last steam passenger run, but most likely it was a ski train between Denver and Winter Park, hauled by Number 1709 in early March. Diesel-electric locomotives had been contemplated for the replacement of steam power on the narrow-gauge lines, but such a large investment for the small amount of traffic was not considered worthwhile.

CONSTRUCTION

Salida to Monarch—26m N-G to S-G.
　　This conversion eliminated the transfer of limestone from N-G into S-G cars at Salida, and the remaining N-G equipped (at Salida) was "piggy-backed" via S-G trackage to N-G rails at Alamosa.

DISPOSITION

Cement Quarry to Alexander—Removed.
Kingsville Junction to Farnsworth—Removed.
　　These Utah branches were no longer needed, their traffic having diminished to almost nothing.

MOTIVE POWER

　　In this last year of S-G steam on the D&RGW, the few locomotives in service were assigned as follows:

2-8-0: switching and local freight at Denver (1139, 1163), Pueblo (1185) and Alamosa (1151).

2-8-2: work trains and local freights at Denver (1207, 1224, 1229).

4-8-4: freight helpers from Denver to East Portal and ski trains between Denver and Winter Park (1700, 1701, 1709).

4-6-6-4: limerock trains from Salida to Pueblo (3700, 3708, 3711).

2-8-8-2: freight helpers from Tabernash to Winter Park, and Denver to East Portal (3609, 3612, 3619).

　　Numbers 3609 and 3612 worked as helpers out of Tabernash in the fall, returning under steam to Denver, where the 1163 was still at work. Together with the 3619, these locomotives were hauled, dead, to Pueblo in November for scrapping. When the 1185 dropped its fire on December 20 at Pueblo, there was no more steam there, and the last trip into Alamosa on December 26 by engine 1151 was the D&RGW's last S-G steam run.

5931, 5932, 5933, 5934-5951, 5952, 5953, 5954
　　General Motors　　　　GP9　　　DE B-B 61

5305-5314
　　General Motors　　　　SD9　　　DE C-C 89

The acquisition of these road-switchers brought to a close the conversion from steam to diesel-electric power.

1957

　　The late-1950's ushered in an era of relative calm for the D&RGW; it went about its business efficiently, deliberately, even perhaps monotonously. U. S. Steel's Columbia-Geneva plant at Geneva, Utah, became the railroad's biggest customer, displacing Colorado Fuel & Iron's Minnequa plant which had held that position for three-quarters of a century. The railroad requested the ICC to void a 1923 Central Pacific - Union Pacific agreement to route central and northern California and Oregon freight preferentially over the UP east of Ogden. In effect, this was another means of opening the Ogden Gateway.

CONSTRUCTION

　　With the construction of long passing tracks in new CTC territory, all of the D&RGW's main-lines were being operated as double track, CTC single track or automatic block signal trackage, thus eliminating delays when opposing trains met.

DISPOSITION

Alexander to Sugar House—Removed.
　　This part of the old Park City Branch was no longer needed.

1958

　　The D&RGW acquired almost all of the Northwestern Terminal's stock, but did not absorb the company.

ACQUISITION

Salt Lake City—4m S-G.
　　This track, plus several miles of industrial spurs, had belonged to the recently abandoned Bamberger Electric railroad.

CONSTRUCTION

　　Some of the double track on the west side of Tennessee Pass was converted to single track with CTC control, between Minturn and the summit.

1959

　　The D&RGW arranged to sell the Silverton Branch to a non-profit foundation provided that the ICC would grant its petition to discontinue service on the line.

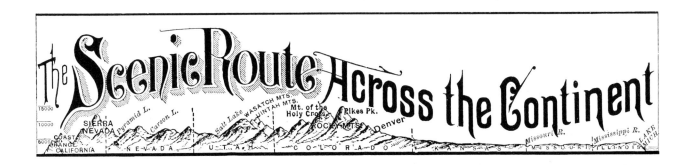

Although 2-8-8-2 3400 was the last of 41 compound articulated locomotives operated by the D&RGW, its green boiler jacket and shiny cylinder-head covers did not prophesy its imminent demise when this photo was taken in Eagle River canyon at Redcliff during 1952.

Only two weeks before its discontinuance, the west-bound "San Juan Express" was photographed while pausing at Gato—which a half-century previous had been a bustling lumber town and the junction of the branch to Pagosa Springs. At that time Gato was called Pagosa Junction.

LE MASSENA

The daily local train—running between Denver and Craig—offered RPO, express, baggage and buffet facilities to a limited clientele in its sparsely-populated territory. The D&RGW's last two 4-6-2's, Numbers 801 and 804, were assigned to this casual schedule until they were retired in 1953. In this scene the train was about to enter the east portal of Moffat Tunnel.

In its final weeks of service, the 1207—last surviving example of 14 2-8-2's—handled work trains on the former Denver & Salt Lake line. Here, at Coal Creek tank on a foggy November day, the engine had stopped to replenish its tender's water supply.

LE MASSENA

The "Exposition Flyer," steam-powered ancestor of the "California Zephyr," utilized two 4-8-4's, Numbers 1704 and 1801, to hoist its long formation of heavyweight cars up the two-percent grade between Denver and the east portal of Moffat Tunnel. A stop was made at Pinecliffe, 37 miles west of Denver, to refill the water supply of the two tenders.

The 3375—formerly Denver & Salt Lake engine Number 216—was the last 2-6-6-0 to have been built, as well as the last one remaining in active service in the United States. Scarcely more potent than the railroad's 2-8-2's, the locomotive was assigned to local freight service between Denver and Toponas.

LE MASSENA

Track on the Ouray Branch was so light that only 2-8-0's could be used beyond Ridgway, and it became the domain of the 300's obtained from the Florence & Cripple Creek railroad. Number 318—found here in Ouray's cul-de-sac—was the lone operating survivor when the rails were pulled up between Ridgway and Ouray in 1953.

The arrival of a great many diesel-electric units in 1949 and 1950, sent most of the articulated steam locomotives to the scrap yard. The few survivors primarily worked as helpers on main-lines in Colorado. A few of the huge 4-6-6-4's—like the 3710 seen here departing Burnham Yard in 1952—hauled freight between Denver and Pueblo.

LE MASSENA

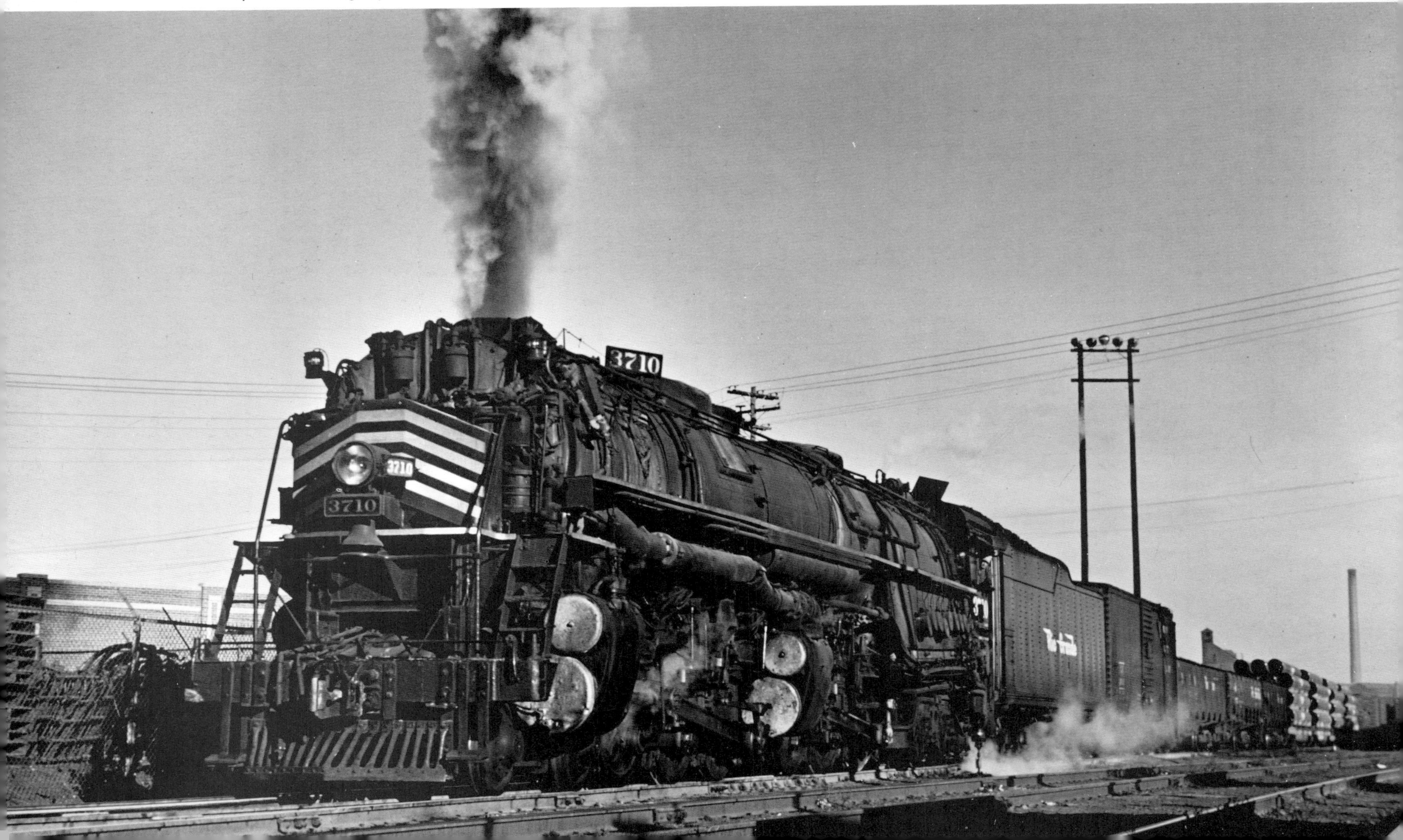

LE MASSENA

Even the relatively short consist of the "Scenic Limited" was sufficent to fill half of the big S-curve which took the track from one side of the valley to the other at Mitchell. The three-percent grade—too formidable for the powerful 4-8-4, Number 1800, which had brought the train from Salt Lake City—demanded the assistance of 2-8-8-2, Number 3612, added at Minturn.

Ordinary freight trains headed south over Tennessee Pass consisted of only 56 cars, requiring three 2-8-8-2's to pull them up the 21 miles of the steep grade in about two hours time. This varied consist—pushed by the 3600, with the 3614 cut into its mid-point—was negotiating the great reverse curve at Mitchell during 1949, the last year of all-steam operations on the hill.

LE MASSENA

LE MASSENA

After the leading 2-8-8-2 entered the Tennessee Pass tunnel it gained speed as it crossed the Great Divide (10,240-feet elevation). The helpers, having only 56-inch diameter drivers, churned furiously to maintain the faster pace set by the leading locomotive, which was equipped 63-inch wheels. The 3552 was the last of 15 compound 2-8-8-2's bought from the Norfolk & Western during World War II.

Iron ore mined in Utah, moved over Tennessee Pass on its way to the blast furnaces at Minnequa. A train of only 24 cars required two 2-8-8-2's—one at each end—to haul it up the three-percent grade. During its final days, the 3400 worked as a helper on these heavy consists, as seen in this smoky portrait at Mitchell.

LE MASSENA

During 1953 the Montrose to Ridgway portion of the Ouray Branch was changed from narrow to standard-gauge by moving one rail outward onto longer ties inserted previously in the track. At the same time, rails were pulled up entirely between Ridgway and Ouray. This scene was near Colonna. The third rail was removed from the trackage at Montrose and the locomotives based there were sold or scrapped. Remaining traffic to and from Ouray had to go by truck.

Some of the powerful Baldwin 4-6-6-4's—which had been designed to haul fast freight trains between Grand Junction and Salt Lake City—ended their careers working in drag-freight service between Denver and Salida on the Royal Gorge route. Number 3708—the last operational survivor—is seen here at Salida during 1954.

184

LE MASSENA

The D&RGW's last operating narrow-gauge 2-8-0 was the 268, which was used to dismantle portions of the lines radiating from Gunnison. After hauling a train of scrap rail and fastenings from Glacier to Gunnison in the summer of 1955, it was withdrawn from service permanently. This scene shows the final wisp of steam fluttering from the drain after the boiler had been emptied.

After their retirement from freight service the D&RGW's half-dozen GM F9-model units were assigned to passenger duties, though they required the attachment of a steam-generator car—in this instance one of the converted ALCO P1-model booster units. The train is the "Rio Grande Zephyr," detouring through Palmer Lake, pulled by the 5771 and 5763.

GREGORY LEPAK

185

Even though the earlier multiple-unit locomotives had been given individual numbers in 1950, and the GM GP7-model units had been given serial-numbers, the 24 GP9-models reverted to the four-unit grouping, 5901 - 5904 through 5951 - 5954.

General Motors SD7 Number 5301, coupled to FT-models, 5443 and 5444, provided an unusual combination of helpers for east-bound freights climbing the hill from Thistle —where this photo was taken—to Soldier Summit. This scene was recorded in 1953.

186

In August, 1955, when 2-8-0 Number 268 rolled into Gunnison with a load of scrap rail from the Crested Butte Branch, an era came to an end. The 268—built in 1882— was the D&RGW's last remaining 2-8-0, and among its final tasks was the dismantling of the narrow-gauge lines radiating from Gunnison to Sapinero, Crested Butte and Castleton. Only moments after this photograph was taken, the 268's steam pressure registered "0" for the last time.

Two of the remaining 2-8-8-2's, 3609 and 3612, worked their last miles as helpers between Tabernash and the Moffat Tunnel in 1956. Upon their return to Denver the era of steam power on the former D&SL railroad came to a close. This photo shows the 3609 leading tonnage upgrade at Winter Park.

DISPOSITIONS

Alamosa to Hooper—Removed.
   There was no further rail traffic on this branch.
Calumet to Kebler—Removed.
   The coal mines at the end of the branch had closed down.

1960

CONSTRUCTION

Idealite Junction to Cement Plant—2m S-G.
   This spur from the Dow plant branch served a concrete aggregate plant northwest of Denver.

1961

A spasm of mergers began to run through the Western

Until the Monarch Branch was converted to standard-gauge and diesel-electric operation (1956) that line provided a spectacular display of narrow-gauge steam locomotives crawling around hairpin-curves and climbing a double switchback. The 486 was obliged to leave half its train at Maysville before tackling the steep grades beyond.

railroads, and the D&RGW found that large blocks of its stock were being acquired by other railroads (AT&SF, CB&Q, Union Pacific) whose intentions toward the railroad were certainly open to question. There was much talk about merging the D&RGW with some other carrier, but little overt action. The D&RGW's last N-G passenger-carrying train, the Silverton-Mixed, was cut back to summertime operations only.

MOTIVE POWER

4001-4003

Krauss-Maffei	ML4	DH C-C	104

These diesel-hydraulic locomotives were purchased with the expectation of reducing the number of units in service and eliminating the diesel-electric's electrical machinery.

All units of the multiple-unit diesel-electric locomotives were reclassified individually since the units of the original locomotives were no longer being kept together.

Original Classification	New Classification
DE 4 (B-B) 228	DE B-B 57
DE 4 (B-B) 232	DE B-B 58
DE 4 (B-B) 235	DE B-B 59
DE 4 (B-B) 237	DE B-B 59
DE 4 (B-B) 238	DE B-B 60
DE 4 (B-B) 239	DE B-B 60
DE 4 (B-B) 241	DE B-B 60
DE 3 (A1A-A1A) 147	DE A1A-A1A 49

189

Number 1709 attained the unintentional honor of having hauled the last steam-powered passenger train on the standard-gauge lines of the D&RGW during 1956. At the time, there was no way of knowing that diesel-electric units would be available for the following weekend's ski train. The 1709 also was the last steam passenger engine on the line.

Three 2-8-0's, constructed between 1906 and 1908, became the last D&RGW standard-gauge steam locomotives to operate on the system. In November of 1956, the 1163—as depicted here—steamed for the last time in Denver's Burnham engine terminal. During their final year the remaining 2-8-0's were used mainly for switching and on local freights.

Always experimenting, the railroad purchased three high-power diesel-hydraulic C-C units manufactured in Germany in 1961. Coupled together to form a locomotive having

12,000 engine-horsepower, the 4001 - 4003 were roaring westward out of the Colorado River's scenic Ruby Canyon at Westwater, Utah, when this photograph was taken.

The 5305—first of the GM SD9-model units—was severely damaged in a wreck. After having been rebuilt at the

Burnham shops, it emerged with a low nose, making it unique among others of that model on the railroad.

191

LE MASSENA

Number 1185, a 1906-vintage 2-8-0 built originally for the RGW, worked on the Creede Branch before having been sent to Pueblo for a final switching assignment, concluding all steam operations there in mid-December, 1956. This location is Sugar Junction, where San Luis Central 1 waited for a tank of oil.

ROSS GRENARD

The last run for a standard-gauge D&RGW steam locomotive came on December 26, 1956. Engine Number 1151, a veteran 2-8-0 with 49 years of continuous service, made a round trip from Alamosa to South Fork. Even though it bore the lowest road number in its group—1151 - 1178—the 1151 was the last 2-8-0 built for the railroad.

The new bridge across the Piedra River near Arboles, constructed as part of the relocation required by a downstream dam, was destined to have a short life, as the railroad itself

was removed in 1971. Though operated for freight only since 1951, the line saw passenger equipment being transferred to the Silverton Branch at the end of May each year.

1962

The ICC refused to void the SP - UP Ogden Gateway Agreement, thus forcing the D&RGW to solicit its own Pacific States traffic. The ICC also turned down the D&RGW's request to dispose of the Silverton Branch, and almost simultaneously passenger traffic on the line began to increase.

CONSTRUCTION

East and west of Arboles—11m N-G.
   This was a new line, relocated above the level of the lake formed by the construction of a dam. It lengthened the N-G main-line by four miles.
Hitchens to Energy—13m S-G.
   This branch was built to serve a new coal mine east of Craig, solid trains being run from the mine to electric generating plants near Denver.
Brendel to Potash—36m S-G.
   Adhering to the undulating profile of local drainage out on the eastern Utah desert, this line dropped into the canyon of the Colorado River to tap a huge new potash mine. However, the first outbound revenue train did not operate until early 1965.

MOTIVE POWER

3001-3013
   General Motors   GP 30   DE B-B 62
   These new units replaced the aging FT model units in freight service.

1963

The "Silverton," no longer mixed, began to handle such

volume that double-heading was occasionally required. Deciding to capitalize on the unexpected popularity of the Silverton train, the Rio Grande Land Company (a subsidiary of the D&RGW Railroad) began to develop the area adjacent to the Durango depot as a tourist attraction.

The "short-fast-frequent" freight train concept was inaugurated to reduce costs and to shorten end-to-end schedules.

CONSTRUCTION

Hayden to Power Plant—3m S-G.
   This short branch, owned by a public utility company, but operated by the D&RGW, was built to transport the material and machinery for a new generating plant.

DISPOSITIONS

Oro Junction to A. V. Sampler—Removed.
   This trackage had not been used for several years.
Fort Logan to Federal Boulevard—Removed.
   This military post near Denver had been abandoned.

MOTIVE POWER

50
   Ex-Sumpter Valley 101   200 HP   DM B
   This N-G diesel-mechanical locomotive became the Durango switcher.
3014-3028
   General Motors   GP 30   DE B-B 62
   These replaced more of the FT model units in freight service.

1964

Once again heavy snows blanketed Cumbres Pass and

JACKSON THODE

Not all of the railroad's diesel-powered locomotives were propelled by traction motors and ran on standard-gauge rails. Number 50, having a mechanical transmission, was the yard-switcher at Durango for a few years—until the installation of a balloon-loop track at Durango eliminated the need to turn Silverton Branch trains after their runs.

the N-G line ceased operating late in December. This was the first time that the railroad was operating without steam locomotives. Furthermore it was the first time that the N-G lines had been completely out of service. In striking contrast, however, the summer season saw such an increase in Silverton Branch patronage that its passenger train ran in two sections, giving the scenic line two passenger trains for the first time since 1921.

A faint ray of hope for a possible opening of the Ogden Gateway was seen when the ICC reopened the case involving the Union Pacific - Central Pacific (Southern Pacific) agreement of 1923. However, the Union Pacific now threatened the D&RGW's back door, asking the ICC for permission to merge with the CRI&P, thus cutting off one of the D&RGW's connections east of Denver.

Passenger service over Tennessee Pass was ended late in the year.

DISPOSITION

Midvale to Sandy—Removed.

There was no further need for this remaining segment.

1965

The N-G line over Cumbres Pass was not opened until May; never before had it been out of service for so long a period. There was so little traffic that it was not considered worthwhile to keep the track cleared with rotary plows; instead, the company's highway subsidiary handled whatever freight was presented.

In mid-June a tornado and violent hail-storm near Palmer Lake produced unprecedented floods which ripped out D&RGW and AT&SF tracks along Plum, Monument and Fountain creeks. Both lines were out of service for two weeks, all Denver - Pueblo trains detouring via the Moffat Tunnel, Dotsero Cutoff and Tennessee Pass.

Freight traffic was accelerated by two departures from the usual operating techniques. CB&Q - D&RGW through freight trains arriving in Denver were interchanged without changing motive power, D&RGW units running as far east as Chicago while CB&Q units operated as far west as Salt Lake City. Furthermore, freight train tonnage was adjusted to the capabilities of a five-unit locomotive, thereby increasing train speeds as well as eliminating the need for largely idle multi-unit helpers. One immediate result of these practices was the scheduling of a Denver - Salt Lake City freight train with essentially the same timing as the "California Zephyr."

The D&RGW offered to buy the Missouri Pacific line between Kansas City and Pueblo, since the latter had expressed apprehension about having to abandon the route in the event of the D&RGW's acquisition of the CRI&P line between Colorado Springs and Kansas City.

CONSTRUCTION

West of Dalton the track was moved to the north side of Bingham Canyon, allowing room for a tailings dump. These three miles of new track joined the original line east of Dalton. Former Bingham Branch track east of Dalton thus became part of the Lark Spur.

MOTIVE POWER

130-139

General Motors	SW 1200	DE B-B 61

These heavy switchers replaced older switchers.

3039-3050

General Motors	GP 35	DE B-B 61

With acquisition of these units the remaining FT model units were retired.

DELL MCCOY

Although the track of the former D&SL railroad had been located in deep canyons, it was remarkably free from snow, and the D&RGW used a spreader to clear the tracks. On this occasion in late 1970, a pair of General Motors GP30-model units—Numbers 3009, 3003 were pushing spreader 042 westward through Byers Canyon.

196

During 1965 and 1966 the D&RGW and CB&Q operated each other's locomotives on freight-trains through Denver, to eliminate terminal delays. In this scene just west of Winter Park, five CB&Q units—led by the 933 and 974—were just commencing their long downhill run along the Colorado River and its tributaries.

This trio of new GM GP35 model units had just come down the steep grade from the Moffat Tunnel, but before they could get through Utah Junction into North Yard another train, following close behind, caught up with it (far right).

The new branch down to the potash mine in Utah passed through a remote and spectacular country to reach the site of the deposit close to the Colorado River in a deep canyon. Three units, led by the 5923, were needed to haul a solid 15-car trainload of potash uphill to the main-line at Brendel.

The Energy Branch was built to a new coal mine from which solid trains were dispatched to power plants at Denver. In this scene the 3004 and 3050 were found assembling one of those consists in 1972.

For 17 years the Denver & Rio Grande Western had not purchased any new switching locomotives—the last previous ones having been half-a-dozen from Fairbanks-Morse in 1948. Ten new General Motors SW1200-model units were purchased in 1965 to replace half of the ALCO units which were delivered in 1941.

Purchased in 1966, one of the six new GM SW1000-model switchers tows the 5771 and 5763, together with the "Rio Grande Zephyr" four-car passenger train out of Burnham Yard toward Denver Union Station shortly after sunrise.

When D&RGW Number 493 ascended the four-percent grade east of Chama and rolled downhill to Alamosa in the autumn of 1967, the railroad concluded nearly nine decades of service through the sparsely-populated hill country along the New Mexico - Colorado border. It was the end of an era—the last narrow-gauge common-carrier

railroad in the Rocky Mountains had ended its operations on the 247 miles of trackage between Farmington, Durango and Alamosa. In this panoramic scene, the 2-8-2 was blasting smoke into the sky at Windy Point, just west of the 10,015-foot summit known as Cumbres Pass. This was a narrow gap in the mighty San Juan Range.

1966

Mail and express shipments had been diverted to highway or air transport, resulting in greatly increased net loss for standard-gauge passenger operations, though the popular narrow-gauge Silverton Branch continued to increase its revenues.

MOTIVE POWER

140-146
General Motors   SW 1000   DE B-B 61

3051-3068
General Motors   GP 40   DE B-B 65
These units, having engines with twice the power of the F3 and F7 models, replaced the older units in high-speed freight service.

1967

All mail and nearly all express was diverted from the railroad, and half of the standard-gauge passenger service was discontinued. The last D&RGW train was operated over Cumbres Pass—an east-bound freight pulled by engine 493—in December, concluding all narrow-gauge operations, excepting those on the Silverton Branch.

CONSTRUCTION

Glenwood Springs to Chacra—7m S-G.
The track was moved across the Colorado River to permit new highway construction on the former roadbed of the railroad.

DISPOSITION

Walsenburg to Calumet Number 2—Removed.
Coal production on this branch had decreased to nearly zero.

MOTIVE POWER

3069-3080
General Motors   GP 40   DE B-B 65

5315-5324
General Motors   SD 45   DE C-C 98
The first six-motor units acquired since 1957, these powerful locomotives were assigned to heavy coal trains on the steep grades in Utah.

1968

The D&RGW finally won its case in the Supreme Court, voiding the SP's agreement to solicit freight traffic preferentially for the UP. The Northwestern Terminal Railroad, formerly operated under a lease, was purchased and its trackage added to the D&RGW system. A new corporation, Rio Grande Industries, was formed with the thought of acquiring the D&RGW Railroad, and engaging in other business which the railroad itself could not legally do.

ACQUISITION

D&SL depot to Denver Union Stockyards—8m S-G.
  This was the trackage of the Northwestern Terminal Railroad in Denver.

DISPOSITION

Woody Creek to Aspen—Removed.
  The last few miles of the Aspen Branch were removed, there being no source of traffic beyond Woody Creek where iron ore was loaded.
Chama to Farmington—Removed.
  Only this portion of the narrow-gauge track was taken up, as there was a possibility that the Chama - Antonito segment could be sold.

MOTIVE POWER

147-149
| General Motors | SW 1000 | DE B-B 61 |
5325-5340
| General Motors | SD 45 | DE C-C 98 |

The six-motor units had been so successful that more of them were acquired, each one replacing two of the F-model units.

1969

In an exchange of stock, Rio Grande Industries acquired 92-percent of the D&RGW's stock, thereby giving RGI control of the railroad.

CONSTRUCTION

Pueblo to Swallows—16m S-G.
  This segment of new line was constructed because a new dam on the Arkansas River west of Pueblo would impound water, and eventually flood the existing trackage.

MOTIVE POWER

3081-3085
| General Motors | GP 40 | DE B-B 62 |

These were replacements for the dwindling fleet of F-series units attaining retirement age.

1970

There was no formal celebration of the railroad's One-Hundredth Birthday, but the company's periodical, the "Green Light," devoted an entire issue to a review of the past century.

In the fall, floods destroyed much of the Silverton Branch, terminating trips for that season.

Two branches were sold to organizations which intended to operate them as tourist lines. Only two passenger trains remained: the former "California Zephyr" and the "Silverton."

At year-end RGI acquired all outstanding shares of railroad stock, and the railroad became an element of a diversified structure which included real estate development, a situation not unlike that of 1870.

DISPOSITION

Antonito to Chama—Sold to the States of Colorado and New Mexico.
Olmstead to Heber—Sold to Wasatch Mountain Railway.

Two decades of General Motors diesel-electric development is illustrated by this pair of units. The 5105, a GP7-model built in 1950, had a 1500-hp engine; the 3101, a GP40-2, built in 1966, was exactly twice as powerful.

GREGORY LEPAK

Some of the D&RGW's new GM SD45 locomotives were teamed with similar ones belonging to the Union Pacific to move solid trains of coal from mines in Utah to a steel mill at Fontana, California. This photograph shows the special loading system at Sunnyside in 1967 which filled the cars while they moved slowly under the pile of coal.

Commencing in 1968, Southern Pacific diesel-electric units ran through Ogden and over D&RGW track to Salt Lake City where freight traffic was interchanged with the Western Pacific. Waiting between runs at Roper Yard are D&RGW 5943 and a trio of Southern Pacific C-C units, two SD45's and an SD40.

"RIO GRANDE GREEN LIGHT"

Rio Grande Southern Railroad
1889 - 1953

1889

The Rio Grande Southern Railroad Company filed its incorporation papers in Colorado on November 5. Its intention was to construct and operate a railroad from the silver mines and mills near Telluride to the Denver & Rio Grande Railroad's Ouray Branch, as well as a line from the silver mines and mills at Rico to Durango, also on D&RG trackage. Ultimately, there would be a connection between the northern and southern segments.

Otto Mears, president and principal owner of the Silverton Railroad, was the first president of the RGS.

1890

Construction of the northern part began in April at Ridgway Junction—a few miles north of Ouray—and by year end, trains were operating into Telluride. Work on the south end, westward from Durango, began in April also, but did not progress so rapidly.

CONSTRUCTION

Ridgway Junction to Telluride—45m N-G.
This northern portion of the line went up Pleasant Valley Creek to a summit at Dallas Divide, then dropped down Leopard Creek to Placerville. Following the San

DELL A. MCCOY

The "California Zephyr" was so popular during the summer tourist season that five diesel-electric units were required to haul the swollen consists. In this scene, midway along the Dotsero Cutoff, the 5771 leads four companions and a 15-car train through Red Rock Canyon of the Colorado River. This wild country in northwest Colorado was so inaccessible during steam days that few photographs exist showing operations along this part of the railroad.

Miguel River upstream for several miles, it by-passed the falls by means of a long loop, then paralleled the upper course of the river to Telluride. Like many other sections of the RGS, this frightful profile, abounding in sharp curves, steep grades and high timber trestles, was an operating man's nightmare.

Durango to Porter—5m N-G.
Following Lightner Creek west for only a short distance, this southern segment headed cross-country to coal mines.

MOTIVE POWER

1-10—Ex-D&RG 242, 256, 243-250	2-8-0	60N
11—Ex-A.T. Sullenberger & Co. 29	2-6-0	40N

Originally this had been D&RG Number 29, having been sold to Sullenberger, who operated it on his lumber railroad at Azotea, New Mexico.

1891

Working more speedily, the northern and southern construction forces completed the entire railroad in December, joining the rails just north of Muldoon. Business was so good that several more locomotives were needed to handle the abundant traffic in silver ores and concentrates, as well as the excellent coal mined to the west of Durango.

CONSTRUCTION

Porter to Muldoon—73m N-G.
After topping a summit at Cima, the line went downhill, still cross-country, and descended into the valley of the Mancos River to Mancos. Proceeding northward, the route crossed a lower summit at Millwood, whence Lost Canyon Creek was followed down to another low point at Dolores. The remainder of the line was built upstream alongside the relatively gentle Dolores River.

The northern terminal of the RGS was at Ridgway, situated in a broad valley 10 miles from Ouray, and a couple of miles beyond the tiny community of Dallas (foreground).

The main-line circled the western end (right) of the high San Miguel Mountains (in the background) to reach Telluride— through some of the most spectacular country in Colorado.

East of Telluride the track ended abruptly at Pandora, encircled by vertical cliffs and sky-scraping pinnacles. Silver and gold ores from the bowels of the mountains were processed there, and shipped to smelters as far away as England. The box canyon at the end of the branch is one of the great scenic wonders of southwestern Colorado.

206

RICHARD KINDIG

The profile of the Rio Grande Southern resembled that of a roller coaster, little of it having less than two-percent grades. The steepest grade was eight miles of four-percent

on the east slope of Dallas Divide, requiring the combined efforts of 2-8-0 Number 42 and 2-8-2 Number 455 to attain 10 mph with 14 freight cars.

Vance Junction to Muldoon—46m N-G.

Even for the otherwise spectacular RGS, this portion of the line was incredible. Heading south from Vance Junction—a few miles west of Telluride—it climbed high along the west wall of the Howard Fork of the San Miguel River, leaping several deep ravines on long high trestles. At the sheer southern end of the valley it crossed to the opposite side and immediately doubled back—across what seemed to be a series of almost continuous trestles built into the precipitous mountainside. Then—somewhat less dramatically—it climbed upgrade along the Lake Fork, crossed Lizard Head Pass at 10,250 feet elevation, and descended alongside the Dolores River to Muldoon.

Telluride to Pandora—2m N-G.

This extension served the great silver ore mills at Pandora, located in perhaps the most beautiful mountain setting in all of Colorado.

MOTIVE POWER

12, 13, 15-21		
Ex-D&RG 251-255, 258-261	2-8-0	60N
14		
Ex-D&RG 105	0-6-0T	48N
22-24		
Ex-RGW 20-22	4-6-0	45½N
(Originally D&RG 158, 159, 165)		
25		
Ex-RGW 31	4-6-0	47N
(Originally Denver Circle 7)		
27-35		
Ex-RGW 71-74, 76-80	2-8-0	56N
(Originally D&RG 71-74, 76-80)		
36		
Ex-D&RG 93	4-4-0	42N

1892

Agitation for the repeal of the Sherman Silver Purchase Act caused a severe decline in silver mining, the industry upon which the RGS was almost totally dependent, and as its traffic began to diminish, the railroad was hard-pressed to meet its financial obligations. Among these were $2-million in bonds held by the Denver & Rio Grande, acquired in exchange for construction funds and equipment. Consequently, the D&RG became even more interested and involved in the activities of the RGS.

207

WILLIAM MOEDINGER

No photograph of the Rio Grande Southern could be more typical of the line: double-headed second-hand motive power, high wooden trestles, and precipitous mountains.

Number 20, a trim 4-6-0, and Number 455, a squat 2-8-2 "Mudhen," labor across the trestle at Leonard on the three-percent climb to Dallas Divide.

CONSTRUCTION

Rico to Enterprise—5m N-G.
This branch required four switchbacks to reach silver mines high above Rico.

Ute Junction to Ute Mine—2m N-G.
This was another spur tapping the coal fields west of Durango.

MOTIVE POWER

34 (second)

Ex-Silverton 269	0-4-4-0TG	Shay N

This geared locomotive was needed for the steep Enterprise Branch.

1893

The closing of so many silver mines along the RGS brought the full effect of the Silver Panic of 1893 to the railroad, and it could no longer pay its expenses or sell more bonds or stock to pay for construction. Seeking court protection, it applied for receivership, and in August D&RG President Edward T. Jeffery was appointed as receiver.

1894

Jeffery and Mears worked out a plan to rescue the RGS from complete collapse; in return for financial assistance, the RGS would transfer half of its stock to the D&RG—thus giving the D&RG a majority—to be deposited with a trustee. In addition, sufficient bonds would be transferred to give the D&RG a majority of them, also. These financial transactions made the Rio Grande Southern a subsidiary of the D&RG.

1895

The other stock and bond-holders, principally associates of Otto Mears, agreed to the reorganization plan, and by December the receivership was over. Jeffery replaced Mears as president—and during the ensuing years D&RG presidents would serve as presidents of the RGS, also. While the RGS would be managed locally, all major decisions would come from D&RG headquarters.

1896, 1897, 1898

During these years the RGS resembled a distant branch

The first locomotives which came to the RGS were ten 2-8-0's from the D&RG, which had been in service for ten years and two of them were not scrapped until 1942. Number 1 is seen here atop Lizard Head Pass with a northbound special train in 1895.

The RGS used D&RG terminal facilities at Durango for forty years, moving its engine terminal on its own line just west of town in 1931. In this scene, 4-6-0 Number 20 with eight loaded cars prepares to leave the Durango yards for Dolores and beyond.

LAD AREND

The two segments of the Rio Grande Southern were joined near Muldoon siding in 1891. Half-a-century later, 2-8-0

Number 40 lumbers past that historic spot with 11 cars of assorted freight, headed for Rico.

of the D&RG, doing as well as it could under conditions of greatly reduced traffic. Had it not been for the "die-hards" of the silver-mining towns, the RGS could have been dismantled.

1899

Traffic showed so little promise of immediate recovery that seven unneeded locomotives were sold to other railroads.

1900

The Enterprise Branch at Rico was disconnected, the mills having closed down. Four more locomotives departed from RGS rails.

1901

The D&RG had come under the influence of George

Ophir station—shown on the page opposite—was situated on a steep hillside between two trestles over Howard Fork, and inside a 24⁰ half-circle curve. Gold and silver ores were brought here by trains of pack-mules from mines in the surrounding mountains, then the ore was shipped by rail to distant smelters.

Gould, who was using its resources to finance the Western Pacific railroad, an extension from Salt Lake City to the Pacific Ocean. The RGS, having nothing to contribute to this cause, was all but abandoned by its step-parent. Another locomotive was sold.

1902, 1903

Completely preoccupied with its acquisition of the Rio Grande Western Railroad and the planning for the Western Pacific, the D&RG left the RGS to get along by itself. Lumbering operations began to be established around Dolores, adding new revenues to those obtained from the hauling of coal.

1904

The RGS roster finally reached bottom with the disposition of locomotives which could not be sold, only 17 remaining.

1905

Despite the loss of considerable ore and concentrate tonnage, the railroad had been making sizable operating profits, and even though bond interest payments had increased, it had been able to accumulate a surplus of $250,000 by 1905.

211

The southern segment of the Rio Grande Southern abounded in hairpin curves, one of which—at East Mancos—nearly closed-in upon itself, as shown here. Both the freight train, pulled by a pair of 2-8-0's, and the special passenger train, with 2-8-0 Number 9, were east-bound from Dolores to Durango. This scene was photographed in 1891.

Among the various mechanical oddities acquired by the Rio Grande Southern was a lone 2-6-0, Number 11, which had been purchased originally by the D&RG. Apparently, its intended use was for passenger trains on the steeply graded track between Ridgway and Telluride.

Access to Telluride was gained by means of a hairpin curve alongside the main-line. Diverging at Vance Junction, the line climbed the east wall of the Howard Fork valley until the rails had reached the top of the cascades of the San Miguel River. (See view on the facing page.)

LE MASSENA

After working for five years on the Denver Circle railroad, Number 7 went to the RGW, becoming their Number 31 for two years. Somewhat modified, it was sold to the RGS in 1891. It is seen here—numbered 25—awaiting departure from Durango with the 8:00 a.m. train to Rico.

Stub switches were common on the RGS. Two of them—accommodating three tracks each—led to the engine-house and yards at the northern extremity of Rico. At this point, the railroad was following an old Ute Indian trail along the banks of the Dolores River.

The Rio Grande Southern possessed only one switching engine, an 0-6-0T numbered 14, which had been obtained from the Denver & Rio Grande's collection of discarded

narrow-gauge motive power—former D&RG Number 105— It pulled the first train into Rico and was used later in the terminal at Ridgway.

Three of the 4-6-0's acquired by the Rio Grande Southern, numbered 22 - 24, were third-hand, having been purchased originally by the Denver & Rio Grande in 1882. They were sold to the D&RGW Railway in 1886, and were taken

over by its corporate successor, the Rio Grande Western, which sold them to the RGS in 1891. This photograph of Number 22 was taken at the original locomotive terminal in Ridgway.

A second batch of nine smaller 2-8-0's (ex-D&RG) came from the Rio Grande Western. None of them remained on

the Rio Grande Southern more than a decade—Number 32 having been among the first sold to other railroads.

This early panorama of Lizard Head Pass—at an elevation of 10,250-feet—shows the summit before the snowshed was constructed over the wye. At the tail of the wye (right) was the sawmill which supplied ties and bridge timbers for the railroad. Snow-covered Vermilion Peak, 13,894 feet above sea level, stands out along the ridge to the right.

Number 41 (ex-D&RG Number 409), one of two such 2-8-0's purchased in 1916, was commencing its sixth decade of service when this picture was taken of it rolling downgrade, across one of the spidery trestles on the upper level of the Ophir Loop. The lower level can be seen toward the top of the photograph.

The mine at Enterprise—above Rico—required switchbacks with five-percent gradients, the steepest trackage of the Rio Grande Southern. The right-of-way can be traced very easily on the mountainsides across the center of the photograph. At the bottom of the scene is the main-line and depot of the railroad.

Still another unique locomotive on the RGS was a 4-4-0, Number 36, which as Number 93 on the D&RG had pulled the paycar. It broke down while hauling a special train at Trout Lake in 1893 and was not used thereafter.

The Rio Grande Southern's water tank at Trout Lake was situated in an incredibly exquisite mountain setting north of Lizard Head Pass. The track climbed across the sublime hillside at the right of the azure lake to surmount the pass three-and-one-half miles further up the line. The Trout Lake tank was a favorite spot for railfan photographers.

In 1892 the Rio Grande Southern traded 2-8-0 Number 34 for the Silverton Railroad's two-truck Shay locomotive, using it on the steep switchbacks to the Enterprise and Black Hawk mines. The mines closed; the Shay was sold in 1899; and the track was disconnected in 1900. The Shay had been named, "Guston," on the Silverton Railroad.

In 1916 the RGS bought three well-used 4-6-0's from the Florence & Cripple Creek railroad, numbering them (second) *20, 22, and 25. They replaced three much older locomotives of that type, which were speedily dismantled.*

DISPOSITION

Rico to Enterprise—Removed.
This branch was no longer needed since its source of traffic had ceased operating.

1906

The excellent coal mined west of Durango was beginning to attract more outside attention, and this added further to RGS revenues. The Boston Coal & Fuel Company branch was purchased by the Calumet Fuel Company, a subsidiary of the Rio Grande Western, and leased to the RGS for operation, using the CF Company (ex-RGS) engine.

CONSTRUCTION

May Day Junction to May Day—2m N-G.
This last new trackage to be built by the RGS extended to a gold mine west of Durango.

MOTIVE POWER

1 (second)—leased from Calumet Fuel Company.
Ex-Boston Coal & Fuel Company Number 1.

1907

The D&RG was perfecting its arrangements for merger with the RGW and several other wholly-owned subsidiaries similar to the RGS. What this would mean for the RGS only time would tell.

1908

The D&RG consolidated all of its subsidiaries except the RGS. Although the D&RG had the power to absorb the RGS also, since it owned a majority of the stock, there appeared to have been two reasons for exclusion of the little line: It could contribute nothing in the form of mortgagable assets, yet it could produce some income from bond interest and equipment rental. Hence, although the D&RG owned substantially less than 100-percent of the RGS stock, it could siphon off 100-percent of any profit.

DISPOSITION

Ute Junction to Ute Mine—Removed.
There was no further need for this trackage, the mine having closed down.

1909 - 1915

In 1913, the year in which the Rio Grande Southern, Denver & Rio Grande, Missouri Pacific, and Western Pacific railroads were combined into a single operating system, the $141,000 accumulated surplus of the RGS vanished, being replaced by a $183,000 deficit. Although the accounts showed extraordinarily large charges — $324,000 — to "maintenance," it is more than likely that the funds found their way into the system's treasury, which was desperate for cash to keep the Western Pacific going.

1916

During the preceding few years the D&RG had been made the victim of a financial manipulation which resulted in the loss of its entire investment in the Western Pacific railroad. In addition, a judgment was levied against it, a circumstance which eventually was to affect the RGS as well.

After modifying its rail-borne motor-busses to accommodate passengers in the freight compartment, the RGS operated these unusual vehicles for excursions between Ridgway and Lizard Head Pass. "Galloping Goose" Number 4 halted at Trout Lake tank to let its passengers enjoy the brisk air and incomparable scenery.
BETTY LE MASSENA

Another one-of-a-kind engine on the Rio Grande Southern was Number 42, an 1887-model 2-8-0 built for the Denver & Rio Grande, and bought by the RGS in 1916.

Assisted by D&RGW "Mudhen" 2-8-2 Number 464, it was nearing the end of the three-percent grade ascent from Placerville to Dallas Divide.

MOTIVE POWER

20 (second), 22 (second), 25 (second)
  Ex-Florence & Cripple Creek

20, 24, 21	4-6-0	85N

40-42
  Ex-D&RG 402, 409, 420

	2-8-0	70N

These were replacements for locomotives which had been scrapped.

1917

Although World War I generated some additional traffic for the RGS, the line failed to make a net profit. As expected, the D&RG was siphoning off almost all net operating income produced by its stepchild railroad.

1918 - 1920

The United States Railroad Administration took over operation of the RGS on January 1, 1918, and by not paying any bond interest, the road showed a fictitious net profit. In spite of this technique, there was a small net loss for 1919. The USRA departed in February, 1920, leaving the RGS to suffer with a six-figure loss for the year.

1921

The court judgment of 1916 against the D&RG had forced it into bankruptcy. During the subsequent financial juggling incident to the D&RG's reorganization, its RGS stocks and bonds were transferred to the Western Pacific Railroad Corporation, a holding company which had acquired the Western Pacific railroad property. As of August 1, 1921, the RGS was no longer controlled by the D&RG, and the stepchild became an abandoned orphan in the great struggle between the financial giants of Wall Street.

1922

Though business was improving all over the nation, the deficit for the RGS soared beyond the $100,000 mark. It failed to pay its bond interest, resulting in the formation of a committee to protect the bondholders' interests.

1923

The financial situation was relieved somewhat by the movement of oil from Farmington, New Mexico, on the D&RG, to Durango, thence via the RGS to Ridgway for transfer back to the D&RG. The latter, being both the originating and terminating carrier, received the lion's share of the revenue for performing the easier portions of the joint haul.

1924

The RGS operating ratio touched 125-percent, a national record in those relatively prosperous times.

1925

The days of accumulated surpluses had departed forever; instead, the accumulated deficits now totalled almost $2-million by year-end.

1926

Coal was becoming available from more economical sources, and the mines west of Durango began to close down completely, reducing RGS traffic even more. The Calumet Fuel Company also terminated its operations.

DISPOSITION

May Day Junction to May Day—Removed.
  There was no further use for this track since the mine had shut down.

1927 - 1929

The general prosperity of the "Roaring Twenties" never touched the RGS as its accumulated deficits headed for $3-million. In December, 1929, while practically every other railroad was contemplating an extra dividend for

Four more motor-cars, having three trucks, were fabricated from Pierce-Arrow sedans, complete with fender-mounted

headlights; Number 5 still retained its "Diana" radiator ornament. Note the "Fast Freight" legend on the carbody.

Christmas, the RGS went into receivership under Victor A. Miller, a Denver attorney.

The last operating ore mill at Pandora closed down and a rock-slide at Ames blocked the line, costing the RGS its oil traffic plus much of its livestock and lumber business.

1930 - 1931

With the RGS freed from the policies of absentee management, receiver Miller began to revive the deteriorated railroad and to reduce its expenses. The Ames slide was conquered by means of a by-pass built on the slide itself.

During the Great Depression, the RGS modified motor vehicles to be used in lieu of passenger trains which ran nearly empty most of the time. The first one—placed in service between Durango and Dolores—was fabricated from a Buick touring car. These were hard times in the San Juans, calling for great adaptability.

Motive power and rolling stock were no longer rented from or repaired by the D&RGW. Steam-powered passenger trains were replaced by home-built hybrid passenger-mail-LCL motor vehicles, humorously termed, "Galloping Geese." Although the future did look more promising in these still prosperous times, the Western Pacific Railroad Corporation applied (unsuccessfully) to the ICC for permission to transfer its RGS securities back to the D&RGW.

MOTIVE POWER

1, 2			
	RGS shops, 1931	2-truck bus	passenger-freight
3			
	RGS shops, 1931	3-truck bus	passenger-freight

1932 - 1938

The Great Depression, which dealt mortal blows to many another railroad, robbed the RGS of 85-percent of its traffic, forcing it to suspend payment of property taxes. Nevertheless, Miller bought several freight cars, acquired a new (to the RGS) locomotive, and presented a plan for reorganizing the railroad. When this plan met with opposition, Miller resigned in 1938, Cass M. Herrington, another Denver attorney, replacing him. In 1933, before the D&RGW went into trusteeship, the Western Pacific Railroad Corporation transferred its RGS securities to the D&RGW, thus returning stock control of the RGS to its original foster parent.

MOTIVE POWER

4			
	RGS shops, 1932	3-truck bus	Passenger-freight-mail
5			
	RGS shops, 1933	3-truck bus	Passenger-freight-mail
6			
	RGS shops, 1934	2-truck bus	Maintenance-of-way
7			
	RGS shops, 1936	3-truck bus	Passenger-freight-mail

223

Motor Number 2 was made from a Buick sedan, providing more seating for the few occupants who rode in it between

Ridgway and Telluride. A four-wheel truck was installed at the rear to support the enclosed mail and express space.

1939 - 1948

Herrington's regime, terminated by his death in 1948, was marked by a further loss of business and considerable confusion among Federal Government agencies. After Herrington applied for abandonment in 1941, local people talked the Reconstruction Finance Corporation into lending the RGS some money. In 1942, the Defense Supplies Corporation bought the railroad's equipment, leasing it back to them. Late in that year the Office of Defense Transportation requisitioned the entire line, but withdrew its order when the Defense Supplies Corporation objected. Another Federal loan was obtained in 1945, but the RGS was too far gone to survive, even with the assistance of these financial transfusions. Starting in 1941, passengers, mail and LCL were carried by highway truck between Durango and Dolores.

MOTIVE POWER

3-5 Busses—Rebuilt with new engines and passenger compartments.

455
    Ex-D&RGW 455 (1939)   2-8-2   K27N

Nine locomotives were dismantled to salvage their scrap metal for World War II.

1948 - 1953

Another Denver attorney, Pierpont Fuller Jr., succeeded Herrington, serving until the very end of the RGS.

The last sources of traffic to the RGS, (sheep and lumber) were being diverted to trucks, and in 1948 the mill of its biggest lumber shipper, near Dolores, burned to the

The view shown on the preceding page is of the last RGS passenger train—which ran from Ridgway to Lizard Head Pass and return on September 1 and 2, 1951. Led by 2-8-0 Number 74, the "special" was recorded as it passed the depot at Ophir and began the climb to the upper level of the loop.

ground. During 1949 passenger service was discontinued between Ridgway and Dolores, and in the following year U. S. Mail was diverted to highway truck. In 1950 and 1951, Galloping Geese 3, 4, 5 and 7 were modified to seat passengers in the freight compartment, and were operated during the summer months, taking tourists from Ridgway to Lizard Head Pass, and from Durango to Dolores.

The last passenger run was operated on September 1 and 2 of 1951 from Ridgway to Pandora and Lizard Head Pass for the Rocky Mountain Railroad Club, using engine 74. By year-end every variety of train had made its final run. The ICC approved abandonment of the line in 1952, and dismantling by a junk company began immediately. By mid-1953 the RGS was hardly more than a memory, its legal last rites having been pronounced in December.

DISPOSITION

Entire railroad—Dismantled 1952-1953.

MOTIVE POWER

74
    Ex-Colorado & Southern
    74 (1949)   2-8-0   B4fN
461
    Ex-D&RGW 461 (1950)   2-8-2   K27N

2 Bus—Sold (1952). (Preserved at Golden, Colorado.)

3 Bus—Sold (1952). (Preserved at Anaheim, California.)

4 Bus—Sold (1953). (Preserved at Telluride, Colorado.)

5 Bus—Sold (1953). (Preserved at Dolores, Colorado.)

6 Bus—Sold (1953). (Brinkerhoff Bros., Rico, Colorado.)

7 Bus—Sold (1953). (Brinkerhoff Bros., Rico, Colorado.)

20 (second)—Sold to Rocky Mountain Railroad Club (1952). (Preserved at Golden, Colorado.)

41—Sold (1952). (Preserved at Anaheim, California.)

42—Sold to Narrow Gauge Motel (1953). (Later operated by Magic Mountain Railroad.)

74—Sold to City of Boulder (1952). (Preserved at Boulder, Colorado.)

455, 461—Scrapped (1953).

The substitute for a short work-train was Number 6 which was equipped with two four-wheel trucks. Like the others, *its rear axle was driven by outside-mounted roller-chains, an arrangement causing frequent operating difficulties.*

Number 20 was temporarily renumbered "1" and repainted in brilliant colors—including a painting of a clipper ship on the tender—for a motion picture filmed on the D&RGW's Silverton Branch in 1949. Bearing the name, "Emma Sweeny," it is shown in this photograph at Silverton.

In 1939 the RGS acquired its biggest locomotive, a 36-year-old 2-8-2 from the D&RGW. Four years later it ran away on the east side of Dallas Divide and was buried for months beneath the wreckage of 24 cars of ore. It was not returned to active service until 1947.

226

OTTO PERRY

In 1949 the Rio Grande Southern added another member to its collection of operating relics by purchasing a 2-8-0 which had previously carried the names of three other railroads on its tender. The 74 is seen in this scene west of Pandora, bringing a special train into Telluride for an overnight stop.

In mid-November, 1951, the last freight train ran from Durango to Ridgway, bringing in D&RGW cars and any RGS cars which would be stored at Ridgway. Engine 461 leads the final train of ten cars—including three cabooses—over the trestles on the upper level of the Ophir Loop.

ROBERT RICHARDSON

LAST NARROW GAUGE
ORE TRAIN
OPHIR LOOP
COLORADO

ROBERT RICHARDSON

During 1916 the Rio Grande Southern purchased three 4-6-0's from the Florence & Cripple Creek. The only one to last until the end of the RGS was Number 20, shown in this view working upgrade along the San Miguel River near Sawpit. This colorful red sandstone canyon is located between Placerville and Vance Junction. Number 20 was a Schenectady product built in 1899 and was originally named the "Portland." This engine was sold to the Rocky Mountain Railroad Club in 1952 and currently is on display at the Colorado Railroad Museum in Golden.

RICHARD KINDIG

With a certain amount of truth, it could be said that the "final run" on the RGS was made by these two cars which got loose during dismantling operations on the south side of Lizard Head Pass. They derailed at Burns after their unscheduled speedy trip down three miles of two-and-one-half-percent-grade.

228

SECTION TEN

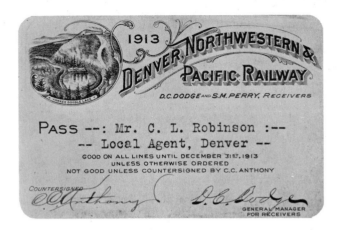

Subsidiary Railroads

The railroad companies included in this section are those which became members of the Rio Grande system by various means. These railroads were built originally for diverse purposes, and several were dismantled when their sources of traffic became depleted or uneconomic. Some owned only track; others owned both track and locomotives, many of which eventually became lettered "D&RG" or "D&RGW."

BINGHAM CANON & CAMP FLOYD

The Bingham Canon & Camp Floyd Rail Road (incorporated in Utah, September, 1872) was organized to haul precious metal ores from mines in upper Bingham Canyon to a smelter at Sandy, Utah, just south of Salt Lake City. Construction was completed in the following year, narrow gauge track being laid in a narrow and steep canyon. The mines were unusually productive, and the consequent railroad traffic attracted the attention of the Denver & Rio Grande in Colorado as a feeder to its contemplated westward extension into Utah. Eventually the management of the D&RG obtained control of the BC&CF's securities, then transferred ownership to a new company, the Denver & Rio Grande Western, in September 1881, at which time the BC&CF became extinct. The BC&CF was operated in coordination with the Wasatch & Jordan Valley with which it connected at Sandy, but neither was joined to the D&RG system until 1883 when the D&RGW's main-line was built across eastern Utah to Colorado.

Locomotive List

1	0-6-0	Porter, Bell	1874	D&RGW	2
2	0-6-0	Porter, Bell	1874	D&RGW	4
3	0-6-0	Porter, Bell	1874	D&RGW	6
4	0-6-0	Porter, Bell	1874	D&RGW	8

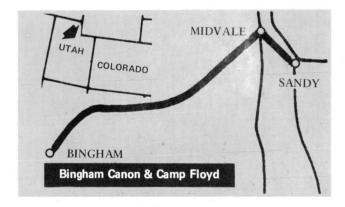

Bingham Canon & Camp Floyd

CALIFORNIA SHORT LINE

The California Short Line Railway (incorporated in Utah, June, 1882) was planned to run from Manti, Utah, to coal mines north of the town. During 1885 about eight miles of track were laid between Chester and Draper, reaching neither Manti nor the coal mine. Lacking money, equipment and a railroad connection, the project languished until 1889 when it was acquired by the San Pete Valley Railroad company which—oddly enough—had no track either.

Copper Belt trackage connected the end of the Bingham Branch and new low-grade line with the tracks of mining companies on the mountain sides above Bingham. Almost hidden in the center of this picture are a pair of slope-tank 0-6-0's of the Utah Copper company.

Unwelcome in Denver's Union Station, the Denver, Northwestern & Pacific (later Denver & Salt Lake) erected its own depot nearby. On this occasion, 2-8-0 Number 109 heads the daily local, while an excursion train loads passengers at the extreme right.

The Porter, Bell company's locomotives built for the Bingham Canon & Camp Floyd Rail Road were essentially identical to those delivered to the Colorado Central railroad the following year.

CASTLE VALLEY RAILWAY

One of George Gould's plans for expanding his transcontinental system westward included a segment of railroad from the vicinity of Green River, Utah, to a junction with the San Pedro, Los Angeles & Salt Lake railroad near Milford, Utah. Although considerable grading was done along this route, only a short portion in strategic Salina Canyon — between Salina and Nioche — was equipped with track laid in 1903 by the Castle Valley Railway (incorporated in Utah, January, 1901). This company was absorbed in the D&RG consolidation of 1908.

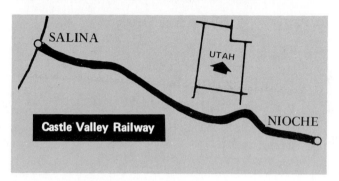

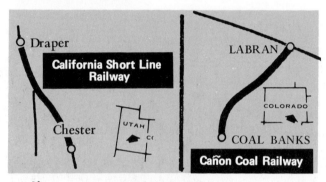

CAÑON COAL RAILWAY

The Cañon Coal Railway (incorporated in Colorado, August, 1872) owned the branch from Labran, Colorado, to coal mines a couple of miles to the south. The D&RG was not able to absorb this company upon completion of construction, due to depressed business conditions, but did purchase and merge it in 1878.

CARBON COUNTY RAILWAY

Two branches entirely in Utah, were constructed by the Carbon County Railway, (incorporated in Utah, November, 1899): Mounds to Sunnyside coal mines, and Scofield to Clear Creek coal mines. The RGW bought all CC stock in 1900 and transferred it to the D&RG in the consolidation of 1908.

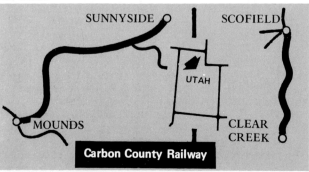

The profile and location of the Castle Valley were impractical for a main-line by-passing Salt Lake City, and the coal mine never produced sufficient traffic. Its abandonment left 20 miles of roadbed and four tunnels, two of which were very close together alongside the new highway at Sumner.

232

Among the rarest locomotives of the Rio Grande system were the five three-truck Shays belonging to the Copper Belt. In this scene Number 2 was poised atop the wooden trestle spanning Bingham Canyon.

COPPER BELT RAILROAD

During the mining of precious metal ore deposits around Bingham, Utah, immense amounts of copper ore were discovered. The various mining companies brought the ore down to storage bins and smelters near Bingham. To connect these facilities with the Bingham Branch of the RGW, the Copper Belt Railroad (incorporated in Utah, May, 1901) was built, replacing a horse-drawn tramway of limited utility. The CB, though operated by the RGW, was merged into the D&RG system in 1908.

Locomotive List

1	3-T Shay	Ex-Salt Lake & Mercur 7	D&RG (C) 1
2	3-T Shay	Lima	1904	D&RG (C) 2
3	3-T Shay	Lima	1904	D&RG (C) 3
4	3-T Shay	Lima	1905	D&RG (C) 4
5	3-T Shay	Lima	1906	D&RG (C) 5

DENVER, CLEAR CREEK & WESTERN

Despite its corporate pretensions, the Denver, Clear Creek & Western Railway (incorporated in Colorado, December, 1888) never came any closer to Clear Creek than Fort Logan, Colorado, at the end of a short branch from Petersburg, Colorado, constructed in 1889. Operated by the D&RG with its own equipment, the DCC&W was sold to the D&RG in 1899.

DENVER, NORTHWESTERN & PACIFIC

The motivation behind construction of the Denver, Northwestern & Pacific Railway (incorporated in Colorado, May, 1902) was to provide a shorter locally-owned transmountain outlet for Denver. Lying between the D&RG and Union Pacific routes, the line would pass through Craig, Colorado, thence to Salt Lake City, Utah, gateway to the Pacific Coast. Operations began at Denver in 1903, and were extended to Steamboat Springs, Colorado, by 1909, serving the numerous coal mines in that area. The railroad was extremely expensive to build, there being 56 tunnels bored through the Rocky Mountains. It was expensive to operate, too; the first 50 miles being almost continuous two-percent grade to what is now the east portal of the Moffat Tunnel. From there the track climbed another 2500 feet on three to four-percent grades to the Continental Divide at 11,660-feet altitude, the west side dropping 2600 feet similarly. Clearing snow on this segment consumed revenues almost as fast as the railroad earned

233

them hauling coal. Lack of additional capital prevented construction of a tunnel underneath the Divide, and the extension to Salt Lake City. Failure was inevitable; receivership began during 1912, and the railroad was sold during 1913 to a new company, the Denver & Salt Lake Railroad.

Construction and early operations utilized two ex-Chesapeake Beach 4-4-0's, two six-wheel switchers, four 4-6-0's and several 2-8-0's whose number eventually reached 24. Ten 0-6-6-0 Mallets were purchased to handle freight tonnage over the Divide. Excepting the 4-4-0's built by Pittsburgh, all locomotives were built by American, and all were acquired by the D&SL.

Locomotive List

20, 21	0-6-0	American	1904	D&SL 20, 21
100-123	2-8-0	American	1904-1910	D&SL 100-123
200-209	0-6-6-0	American	1908-1910	D&SL 200-209
300-303	4-6-0	American	1904-1910	D&SL 300-303

390, 391	4-4-0	Ex-Chesapeake Beach 3, 4		D&SL 390, 391

DENVER & SALT LAKE RAILROAD

The Denver & Salt Lake Railroad was organized (incorporated in Colorado, December, 1912) to take over the DNW&P which had failed financially. By 1915 track had been extended from Steamboat Springs, Colorado, to Craig, Colorado; but there it ended forever, as history would develop. Financially, the new company did no better than the old one; it lost money every year except one and went into receivership in 1917. However, the railroad had been instrumental in persuading those counties through which it ran to finance a long tunnel through the Continental Divide, and work on it commenced in 1923. Meanwhile, despite a small profit in 1925, the D&SL underwent financial reconstruction in 1926 when the railroad was sold to another new company, the D&SL Railway.

Locomotive List

20, 21	0-6-0	Ex-DNW&P	20, 21	NWT 20, 21
100-123	2-8-0	Ex-DNW&P	100-123	D&SL 100-123
200-209	0-6-6-0	Ex-DNW&P	200-209	Modified
200-209	2-6-6-0	Modified in railway shops		D&SL 200-209
210-216	2-6-6-0	American	1913-1916	D&SL 211-216
210—destroyed				
300-303	4-6-0	Ex-DNW&P	300-303	D&SL 300-303
390, 391	4-4-0	Ex-DNW&P	390-391	D&SL 390, 391

DENVER & SALT LAKE RAILWAY

The Denver & Salt Lake Railway (incorporated in Delaware, November, 1925) was essentially a financial

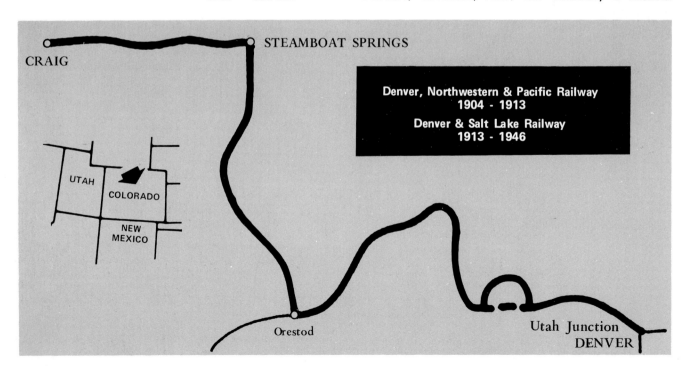

CRAIG   STEAMBOAT SPRINGS

UTAH
COLORADO
NEW MEXICO

Denver, Northwestern & Pacific Railway
1904 - 1913

Denver & Salt Lake Railway
1913 - 1946

Orestod

Utah Junction
DENVER

At Leyden Junction the Denver, Northwestern & Pacific connected with the affiliated electrified Denver & Northwestern interurban line—behind the train. In this scene,

2-8-0 Number 101 pauses for water while en route to the coal mines with a string of empty and very new Pullman-built coal gondolas.

The DNW&P's first locomotives were a pair of 0-6-0's numbered 20 and 21, which were used during construction.

One of them was moving a supply train across the Coal Creek trestle when this photograph was taken.

Rugged walled Gore Canyon presented difficult location problems, requiring the boring of six short tunnels through rocky promontories. There was hardly any straight track in this precipitous gorge where the track was far above the stream bed.

DNW&P 0-6-6-0 Number 200 was neither the first articulated nor the first compound locomotive in Colorado, but it was the first to combine those features in a single machine, preceding by two years the Mallets of the D&RG.

236

Another spectacular feat was the Rifle Sight Notch loop on the west side of Rollins Pass. The track encircled the hill at the left, then tunneled beneath the notch, thereby reaching a better location for the track on a lower level.

"THE MOFFAT ROAD"

After the track had been advanced into South Boulder canyon the railroad bought a pair of second-hand 4-4-0's to handle the track-laying train, thus releasing the two 0-6-0's to move supplies between Denver and the advancing end-of-track.

Confronted by the steeply tilted rocks of the Front Range, the DNW&P's surveyors curved the right-of-way back upon itself, then curled it around the rim of a convenient tongue- *mesa—thus gaining sufficient altitude to maintain a two-percent gradient through this difficult transition between the high plains and the mountains.*

reorganization of the D&SL Railroad to reduce obligatory interest charges on debt; management remaining unchanged. The Moffat Tunnel was completed in 1928, eliminating the worst operating difficulties, but even so, the railroad barely earned enough to cover its fixed charges. The new tunnel, on the other hand, made practical a new route through the Rockies; only a short link between the D&SL and D&RGW was missing. The D&RGW bought control of the D&SL, took over a separate company (D&SLW), to build the connection and inaugurated service over this new route in 1934. In the process the D&RGW used its D&SL stock to borrow money from the Reconstruction Finance Corporation, which then held D&SL control until merger into the D&RGW in 1947. During construction of the tunnel, electrification was considered, but nothing became of the plans.

Locomotive List

20, 21	0-6-0	Ex-NWT	20, 21	Scrapped
100-123	2-8-0	Ex-D&SL	100-123	Scrapped
111-113, 118-123		D&RGW	1031-1039	
200-209, 211-216	2-6-6-0	Ex-D&SL	200-209, 211-216	
		D&RGW	3360-3375	
300-303	4-6-0	Ex-D&SL	300-303	Scrapped
302, 303		D&RGW	795, 796	
390, 391	4-4-0	Ex-D&SL	390, 391	Scrapped
400-407	2-8-2	Lima	1915	D&RGW 1220-1227
408, 409	2-8-2	American	1916	D&RGW 1228, 1229

The DNW&P's first passenger locomotive, a 4-6-0 Number 300, poses in South Boulder canyon at Tunnel 28. This may have been the first train, as indicated by the white flags carried on the locomotive.

239

The side of the D&SL's 2-6-6-0's, equipped with two power-reverse devices, was a nightmare of piping and reciprocating machinery. In this afternoon view, two of them were drifting down the two-percent grade just north of Plainview.

After extricating itself from the main canyon of the Grand (Colorado) River the DNW&P wriggled into and out of Rock Creek Canyon through a remarkable succession of tunnels and hairpin curves. This panorama from Volcano looks directly into one of the narrow side canyons (above the engine).

240

When the Dotsero Cutoff between the D&SL and D&RGW was completed, the latter commenced operating a fast freight train via the shorter route. Here D&SL 2-8-2

Number 403 escorts D&RGW 2-8-8-2 Number 3612 into the yards at Utah Junction.

As illustrated by this photograph looking westward from the end of D&SL track, there was practically nothing

between Craig and Salt Lake City, 225 miles distant across an unknown and unsettled region.

241

OTTO PERRY

The first Denver & Rio Grande Western passenger train to be operated via the Moffat Tunnel - Dotsero Cutoff route was the "Panoramic," whose regular motive power *was initially one of the D&RGW's fourteen 2-8-2's. This one was Number 1200, negotiating the upper level of the Fireclay Loop in the late afternoon.*

DENVER & SALT LAKE WESTERN

The D&SL, having no resources of its own to build the cutoff between Orestod, Colorado, on its line and Dotsero, Colorado, on the D&RGW, organized the Denver & Salt Lake Western Railroad (incorporated in Wyoming, October 1924) to build the line. When D&RGW gained control of the D&SL, ownership of the D&SLW was transferred to the D&RGW, and after some delay, the track was laid in 1934. The D&SLW was merged into the D&RGW in 1947.

The scene on the preceding page shows one of the Denver & Salt Lake's 2-8-2's—assisted by a compound 2-6-6-0 whose boiler was no larger—ascends the middle section of the huge loop at Fireclay. Both locomotives have been equipped with auxiliary tanks to eliminate stops for water on the long, steep climb to the Moffat Tunnel.

RALPH HALLOCK

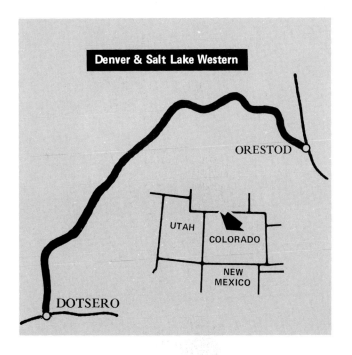

Out of four 4-6-0's owned by the D&SL, only one, Number 302, was operated by the D&RGW when it absorbed the smaller railroad in 1947. In pre-merger times that same locomotive, pulling the daily local from Denver to Craig, was found at Hayden—just before sunset—waiting for a meet with the overnight mixed train to Denver.

Following the three special trains carrying dignitaries from Denver to the opening ceremonies at Bond was the first freight train to roll over the Dotsero Cutoff. The scene on the preceding page shows the train slowly rolling past the crowd at Bond—pulled by 2-8-8-2 Number 3600, the first of 20 such powerful D&RGW locomotives.

D&RGW COLLECTION — COURTESY JACKSON THODE

After the D&SL had been merged with the D&RGW in 1947, the NWT remained a leased line, and was not integrated into the latter company's corporate structure until 1970. On this occasion the 601 (A, B, C) was accelerating the "California Zephyr" over NWT track between Union Station and Utah Junction, shortly after the train's inauguration.

The Denver & Rio Grande Western's articulated locomotive Number 3618, a single-expansion 2-8-8-2, leads 52 freight cars—mostly empty refrigerator cars—along the Dotsero Cutoff, en route to Salt Lake City. The new cutoff saved 175 miles and bypassed the three-percent grade over Tennessee Pass. At Range the landscape was barren and lonely.

For a few years the Northwestern Terminal line owned the two 0-6-0's, numbered 20 and 21, which had been purchased

originally by the DNW&P railroad. This portrait of the 21 at Utah Junction reveals the lettering "N W T Co." on its cab.

GOSHEN VALLEY RAILROAD

The Goshen Valley Railroad (incorporated in Utah, December, 1918) was built in 1919 from Pearl, Utah, to copper mines at Iron King and Dividend, Utah, the mine owners paying two-thirds of the cost. The D&RGW operated the branch with its own locomotives, and in 1927 bought out the mining companies' interests. The railroad was merged into the D&RGW in 1947.

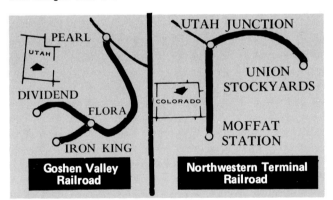

NORTHWESTERN TERMINAL RAILWAY

When the DNW&P was built, its tracks ended at Utah Junction, a few miles north of its passenger and freight terminal in lower Denver. This terminal line and associated yards belonged to the Northwestern Terminal Railway (incorporated in Colorado, August, 1904) which was owned by and leased to the DNW&P. The arrangement was continued by the D&SL, successor to the DNW&P, but when the D&SL failed, the NWT did likewise, going into receivership in 1920. It was sold in 1926 to a reorganized company, the NWT Railroad.

Locomotive List

20, 21   0-6-0   Ex-D&SL   20, 21   D&SL   20, 21

NORTHWESTERN TERMINAL RAILROAD

The Northwestern Terminal Railroad (incorporated in Nevada, July, 1926) was organized to take over the property of the NWT Railway which had failed, and to lease it to reorganized D&SL railroad. The D&RGW gained control of the D&SL in 1934, and assumed the lease of the NWT in 1947, but did not absorb it until 1969.

RIO GRANDE RAILROAD

The D&RG used subsidiary companies to build and own branches to sources of special traffic. One of these was the Rio Grande Railroad (incorporated in Colorado, July 1900) which constructed the following lines: Texas Creek, Colorado, to Westcliffe, Colorado, (precious metal mines—1901); Delta, Colorado, to Somerset, Colorado, (coal mines—1902); Maitland, Colorado, to Big Four, Colorado (coal mines—1904, 1908). The RG was absorbed into the D&RG system in the consolidation of 1908.

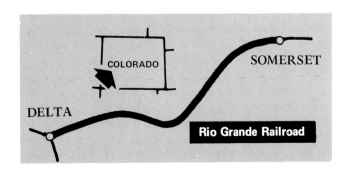

247

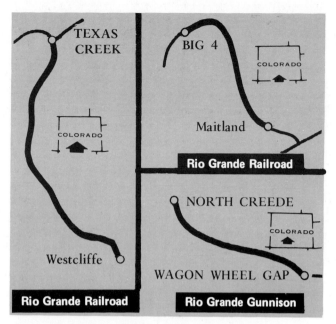

RIO GRANDE GUNNISON RAILWAY

Through a subsidiary company, the Rio Grande Gunnison Railway (incorporated in Colorado, September, 1891), the D&RG extended a branch from Wagon Wheel Gap, Colorado, to silver mines around North Creede, Colorado, in 1891. The D&RG leased the trackage, reimbursed the mining company for its contributions, and absorbed the company in 1908.

RIO GRANDE JUNCTION RAILWAY

Owned 50-percent each by the D&RG and Colorado Midland, the Rio Grande Junction Railway (incorporated in Colorado, June, 1889) was formed to provide a link between Rifle, Colorado, where D&RG rails ended, and Grand Junction, Colorado, where D&RG track connected with the Rio Grande Western. The D&RG and CM jointly leased the RGJ and operated over it, the CM having trackage rights over the D&RG between Rifle and New Castle. In 1900, the D&RG and Colorado & Southern bought the CM on a 50:50 basis, and in subsequent years the D&RG acquired RGJ stock from the CM, obtaining all of it by 1914. Although the CM suspended operations in 1918, it was not until 1947 that the RGJ was absorbed into the D&RGW's corporate structure.

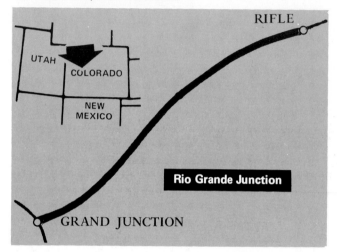

As could be expected, the Rio Grande, Pagosa & Northern used Denver & Rio Grande equipment during construction, as well as in regular operations. This scene near Dyke shows 2-8-0 Number 66 and a complement of stalwart track layers.

248

RIO GRANDE, PAGOSA & NORTHERN

Lumber companies logging the forests of southwestern Colorado joined with the D&RG during 1900 in building a branch, known as the Rio Grande, Pagosa & Northern Railroad (incorporated in Colorado, April, 1899), from Gato, Colorado, to Pagosa Springs, Colorado. Over a period of years the D&RG bought the lumber companies' interests, obtaining complete ownership by 1904.

Various narrow-gauge 2-8-0's were leased from the D&RG to haul trains of raw timber and finished lumber.

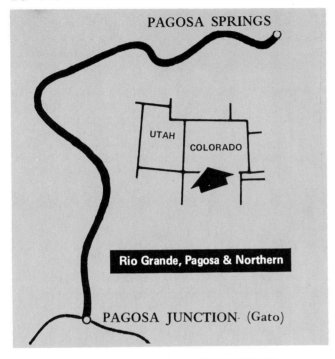

RIO GRANDE, PUEBLO & SOUTHERN

During 1902 the D&RG constructed a branch from Zinc Junction, Colorado, to a smelter at Blende, Colorado, using a subsidiary company, the Rio Grande, Pueblo & Southern Railroad (incorporated in Colorado, April, 1902) for this purpose. The RGP&S was absorbed into the D&RG system in the 1908 consolidation.

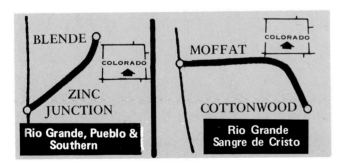

RIO GRANDE, SANGRE DE CRISTO

When copper mines at Cottonwood, Colorado, required a railroad connection in 1901, the D&RG obliged by forming a new company, the Rio Grande, Sangre de Cristo Railroad (incorporated in Colorado, January, 1901), which would join with the mining company in constructing track from Moffat, Colorado. The D&RG leased and operated the line, and in time bought the mining company's interest. The RGSdeC was merged into the D&RG system in 1908.

RIO GRANDE & SANTA FE' RAILROAD

Though barred by an 1880 agreement from building south of Española, New Mexico, the D&RG reached Santa Fe, New Mexico, by purchasing an independent railroad between those cities, the Santa Fe' Southern, in 1895, using a subsidiary, the Rio Grande & Santa Fe' Railroad (incorporated in New Mexico, July, 1895), for that purpose. The RG&SF became part of the D&RG system in the consolidation of 1908.

SALT LAKE & EASTERN RAILWAY

The Salt Lake & Eastern Railway (incorporated in Utah, September, 1888) was built in 1888-1889 to bring silver and lead ores from the Park City, Utah, area to smelters around Salt Lake City. Its narrow-gauge track climbed six-percent grades to surmount the Wasatch Mountains; fortunately, however, loaded cars moved downhill. Operations were conducted in cooperation with the Salt Lake & Fort Douglas and Utah Central railroads, the combination being known familiarly as "Utah Central." Operating costs were excessive and the railroad went into receivership during the silver panic of 1893. In 1898 it was sold to a newly organized Utah Central company.

Locomotive List

Unkown	2-6-0	Ex-Utah Northern	UC

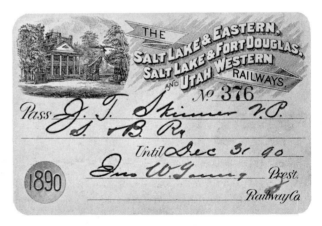

SALT LAKE & FORT DOUGLAS RAILWAY

Although the Salt Lake & Fort Douglas Railway (incorporated in Utah, December, 1884) had been organized to serve Fort Douglas, Utah, construction of its narrow-gauge track did not commence until 1887 when sandstone from the Red Buttes quarry was needed for some of the Mormon Church edifices then being erected in Salt Lake City. Grades and curvature were unusually severe: 10-percent and approximately 80°. Passenger and freight

Pagosa Springs, at the northern end of the RGP&N, was the center of a vast lumbering industry dominated by the Pagosa Lumber Company. Engines were turned on a loop, part of which can be seen in the foreground of the picture.

Any photograph of the Salt Lake & Eastern is most rare. This one shows one of its 2-6-0's at Park City, and one

can only wonder how it managed to climb the six-percent grade over the mountains from Salt Lake City.

operations were coordinated with the Salt Lake & Eastern and Utah Central railroads, commonly called "Utah Central." Like the SL&E, the SL&FtD failed to cover its expenses and went into receivership during 1897, afterward being sold to the new Utah Central company in 1898.

Locomotive List

| Unkown | 2-6-0 | Ex-Utah Northern | UC |
| 226 | 2-T Shay | Lima, 1888 | UC |

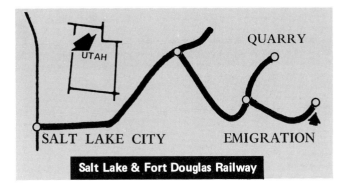

Salt Lake & Fort Douglas Railway

SAN PETE VALLEY RAILWAY

Though formed by an English group at an early date, the San Pete Valley Railway (incorporated in Utah, June, 1874) accomplished little until 1889 when it purchased the uncompleted track of the California Short Line. Thereupon the railroad was completed promptly from a coal mine at Wales, Utah, to Nephi, Utah, and by 1893 tracks had reached Manti, Utah. Next, a local group, having purchased the railroad from its former owners in 1894, extended the rails from Manti to a quarry at Morrison, Utah, and in 1896 widened the track to standard-gauge, thus matching connections at both ends of the line. Its last trackage was a branch from Nebo Junction, Utah, to Wales in 1894. In 1907 the D&RG acquired the stock of the SPV and merged it into their system in 1908.

Locomotive List

| 1, 2 | 2-6-0 | Ex-Utah Northern | Sumpter Valley |
| 50, 51 | 2-8-0 | Baldwin 1896 | D&RG (C) 680, 681 |

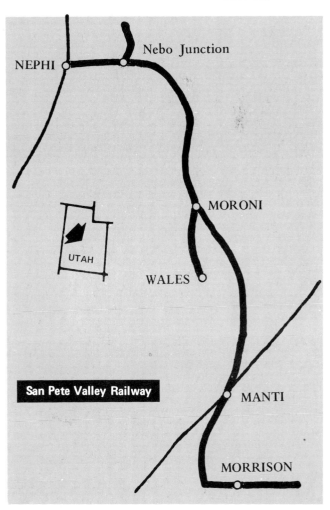

San Pete Valley Railway

"INTERMOUNTAIN RAILROADS"

The Salt Lake & Fort Douglas hauled its local trains with 2-6-0's between Salt Lake City, the military post, peniten- tiary and Emigration Point. This one was acquired from the Utah Northern when that road converted to standard-gauge.

ALLEN COUNTY HISTORICAL SOCIETY

This tiny two-truck Shay, whose road number was the same as its builder's serial-number—226—was used on the steep branch to stone quarries east of Salt Lake City. The SL&FtD obtained stone here for the city's buildings.

The western terminal of the San Pete Valley Railway was at Nephi, a station on the Utah Southern south of Salt Lake City, where this photograph was taken. Initial motive power *consisted of two 2-6-0's obtained from the Utah Northern, one of which is seen here with a rather short freight train. Notice that the car next to the engine is a four-wheeler.*

After the SPV changed its gauge, it bought two new standard-gauge 2-8-0's which were among the smallest of their type. Compare the diameters of the pilot-truck wheel and the front of the smokebox.

The condition of the open platforms belonging to the combination car of Union Pacific ancestry hardly inspired universal confidence in the transportation facilities of the San Pete Valley. This station served the community of Chester.

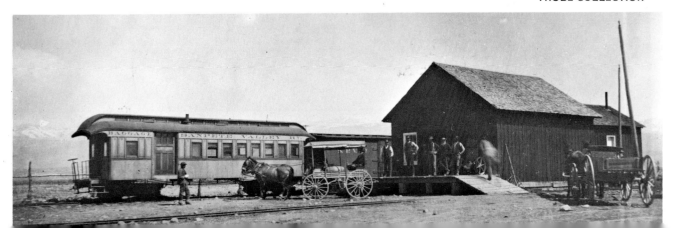

Biggest engine on the SFS was a 2-8-0 which was almost identical to those of the D&RG. In this scene of a minor *accident involving Number 3, passengers appear to have been accepting the cataclysm with utmost complacency.*

The two 2-6-0's used by the Santa Fé Southern had been obtained from the St. Louis & Cairo railroad when it changed its track gauge. They were near-twins to the Pittsburgh & Western locomotives erected by Pittsburgh Locomotive Works a couple of years later.

SANTA FÉ SOUTHERN RAILROAD

After the Texas, Santa Fé & Northern, which operated a railroad between Española, New Mexico, and Santa Fé, New Mexico, had run out of money, the company was reorganized as the Santa Fé Southern Railroad (incorporated in New Mexico, January, 1889). By 1894 the SFS was in receivership, its expenses exceeding the revenues from insufficient traffic. When the railroad was put up for public sale in 1895 to satisfy its creditors, the D&RG bought the line with Rio Grande Southern bonds, and renamed it Rio Grande & Santa Fé.

Locomotive List

1 unkown	Ex-TSF&N 5	Scrap
2 unkown	Ex "General Meily"	Scrap
3 2-8-0	Ex-Connotton Valley 6	D&RG 71 (2)
4 2-6-0	Ex-St. Louis & Cairo 26	D&RG 24 (2)
5 2-6-0	Ex-St. Louis & Cairo 27	D&RG 25 (2)

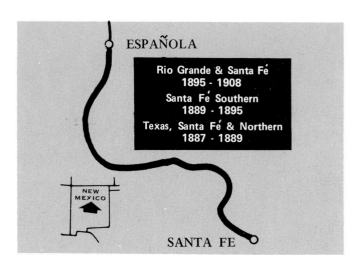

SEVIER RAILWAY

The Sevier Railway (incorporated in Utah, May, 1891) was created by the Rio Grande Western to construct and own an extension of the branch to Manti, Utah. Rails reached Salina, Utah, in 1891, Belknap, Utah, in 1896, and Marysvale, Utah, in 1900. The RGW leased the trackage until 1908 when both companies were absorbed into the D&RG system.

STATE LINE & DENVER RAILROAD

The State Line & Denver Railway (incorporated in Colorado, May, 1889) was organized solely to enable (by means of a merger) the D&RGW Railway to own and operate a railroad in Colorado. The union of these two companies was called Rio Grande Western, and it had corporate authority to extend its trackage as far east as Glenwood Springs, Colorado.

TEXAS, SANTA FE' & NORTHERN

Though the TSF&N had been formed (incorporated in New Mexico, December, 1880) to link Santa Fe, New Mexico, with the D&RG—which was forbidden to build south of Española, New Mexico — nothing much was accomplished until the arrival of Luther M. Meily, who had built the Denver, Utah & Pacific. With outside financial aid, Meily started laying track in December, 1886, completing the work in January, 1887. The TSF&N was unable to meet its financial obligations and was sold to a new company, the Santa Fe' Southern, in 1889.

Locomotive List

5	unkown	unkown	SFS 1
"General Meily"	unkown	unkown	SFS 2

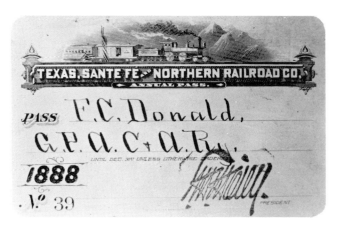

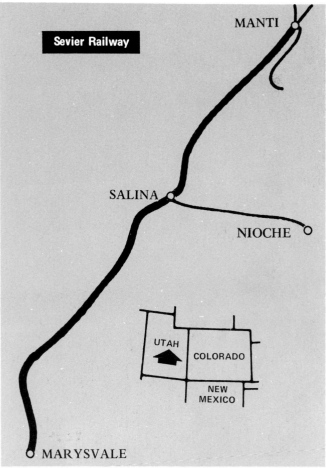

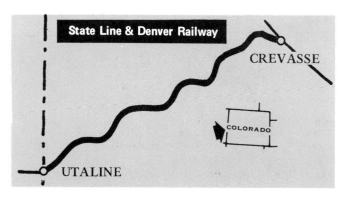

"AMERICA'S WONDERLANDS"

The quality of Texas, Santa Fe & Northern track along the Rio Grande did not inspire confidence among passengers, *whose attentions were doubtless diverted by the remarkable scenery visible from the car windows.*

TINTIC RANGE RAILWAY

Silver mining near Eureka, Utah, interested the Rio Grande Western sufficiently for it to organize the Tintic Range Railway (incorporated in Utah, May, 1891) for the purpose of building and owning track from Springville, Utah, to the mining area, then leasing it to the RGW which would operate it with their own locomotives. The line was built in 1891; extensions reached Mammoth in 1892 and Silver City in 1893. Several miles of long spurs were removed in 1896, the silver panic having forced the closure of mines. The TR was absorbed into the D&RG's system in 1908.

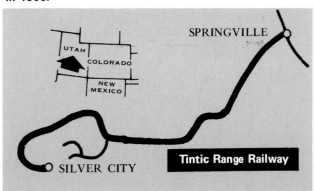

TRINIDAD & DENVER RAILROAD

Unable to extract enough money from its own treasury to build a short branch from El Moro, Colorado, to coal mines at Engleville, Colorado, the D&RG formed a separate company, the Trinidad & Denver Railroad (incorporated in Colorado, August, 1886), to provide the necessary trackage. Construction was completed in 1887, and in 1888 the D&RG bought the railroad and merged it.

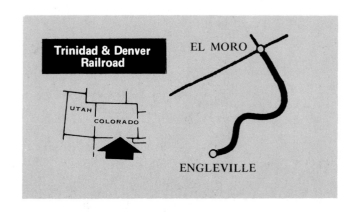

256

"TITAN OF THE TIMBER"

No photographs of the Utah Central Railway's two-truck Shay—Construction Number 327—have been discovered, however, this photograph of a sister locomotive—Construction Number 323—was a nearly identical duplicate.

UTAH CENTRAL RAILWAY

The Utah Central Railway (incorporated in Utah, April, 1890) owned but two miles of track connecting Lincoln Park station on the Salt Lake & Fort Douglas with Sugar House depot on the Salt Lake & Eastern, both points being located on the southeastern outskirts of Salt Lake City, Utah. After this track was laid in 1890 the three railroads were operated under common management and name: Utah Central. This enterprise did not prosper, however, and by 1893 it was in receivership. In 1897 it was reorganized by the bondholders as the Utah Central Railroad.

Locomotive List

1	2-6-0	Ex-SL&E/SL&FtD	Unknown
1	2-8-0	Baldwin, 1895	RGW 01
2	2-8-0	Ex-Connotton Valley 13	RGW 02
3	2-8-0	Ex-Great Falls & Canada 3	RGW 03
4-7	2-6-0	Ex-SL&E/SL&FtD	Unknown
226	2-T Shay	Ex-SL&FtD 226	Oregon Lumber Company
327	2-T Shay	Lima, 1891	Doty Lumber Company

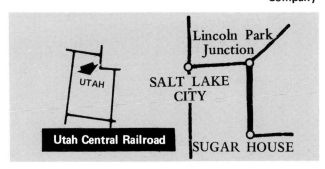

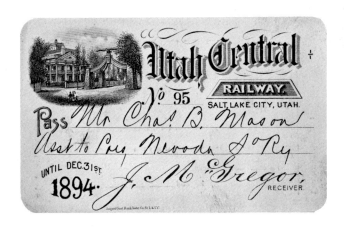

UTAH CENTRAL RAILROAD

The Utah Central Railroad (incorporated in Utah, December, 1897) had been barely organized when it was approached by the Rio Grande Western with an interesting proposition. If the new company (which would include the old UC, SL&FtD and SL&E companies) gave the RGW its stock, the RGW would pay the bond interest, lease the property, and operate it. This arrangement took effect in January, 1898. The D&RG took over the lease in 1902, then absorbed the UC in the D&RG-RGW consolidation of 1908. In 1900 the RGW removed almost all of the former SL&FtD N-G trackage and converted the Park City, Utah, line to standard-gauge, somewhat reducing the steep grades at the same time.

Excepting a two-truck Shay and a new Baldwin 2-8-0, Utah Central motive power was entirely second-hand, and photos of any of them in their original habitat are not known. In this imperfect rendition of Sumpter Valley railroad Number 8, the reader will perceive a 2-8-0 which had been Utah Central Number 2.

Sumpter Valley 2-8-0 Number 15 had been constructed originally for the Great Falls & Canada Railroad as its Number 7. GF&C Number 3, constructed on the same order, became UC Number 3—of which no photos are known, despite four subsequent renumberings in the Rio Grande System.

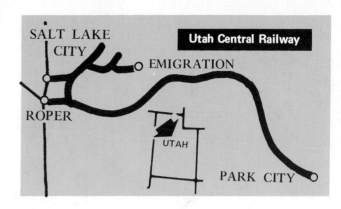

UTAH EASTERN RAILWAY

The Utah Eastern Railway (incorporated in Utah, December, 1897) was a subsidiary of the Rio Grande Western, organized to construct and own an extension of the Provo Canyon Branch from Milepost 11 to Heber, Utah. Track was laid during 1898 and the company was merged into the RGW in 1900.

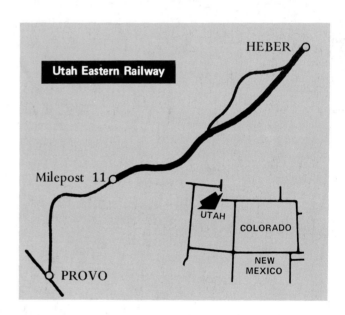

UTAH & PLEASANT VALLEY RAILWAY

The Utah & Pleasant Valley Railway (incorporated in Utah, December, 1875) was perpetrated to haul coal from mines at Pleasant Valley, Utah, to the Utah Southern Railroad at Provo, Utah. The enterprise languished for lack of money until 1878 when construction began, narrow gauge track being completed in the following year. An interesting feature of the line was a U-shaped switchback atop the Wasatch Mountain ridge. The railroad was entirely too long to be successful and, consequently, defaulted on its bond payments in 1880, then went into receivership in 1881. In the next year the D&RGW acquired the company after a foreclosure sale.

Locomotive List

7	2-6-0	Baldwin	1877	D&RGW 7
8	0-6-0	Porter, Bell	1877	D&RGW 9

The rolling stock and motive power of Utah's earliest railroads are among the great rarities of photographic history. In this portrait of construction at Castle Gate, a Utah & Pleasant Valley locomotive was found working with cars bearing designations of the Wasatch & Jordan Valley and perhaps the Bingham Canon & Camp Floyd, also.

The obvious crudity of Utah & Pleasant Valley track revealed in this picture was no greater than that of other hastily constructed early-day railroads, including the Union Pacific, whose track differed only in gauge.

259

A switchback from the "main-line" of the Wasatch & Jordan Valley Railroad led to a granite quarry where stone for the Morman Temple in Salt Lake City was quarried.

The mule and horse motive power and associated rolling stock did not appear in contemporary tabulations of equipment, however.

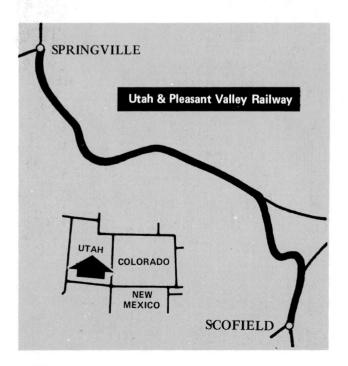

SPRINGVILLE

Utah & Pleasant Valley Railway

UTAH

COLORADO

NEW
MEXICO

SCOFIELD

The W&JV's two 0-6-0's, constructed by Dawson & Baily in 1873, closely resembled a contemporary locomotive, Number 1 of the Colorado Central.

Though a few photographs have recorded the appearance of Wasatch & Jordan Valley freight cars, no picture of the railroad's three narrow-gauge locomotives seem to have *been preserved. However, this photograph of a Columbia & Puget Sound engine built at the same time was a twin to the W&JV's lone 4-4-0.*

WASATCH & JORDAN VALLEY RAILROAD

Built initially from Sandy, Utah, to a granite quarry southeast of Salt Lake City, Utah, in 1873, the Wasatch & Jordan Valley Railroad (incorporated in Utah, October, 1872) was extended to the precious metal mines at Alta, Utah, in 1876. Much of this latter portion was covered by a snowshed. The W&JV was operated in coordination with the Bingham Canon & Camp Floyd, this association becoming closer in 1879 when the W&JV filed Articles of Consolidation in Utah as part of a plan to sell additional bonds in New York. The consolidation was not consummated, however, and the W&JV failed to pay its bond interest, throwing it into receivership in 1880. The railroad was sold to the D&RGW during 1881.

Locomotive List

1	0-6-0	Dawson & Baily	1873	D&RGW 1
2	0-6-0	Dawson & Baily	1873	D&RGW 3
3	4-4-0	Dawson & Baily	1874	D&RGW 5

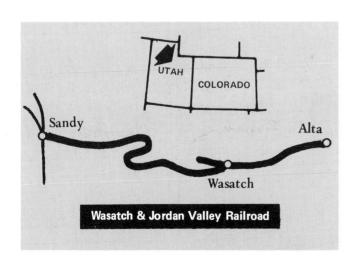

Wasatch & Jordan Valley Railroad

IN SPANISH FORK CAÑON.

Spanish Fork Canyon provided the only practical access for a railroad through the lofty Wasatch Range southeast of Salt Lake City to the coal deposits on the eastern slopes. Later, it became the route for the D&RGW's main-line across the Rocky Mountains between Denver and Salt Lake City.

261

The exceedingly deep snows of Alta—the delight of modern skiers—plagued the Wasatch & Jordan Valley, causing the railroad to encase much of its trackage in wooden snowsheds which clung precariously to the steep mountain slopes.

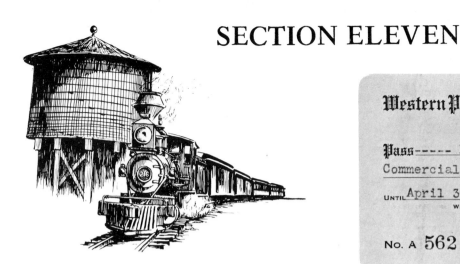

WESTERN PACIFIC

Prior to 1900 the Denver & Rio Grande railroad had maintained traffic relationships with the Rio Grande Western, a railroad which the D&RG had fostered originally as the Denver & Rio Grande Western Railway. After the D&RG's reorganization in 1886, the D&RGW had become independent of its former parent, and had changed its name to "Rio Grande Western" concurrently with widening its track from narrow to standard-gauge in 1889. The D&RG had wanted to absorb the D&RGW (as well as the RGW), but had been unable to do so; however, in 1900 the outlook suddenly changed. The reason for this abrupt alteration was the entry of the Gould family — headed by George Jay Gould — into D&RG management.

After his father's death in 1892, George had been entrusted with managing the Gould railroad empire and one of his ambitions was to assemble a system which would span the nation from ocean to ocean. West of the Mississippi River Gould had used the Missouri Pacific railroad as the foundation for his transportation edifice, and in 1900 the MP began to purchase D&RG stock, obtaining enough for control before the year ended. Gould management replaced the former one and the D&RG began to purchase RGW stock, thus extending the Gould system to Ogden and Salt Lake City. Here, in the midst of a vast territory dominated by the Union Pacific railroad, George Gould reached the end-of-track. The Central Pacific railroad, one of two possibilities open to him, fell to Union Pacific control in 1901, while his only existing alternative, the San Pedro, Los Angeles & Salt Lake railroad, also was placed beyond his grasp in 1902 by an ownership agreement with the UP.

Having gained control of both routes to the West Coast, the UP was in a position to divert all traffic over its own line east of Salt Lake City, unless a shipper were to pay a combination of local rates (at higher cost) for routing his shipment via RGW-D&RG-MP. For Gould it was no longer a question of buying a railroad just to have a transcontinental system; instead, he was being forced to build a railroad— a new experience for the Gould clan—to prevent traffic starvation of his most recent acquisitions. The odds against

him were formidable, but Gould had no other choice even though the D&RG-RGW route between Salt Lake City and Denver was 100 miles longer than that of the UP, and a new route between Salt Lake City and Oakland would be 150 miles longer than the CP's line.

To accomplish his objective, Gould would have to finance and construct somewhat more than 900 miles of railroad through enemy territory at a cost approximating the value of the family fortune, about $80-million. This new railroad, the Western Pacific Railway, was to be known as the Denver & Rio Grande's "Western Extension," the D&RG being responsible for construction and expenses, just as though it were a branch of the D&RG. In addition, Gould would have to keep his activity secret until he could be assured of both physical and financial success, a most difficult proposition since UP people infested not only MP and D&RG Directorates but also the managements of banking houses which supplied funds for Gould's activities.

It is known that Gould, operating through the D&RG's engineering department, authorized some surveys in California during 1902, and he was behind dummy lumber and mining enterprises which obtained claims to rights-of-way in the state. Moreover, he talked with well-known Californians whose ideas and activities coincided with his own. One can conceive how Gould might have kept his contacts secret, but how the work was paid for is another matter. One possibility is that they were handled through the D&RG's Castle Valley Railway subsidiary which was supposed to build a cutoff between Farnham (on the main-line) and Salina (on the Marysvale Branch), thence perhaps to Milford (on the SPLA&SL railroad), all in Utah. The 1902 Annual Report contains this intriguing comment: "The Castle Valley cutoff on the RGW was commenced last spring. The surveys and location were completed and a contract was let for 21 miles of grading. The cutoff will extend from Farnham to Salina, a distance of 116 miles, and when completed will afford a route 38 miles shorter than the present one to Southwestern Utah. Important coalfields in the vicinity of Salina Canyon and in contiguous districts can be opened up and the coal made avail-

The D&RG did more than just pay the cost of constructing and operating the WP; it supplied locomotives and cars also. D&RG 4-6-0 Number 507, converted to burn oil, was one of three used between Oakland and Oroville in California.

Quite understandably, the Western Pacific's first locomotives resembled those of the D&RG in both appearance and dimensions. After Baldwin delivered the first 20 2-8-0's in 1906, a quarter-century was to pass before that company received a second order.

able for commercial use to meet the growing demands for Utah fuel. The construction of the cutoff will be prosecuted from time to time according to the requirements of the various classes of traffic which it is believed can be developed in the territory to be traversed." The 1903 Report stated that 21 miles of the CV had been completed; that it was not contemplated to extend the CV during the current year; and that $400,000 of RGW bonds were issued to pay for the work. Never again was the CV mentioned in a D&RG Annual Report, and its actual status is open to inquiry. Was it to be a cutoff, affording a shorter route to the coast? If so, its severe gradients and curvature were not of main-line calibre. Was it to open up coal deposits? If so, the line was built in the wrong location. If it were important, why were its objectives and completion so indefinite? The timing of the CV's birth, and the peculiarities of its brief active existence, are highly suggestive that the CV may have been used by Gould to cover his preliminary Western Pacific activities.

During 1902 Gould's agents brought together the elements needed for the formation of the Western Pacific Railway, and in March, 1903, the railroad was incorporated in California. Capitalized for $100-million (half stock, half bonds), its officers and directors were local personages, presumably known only to Gould. Originally, the WP was a consolidation of four "paper" companies (Stockton & Beckwith Pass Railway, Sacramento & Oakland Railway, San Francisco Terminal Railway & Ferry Company, and Oakland Realty & Improvement Company) organized by W. J. Bartnett and A. W. Keddie, plus the two D&RG dummies (Butte & Plumas Railway and Indian Valley Railway). The existing Alameda & San Joaquin Railroad was added in July, 1903, at which time also the D&RG purchased 51-percent of the Boca & Loyalton Railroad, a lumber line which traversed the western approaches to strategic Beckwourth Pass. All of this was kept out of Poor's Manual of Railroads though, of course, the UP and its bankers were well aware of unusual activity along the proposed route in California.

During 1903, in the midst of widespread speculation, Gould perfected his plans for constructing the WP, and explored methods of financing it until it could become self-supporting. The amount of money needed was enormous, far greater than any sum which could be spirited away from the MP, D&RG and RGW treasuries through subsidiary companies without immediate detection. Nor could Gould borrow what was needed without pertinent questions being asked. And as for selling stock in his new railroad; who had that kind of money? Eventually Gould was obliged to rely on his own resources, and in so doing was forced to reveal his project. His own Bowling Green Trust Company would underwrite a $50-million issue of first-mortgage bonds on a non-existent railroad, just the reverse of the usual procedure. Ordinarily, such bonds were unsalable, but Gould included three provisions which made them marketable. The D&RG would guarantee payment of principal and interest if the WP's revenues were inadequate. In return for these payments and any operating deficits the WP would give promissory notes to the D&RG and RGW. And the D&RG would advance its own funds for construction, accepting up to $25-million in second-mortgage bonds at a suitable discount.

When these agreements were recorded at Salt Lake City in February, 1904, Gould's intentions were no longer a secret. Gould resigned from his position on the UP board and E. H. Harriman departed from the D&RG's board. E. T. Jeffery of the D&RG and W. H. Taylor of the trust

company appeared on the WP board. A syndicate (Blair & Company, William Salomon & Company, W. A. Read & Company, all of New York) agreed to sell the WP first-mortgage bonds, yielding 90-percent of par to the trust company which would advance the funds as needed by the WP for construction. The battle to the Pacific's shores had begun, a fact not revealed to D&RG stockholders until the 1905/1906 Annual Report, the text of which was a masterpiece of evasive literature. One paragraph is worthy of close interpretation because it reveals an aspect of Gould's motives: "The D&RG Railroad Company and The RGW Railway Company will, together, hold in their treasuries 500,000 shares, of a par value of $50,000,000, out of a total capitalization (ignoring the $50-million issue of bonds!) of the WP Railway Company of 750,000 shares, of a par value of $75,000,000. This will place your Company in the absolute control of the WP Railway Company without any immediate money outlay, and with only a contingent liability for the future."

This is a most remarkable statement. Gould was telling D&RG stockholders (principally, the MP railroad, which he owned) that their company possessed $50-million face-value of WP stock (which would never have any real value because the D&RG was not going to pay for the stock, and all WP expenditures would be made with borrowed funds represented by bonds and notes). Of even greater importance was his minimizing the D&RG's future liability for WP debt, as provided by the terms of its mortgage. This liability could be at least $50-million principal plus $150-million interest (5-percent for 30 years) plus whatever other amounts might be needed to complete the WP and operate it until it became self-supporting. There was no need for Gould to make such a statement for the benefit of the D&RG or MP stockholders; he would have been talking to himself. Most probably he was addressing the financial world with the thought of boosting the prices of D&RG and MP stock, enabling him to sell these securities at handsome profit, or to use them as collateral in additional borrowing for empire-building purposes. He may even have been considering offering the D&RG-RGW-WP to the Chicago & North Western; Chicago, Burlington & Quincy; or Chicago, Rock Island & Pacific, thus forcing the UP-CP-SP system to buy his railroads for no other reason than to preserve their monopoly.

Despite this strange financial background of the WP, track-laying began at Oakland on January 2, 1906, and at Salt Lake City on May 24, 1906. The most difficult construction was in the Sierra Nevada mountains of California where the grade was held to one-percent and the summit was crossed at 5000-foot elevation. (The CP's grades were 2.2-percent, and its elevation was 2000 feet higher.) Besides the various obstacles interposed by the UP-CP-SP forces, the WP also was impeded by the San Francisco earthquake of April, 1906, and the money panic of 1907 (which was somewhat beneficial in that it increased the availability of construction workers). By mid-1907 177 miles of track had been laid and completion was expected in the fall of 1908. Just a year later the D&RG reported that over 400 miles of WP track had been laid, and that 225 miles in California and 260 miles in Utah and Nevada could be opened for traffic by the end of 1908.

Optimistic though these first events may have been, the WP was only half finished, and it had run out of money. Accordingly, after the consolidation of the RGW and D&RG on August 1, 1908, the (new) D&RG company floated a $150-million bond issue, part of which was sold

*The second group of 2-8-0's for the Western Pacific —
numbered 21 - 65 — came from the American Locomotive*

*Company, which had just completed an order for 68 simi-
lar engines for the D&RG and the RGW.*

*The WP's first 13 0-6-0 switchers were part of a group of 16,
of which the D&RG ordered three; however, those delivered
to the WP burned oil as fuel instead of coal.*

*The 122 was one of five RGW 2-8-0's which were changed to
oil-burners and used by the WP to haul construction trains
on the western end of the WP.*

promptly, and $16-million of the proceeds turned over to the WP in exchange for $17-million of WP second-mortgage bonds. (Later, the WP received $7-million more for $8-million of its bonds.) Among the D&RG assets pledged under the mortgage was the $50-million face-value of worthless WP stock, as well as the WP's $25-million bond-issue! Oddly, the trustee was the Bankers Trust Company, a Kuhn, Loeb & Company subsidiary! Apparently, Gould was obtaining money from enemy sources, and he was using valueless collateral for his loans. Nor was this all. In 1908 also, Gould's Bowling Green Trust Company was merged into the Equitable Trust Company of New York, one-sixth of which was owned by Kuhn, Loeb & Company. Equitable Trust was one of the UP's sources of funds, and Kuhn, Loeb had been characterized as the UP's General Staff. Here was Gould, to all outward indications joining forces with his enemies But was this conceivably the price which was exacted in return for the $150-million loan to the D&RG?

Whatever the motives, Gould's actions in 1908 had given the UP's bankers the means by which they could obtain control of not only the WP, but also the D&RG itself. The MP-D&RG-WP system was in a state of delicate financial balance. The D&RG could continue to "own" the WP so long as it continued to pay the interest on the WP's first-mortgage bonds; failure to do so would transfer control to Equitable Trust and ownership to the bondholders. The D&RG itself, having advanced about $25-million of its own funds to the WP, was suffering acutely from neglected maintenance of its track and equipment. Moreover, the MP was contemplating the approaching maturity of a bond issue which it could not redeem. Gould's system, though it was attaining its objective of reaching the Pacific Ocean, was on the verge of internal collapse, a matter certainly known to Gould and which may account for his actions during the next few years.

Even nature conspired against the completion of the WP; unprecedented rains in California in early 1907 caused landslides and flooding which hampered new construction and necessitated reconstruction of previously built railroad. Some freight service had been instituted in late 1907 between Salt Lake City and Shafter, Nevada, where the WP connected with the Nevada Northern, a carrier of copper ore, but further traffic could not be handled until the entire railroad had been completed. This did not occur until November 1, 1909, when the last spike was driven just west of Keddie, California, without either celebration or ceremony. One month later through freight service commenced on the 940-mile line, though the first passenger train did not arrive at Oakland until August 22, 1910. Meanwhile, the D&RG and WP had been erecting a joint station in Salt Lake City; it was completed in time for the departure of the WP's inaugural westbound passenger run.

At this point the WP had cost a little over $70-million! Forty-eight-million dollars had come from the sale of $50-million first-mortgage bonds and $23-million had been provided by the D&RG against the $25-million second-mortgage bonds, which meant that the $50-million issue of WP stock, pledged under the D&RG's $150-million loan, was still without tangible value, although it represented legal ownership of the WP by the D&RG.

The three years following the WP's completion produced some changes which were to greatly affect its future. B. F. Bush, president of Gould's Western Maryland railroad, was installed as president of the MP, D&RG and WP companies. WP promissory debt to the D&RG, representing operating deficits and additional construction costs,

had soared beyond $10-million. Most important of all, the Goulds sold essentially all of their MP and D&RG securities. MP stock, valued around $100 per share in 1903, brought only half that price in 1911, and by 1913 changed hands at a mere $8 to $30. As the Goulds sold out Kuhn, Loeb and their allies bought in; by the end of 1913 the UP, through its bankers, had obtained control of the MP-D&RG-WP system. Why the Goulds cashed their MP chips is not explained. In view of the decline in price of MP stock, the Goulds may have wanted to save as much of the family fortune as possible. Furthermore, they must have been aware that the continued decline in MP net income might result in a financial reorganization which would completely wipe out their stock. In any event, by the end of 1913 the Goulds no longer determined the future of the MP, the D&RG or the WP.

At this point it is interesting to observe that the WP's balance sheet showed capital stock valued at $75-million, supposedly represented by investment in the railroad! The D&RG wasn't quite so unconscionable; it valued its $50-million holding at a more modest $4-million.

In the business world there are three varieties of profiteers: those who profit exorbitantly from building an enterprise, those who profit from operating it, and those who profit from its destruction. As far as the Goulds were concerned, in the WP they were none of these, perhaps for the only occasion in their careers! They made nothing from the WP's construction, neither from contracts nor from stock promotion. The WP was worth every dollar expended on it. The WP had no operating monopoly, and it performed a service worthy of its cost. The Goulds were gone before the WP became involved in financial manipulation and reorganization. The same cannot be said for the managements which succeeded the Goulds in the MP, D&RG and WP. What they did to the financial structures, the bondholders and stockholders of those railroads is considered by many to be a monumental exemplification of corporate infidelity.

The first move in this new era of WP history began with a request from the MP board of directors to the D&RG board, recommending that the D&RG not pay the WP bond interest due September, 1914. Somewhat astounded by this proposal, the D&RG board debated, then paid the interest. The implications of such action were most sinister for the D&RG. It was financially able to make the necessary payment; in fact, during the 1910-1914 period it had purchased 44 new locomotives of exceptional size; it had built 122 miles of new trackage and had improved another 103 miles. On the other side of the ledger the D&RG stood to lose its entire investment in the WP: $23-million in second mortgage bonds and $17-million in promissory notes. Furthermore, the WP was fast approaching the break-even point, and thus would no longer be a burden to the D&RG. Yet, in March, 1915, the D&RG board, by not deciding to do anything about the WP's March interest, allowed the default to occur!

Eight months later the Trustee under the first mortgage (Equitable Trust) declared the $50-million principal due. Immediately after the default the Trustee of the WP Railway applied for a receivership which was granted by the courts. In May a Bondholders' Protective Committee was formed, with A. W. Krech (President of Equitable Trust) as chairman.

Working with unusual speed, and without any protest on the part of the D&RG board or Central Trust (Trustee of WP second-mortgage), the Committee bought the WP for its $18-million bid at the foreclosure sale in June, 1916.

On the day before the inauguration of through service
between Salt Lake City and Oakland, the WP assembled
a train composed of D&RG equipment, and gave representa-
tives of the public press a grand tour of the newly-completed
railroad. On its westward trip the special train–pulled by
4-6-0 Number 71–paused on the salt flats at Salduro for a
panoramic portrait.

By this inaction of the D&RG board and the Trustee for the WP second-mortgage bonds which it held, the D&RG threw away its $55½-million investment in the WP, more than half of the railroad's cost!

Two new Western Pacific companies now entered the picture, both incorporated in June, 1916. One—the WP Railroad Company—was a California company, while the other, the WP Railroad Corporation, was based in Delaware. The WP Railroad Company issued to the WP Railroad Corporation $50-million in common stock, $30-million in preferred stock, and $20-million in first-mortgage bonds in return for the entire WP railroad plus $17.1-million cash which had been contributed by former WP Railway bondholders. For each $1000 bond these bondholders received 10 shares WP Railroad Corporation common stock ($1000 par value) and six shares WP Railroad Corporation preferred stock ($600 par value), provided they paid $360 for 4/5 of a WP Railroad Company bond ($1000 par value). The WP Railroad Corporation kept the WP Railroad Company stock and the WP Railway Company bonds, thus retaining a claim for further recovery against the D&RG. (Using 1917 prices, a participating bondholder received stock selling for about $390, while a non-participating holder received $360, less a $5 fee.)

Waiting hardly long enough for the ink to dry on its charter, the WP Railroad Company immediately began a program of acquisition and construction to provide the railroad with new sources of traffic. It purchased the ailing Boca & Loyalton from the D&RG for $35,000, and through a subsidiary, Standard Reality & Development Company, invested $75,000 in the Indian Valley Railroad, which extended from Paxton, California, to the Engles copper mine. Then it spent almost $500,000 on the Deep Creek Railroad, running south from Wendover, Utah, to mines at Gold Hill, Utah. Furthermore, for $1.1-million it purchased two-thirds of the stock of the Tidewater Southern Railway out in California, an electric interurban line serving the area south of Stockton down to Turlock and nearby towns. In 1917 the WP began construction of a branch from Niles to San Jose, but the entry of the nation into the World War caused this work to be discontinued. A more successful project in that year was the acqustion, at a cost of $700,000, of the southern end of the narrow gauge Nevada-California-Oregon Railway. Widened to standard gauge and partially relocated, this trackage became the Reno Branch, and operations commenced over it in 1918. In addition two short branches were built at the south end of the Great Salt Lake: one from Burmester, Utah, to Tooele Junction, serving a copper smelter supplied with ore by the Tooele Valley railroad, the other from Ellerbeck to limestone quarries at Dolomite and Flux. By the end of 1918 the grand total of this new trackage was 218 miles, and the cost had amounted to about $3.6-million.

Like other railroads, the WP was operated by the USRA during 1918, 1919 and early 1920, after which the railroad was returned to its owners, who received $8.6-million in compensation for war-caused wear and tear. Among the changes wrought by the USRA was an arrangement with the Southern Pacific for the use of Central Pacific and Western Pacific tracks between Wells and Winnemucca, making this 180-mile segment across Nevada the equivalent of double track. Though the WP did not like the plan at first, it agreed to a 50-year extension in 1924.

Despite a severe business recession in 1921, the WP management continued its program of branch-line acquisi-

tions and construction to add new sources of traffic. The San Jose Branch was finally completed and a new one was begun into the forest south of the Hawley, Nevada. This, the Calpine Branch, was completed in 1923. Late in the year the WP Railroad Corporation bought the securities of the Sacramento Northern electric interurban railroad between Sacramento and Chico, turning the line over to the WP Railroad Company for operation. In 1924 the WP "company" acquired the SN by selling bonds, using the cash to purchase the SN securities from the WP "corporation."

Going back now several years to the time when the WP was constructing its railroad — James J. Hill, who controlled the Northern Pacific, and Great Northern railroads (and through them the Chicago, Burlington & Quincy; and Spokane, Portland & Seattle railroads), began to build southward into central Oregon, with the thought of connecting his system with the WP to gain an entry into California where the SP-CP-UP system enjoyed a virtual monopoly. Backed by the financial resources of J. P. Morgan, Hill pushed this new line, the Oregon Trunk Railway, as far as Bend, Oregon, by 1911. Here, Hill was blocked by the UP, which was financed by Kuhn, Loeb & Company, Morgan's rival in the field of high finance. Consequently, the OT terminated out in the middle of nowhere. In 1916 Hill died, leaving the northern trans-mountain lines without its adroit strategist, and nothing more was accomplished toward a connection between the OT and WP. However, in 1924 things began to change within the SP-CP-UP system. The SP purchased the El Paso & Southwestern railroad and its subsidiaries from one Arthur C. James, who then began to buy WP Railroad Corporation stocks and bonds; by 1926 his holding company owned enough to give him control. Since James had previously acquired control of the GN-NP-CB&Q-SP&S-OT system, the Great Northern applied for and received authority to construct the OT-WP link, but the project lay dormant for another five years, and while the ICC deliberated, the WP improved its trackage and acquired additional feeders.

One of these new acquisitions was the Alameda Belt Line, a switching proposition built in 1926, and owned jointly with the Atchison, Topeka & Santa Fe. Another one was an 88-mile electric interurban line, the San Francisco-Sacramento Railroad, running between Oakland, California, and Sacramento. A majority of the stock was purchased by the WP Railroad Corporation in 1927, the interurban company being merged into the SN two years later. Still another was the 54-mile Central California Traction Company, which operated an electric interurban railroad extending from Sacramento to Stockton. The securities of this company were purchased in equal proportions by the WP, SP and AT&SF in 1928. A short branch, from Kingdon to Terminous, California, was constructed in 1928. Still another subsidiary, the Western Pacific-California railroad, was organized in 1930 to build a line from Niles, California, to San Francisco, thus giving the latter city a second all-rail connection. Work was to have commenced in 1931, but the great business depression caused the WP to abandon the project during 1933.

The ICC granted final approval for the OT-WP connection in 1930, after allowing the SP to complete its roughly parallel Alturas Cutoff first. The GN built south from Bend, Oregon, into Chemult, Oregon, on the SP, thence from Klamath Falls, Oregon (also on the SP), south to Bieber, California. Meanwhile the WP laid track northward from Keddie, California, to Bieber, California, 112

The vast emptiness of the Nevada desert is well-illustrated by this view from the cab of a Western Pacific diesel-electric F-unit. This scene is at WP milepost 404.5 eastbound, at Sano, Nevada. Through much of this region stretches of tangent track are the rule, rather than the exception.

When the Western Pacific's last spike was driven at Keddie, California, on November 1, 1909, the Rio Grande System had been completed between Denver and the Pacific Coast. This was the final link in Gould's railroad empire, the only one under a single management to have spanned the United States from coast to coast.

miles, of which five miles was on SP track. The rails were joined with appropriate ceremony on November 10, 1931, as Arthur James drove the final, gold spike between GN 2-8-2 Number 3351 and WP 2-6-6-2 Number 204, which faced each other at the head of special trains.

The completion of the Northern California Extension, as the new line was called, could hardly have occurred at a more dismal time for the WP. Its earnings had reached $2400 per mile-operated in 1926; they were less than $400 in the next year, and in 1931 a loss of $2000 per mile was recorded. The cause was the fatal combination of a major business depression which reduced traffic and substantial additions to bonded debt (for acquisitions and extensions) which increased obligatory expenses. As if these were not enough, the interurban lines brought into the WP almost immediately began to lose passenger traffic to highway busses and private automobiles. Furthermore, the WP's aged cars and locomotives were becoming inadequate to handle the traffic competitively, while maintenance costs were increasing. Replacement equipment, bought with borrowed money, added further burden to the WP's strained treasury. Another unfavorable factor was the large proportion of non-originated traffic 60-percent of which was routed over the D&RGW between Salt Lake City and Pueblo-Denver. This circuitous and difficult route could not compete with the CP-UP on either a time or rate basis.

The opening in 1934 of the D&RGW's Dotsero Cutoff in Colorado, which initiated the CB&Q-D&SL-D&RGW-WP route (175 miles shorter than the former one), enabled these railroads to match CP-UP schedules, but this by no means alleviated the WP's serious financial predicament. Even before the Cutoff was opened, the WP asked its bondholders, including A. C. James, to defer interest payments until 1937. In 1935 it was unable to pay any bond interest and applied for reorganization under the Federal Corporate Bankruptcy Act, resulting in a trusteeship. Over the next few years five plans of financial organization were proposed, as well as one which embraced a merger with the D&RGW. A modified ICC plan received Court approval in 1939, thus setting the scene for a multi-sided legal fracas which was to last four years.

Otherwise 1939 was an eventful year for the WP. Operation of the Deep Creek railroad was discontinued and the track was sold for scrap. Indian Valley trackage was removed for lack of traffic. And the first diesel-electric locomotives (three switchers) arrived. Lastly, a new passenger train, the "Exposition Flyer," was inaugurated between Chicago and Oakland via CB&Q, D&SL, D&RGW and WP lines. Despite its longer journey, this train equalled the schedule of comparable trains on the CP-UP-Chicago & North Western route.

Of equal importance was a reduction in the annual deficit from a peak of $3700 per mile in 1938 to $1600 in 1939, an effect produced by the war in Europe. By 1941 this traffic had enabled the WP to make its first profit in several years, a feat which would have brought joy to Arthur James had he not died that year. A year earlier the WP had ceased operating the Calpine Branch where lumber traffic had dwindled to nothing. By contrast, in the Bay Area, traffic was almost double what it had been only five years earlier, a situation which caused the AT&SF and WP to form another jointly-owned company the Oakland Terminal Railway. This rail line was created in 1942 to serve harbor and industrial facilities.

As war traffic surged along the WP's rails (attaining a peak four times the tonnage handled in 1932) the railroad's facilities were taxed to their utmost. Steam locomo-tives were borrowed from the D&RGW and the Duluth, Missabe & Iron Range; in 1944 a Centralized Traffic Control system was installed between Portola and Spring Garden, thence down Feather River Canyon as rapidly as the equipment could be obtained and installed. During these years it was usual for the "Exposition Flyer" to run six hours late eastbound from Portola, so great was the volume of the westbound freight dropping down the hundred-mile, twisting, one-percent grade in the canyon.

While the WP's operating people were struggling with their problems of train movement, its Trustees and Directors were wrestling with the railroad's financial structure and the massive burden of debt which could be borne only in times of saturated prosperity. Among the contenders were Federal agencies (Railroad Credit Corporation, Reconstruction Finance Corporation, Interstate Commerce Commission), holding companies (WP Railroad Corporation, A. C. James Company, Western Realty Company), and mortgage trustees (Crocker First National Bank, Irving Trust Company), all arguing their various propositions in the halls of justice, including the U. S. Supreme Court. A modified ICC plan was approved by the Supreme Court and qualified security holders in 1943, though the plan (retroactive to January 1, 1939) was not to become final until the end of 1944. The WP's two trustees were discharged in mid-1945, being replaced by a reorganization committee which served until March, 1946. As a result of this prolonged financial contest, the WP Railroad Corporation holdings of WP Railroad Company stock, which had been valued at $80-million in 1916, were now found to be worthless! The Junior Bonds held by the A. C. James Company were liquidated for about 30 cents per dollar, paid in cash and new securities. The railroad and its assets were, in effect, delivered to the first-mortgage bondholders (who had invested only $27-million!), an action which eliminated control of the railroad company by the two holding companies. This procedure also severed the financial link between the WP Railroad and the former D&RG Railroad, through the WP Railroad Corporation. The holding company had gained control of the D&RG in the latter's bankruptcy of 1918 and its reorganization as the Denver & Rio Grande Western Railroad in 1921. The D&RGW failed twice more, in 1922 and 1935, and when it was reorganized in 1947 the WP Railroad Corporation's interest was completely eliminated. (There being no relationship between the WP and D&RGW Railroads after 1947, the WP's subsequent history will be presented only briefly.)

Now, for the first time, the WP railroad was free of external control. Its debt had been reduced to a mere $17-million outstanding and its asset-value had been halved to $125-million. But this was not the end of wrangling over money. The WP Railroad Corporation sued the reorganized WP Railroad Company for $18-million, the amount of tax-savings gained by the railroad company when the two organizations filed consolidated income statements which reduced war-inflated railroad income with corporation losses ($76-million) due to reorganization of the railroad company. Fortunately for the railroad company this suit was decided against the corporation in 1949, though it continued litigation for the next few years.

Having disentangled itself from the vicissitudes of finance, the WP continued its program of signalling (completed in 1952), centralized traffic control (completed in 1953) and motive power conversion (last regular steam operation, 1954). In the 10-year period, 1946-1955, the WP spent $47-million for new locomotives and cars, and

The earliest component of the WP was the Alameda & San Joaquin railroad, which was acquired before any WP track *was laid. With that short-line came two new 4-6-0's the WP's first motive power, renumbered 121 and 122.*

On August 22, 1910, the Western Pacific Railway's first passenger train from Salt Lake City, Utah, arrived in *Oakland, California, pulled by 4-6-0 Number 94—and was greeted by an enthusiastic crowd.*

$32-million for track improvements, part of which was spent for a new tunnel in Feather River Canyon to bypass an area susceptible to severe flood damage.

But the calm lasted for but a decade; nation-wide merger fever attacked the WP in 1960 when four Western railroads, acting through subsidiary companies, acquired half of the WP's outstanding stock. Southern Pacific bought 10-percent; Great Northern, 10-percent; Atchison, Topeka & Santa Fe, 20-percent; Union Pacific, 10-percent. SP, backed by UP, applied to the ICC for permission to purchase all WP stock, and as could be anticipated the AT&SF, supported by GN, asked for the same thing. ICC hearings were conducted during 1961, but the decision was not immediately forthcoming. In 1963 an ICC examiner recommended that the SP acquire the WP, suggesting a basis for the acquisition. Believing this basis to be unfair to its stockholders, WP management promptly protested the recommendation, and demanded an evaluation of WP property if the ICC ordered the acquisition. Two years later the ICC ruled that the WP should remain independent, and the AT&SF, thereupon, disposed of its WP stock; the other roads, however, retained their interests. (The AT&SF; Chicago, Burlington & Quincy; and Union Pacific railroads bought substancial quantities of D&RGW stock in 1961, thus establishing a measure of "remote control" over the WP and D&RGW railroads.)

Despite opposite views regarding WP ownership by the SP, the two railroads negotiated an arrangement in 1963 permitting the SP to operate over the WP between Flanigan, Nevada, and Winnemucca, Nevada, thus shortening the SP's route between Ogden, Utah, and northern California via its Alturas line. Also in 1963 a dam was built across the Feather River a few miles east of Oroville, California. Its impounded water would have inundated several miles or WP track; consequently, the constructors built a 23-mile permanent relocation around the site for the WP.

During the 1960-decade the WP had nearly doubled its GTM/TH to 114,000, and two-thirds of its freight tonnage was received from connecting railroads. Yet, operational deficits were incurred in 1969 and 1970, despite the discontinuance of all passenger service in the latter year. A new management felt that industrial diversification would be beneficial; consequently, at the end of 1971 a new company, Western Pacific Industries, acquired the railroad by means of a stock exchange. Afterward, WPI was owned 10-percent each by corporate subsidiaries of the SP, UP and Burlington Northern (which had acquired the GN's stock in a merger). In turn, the WP owned the Sacramento Northern railroad outright, and half of the Alameda Belt Line and Oakland Terminal railroads, the other half being owned by the AT&SF. Together with the AT&SF and SP, it shared equally in the ownership of the Central California Traction Company.

At the time of this writing, despite fractional ownership of the WP and D&RGW companies by other railroad corporations, the two railroads are unrelated otherwise. Hence, the account of the WP will be concluded at this point.

WESTERN PACIFIC MOTIVE POWER

1903

121	4-6-0	Richmond	1896		TF 17
Ex-Alameda & San Joaquin 1					
122	4-6-0	Richmond	1896		TF 17
Ex-Alameda & San Joaquin 2					

1905

34	4-6-0	Leased from RGW			
121, 122, 124, 128, 149					
	2-8-0	Leased from RGW			
532	4-6-0	Leased from D&RG			

1906

1-20	2-8-0	Baldwin	1906		C 43

1908

71-85	4-6-0	American	1908		TP 29
Ordered as D&RG 745-759					

1909

86-106	4-6-0	American	1909		TP 29
21-65	2-8-0	American	1909		C 43
151-162	0-6-0	American	1909		S 31
Ordered as D&RG 844-855					

1910

507	4-6-0	Leased from D&RG			

1914

661	2-8-0	Leased from D&RG			
668	2-8-0	Leased from D&RG			
714	4-6-0	Leased from D&RG			

1916

123	2-6-0	Baldwin	1876		EF 14
Ex-Boca & Loyalton 4					
124	2-8-0	Baldwin	1882		C 23
Ex-Boca & Loyalton 5					
125	2-8-0	Pittsburgh	1888		TF 21
Ex-Boca & Loyalton 7					

1917

126	4-6-0	New York	1891		TF 18
Ex-D&RG 546					
127	4-6-0	New York	1891	TF 19	
Ex-D&RG 549					
201-205	2-6-6-2	American	1917		M 80

1918

301-305	2-8-2	American	1918		MK 60

1919

321-325	2-8-0	Baldwin	1918		MK 55

1920

306-310	2-8-2	American	1919		MK 60
Ex-Elgin, Joliet & Eastern 802-806					

Although the Western Pacific was 150 miles longer than its immediate competitor, the Central Pacific (later Southern *Pacific), it crossed the Sierra Nevada range in California at an altitude 2000-feet lower and maintained a one-percent*

1922

| 311-315 | 2-8-2 | American | 1921 | MK 60 |

1923

| 316-321 | 2-8-2 | American | 1923 | MK 60 |

1924

| 322-326 | 2-8-2 | American | 1924 | MK 60 |
| 206-210 | 2-6-6-2 | American | 1924 | M 80 |

1926

| 327-331 | 2-8-2 | American | 1926 | MK 60 |

1927

| 163 | 0-6-0 | American | 1915 | S 34 |

Ex-United Verdi Copper 3

| 164-166 | 0-6-0 | American | 1919 | S 34 |

Ex-United Verdi Copper 86-88

1929

| 332-336 | 2-8-2 | American | 1929 | MK 60 |

1931

| 251-256 | 2-8-8-2 | Baldwin | 1931 | M 137 |

1936

| 171-180 | 4-8-2 | American | 1924 | MT 44 |

Ex-Florida East Coast 403-408, 410, 412, 414, 415

1938

| 257-260 | 2-8-8-2 | Baldwin | 1938 | M 137 |
| 401-407 | 4-6-6-4 | American | 1938 | M 100 |

1939

| 501-503 | B-B | General Motors SW 1 | 1939 | S 50 |

1941

| 901-903 | 4 (B-B) | General Motors FT | 1941 | D 225 |

1942

| 504-511 | B-B | American S 1 | 1942 | S 50 |

274

gradient. A circular loop was required west of Spring Garden Tunnel to circumvent a short stretch of three-percent grade, *which was an extension of the temporary track surmounting the ridge above the tunnel.*

1943

481-486	4-8-4	Lima	1943	GS 64
551-558	B-B	American S 2	1943	S 57
904-906	4 (B-B)	General Motors FT	1943	D 225

1944

| 907-912 | 4 (B-B) | General Motors FT | 1944 | D 225 |

1945

| 581-585 | B-B | Baldwin VO 1000 | 1945 | S 60 |

1947

| 801-803 | 3 (B-B) | General Motors F 3 | 1947 | D 176 |

1950

559-562	B-B	American S 2	1950	S 57
804-805	3 (B-B)	General Motors FP 7	1950	D 176
913-921	4 (B-B)	General Motors F 7	1950	D 239

1951

| 563-564 | B-B | American S 4 | 1951 | S 57 |
| 922-924 | 4 (B-B) | General Motors F 7 | 1951 | D 238 |

1952

| 601-606 | B-B | General Motors SW 9 | 1952 | S 62 |
| 701-709 | B-B | General Motors GP 7 | 1952 | RS 62 |

1953

| 710-713 | B-B | General Motors GP 7 | 1953 | RS 62 |

1955

| 725-732 | B-B | General Motors GP 9 | 1955 | RS 62 |

1959

| 2001-2006 | B-B | General Motors | GP 20 | 1959 | RS 64 |

1960

| 2007-2010 | B-B | General Motors | GP 20 | 1960 | RS 64 |

1963

| 3001-3010 | B-B | General Motors | GP 35 | 1963 | RS 65 |

1964

| 3011-3012 | B-B | General Motors | GP 35 | 1964 | RS 65 |

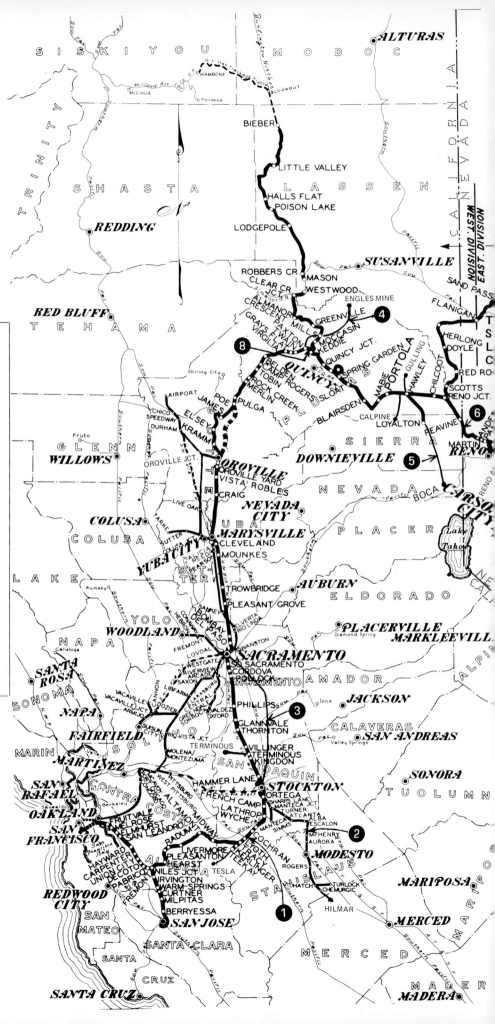

WESTERN PACIFIC SYSTEM MAP

MAP LEGEND

— **WESTERN PACIFIC**

— SACRAMENTO NORTHERN

— NORTHERN ELECTRIC
   SN lines north of Sacramento

— SAN FRANCISCO - SACRAMENTO
   SN lines south of Sacramento

1 ALAMEDA & SAN JOAQUIN
   Tesla to Stockton

2 TIDEWATER SOUTHERN
   Stockton to Hilmar

3 CENTRAL CALIFORNIA TRACTION
   Sacramento to Stockton

4 INDIAN VALLEY
   Paxton to Engles Mine

5 BOCA & LOYALTON
   Gulling to Boca
   Hawley to Portola

6 NEVADA - CALIFORNIA - OREGON
   Reno Jct. to Reno

7 DEEP CREEK
   Wendover to Gold Hill

8 LAST SPIKE DRIVEN HERE

276

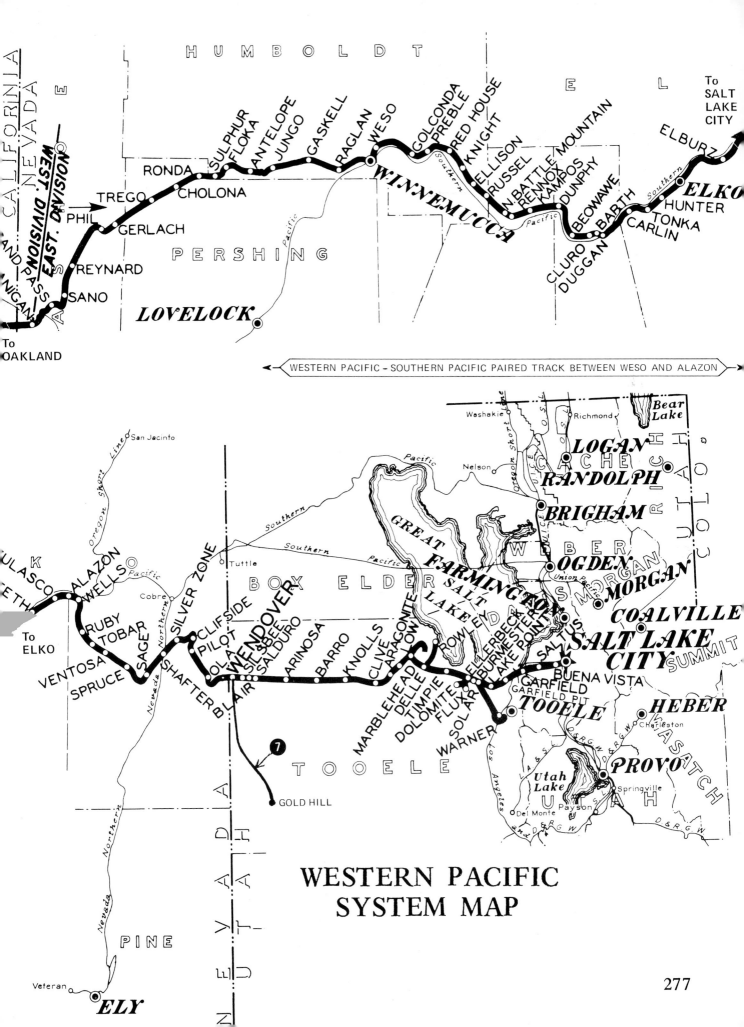

WESTERN PACIFIC
SYSTEM MAP

277

1965

3013-3022 B-B General Motors GP 35 1965 RS 65

1966

3501-3510 B-B General Motors GP 40 1966 RS 68

1967

607 B-B General Motors NW 2 1939 S 62
Ex-Stockton Terminal & Eastern 1000

608 B-B General Motors NW 2 1940 S 62
Ex-Stockton Terminal & Eastern 1001

751-755 B-B General Electric U 30B 1967 RS 70

801 D B-B General Motors F 3 1948 D 62
Leased from Sacramento Northern

806 B Renumbered from 920 B

3511-3516 B-B General Motors GP 40 1968 RS 68

1968

756-759 B-B General Electric U 30B 1968 RS 70
925 A, 925 D Renumbered from 801 A, 802 A

926 A Renumbered from 801 D

1969

554 B-B American S 2 1948 S 57
Ex-Tidewater Southern 744

760-769 B-B General Electric U 30B 1969 RS 70

1970

552 B-B American S 2 1949 S 57
Ex-Tidewater Southern 745

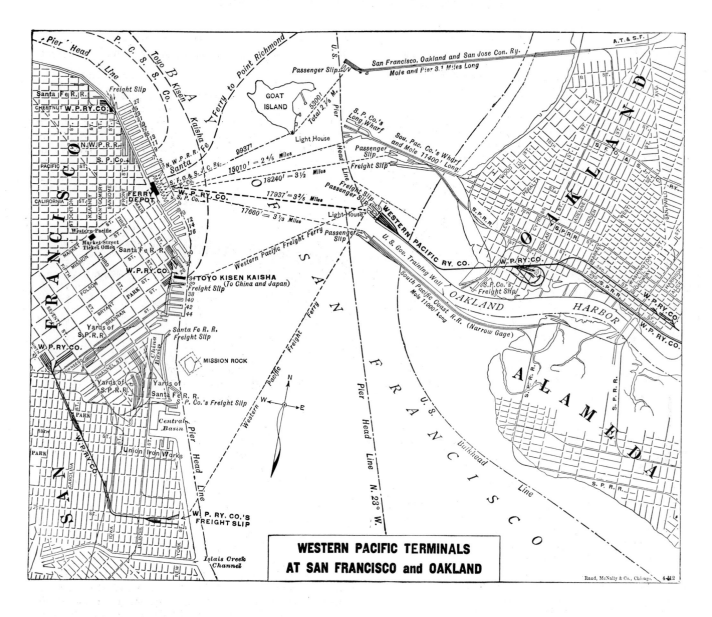

Western Pacific's terminals in the San Francisco Bay Area— *taken from the WP's public time-table of November, 1912.*

SECTION TWELVE

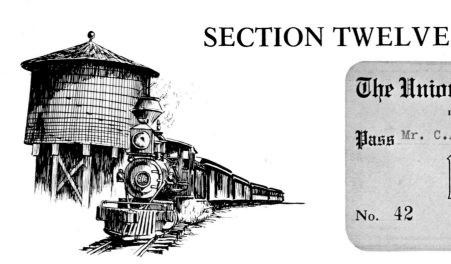

The Union Depot and Ry. Co.

DENVER, COLORADO

Pass Mr. C.A.Chisholm & Party

1914

No. 42

SUPERINTENDENT

Associated Railroads

Various members of the Rio Grande system were involved in operational associations with other railroads, principally the usage of their rails under trackage-rights agreements, most of which are still in effect.

AMERICAN SMELTING & REFINING CO.

Formed in 1899, this company was a consolidation of several smelters and associated facilities in Colorado and elsewhere, including a coal mine at Bon Carbo and a coke works at Cokedale, both located west of Trinidad, Colorado. In 1920 AS&R leased a D&RG locomotive and a few passenger cars to carry miners over its own track between the coke plant and coal mine. This arrangement lasted until 1929 when the coke works was closed, the D&RGW acquiring about a mile of AS&R track through Cokedale at that time, though it did not acquire the track to the mine over which it had operated freight trains between 1917 and 1950.

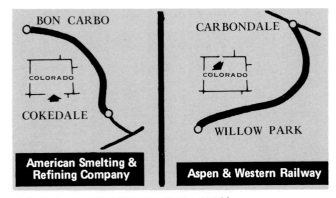

ASPEN & WESTERN RAILWAY

During 1888 the D&RG built the A&W, a subsidiary of the Colorado Coal & Iron Company, from Carbondale, Colorado, to coal mines at Willow Park, Colorado. The D&RG operated the narrow-gauge line with its own locomotives under contract for just one year, much of the track being heavily damaged by a cloudburst in 1889, after which operations were discontinued permanently.

ASSOCIATED RAILROADS

This company, owned by the AT&SF, CB&Q, CRI&P,

C&S, and D&RGW railroads, was organized in 1953 to acquire the Denver & Intermountain trackage between lower Denver and the Denver Federal Center. Following three years of C&S operation (for AT&SF, CB&Q, C&S), the D&RGW operated the line (for CRI&P, D&RGW) for two years, each operating company alternately using its own equipment. After the flood of 1965, which took out the bridge across the South Platte River in Denver, the D&RGW ran over the C&S West Side line to reach Associated's track.

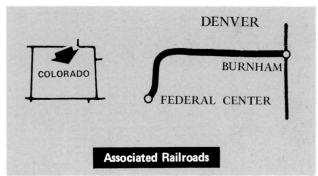

ATCHISON, TOPEKA & SANTA FE

For a few months during 1879 and 1880, the AT&SF controlled the D&RG through a lease, which was terminated after a rowdy legal fracas. In 1881 the D&RG added a standard-gauge third rail between Denver and Pueblo, primarily to enable the AT&SF to operate its trains into Denver. This situation was terminated in 1887 when the AT&SF built its own track paralleling the D&RG. In 1906 the D&RG built a short piece of track from Longsdale, Colorado, to a coke plant at Cokedale, Colorado, and operated over the AT&SF from Trinidad, Colorado, to Jansen, Colorado, thence over the Colorado & Wyoming to Longsdale. Though operations over the C&W were discontinued in 1950, the D&RGW still uses the AT&SF track to handle coal originating on the C&W. During 1918 the AT&SF and D&RG installed connections at four points along the route between Denver and Pueblo

279

Remains of the ill-fated Aspen & Western Railway—despite the ravages of floods and severe weather—are in remarkably good condition today, as this red sandstone bridge abutment so eloquently testify to onlookers.

where their lines crossed, permitting their use as double-track. Since 1921, when a flood destroyed AT&SF track between Clelland, Colorado, and Pueblo, its trains have operated over D&RGW rails to reach coal mines south of Cañon City.

BALLARD & THOMPSON RAILROAD

This railroad between Thompson, Utah, and Sego, Utah, was built and owned by coal-mining companies, though operated by the D&RG with its own locomotives under contract from 1913 to 1950 when the line was abandoned.

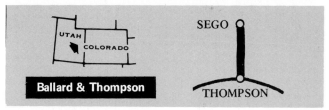

BAMBERGER ELECTRIC RAILWAY

In 1958, when this electric interurban line ceased operating, the D&RGW purchased a few miles of trackage, principally that serving industries in the Salt Lake City and Ogden areas.

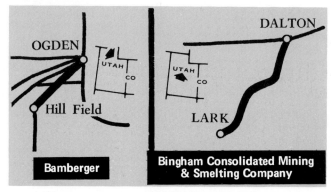

BINGHAM CONSOLIDATED MINING & SMELTING COMPANY

To serve its giant copper mine and mill at Lark, Utah, this company built a line from Dalton, Utah, on the RGW in 1901. After being operated by the RGW with its own locomotives for another two years, the track was purchased by the Rio Grande Western.

Operated alternately by the Colorado & Southern and the Denver & Rio Grande Western, over former Denver & Intermountain electric interurban track, Associated Railroads *serves local industries and the sprawling Federal Center, west of Denver. This scene, near the end of the line, looks eastward toward the central business district.*

OTTO PERRY

In this smoky portrait—taken just south of Castle Rock— D&RGW 2-8-0 Number 1162 and Chicago, Burlington & Quincy 2-8-2 Number 4999 combine their efforts to haul a Colorado & Southern freight train on Atchison, Topeka & Santa Fe rails up the hill to Palmer Lake.

The Boston Coal & Fuel's only engine, Number 1, had been built as D&RG Number 80 and had carried that same number on the D&RGW and RGW before having become RGS 35. Later, it was Calumet Fuel engine 1, and when it was returned to the RGS, it became that railroad's second Number 1.

VEST DAY COLLECTION

281

Hidden among the buildings and underbrush was the balloon loop of the Calumet Fuel Company's railroad at its coal

mine adit atop Perin's Peak—visible from Durango, only five miles distant. This railroad connected with the RGS.

BOSTON COAL & FUEL COMPANY

Constructed in 1901, the BC&F company's railroad extended from Franklin Junction on the Rio Grande Southern to a coal mine at Perin's Peak. The company purchased RGS 2-8-0 Number 35, and renumbered it 1. In 1906 the Boston financiers sold the company to the Utah Fuel Company, a subsidiary of the Rio Grande Western; thereafter it was known as the Calumet Fuel Company.

CALUMET FUEL COMPANY

This was a subsidiary of the Utah Fuel Company (owned by the Rio Grande Western) which had taken over the Boston Coal & Fuel Company's railroad and coal mine west of Durango. It leased the railroad to the Rio Grande Southern for operation, and transferred the BC&F's engine to the RGS, which numbered it (second) 1. After 1913, when this engine was dismantled, the RGS used its own motive power until operations were discontinued in 1926.

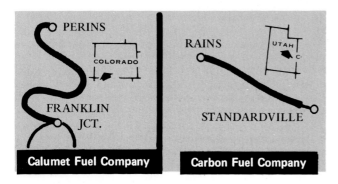

CARBON FUEL COMPANY

An extension of the Spring Canyon Branch, from Standardville, Utah, to Rains, Utah, was purchased from this coal mining company in 1914.

CASTLE VALLEY RAILROAD

Castle Valley Railroad trackage consisted of a few miles of line between Castle Junction, and coal mines at Mohrland, Utah, and a main-line — owned jointly with the Southern Utah railroad — from the junction to Price on the D&RG. Upon completion in 1913, the railroad was leased to the D&RG which operated it with CV motive power. This arrangement was terminated in 1917, when the Utah Railway absorbed the CV, and discontinued operations over the joint track.

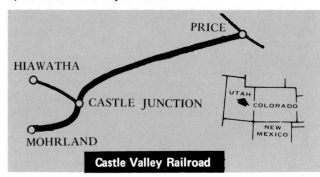

COLORADO MIDLAND RAILWAY

The CM completed a standard-gauge line from Colorado Springs to Leadville, Aspen and New Castle by the end of 1888. Although independent at first, it became part of the AT&SF system in early 1891. During 1890 the Rio Grande Junction railroad was constructed between Rifle Creek and Grand Junction, where a connection was made with the standard-gauge Rio Grande Western railroad. This company was owned equally by the D&RG and CM, and gave the AT&SF access to Salt Lake City and Ogden, and the D&RG a new (standard-gauge) line between Denver and Utah. Both the AT&SF and CM failed financially in 1894, the CM having been reorganized in 1897 free from AT&SF control. In 1900 the D&RG and Colorado &

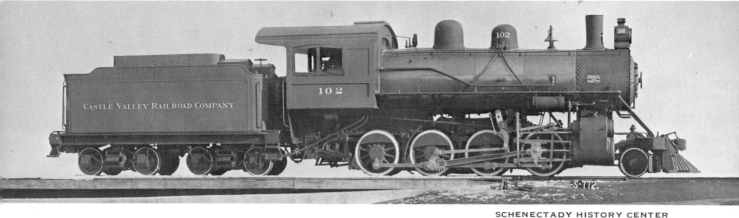

SCHENECTADY HISTORY CENTER

The Castle Valley owned only three locomotives, which were operated by D&RG crews under a contract arrange-

ment until the short-line became a part of the Utah Railway in 1917.

GLENWOOD SPRINGS

NEW CASTLE

SPRING GULCH

ASPEN

LEADVILLE

UTAH

COLORADO

Colorado Midland Railway

BUENA VISTA

COLORADO SPRINGS

RICHARD KINDIG

In 1936 the D&RGW abandoned its own track between Walsenburg and Trinidad, and operated its trains over the parallel C&S track. On this occasion the 1520, a

monstrous booster-equipped 4-8-2, was photographed at Monson while returning empty cars to the coal mines.

283

The Kenilworth & Helper's track was so steep that three-truck Shays were needed to handle trains between the D&RG's main-line and the loading dock at the foot of *a two-track tramway (above the engine's cab) leading to the mine. The K&H's two locomotives were sold to logging companies in the Pacific Northwest.*

Southern railroads bought the CM railroad, which failed again in 1912. Both railroads lost their investment when the CM was reorganized in 1917, then dismantled during 1921.

COLORADO & SOUTHERN RAILWAY

The C&S and D&RG/W have been associated in various ways for a great many years, beginning in 1900 when they jointly bought the Colorado Midland. The foreclosure sale of the CM in 1917 ended this venture. In 1911 the two companies (through subsidiaries) built a new double track line between Minnequa, Colorado, and Walsenburg, Colorado, and have used it jointly since then. Also during 1911 the D&RG suspended operations between Leadville, Colorado, and Dillon, Colorado, allowing the C&S to handle all traffic. (This arrangement was concluded in 1924 when D&RG/W rails were removed.) In return for this corporate courtesy the C&S arranged for the D&RG to operate C&S branches from Gunnison to Baldwin, Colorado, and Quartz, Colorado, this trackage having been isolated by the collapse of the Alpine Tunnel. The Quartz Branch was removed in 1934, and the D&RGW was given the Baldwin Branch in 1937. In 1918, when the AT&SF and D&RG instituted paired-track operation between Denver and Pueblo, the C&S (which had an operating agreement with the AT&SF) began running its trains over D&RG/W rails between those cities. This routing continues in effect today. In 1936 the D&RGW abandoned its track south of Walsenburg, Colorado, and has been operating over C&S trackage to Trinidad, Colorado, since that time. And, finally, in 1953, the D&RGW and C&S became alternate operators of the Associated Railroads line west of Denver.

COLORADO & WYOMING RAILWAY

The C&W, owned by the CF&I Steel Corporation (formerly Colorado Fuel & Iron Corporation), owned four segments, one of which was a short branch from the C&S/D&RG main-line to a company coal mine at Hezron, Colorado. From its construction in 1903 until its removal in 1936 this branch was operated by the D&RG/W with its own engines, leasing the track from the C&W. In 1906 the D&RG built a branch from Longsdale, Colorado, to a coke plant at Cokedale, Colorado. To reach this section of otherwise isolated track, the D&RG/W operated over AT&SF rails from Trinidad to Jansen, thence over the C&W to Longsdale. This arrangement with the C&W was terminated in 1950 when the D&RGW dismantled its branch.

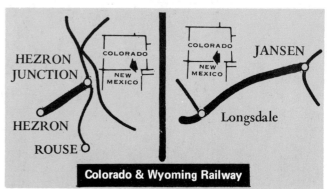

Colorado & Wyoming Railway

This contemporary panorama of Denver's Union Station reveals architectural evolution over a span of nine decades. The original wings are seen flanking the newer central structure. The umbrella-platforms and miscellaneous appendages were added at various times for handling passengers (left) and United States mail (right).

DENVER UNION TERMINAL

The D&RGW has been a part-owner of Denver's Union Station ever since its completion in 1881. The station company provides facilities for passengers and related traffic, but does no switching, that function being performed by railroads using the trackage. The station company has had three names indicating internal rearrangements in its financial structure. The above name is the third and dates from 1912.

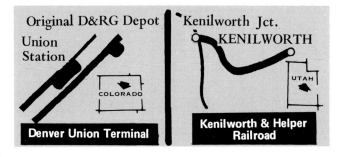

285

The west-bound "California Zephyr" of the Denver & Rio Grande Western is seen here leaving former Denver & Salt Lake track—commencing its six-mile trip on Moffat Tunnel *Improvement District trackage through the tunnel of the same name. At one time both the D&RGW and the D&SL used this famous tunnel beneath the Continental Divide.*

KENILWORTH & HELPER RAILROAD

After the K&H (owned by a coal mining company) had been built in 1911 from Independent, Utah, to the mines at Kenilworth, Utah, the railroad was operated by the company until 1914 when the D&RG began operations under a lease, using two K&H Shay locomotives. In 1926 the D&RGW built its own track to the mines, thus ending the need for the K&H.

MOFFAT TUNNEL IMPROVEMENT DISTRICT

The district, composed of areas adjacent to Denver & Salt Lake railroad trackage, was created by the Colorado State Legislature in July, 1922, to bore, own and administer the Moffat Tunnel through the Continental Divide. Begun in the fall of 1923, the tunnel was completed for traffic in early 1928 and was leased to the D&SL. Although plans were considered to use electric locomotives through the tunnel, as well as to haul automobiles and trucks

through it on flat cars, neither scheme was executed. The D&RGW began operations through the tunnel in 1934, becoming its exclusive user in 1947 when the D&SL was absorbed.

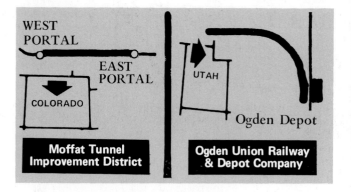

The first "Scenic Limited" passenger train lasted only three months—during the summer of 1906. Here the first eastward *consist is ready to depart from Ogden's Union Station with Rio Grande Western 4-6-0 Number 33 on the point.*

286

OGDEN UNION RAILWAY & DEPOT CO.

In 1883, when the D&RGW Railway built into Ogden, Utah, the Union Pacific tried to keep the narrow-gauge line from entering the terminal, which was owned jointly by the UP and Central Pacific. The CP, however, did not object and permitted the D&RGW to lay a track on its property. The terminal property was incorporated separately in 1888, the D&RGW paying rental since that time until 1953 when the D&RGW discontinued passenger service into Ogden.

PUEBLO & ARKANSAS VALLEY RAILROAD

The P&AV, a subsidiary of the AT&SF, built that system's initial trackage through Colorado. A subsidiary of the P&AV, the Cañon City & San Juan, graded the line between Cañon City, Colorado, and Texas Creek, Colorado, on which the P&AV laid track and constructed the famous Hanging Bridge in 1879. In 1880 the P&AV sold this line, plus graded portions as far as Leadville, Colorado, to the D&RG as a condition of settlement in the Royal Gorge-Raton Pass "war."

PUEBLO UNION DEPOT & RAILROAD CO.

The PUD & Railroad Company was organized to construct and operate a passenger terminal for the D&RG, AT&SF, CRI&P, UPD&G (later C&S) and MP railroads. The station was opened in 1890; its trackage and passenger station were severely damaged in the flood of 1921; and the CRI&P withdrew in 1925. All train movements have been handled by the individual railroads using the terminal.

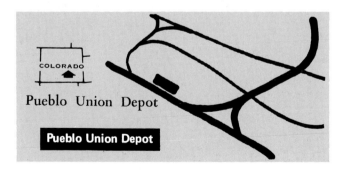

RIO GRANDE & SOUTHWESTERN

When the D&RG supplied rails and fastenings for the RG&SW in 1903 the intent was to reimburse the lumber company for its expenditures on grading and tracklaying between Lumberton, New Mexico, and El Vado, New Mexico. Operated with its own locomotives, the RG&SW was not notably prosperous, and although the D&RG acquired a controlling quantity of stock, the RG&SW was not merged into the D&RG system, the track being dismantled in 1923 when the lumber company moved its operations elsewhere.

The D&RGW's famous "hanging bridge"—as well as the track through the Royal Gorge of the Arkansas River—was not constructed by the D&RG, but by the Pueblo & Arkansas Valley, a subsidiary of the AT&SF. This rare photograph shows the bridge while it was being erected during 1879.

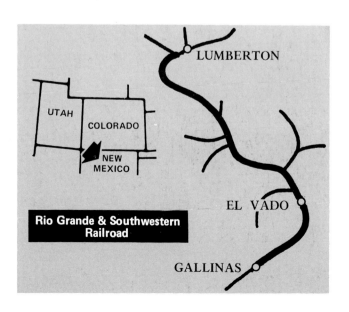

Familiar indeed is the trackside facade of Pueblo's Union Station, but its downtown aspect—virtually unknown to D&RG passengers—was a gem of 1889 architecture, its great tower resembling those of depots in Chicago and St. Louis.

SALT LAKE CITY UNION DEPOT

The building of the Western Pacific required a new passenger depot for that railroad and the D&RG in Salt Lake City. A separate company, the Salt Lake City Union Depot & Railroad (incorporated in Utah, May, 1907) owned 50½-percent by the D&RG and 49½-percent by the WP, was organized for this purpose. The station was opened in 1910 when the WP began passenger operation. In subsequent years, although both D&RGW and WP experienced a multitude of financial reorganizations and control, their ownership has remained undisturbed. All switching was performed by the D&RGW for both railroads.

SALT LAKE & UTAH RAILROAD

When the SL&U electric interurban ceased operating in 1946 the D&RGW purchased its trackage between Provo, Utah, and Orem, Utah.

SOUTHERN UTAH RAILROAD

Southern Utah Railroad trackage consisted of a few miles of line between Castle Valley Junction and coal mines at Hiawatha, Utah, and a main-line—owned jointly with the Castle Valley Railroad—from the junction to Price on the D&RG. Upon completion in 1910, the railroad was leased to the D&RG which operated it with SU motive power. This arrangement was terminated in 1915, when the SU commenced its own operation. The Utah Railway absorbed the SU in 1919 and dismantled the joint track.

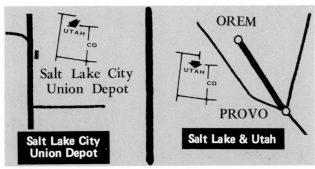

The official opening of the Salt Lake City Union Depot in August of 1910 coincided with the departure of the Western Pacific's first passenger train destined for the Pacific shores. The trains in this picture are Denver & Rio Grande locals headed for Park City, Bingham and Marysvale, towns located on branch lines in Utah.

SPRING CANYON COAL COMPANY

During 1913 this company arranged with the D&RG for the construction of a branch from a junction near Helper, Utah, to coal mines at Storrs, Utah. The D&RGW purchased this trackage in 1913, and with it obtained the new Baldwin 2-8-0 which the coal company had ordered.

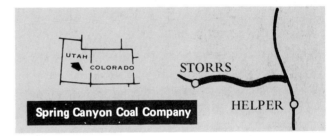

The coal mines in Spring Canyon were served by two railroads. Utah Railway track is seen at the lower left, and the former Spring Canyon Coal Company's rails are across the canyon at the far left.

The D&RG's original main-line is in the foreground of this view, while the cars are standing on the three-rail track of the Colorado Central (narrow-gauge) and Union Pacific (standard-gauge) railroads. The six-track yard serving Denver's Union Station was situated behind the building.

STANDARD COAL COMPANY

This company paid for an extension of the branch from Storrs, Utah, to its own mines at Standardville, Utah, built during 1914. The D&RG acquired this track immediately upon completion.

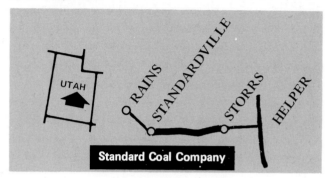

TIERRA AMARILLA SOUTHERN RAILROAD

In 1892 the D&RG laid track from the end of the Chama lumber spur to Brazos , thence to Tierra Amarilla in 1896, for the use of lumber companies. By 1902 it had acquired the line, but dismantled it a year later, using the rail and fastenings for the Rio Grande & Southwestern railroad.

The Utah Railway was comprised of two segments—con- nected by Denver & Rio Grande track between Castle Gate

and Thistle. This pair of rare photographs portrays a west- bound Utah coal train approaching the crest of Soldier

290

This panoramic view of Denver Union Station was photographed after the fire of 1893. It shows the yard enlarged to 11 three-rail tracks, the new depot tower and the new canopy along the entire southwest face of the structure.

Summit. The locomotive on the head-end is a 2-10-2, while a compound 2-8-8-2, cut into the train toward the rear, was both pushing and pulling. The big articulated locomotive remained in the trains in both directions over the hill.

291

RICHARD KINDID

Between Provo and Thistle the Denver & Rio Grande Western and Utah railroads shared each other's tracks. In this photograph taken at Castilla, Number 1403, a 2-10-2, was headed eastward upgrade on the Utah Railway's track.

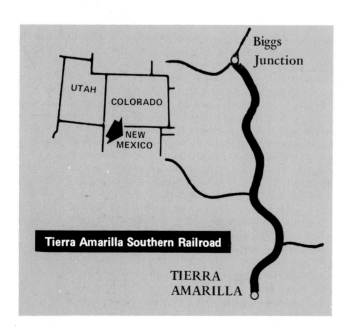

Tierra Amarilla Southern Railroad

UNION DEPOT & RAILROAD

Denver's Union Station was erected during 1880-1881 to replace the individual depots of the railroads serving Denver — Colorado Central; Denver Pacific; Denver & Rio Grande; Denver, South Park & Pacific; Kansas Pacific — although the Union Pacific, which had absorbed the DP and KP in 1880, initiated the project and advanced most of the money to construct it. The formation of the Colorado & Southern railroad in 1899 required a rearrangement of ownership in the station company; accordingly, it was reorganized and renamed Union Depot & Railway in that same year.

UNION DEPOT & RAILWAY

This company was little more than a financial successor in 1899 to the previous company of similar name, the D&RG maintaining its nominal 20-percent interest in both companies. Part of the structure was razed and rebuilt, and the depot trackage was entirely relaid during 1912-1914. This work, combined with a change in railroad ownership, produced another financial reorganization in 1912, the succeeding company being named Denver Union Terminal.

UTAH RAILWAY

During 1914 the Utah Railway built a track adjacent to that of the D&RG between Provo and Thistle, Utah, and from Castle Gate to Castle Junction — arranging for the D&RG to operate trains with its own locomotives. This operation was concluded in 1917 when the Utah commenced operation, using D&RG track between Castle Gate and Thistle. In exchange, the D&RG ran over Utah Railway track between Provo and Thistle, under an agreement which is still in effect.

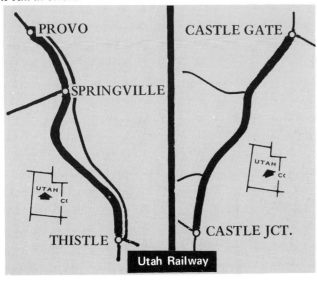

VICTOR COAL & COKE COMPANY

This coal-mining company owned yard trackage between Pictou, Colorado, and Maitland, Colorado, constructed in 1896. The D&RG bought that trackage in the same year.

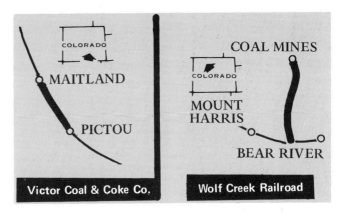

WOLF CREEK RAILROAD

Although the Wolf Creek Railroad (incorporated in Colorado, May, 1915) had intended to reach coal mines several miles north of Mount Harris, Colorado, its track extended only a couple of miles to much closer mines. The D&SL and its successor, the D&RGW, used this trackage as a mine spur, discontinuing that usage in 1951 when the last mine ceased production.

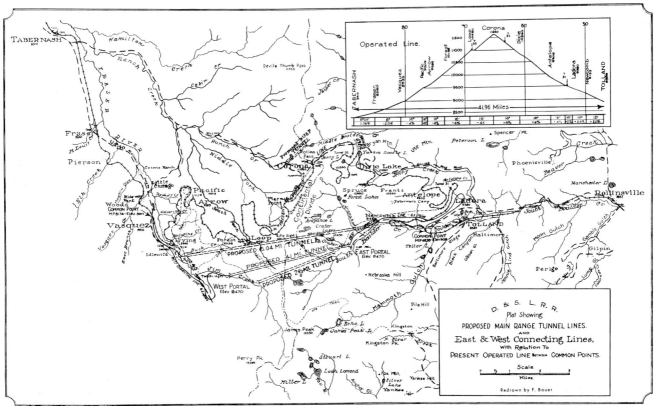

The above map from the book, "The Moffat Road," by Edward T. Bollinger and Frederick Bauer, shows the proposed routes for the "Main Range Tunnel"—which came to be known as Moffat Tunnel. This six-mile tunnel beneath the Continental Divide eliminated 25 miles of track on both flanks of 11,660-foot Rollins Pass, highest point attained by an ordinary standard-gauge railroad in North America.

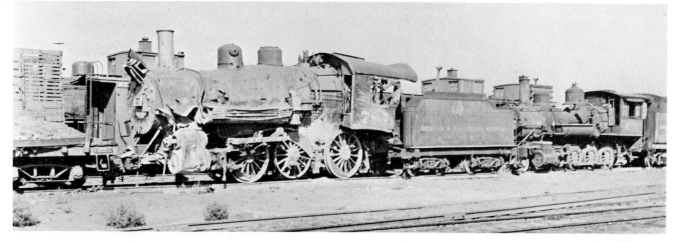

DON E. A. ROGERS

The appearance of 4-6-0 Number 787 at Grand Junction in 1935 reflected the general condition of the railroad at that critical time. Its pilot truck was missing; its main and connecting rods had been removed. Nearly all of its valve motion had been taken, and even the tire from its main driving-wheel had been appropriated for use on some sister engine.

Draws—which shifted the narrow-gauge inside rail from one side to the other in three-rail track—were required in Denver Union Station, where the D&RG's three-rail track differed from that used in the Station's trackage. Draws were also needed in three-rail wyes, like this one at Alamosa.

STANLEY McGUIRE

Idler cars, riding on standard-gauge trucks and having offset couplers, enabled narrow-gauge locomotives to handle cars of the wider gauge on three-rail track, as seen here at Montrose.

ROSS GRENARD

SECTION THIRTEEN

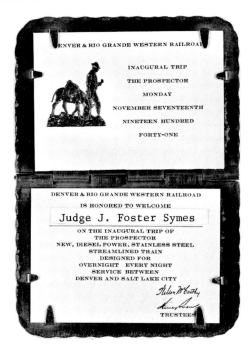
Curiosity Salon

In a work of this magnitude, a great many worthy pictures of possible interest to the readers become available—showing locomotives, cars, trains and trackage—yet they do not fit logically within the established structure of the book. Rather than reject them, the author and publisher have grouped them in this special section for the enjoyment of the readers. If no other description applies to the subject matter of these photographs, at least they can be classified as unusual or little-known to the ordinary railfan.

STANLEY MCGUIRE

The 319 and its freight train, specially painted and lettered "D&RG," did not last very long. A head-on collision, staged in Animas Canyon for a motion picture, ended the career of this assemblage.

There was nothing unusual in having narrow-gauge engines haul standard-gauge freight cars between Alamosa and Antonito, but a standard-gauge freight locomotive at the head of a narrow-gauge passenger train was most uncommon.

One cannot always believe what has been recorded in photographs. Even though the front number-plate bears a numeral "1," mechanical details reveal that this 2-4-0 was actually Number "4" temporarily renumbered for pay-car service.

The 1104 and 731 were so forcefully interlocked in a head-on collision that they could not be separated, and were hauled to the Burnham shops, still locked together, after their pilot trucks had been removed.

The severe snowstorms of early 1949, which blocked the Union Pacific's main-line, caused the diversion of much of its freight traffic over the D&RGW via Tennessee Pass. The UP lent four of its 4-6-6-4's to help trains up the three-percent grade on the west side of the hill. En route back to Denver, the 3986 and 3944 were taking water at Colorado Springs.

When the D&RGW commenced operating the electrified line of the former D&IM interurban route through the suburban area west of Denver, switcher 100 was equipped with a trolley pole to actuate the grade-crossing signals.

GEORGE TROUT

Doubleheaded 3600's were not common, but in 1950 the 3613 helped the 3606 to haul a long drag from Denver to Pueblo. Both tenders were filled with water at Sedalia before starting the arduous climb to Palmer Lake. After that ascent it was downhill for the remaining 70 miles into Pueblo's yard.

There was a short segment of four-rail track on the spur into the tie plant at Salida. The rails were standard gauge, three-foot narrow gauge, and 20-inch narrow-gauge for the tie plant's own railroad.

HERBERT O'HANLON

Duluth, Missabe & Iron Range Number 225 was one of eight 2-8-8-4's leased by the D&RGW during the winter of 1942 - 1943. Weighing 30,000 pounds more than the D&RGW's 2-8-8-2's, they were the heaviest steam locomotives operated by the railroad.

Despite the obvious evidence, this is not the famous locomotive which pulled the Central Pacific train to Promontory Summit on May 10, 1869. It is D&RGW 2-8-0 Number 315, all decorated and spuriously inscribed for a motion picture.

299

After the merger of the D&SL into the D&RGW in 1947, their 10 2-8-2's worked out of Denver in local freight service, but one of them—D&RGW 1222 (ex-D&SL 402)— was given a huge tender which had been removed from an ex-N&W 2-8-8-2. This locomotive was used for branch-line duties at Salt Lake City where this photo was taken.

The first special passenger train to leave Denver for the opening of the Dotsero Cutoff was the Burlington's "Pioneer Zephyr." While heading west, CB&Q Zephyr Number 9900 paused momentarily in the depths of Gore Canyon beside the roaring Colorado River. The date was June 16, 1934 — and the Zephyr was only a short time away from her 11:58 a.m. arrival at Orestod, the only one of four "specials" to arrive on time. This train was the first diesel-electric streamliner to travel on the D&SL.

Despite the extremely low winter temperatures and long-lasting snow-cover in Colorado's mountainous regions, the Denver & Rio Grande Western's steam locomotives had open cabs, equipped with only canvas curtains to keep out the frigid elements. One 2-8-8-2 — Number 3604 — was given an enclosed all-weather cab, a feature which was later incorporated into the railroad's 4-8-4's and 4-6-6-4's, the only new locomotives having that important component for the comfort of engine crews.

To escape the canyon of the Colorado River, the rails of the D&SL climbed a tortuous alignment along Rock and Egeria creeks—the grade being held to two-percent by strategems like this spectacular double-horseshoe curve near Crater.

This long consist—headed for Craig—was pulled by five B-B diesel-electrics, a pair of GM GP30 units separated by a trio of GP35's.

During 1927 the twisting alignment of the D&RGW's main-
line along the Arkansas River between Buena Vista and
Granite was reconstructed to eliminate the severe curvature
which restricted train speeds. Excavated rock was hauled

away by work trains such as this one, composed of flat cars
carrying small dump cars in an early version of piggy-back
operations.

303

The Denver & Rio Grande Western did not have a narrow-gauge 2-8-2 numbered "7." This locomotive—bearing that number—was actually the 476, temporarily altered for a motion picture session.

The usual technique for plowing out a snowslide in the canyon of the Rio de Las Animas was to use two locomotives—the first one, 2-8-2 Number 453 (uncoupled from the train), doing the plowing. If it became derailed the second engine—2-8-2 Number 463—could pull it back onto the rails.

Corporate Control

A corporation is owned by its stockholders, who control its destiny through an elected Board of Directors and a group of management officials. Bondholders lend their own money to the corporation, and ordinarily have no direct influence on policy. If a corporation prospers, the stockholders receive a return (dividends) on their invested capital, but if it fails they frequently lose their entire investment and the bondholders take possession of the corporate property. In the subsequent financial reorganization bondholders in the "old" corporation usually become stockholders in the "new" one. In theory, this was the manner in which corporate enterprises were guided, but all too often this was not the way events actually transpired. The whole corporate edifice of today's D&RGW railroad furnishes an excellent example of this latter consideration.

In the very beginning, William J. Palmer and his business associates exercised effective control of the D&RG, frequently disregarding the stockholders who were English, Dutch and German investors. This managemental control, with only minor interruptions, lasted from 1870 to 1883, when Palmer left the D&RG and devoted his attention wholly to the D&RGW Railway, which also was controlled primarily by its management.

For a short interval during 1879 and 1880 Jay Gould obtained personal control of the D&RG by purchasing its stock, but withdrew when he turned his financial scheming in the direction of the Missouri Pacific railroad.

During this same period the D&RG had been leased to the Atchison, Topeka & Santa Fé, which had its own ideas concerning the smaller railroad. The result was a three-way conflict among Palmer, the AT&SF, and Gould. Gould dictated a peace which left Palmer in sole control of the D&RG.

The 1890-decade was characterized by stockholder-management control by eastern investors. This combination did as little as possible, although it did succeed in avoiding the financial failure which overwhelmed the Union Pacific, AT&SF, and many other railroads in the nation.

Beginning in 1890 the Missouri Pacific railroad began to buy D&RG stock, which by 1900 gave it working control over both the D&RG and the Rio Grande Western, because the D&RG had bought the RGW's stock. The MP belonged to the Gould family: Jay, his four sons (George, Frank, Edwin, Howard) and two daughters (Helen and Anna). They owned enough stock to exercise control of the railroad's management, and participated in it themselves, led by George after Jay's death in 1892. Jay's ambitions extended little beyond the accumulation of money derived from the financial manipulation of railroad corporations, but George entertained visions of assembling a coast-to-coast network with the MP as its cornerstone. After obtaining control of the D&RG and RGW, plus half of the Colorado Midland, George anticipated the construction of a cutoff across central Utah toward a connection with the eastward-building San Pedro, Los Angeles & Salt Lake railroad. The UP blocked this gambit by adding the SPLA&SL to its system, and forced Gould to build his own railroad (Western Pacific) to the Pacific Coast.

After the WP was completed it was controlled by the D&RG (which had been consolidated with the RGW in 1908) by ownership of all stock. The stock was without value otherwise, because the D&RG had not paid anything for it, contributions from the D&RG's treasury having been in the form of WP second-mortgage bonds—for construction—and promissory notes—for operating deficits. The Goulds were unable to hold their 18,000-mile system together however, and by 1914 they had disposed of their control of the MP to that railroad's bankers. Because of its D&RG stock ownership the MP continued to control the D&RG until 1918, when the D&RG went into receivership.

The D&RG was reorganized as the D&RGW in 1921, eliminating the MP-owned stock; it failed immediately, and was again reorganized in 1924. At that time the MP acquired half of the new D&RGW's stock from the Western Pacific Railroad Corporation. (This latter company, not to be confused with the Western Pacific Railroad or Western Pacific Railway companies, will be treated later in this chapter.) The MP effectively controlled the D&RGW from 1924 to 1930, when the Alleghany Corporation obtained stock-control of the MP, thus indirectly controlling the D&RGW until its financial collapse in 1935. The MP's and

WP Railroad Corporation's D&RGW stockholdings were eliminated in the 1947 reorganization of the D&RGW.

A receivership places corporate property under court control, superseding control by any other organization. A very short protective receivership came in early 1879, then another which lasted from 1879 to 1880. A financial-difficulty receivership lasted from 1884 into 1886, and another one endured from 1918 into 1921. Yet another such receivership began in mid-1922 and terminated at the end of 1924. The railroad's final financial failure in 1935 was followed by a Federal Court trusteeship which was ended with a reorganization in 1947. To prevent control of the D&RGW by outside interests, the court ordered the railroad's stock placed in escrow until 1955, thus insuring management control during that period.

Following release of the D&RGW's stock from escrow in 1955 the railroad's management remained in full control, and retained it even though subsidiaries of the AT&SF, CB&Q, and UP each bought about 10-percent of the stock (for possible use in any merger proceedings). In 1970, after an exchange of stock, control of the railroad passed entirely to Rio Grande Industries, an industrial company which engaged in other (non-railroad) businesses, including real-estate development. Thus, the railroad was in a position very much like its original one a century previous.

The most intriguing control of the D&RGW was that of the Western Pacific Railroad Corporation, formed in 1916 following the financial failure of the WP Railway Company in 1915. This was caused by the failure of the D&RG to pay WP bond-interest, as it had agreed to do when the bonds were issued originally in 1903 to provide funds for the construction of the WP. After a series of complicated financial and legal maneuvers, (details of which are given in the chronology of the D&RG 1915-1917), the D&RG lost its entire investment (about $50-million) in the WP. Moreover, it owed $38-million to the WP Railroad Corporation as a deficiency judgment when the WP was sold in the foreclosure proceedings. The WP Railroad Corporation owned all the stock ($80-million) of the new WP Railroad Company. Bondholders of the old WP Railway Company owned all $20-million of bonds in the new railroad company, and all stock ($75-million) of the WP Railroad Corporation (for which they had paid $18-million cash). The WP Railroad Corporation then began to attach the D&RG's cash deposits, security holdings, and subsidiary properties in an effort to satisfy the judgment amount. It collected more than half of the total before the D&RG was forced into receivership in 1918. This one ended in 1920 with the foreclosure sale of the D&RG railroad to the WP Railroad Corporation for only $5-million! Four days later officers of the WP Railroad Corporation and the new D&RGW Railroad Company celebrated the beginning of a new era at a gala dinner held in Denver's foremost hostelry.

Within a year the D&RGW failed, and it was sold again in 1924 to its bondholders for $18-million. Reorganized once again, it emerged owned equally by the WP Railroad Corporation and the Missouri Pacific railroad, which had bought its half-interest from the WP Railroad Corporation for $10-million. In subsequent years the MP controlled the D&RGW, while the WP Railroad Corporation exercised its control over the WP Railroad Company. After the great business depression of the early 1930's both the D&RGW and WP Railroad Company succumbed financially, and eventually the WP Railroad Corporation lost its investment in both railroads.

Having thus lost its principal assets and sources of income, the WP Railroad Corporation went into receivership in 1949, where it has since remained, although effectively defunct.

(The Western Pacific Railroad Corporation deserves much fuller treatment because of its influence on three railroads: WP, D&RGW, MP. Only a small portion of its interesting history can be given herein, however, without straying too far from the principal subject matter of this work.)

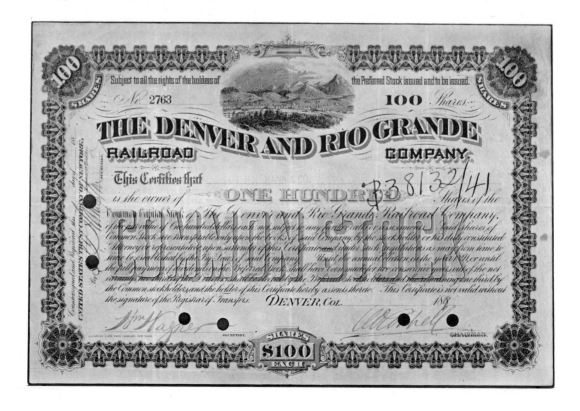

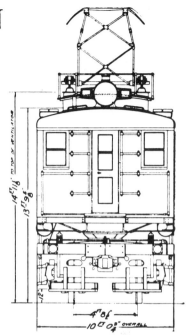

Electrification

Railroad electrification is economically advantageous wherever there is a high concentration of motive power. These are places where grades are steep, where speeds are high, where traffic is dense. Long continuous grades and nearby sources of coal favored electrification. For such reasons the railroad attracted advocates of all-electric motive power early in this century. At that time a 1000-hp B-B locomotive was considered a large machine; four decades later a 13,200-hp B-D+D-B unit was proposed. For various reasons none of the plans were adopted, and the railroad converted from steam to diesel-electric motive power. During the past quarter-century all-electric units have advanced to a B-B-B arrangement of 11,000-hp, and the railroad itself has been changing, demanding increased power from its diesel-electric units. The arguments in favor of electrification seem more compelling than ever at the moment, but there is no outward evidence to indicate that it is being considered.

Plans for electrification date back to 1907 when the D&RG, then controlled by the Missouri Pacific Railroad, was preparing for its imminent merger with the Rio Grande Western, and its Western Extension (as the Western Pacific was called) was laying track somewhere out in the vast desert west of Salt Lake City. The railroad's own engineering department, however, had been surveying a new route between Walsenburg and Minnequa, Colorado, to handle the enormous traffic from the southern Colorado coal fields. Originated by both the D&RG and the Colorado & Southern, this immense volume of high-grade bituminous coal converged upon Walsenburg for movement northward over the D&RG's original rollercoaster alignment to the Colorado Fuel & Iron Company's gigantic steel mill at Minnequa on the southern outskirts of Pueblo, with considerable tonnage going beyond to Denver. The Colorado & Southern's engineers also had surveyed a new route hugging the foothills where water was more readily available, but D&RG men favored the more direct line, shorter by about 12 miles.

Meanwhile, H. A. Goodridge, the D&RG's Electrical Engineer, had been devoting his attentions to something

considerably more exciting than just signal circuits, station lights and car batteries. Furthermore, General Manager A. C. Ridgway had not been confining his own thinking to transportation entirely in terms of coal and steam. At this early date in the very infancy of electrified railroading the D&RG was quite seriously considering what appeared to be deliberate heresy — the hauling of coal with electric, instead of coal-burning, locomotives. For a railroad which had always relied on the iron horse, this was rather unfriendly behavior!

Goodridge's report, submitted to Ridgway in early March 1907, contained a comparison of investment and operating costs for steam and electric locomotives over the proposed new line between Walsenburg and Minnequa. Twelve 85-ton freight locomotives, and two 70-ton passenger locomotives would replace 23 steam locomotives then in service on the old line. While no mention was made of the kind of system, it appears to have been single-phase AC. An annual saving of $25,000 in operating costs was predicted for electric locomotives, but this was completely overshadowed by a $37,000 yearly charge to electric operations for depreciation. Goodridge explained that the anticipated savings were not so great as those experienced by other railroads. He did not feel that the "fireman" should be eliminated; power would not be quite so cheap as reported; nor were certain minor items justified on the D&RG. The sum of these charges came to $34,000, which would have favored electrification were these savings to have been realized in actual operations. Goodridge felt unfavorable about them, and steam emerged triumphant by a $22,000 annual margin.

At the end of March Goodridge made another proposal for A. C. Ridgway. This one was for a Rio Grande Western subsidiary, known as the Copper Belt, which operated about eight miles of exceptionally steep twisting standard-gauge track out of Bingham, Utah, to open-cut copper mines along the steep hills of the valley in which Bingham was situated. Some of its grades were 8½ percent, while curvature was often as sharp as 40°. Five three-truck

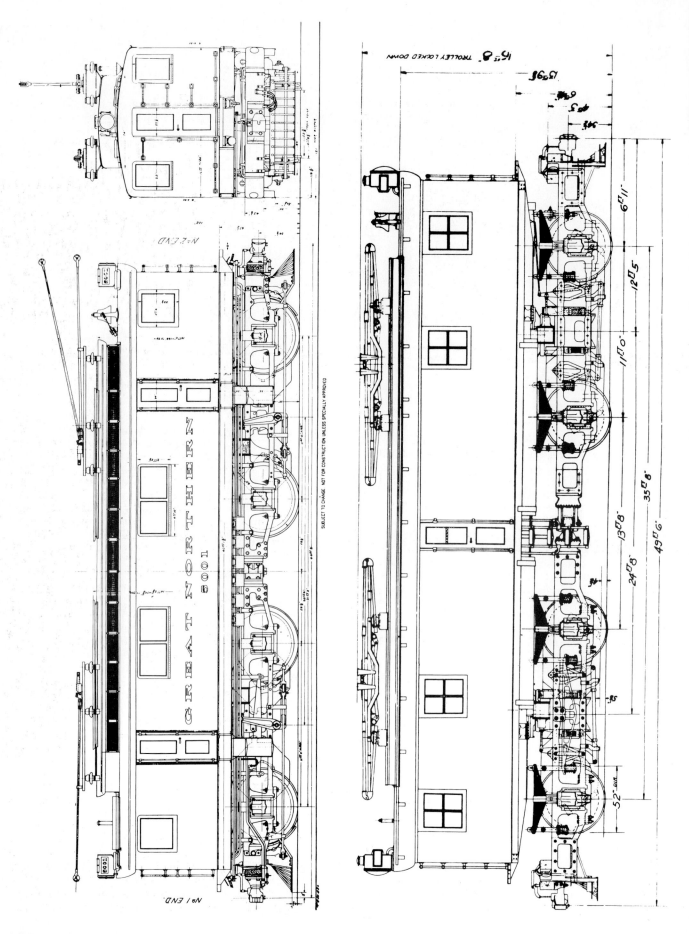

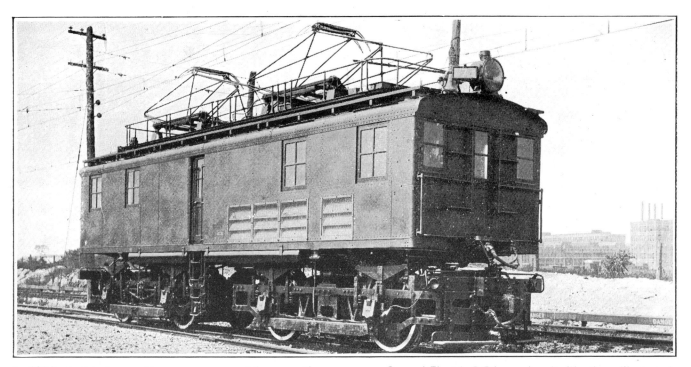

In 1926, electric locomotives were proposed for operation through the six-mile Moffat Tunnel—which became filled with smoke from Denver & Salt Lake locomotives. They were General Electric B-B box-cab units like those illustrated in the photograph above and in the drawing on the opposite page (right-hand view)—a 1000-HP locomotive.

Shays, frequently double heading, snaked cars in and out of the mine spurs, pushing one load or four empties apiece. Goodridge felt that three 55-ton DC locomotives could replace the Shays. A sub-station to convert power (purchased from the Telluride Power Company) would be needed, plus lines, feeders and track-bonding.

Here, the figures favored electric operations by a total of $10,000. In addition Goodridge pointed out the faster speed of the electrics, as well as their ability to use electric braking on the steep pitches. Top management didn't go for the idea, however, despite the 10-percent return on the additional investment. The reason does not appear to be known, but two possibilities can be advanced. The Western Pacific was consuming all available cash, or perhaps it may have been felt that the trackage involved would be relocated as the open-cut mines advanced into the hillsides, as indeed they did.

During the spring and summer of 1907 Goodridge was a busy man; he was working on another proposal: the electrification of the main line from Glenwood Springs to Tennessee Pass, his report going to C. H. Schlacks, vice-president, on August 1. The entire project involved 79 miles of railroad: 17 through precipitous Glenwood Canyon of the Grand River between Glenwood Springs and Dotsero with an average grade of 1¼-percent; 41 miles up the broad valley of the Eagle River on a 1¼-percent average grade to Minturn; and 21 miles of 3-percent average grade from Minturn to the summit of the pass. The power was to be three-phase AC, transmitted at 60,000 volts, and fed to the dual catenaries at 6600 volts per phase. (This system

All-electric locomotives—using three-phase power like those built for the Great Northern railroad's original Cascade Tunnel—were proposed for the Soldier Summit electrification project.

was like that being installed for the Great Northern's Cascade Tunnel electrification.) Goodridge was in favor of the conversion, not so much from the standpoint of regenerated power when the trains coasted downhill, but more so from the saving in brake shoes and wheels, plus increased safety in the handling of heavy trains down the steep grades.

The proposed 100-ton locomotives were to have been identical, except for their gearing. Operating speeds were estimated at 15 mph for freight service or 25 mph for passenger. The wheel-arrangement was B-B with four induction motors producing 1600 HP at the drawbar for a one-hour rating. Two speeds, 16½ and 27½ mph, were available for downgrade running. Two locomotives were to be given 750 tons of freight eastbound Glenwood Springs to Minturn, while a single one would handle a 400-ton passenger train. Operation up the grade between Minturn and Tennessee Pass was fairly simple in concept; the number of units would be doubled. Downhill westbound tonnage limits were 950 for freight and 450 for passenger runs.

The power house was to be located close to Glenwood Springs, where hydro-power from the Colorado River would be available. (Such a plant is now located at Shoshone, a few miles east of Glenwood Springs, generating power for Denver.) It was to have had three 3000 KW turbo-generators capable of handling a continuous summer load of 8000 KW. Five stations were to be located about 15 miles apart to feed the dual trolley-wires. The total cost came to $2.5-million, a substantial sum even for the Gould dynasty of railroads.

The use of electricity would have saved about $70,000 per year in direct operating costs, but when depreciation was included, steam power came out ahead by $73,000 net. However, it was suggested that if power could be purchased for $16 per horsepower per year, the $900,000 investment in a generating plant could be eliminated, and then it

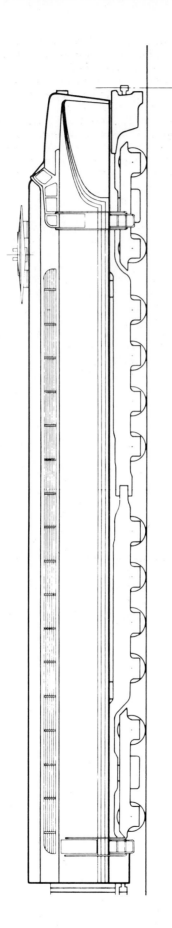

The most unusual locomotives proposed for the D&RGW were these 5000-HP hybrid units utilizing diesel-electric propulsion for the eight main axles and straight-electric power for the four truck axles, which would have received external power from an overhead wire installed over short stretches of steeply-graded trackage.

One of these 7500-horsepower electric locomotives — having motors on all axles — would have replaced two of the D&RGW's huge 2-8-8-2 articulated steam locomotives or six B-B diesel-electric units on heavy main-line freight trains operated between Denver and Pueblo, or over the mountains to Salt Lake City.

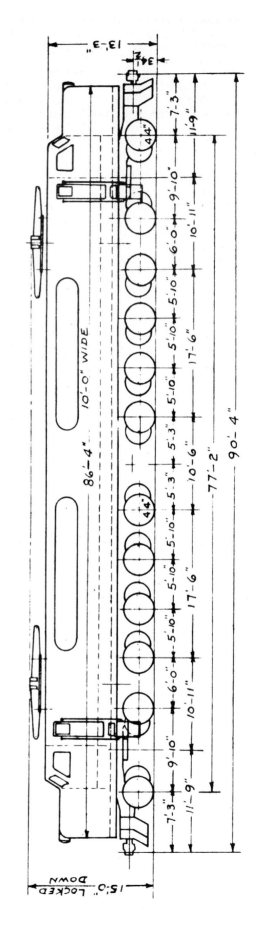

would be economical to electrify the railroad as otherwise proposed. George Gould didn't accept the proposal. He knew as well as anyone that it took money to make money, and at that moment his Western Pacific was keeping him and his Rio Grande system perpetually broke.

Though the railroad's own people ceased their studies of substituting electricity for steam, General Electric was at work on the same idea. During the fall of 1908 it studied the possibility of electrifying the line over Soldier Summit in Utah, between Thistle and Helper. Between these two points lay 50 miles of brutal railroad, with a 2½-percent maximum westbound grade against loaded movements, and a 4-percent maximum eastbound grade against empty movements. That 4-percent grade, only seven miles long, was a real hair-raiser though; passenger trains with five locomotives, and freights with six engines, were not unknown. This proposal reached the D&RG's offices in early December.

In certain respects it suggested a scheme much like that envisioned for the Glenwood Springs — Tennessee Pass trackage. The locomotives were a bit heavier — 115 tons — with four 400-HP motors. The overhead conductors were to be three-phase, but the phase voltage was to be 11,000, to reduce transmission losses of power. Two of these locomotives were to handle 1200 tons from Thistle eastbound to Tucker at the foot of the 4-percent grade, whence three of them could ascend the grade within the

one-hour power-rating of the motors. A total of seven units were estimated for freight service, with a couple of additional ones for passenger service.

Castle Gate, a few miles west of Helper, was selected for the site of a coal-fired generating plant housing two 9000 KW, three-phase, 25-hertz, 2200-volt generators. Transformers would convert this power to 66,000 volts for transmission to sub-stations located at Colton, Tucker, and Rio, at which points the catenary would be connected. A particularly interesting feature was the location of wooden poles on both sides of the track, one pole supporting one three-phase transmission line and one trolley wire, while the opposite pole supported a duplicate transmission line and the second trolley wire. (This arrangement made the catenary for the 14 miles of double track between Colton and Tucker somewhat complicated.)

General Electric admitted that its cost estimate of the installation was quite loose because it did not have very much information from the railroad. Furthermore, it had no basis upon which to base any operating costs, nor did it have adequate data for a cost comparison with steam operation. To quote GE, "The total value of these improved conditions, particularly the broader questions as to the effect of increased speed and capacity, is virtually impossible of accurate determination on a purely engineering basis and must necessarily, therefore, be estimated by the officials who are controlling and directing the Denver &

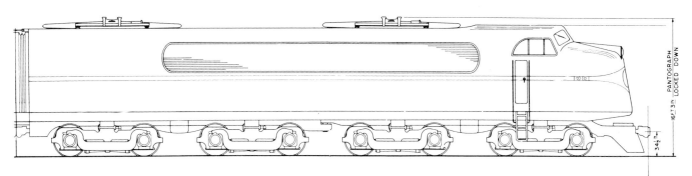

This twin-unit monster was proposed to haul D&RGW main-line freight trains between Salt Lake City and Denver or Pueblo. One unit would have been able to handle the *heaviest passenger consists without helpers, even on the three-percent grades of Tennessee Pass. Two units coupled together measured about 150 feet between knuckles.*

A 6750-HP ELECTRIC LOCOMOTIVE WITH A MILLION POUNDS ON DRIVERS

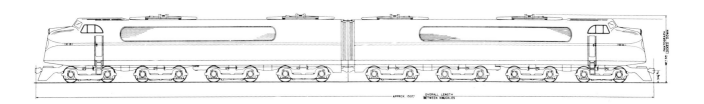

PRINCIPAL DATA AND DIMENSIONS

Wheel Arrangement	2[(B-B)+(B-B)]
Total Weight	1,000,000 lb
Weight on Drivers	1,000,000 lb
Number of Driving Axles	16
Weight per Driving Axle	62,500 lb
Continuous Rating	
At Rail	6,750 hp
Tractive Effort	150,000 lb
Speed	16.9 mph
Adhesion	15.0 per cent

Starting Tractive Effort	
25% Adhesion	250,000 lb
Maximum Operating Speed	75 mph
Number of Traction Motors	16
Line Voltage	12,000
Phases	Single
Length Overall, between Knuckles, Approx.	150 ft
Width Overall	11 ft 0 in.
Height over Pantograph, Locked Down	16 ft 0 in.

311

Rio Grande." Regardless, GE estimated the grand total to be just under $3-million.

Once more the railroad chose not to abandon steam for electricity, probably because it, and the Goulds, were just as broke in 1908 as they had been in 1907, due to the continued drain of Western Pacific construction which was soaring far beyond anticipations. On the other hand, there was no doubt that traffic was stagnating between Walsenburg and Pueblo, and on the steep grades over Tennessee Pass and Soldier Summit. In a mighty attempt to loosen the congestion which was throttling its vital revenues, the D&RG acquired 34 heavy 4-6-0's, 28 heavy 2-8-0's, eight 2-6-6-2's, 14 2-8-2's, six 4-6-2's and 15 2-8-8-2's between 1908 and 1913. In addition it found funds to add some double track on the west side of Tennessee Pass and on both sides of Soldier Summit. Furthermore, it built 14 miles of two-percent double track to eliminate the four-percent grade between Tucker and Soldier Summit, and jointly with the Colorado & Southern it constructed a new low-grade double-track line 54 miles long between Walsenburg and Minnequa. All of these were accomplished with borrowed money, however.

Despite these alternate measures to improve the performance of steam-powered trains, Vice-President and General Manager E. L. Brown proclaimed that the D&RG had been examining a proposal from General Electric for the electrification of the Soldier Summit hill as well as the remaining trackage into Salt Lake City, a total of 115 miles. This belated and surprising revelation appeared in the Electric Railway Journal during November of 1912, and it appears that either Mr. Brown or the Journal's informer managed to confound readers with an unlikely mixture of earlier proposals.

Other railroads with operating difficulties similar to those of the D&RG had electrified portions of their lines. The Great Northern did their Cascade Tunnel project in 1908/1909. In 1917 the Milwaukee inaugurated electric operations between Harlowton, Montana, and Avery, Idaho, across the Rocky Mountains. The Norfolk & Western eliminated steam operations on 77 miles of line in 1915. Meanwhile, in Colorado and Utah, the D&RG plunged into complete financial failure in 1918, followed by another in 1920. Reorganized in 1921 as the Denver & Rio Grande Western (known locally as the Dangerous and Rapidly Growing Worse) the railroad failed once again in 1922, and repeated the performance in 1935. During all of this time the railroad had no funds for electric locomotives, power plants and catenaries, and no sober banker would have advanced it the money for such a project. Ideas of electrification had died in 1908 and they stayed very dead for almost two decades, during which period the railroad suffered from a multitude of financial woes.

After the railroad company had been financially reorganized in the early 1920's it purchased considerable new motive power. Among the additions were 30 huge 4-8-2's (10 of which were equipped with trailing-truck boosters), 10 others having three cylinders, 10 compound 2-8-8-2's, and 10 single-expansion 2-8-8-2's, which were the world's largest locomotives at the time (1927). These latter locomotives had just begun to demonstrate their capabilities between Pueblo and Grand Junction when the General Electric company made a motive power/train-performance/track-improvement study of that same territory.

Issued in 1927, GE's report of the survey was a generalized attempt to persuade the D&RGW to discontinue the acquisition of monstrous steam locomotives, and

to commence planning for the electrification of the most difficult segment of line between Salida and Minturn. GE conceded that existing traffic was being adequately handled by the new and far more powerful engines, operating over a line which had been greatly improved recently, but it believed that only a small increase in traffic would produce a saturation which could be relieved but little by bigger steam engines, and that massive physical modifications would be required.

Electrification, it was claimed, would postpone for several years the need for double-tracking or grade-reduction. Electric locomotives, with multiple-control, would increase train-tonnage and train-speed. Electro-dynamic braking downhill would reduce brake and wheel wear, and could return 20-percent of the power to the distribution system. Electric locomotives were more dependable, more available, safer and more efficient than those powered by coal and steam. In 1926 2500 trains were operated between Salida and Minturn; their gross tonnage came to 5-million. The saturation point was estimated at 2600 trains and 7-million tons. Electrification could prolong that point to 3000 trains and 10-million tons.

Operations were analyzed in considerable detail, but GE made no specific suggestions beyond their estimate that 14 1-C+C-1 locomotives, weighing 250 tons (presumably like those then being delivered to the Great Northern railroad), could replace the 18 2-8-8-2's assigned to the district. A $5½-million investment for the purchase of the locomotives and the electrification of 150 miles of track would produce an annual saving of about $250,000 from operations alone.

An immediate decision for electrification was not indicated in the report, nor were there any startling revelations which might have urged the D&RGW into such action. Hence, it was ignored, and the railroad bought 14 4-8-4's in 1929 and 10 more single-expansion 2-8-8-2's in 1930.

Toward the end of the 11-year trusteeship the prospects for stringing catenary through the Rockies seemed considerably brighter. After somewhat more than half a year of study, Westinghouse submitted a preliminary report on the electrification of the D&RGW between Pueblo and Salt Lake City, plus the Denver & Salt Lake Railway (controlled by the D&RGW and merged during 1947), and the Dotsero Cutoff, which connected the D&SL with the D&RGW. Dated 31 July 1946, the report was signed by Charles Kerr, Jr. and D. R. Campbell, two of the ablest men in the application of electricity to railroad transportation.

Kerr and Campbell thought big; $33.4-million (net) would be required to do the job, presuming that the 153 displaced steam locomotives could provide a credit of roughly $100,000 apiece, their ledger value. Thirteen-hundred track-miles would be strung with 24,000-volt 15-hertz catenary at a cost of close to $17-million. All main-line trains would be handled by 43 B-D+D-B 7500-HP locomotives (10 to be equipped with train heat boilers) which would be the most powerful on Earth. Local main-line trains would be hauled by one of three electric motor-cars, while all branch-line services would be converted gradually from steam to diesel-electric power. The bill for the motive power was anticipated to total $21-million. The 29 6000-KVA substations, and communications and signal modifications accounted for the remaining capital outlay. With this arrangement, 33-percent of the main-line track would be electrified, yet electric operations would account for 88-percent of ton-miles and 70-percent of passenger-miles, based on 1941 traffic.

It was expected that the railroad would purchase commercial power at appropriate locations, and transmit it to the various substations for feeding the trolley-wire. Where the load was to be heavy — Salt Lake City to Woodside, Denver to Glenwood Springs, Dotsero to Yale, Pueblo to Cañon City — this line would be doubled. The scheme was quite ingenious, and it would have saved considerable money in initial investment when compared with the three-phase transmission systems suggested previously.

Outwardly, the locomotives were almost twins to the two Great Northern 5000-HP B-D+D-B monsters then under construction by ALCO/GE. While the GN locomotives had 12 500-HP motors powering 42" drivers, the D&RGW version was to have 12 625-HP motors for its 44" wheels. Its axle load was only 50,000 lbs. (comparable with that of contemporary diesel-electrics) yielding a total weight of 600,000 lbs., 135,000 lbs. lighter than the GN units. On a short-time basis these new behemoths were calculated to produce 180,000 lb. tractive effort up to 20 mph, with an output of 13,200 HP at 45 mph., far surpassing any other single unit of railway motive power. Westinghouse had stated that the railroad's traction problem was a difficult one, requiring high continuous drawbar pull at low speeds together with high continuous horsepower output at fairly high speeds. Yet, after looking at the various solutions, Messrs. Kerr and Campbell felt that they had come up with a practical answer in the form of this new giant of the rails.

To test its analysis, Westinghouse selected dispatchers' train sheets for peak-traffic days in October, 1941, then duplicated those traffic movements with electrified operations. By doing this the total number of locomotives and trains was determined, as were the maximum operating costs. As a by-product it was noted that the all-electric locomotives could accelerate their trains to the maximum allowable speed considerably faster than either the 2-8-8-2 steam locomotives or the 6000-HP diesel-electrics. This inherent characteristic of electric motive power (very high short-time overload power) enabled the proposed locomotives to handle heavier trains at higher speeds than were currently hauled by existing locomotives. In passenger service, for example, the electric locomotive with 14 75-ton cars could run 50-percent faster than a 6000-HP diesel-electric on grades steeper than one-percent.

There remained one final consideration. Would the anticipated savings justify the tremendous investment? Here again, Westinghouse had the figures, right down to the last dollar. Compared with steam operation, direct operating expenses (principally for crews, maintenance, and fuel) were expected to decline from $12-million annually to $5-million. Depreciation, of course, would climb, from $600,000 to $1.2-million. The net result was an annual saving of more than $6-million which was an 18.5-percent return on the added investment required for the electrification. Westinghouse now rested its case, commenting briefly, "The horsepower provided to move this traffic will be at least 50-percent greater per trailing ton than it is economically practical to provide by any other means. This assures a standard of service to the traveling and shipping public which cannot otherwise be furnished."

Aware that the D&RGW's engineering department had been studying motive power of various sorts, and that Westinghouse had submitted its proposal, General Electric joined forces with Westinghouse in another attempt to string catenary across the Rocky Mountains. Their report concerning this project, dated March 3, 1947, was sub-

mitted to assist the railroad in deciding among steam, diesel-electric and all-electric motive power. Again the trackage involved extended from Denver and Pueblo to Salt Lake City, but this time the locomotive was a B+B-B+B, like the ones being built by GE for the Virginian. While the previous plan had compared only electric and steam operations, this one went a bit further, adding diesel-electric operations to the picture, based upon 1941 traffic levels.

At this time, the report claimed, the D&RGW had 17 four-unit diesel-electric road locomotives, either in operation or on order. Another 33 such locomotives (total — 200 1350-HP units) would be required to eliminate steam from all main-line services. However, all-electric operation could be attained with 72 3000-HP units normally coupled back-to-back in pairs. They would draw power from a 12,000-volt, single-phase overhead wire, which would be fed from seven points by frequency-charger sets, using purchased power.

The whole idea took a sizable pile of money — $43½-million more than for steam facilities and equipment, and almost $28-million more than the diesel-electric conversion from steam. If the railroad were to use diesel-electric power, it would show a 15-percent return on its additional investment; all-electric power would show a 14-percent return on the same basis, but the dollar savings would have been twice as large, considering only operating expenses.

Sensing that the all-electric idea had not received immediate acceptance at 1531 Stout Street in Denver, the engineers at Westinghouse made a final attempt to persuade the railroad to power its trains with some sort of electric locomotive. In this last scheme three-phase power would be purchased at suitable points for distribution to the overhead wires which would extend only from Milepost Six (west of Denver) to Tabernash, Colorado, (the western foot of the Moffat Tunnel grade), and from Helper to Thistle, Utah. Freights operating eastbound over Tennessee Pass would still need helpers, however, any other type of operation being considered impractical. The proposal envisioned the use of 17 2-D+D-2 3000-HP diesel-electric locomotives (essentially identical to those built by Baldwin for the Seaboard Air Line and the Pennsylvania railroads) for main-line passenger service. Coupled in pairs, 24 more units would handle freight trains between Pueblo and Helper. (One pair of these would be the Minturn - Tennessee Pass helper.) Twenty-eight combination units (B-D+D-B) with catenary-powered leading and trailing trucks would be assigned between Denver and Bond, Colorado, and between Helper and Salt Lake City, Utah. Except for the powered trucks, associated controls and dynamic braking equipment, these dual-power units would be the same as the diesel-electric locomotives to be used elsewhere. Ordinarily one would operate as a 6000-HP locomotive; beneath the wires it was a 10,000-HP road-helper locomotive, thus eliminating separate helpers.

A total of only $15-million was required beyond the existing investment in steam power and associated facilities, with an estimated net annual saving close to $3-million, generated primarily in fuel and enginehouse-expense categories. It was significant that there was no anticipated saving in locomotive repairs.

In the preface to this report, dated May 21, 1947, it was stated that the elimination or reduction of helper service was a prime objective for the railroad, and it mentioned in passing the "modern requirements of railroad financing" with which these combination locomotives would comply. Hence, it can be presumed that the railroad itself was more interested in the elimination of helpers than in complete electrification. And, even if it had been interested in converting to all-electric propulsion, there seems to have been some doubt that electric locomotives, overhead wires and transmission lines would have qualified for the necessary loans of capital. Concluding, "Although electrification offers the best means of operating the railroad, we are familiar with the factors which militate against its immediate use, and therefore, this report will discuss the most desirable alternative of using trolley/diesel-electric locomotives. — — — The trolley/diesel-electric locomotive offers the most economic means with minimum investment of materially reducing helper service on the railroad." The report produced nothing.

The year, 1947, was a significant one in the D&RGW's history. Restored to health under the guidance of its two hard-working Trustees and a hard-headed Judge, the railroad emerged from 11 years of trusteeship. It absorbed the Denver & Salt Lake Railway over which it had operated through the Moffat Tunnel and via the Dotsero Cutoff. And, without adding any motive power, it attained all-diesel-electric operation of its main-line through-freight trains. Although additional road units were not acquired until 1948 (one four-unit) and 1949 (11 four-unit), the all-electric proposals seem to have experienced a final demise, and nothing further was heard about them.

In retrospect, the relatively recent ideas of electrification involved certain difficulties which weighed most heavily against them. The plans all necessitated considerable outlays in the form of substations, transmission lines, pole lines and overhead wires. The diesel-electric locomotive was free from such vast capital expenditures. Furthermore, all of this electrical system had to be complete, and promptly so, before through service could be inaugurated. As for the internal-combustion unit, its investment could be gradual, with operations converted gradually, too. For these two reasons, the financial strain was much greater with the all-electric system. It was akin to a serious operation on a person; if he survived, he would be in wonderfully excellent health. And, in 1947 hardly anyone in the financial community, including Colorado and Utah, was willing to bet much on the D&RGW's survival. Conservatively recapitalized, its common stock sold for $6 to $19 per share, although par-value was $100. Its $100 preferred stock brought only $26 to $44 in the market. Its two bond issues were changing hands at discounts up to 61-percent for the income series, and 22-percent for the secured series. This sort of Wall Street opinion made it extremely difficult for the D&RGW to borrow money for capital improvements to reduce operating costs, except by conditional-sale agreements or equipment-trusts for property which could be repossessed, if necessary, and resold to some other railroad.

It is possible that Kerr and Campbell and their associates were correct in believing that electrification then would have made the railroad more efficient today; perhaps it could have become a Rocky Mountain Virginian, competing with the AT&SF and Union Pacific without having to work quite so strenuously. In any event, each major decision had to be made within the current context of events and situations. For the Denver & Rio Grande Western in 1947, diesel-electric operation was the only answer, no matter how remunerative the alternatives.

During the early part of the 1950-decade the railroad's research department examined a few propositions for "electrified" operations between Denver and the East Portal of the Moffat Tunnel. Among these schemes were battery-powered helpers which would return automatically while (partially) recharging themselves, and a nuclear-powered generating plant which would furnish power to a catenary from which specially-equipped diesel-electric units could draw the power during their climb up the steep grade. Nothing came of either of these schemes, however.

D&RGW ANNUAL OPERATING STATISTICS FOR 1941

FREIGHT

Train Miles	3,456,760	2,246,894
Principle Locomotive Light Miles	47,632	30,951
Helper Miles	469,370	211,217
Helper Light Miles	394,419	177,489
Train Switching	138,504	138,504
Total Locomotive Miles	4,506,685	2,805,055
Locomotive Ton Miles (Thousands)	1,656,841	841,516
Trailing Ton Miles (Thousands)	6,989,514	6,989,514
Total Ton Miles (Thousands)	8,646,355	7,831,030
Trailing Ton Miles Per Train Mile	2,022	3,106
Trailing Ton Miles Per Locomotive Mile	1,600	2,488
Train Hours	186,735	86,753
Train Miles Per Train Hour	18.5	25.9
Trailing Ton Miles Per Train Hour	1, 37,410	80,550
Tons of Coal or 1000 KWH Used	1 630,090	233,347
Pounds of Coal or KWH Per Locomotive Mile	279.5	83.188
Pounds of Coal or KWH Per 1000 Trailing Ton Miles	180.5	33.385
Pounds of Coal or KWH Per 1000 Total Ton Miles	146.0	29.798
Crew Miles:		
Enginemen — Road	3,642,896	2,416,349
Trainmen — Road	3,456,760	2,246,894
Enginemen — Helper	863,789	388,706

PASSENGER

Train Miles	1,443,483	1,443,483
Principle Locomotive Light Miles	30,726	30,726
Helper Miles	71,260	0
Helper Light Miles	62,761	0
Total Locomotive Miles	1,608,230	1,474,209
Locomotive Ton Miles (Thousands)	510,840	339,068
Passenger Car Miles	11,358,607	11,135,607
Locomotive Miles Per Train Mile	1.113	1.021
Passenger Car Miles Per Train Mile	7.86	7.86
Passenger Car Miles Per Locomotive Mile	7.06	7.70
Tons of Coal or 1000 KWH Used	115,542	38,080
Pounds of Coal or KWH Per Locomotive Mile	143.8	25.831
Pounds of Coal or KWH Per Passenger Car Mile	20.34	3.353
Crew Miles:		
Enginemen — Road	1,474,209	1,474,209
Trainmen — Road	1,443,483	1,443,483
Enginemen — Helper	134,021	0

DEPOT AT PALMER LAKE.

Rio Grande Territory

The region served by the Denver & Rio Grande Western Railroad and its corporate ancestors is one of great variety. Although this is particularly true of the topography—which ranges from vast open prairie-land to the loftiest mountain ranges in the United States—there are also wide differences in geology, weather, agriculture, forests, rivers, industry and history, all of which influence the location of trackage, design of motive power, operating techniques, traffic composition and financial results.

Despite this great diversity, the D&RGW's territory sub-divided itself naturally into districts having homogeneous characteristics and distinct identifications. Eighteen such divisions logically suggest themselves — each of which is described in the text which follows, and whose physical features are delineated on accompanying route maps, newly prepared for this book.

Also included in this section are revised and up-dated D&RGW profile charts, showing both abandoned and existing routes.

——— TABLE OF CONTENTS ———

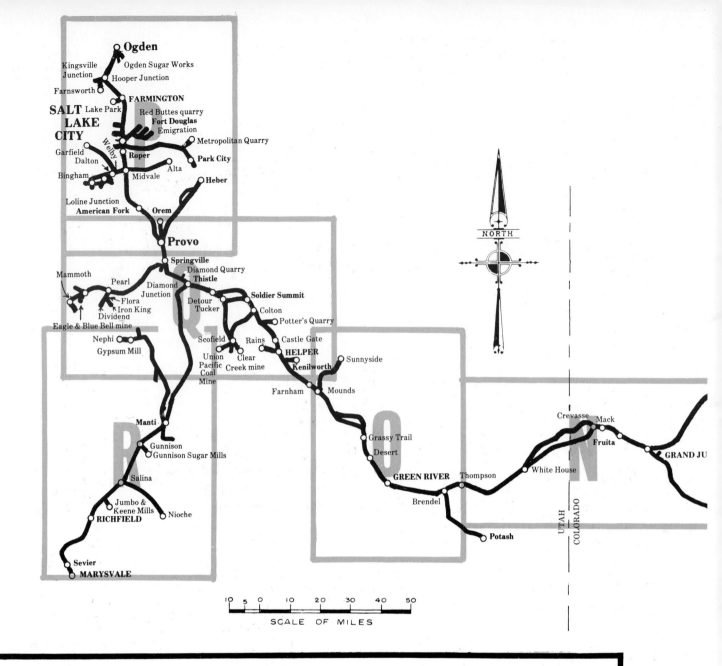

RIO GRANDE TERRITORY
Key Map

The Denver & Rio Grande Western Railroad route maps reproduced in this section of the book consist of 18 segments—each presented on a full page—together with a description of the contiguous territory.

An "index letter" appears on each map segment and on each corresponding territorial description. This "Key Map" shows how the segments have been arranged in alphabetical sequence and they have been placed with each territorial description. The Table of Contents on the preceding page shows where each territorial description begins, followed by the page number for each map segment.

In some areas, the map segments overlap; thus—for example—the track near Ridgway appears on two segments: "K" and "L." All map segments have been drawn to the same scale: approximately 7½ miles to the inch.

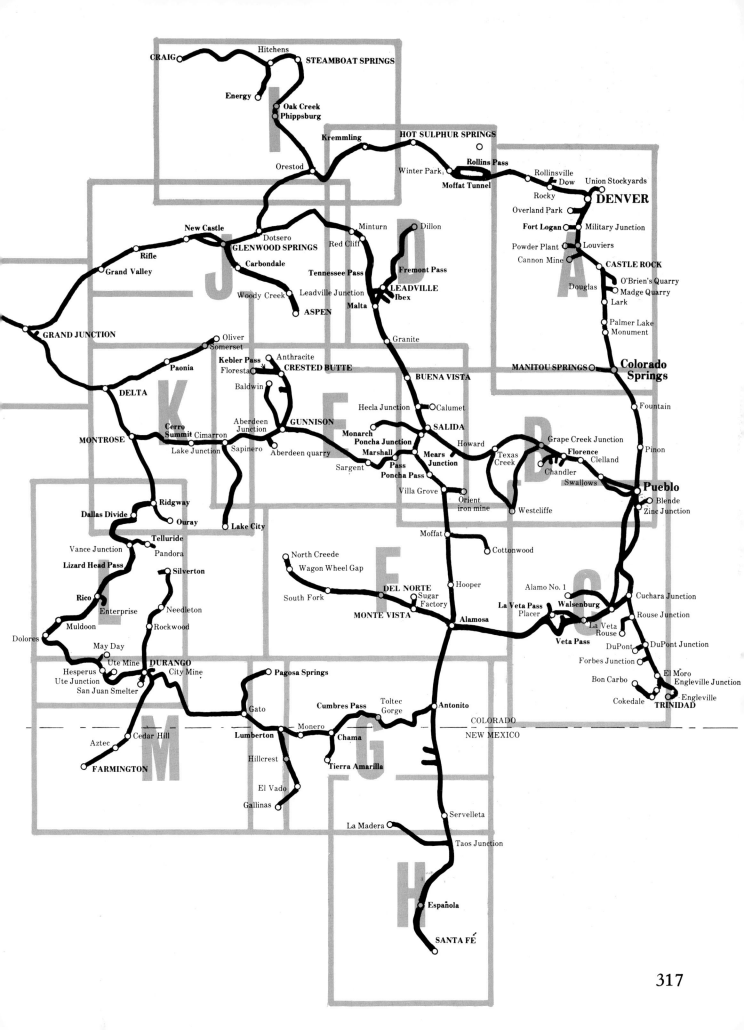

CRAIG
Hitchens
STEAMBOAT SPRINGS
Energy
Oak Creek
Phippsburg
Kremmling
HOT SULPHUR SPRINGS
Orestod
Winter Park
Rollins Pass
Rollinsville
Dow
Union Stockyards
Moffat Tunnel
Rocky
DENVER
New Castle
Dotsero
Minturn
Dillon
Overland Park
Rifle
GLENWOOD SPRINGS
Red Cliff
Fort Logan
Military Junction
Grand Valley
Carbondale
Tennessee Pass
Fremont Pass
Powder Plant
Louviers
Woody Creek
Leadville Junction
LEADVILLE
Cannon Mine
CASTLE ROCK
ASPEN
Malta
Ibex
O'Brien's Quarry
Douglas
Madge Quarry
Lark
Granite
Palmer Lake
Monument
Oliver
Somerset
Paonia
Kebler Pass
Anthracite
CRESTED BUTTE
BUENA VISTA
MANITOU SPRINGS
Colorado
Springs
Floresta
DELTA
Baldwin
Hecla Junction
Calumet
Fountain
Aberdeen
Junction
GUNNISON
SALIDA
Cerro
Summit
Cimarron
Monarch
Grape Creek Junction
Pinon
MONTROSE
Lake Junction
Sapinero
Poncha Junction
Howard
Florence
Clelland
Aberdeen quarry
Marshall
Mears
Texas
Chandler
Sargent
Pass
Junction
Creek
Swallows
Pueblo
Poncha Pass
Blende
Villa Grove
Zinc Junction
Ridgway
Orient
Westcliffe
Dallas Divide
Ouray
iron mine
Telluride
Moffat
Vance Junction
Pandora
North Creede
Cottonwood
Lizard Head Pass
Wagon Wheel Gap
Silverton
Alamo No. 1
Cuchara Junction
Rico
Needleton
South Fork
DEL NORTE
Hooper
La Veta Pass
Walsenburg
Enterprise
Sugar
Placer
Rouse Junction
Muldoon
Rockwood
Factory
La Veta
Dolores
MONTE VISTA
Alamosa
Rouse
DuPont Junction
May Day
Ute Mine
Veta Pass
DuPont
Hesperus
DURANGO
Forbes Junction
Ute Junction
City Mine
Bon Carbo
El Moro
San Juan Smelter
Pagosa Springs
Engleville Junction
Gato
Cokedale
Engleville
Aztec
Cedar Hill
Cumbres Pass
Toltec
Antonito
TRINIDAD
Monero
Gorge
COLORADO
FARMINGTON
Lumberton
Chama
NEW MEXICO
Hillcrest
Tierra Amarilla
El Vado
Servelleta
Gallinas
La Madera
Taos Junction
Española
SANTA FÉ

317

THE COLORADO PIEDMONT

The north-south route of the Denver & Rio Grande Western Railroad marks the dividing line between two regions of strikingly different topography. Eastward from its rails the Great Plains slope gently downward, losing about 5000 feet of altitude in roughly 750 miles. Westward, however, the Rocky Mountains jut sharply upward; 50 miles west of Denver, the peaks of the Continental Divide tower almost 10,000 feet above the city. Between Denver and Colorado Springs, the railroad—following local streams—lies in this great crease of the Earth's surface.

Clinging closely to the foothills, the main-line ascends to the summit of the divide between the South Platte River and Arkansas River watersheds, then descends to Colorado Springs. All of the branches were short, serving industries (DuPont), coal mines (Lehigh), quarries (Hathaway and Madge), or points of local interest (Overland Park, Fort Logan, Manitou). The Atchison, Topeka & Santa Fe also owns a line between Denver and Colorado Springs, paralleling the D&RGW, and although its track crosses at South Denver, Sedalia and Spruce, suitable connections have been installed permitting the two lines to be operated as joint double-track. By virtue of an operating agreement with the AT&SF, the Colorado & Southern runs its trains over both tracks, and until 1966 Missouri Pacific locomotives and cars also used this route into Denver.

Within this same region will be found the D&RGW's other main-line, one which it acquired in 1947, the former Denver & Salt Lake railway. This remarkable railroad runs directly toward the mountains; then, when the underlying rocks tilt upward at a 45° angle, ascends this sheer flank until it is able to follow a rugged canyon to the Moffat Tunnel. With its multiplicity of tunnels and the great loop at Fireclay, the line is a scenic wonder and a marvel of engineering. In addition, it is one of the longest steep mainline grades in the nation, being slightly less than 50 miles of unrelieved 2-percent grade. The only branch (Dow) serves a chemical plant and an aggregate mill.

Denver, understandably, is the focal point of the area, being the junction with many other railroads serving the city. The D&RGW interchanged with the Chicago,

The wooden trestle of the Atchison, Topeka & Santa Fe Railroad spanned spacious Pikes Peak Avenue in Colorado Springs — located at the base of majestic Pikes Peak, *14,110-feet above sea level. Pikes Peak is the easternmost of Colorado's major mountain summits, and dominates the landscape between Denver and Pueblo.*

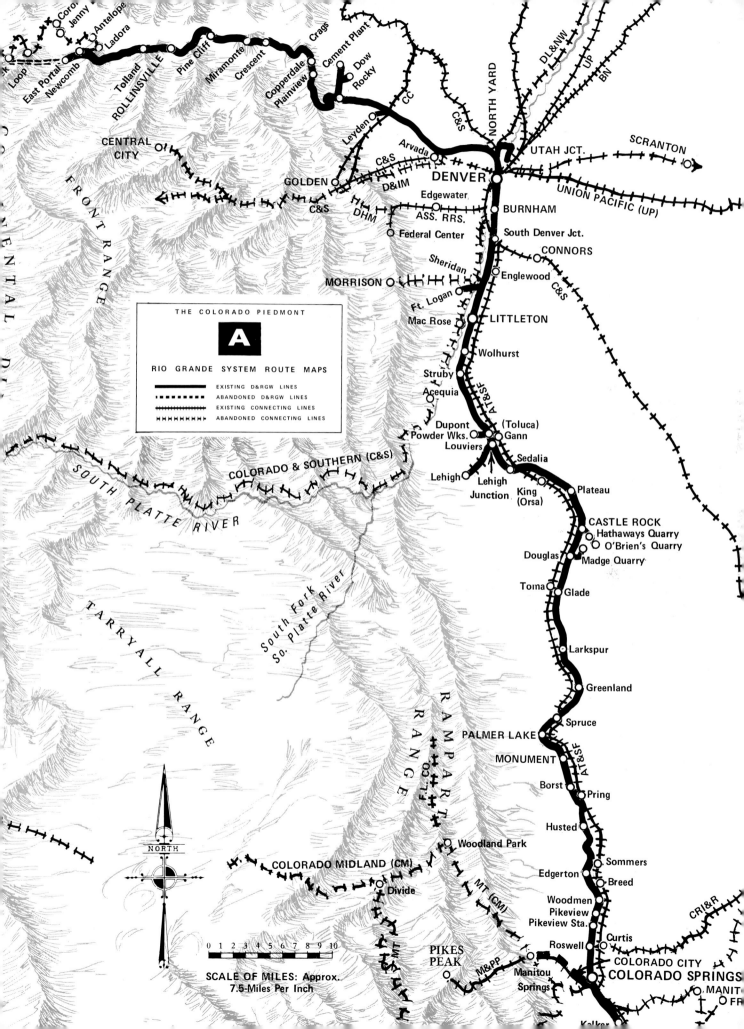

THE COLORADO PIEDMONT

A

RIO GRANDE SYSTEM ROUTE MAPS

EXISTING D&RGW LINES
ABANDONED D&RGW LINES
EXISTING CONNECTING LINES
ABANDONED CONNECTING LINES

SCALE OF MILES: Approx.
7.5-Miles Per Inch

NORTH

Burlington & Quincy; Chicago, Rock Island & Pacific (operating over UP tracks); Colorado & Southern (controlled by the CB&Q, operating over its own tracks to the north and via D&RGW/AT&SF trackage southward); and the Union Pacific. In pre-automobile days Denver had been the terminal of 17 different main-line routes, and its Union Depot had handled upwards of 150 passenger trains each day, not counting following sections and extras. In 1963, the combined passenger traffic of all three roads operating between Denver and Pueblo was less than what the D&RG handled alone in 1871, the first year of operation, when hardly anyone besides Indians, miners and traders lived outside of Denver.

The railroad's first depot in Denver was located between Nineteenth and Twentieth Streets, where its first spike was driven. (This location is now in the midst of the UP's yard trackage, in line with Wynkoop Street and southeast of its freight office.) After using that station for only three years, the D&RG moved into its new building at Sixth and Larimer Streets. Here, in 1874, it was joined by the Denver, South Park & Pacific, and in 1879 both of them began to operate out of the Colorado Central station at Sixteenth and Delgany Streets. After Denver's Union Depot was constructed in 1881, the D&RG transferred its terminal to the new location, but used its tracks in Wynkoop Street in front of the building. Shortly thereafter it laid

Travelers from all over the world have gazed in awe at the snowy summit of Pikes Peak, Colorado's most famous mountain. Towering a mile-and-a-half above Manitou Springs, Pikes Peak is a sublime sentinel, visible for many miles in almost any direction.

North Cheyenne Canyon has been a spectacular scenic attraction for tourists visiting the Pikes Peak Region since the earliest days of railroad construction and settlement. For many years the Denver & Rio Grande was the most popular means of transportation for tourists traveling to and from the region.

track to the rear of the station, where the passenger tracks are today. Freight trains terminated at Burnham (Shops) yards south of the depot, or at North Yard, north of the depot.

Early-day visitors to Colorado Springs and the Pikes Peak Region often stayed at the prestigious wooden Antlers Hotel, which was destroyed in a grand conflagration in 1898. The second Antlers Hotel has since been replaced by a third building of the same name.

THE ARKANSAS VALLEY

As the D&RGW's track, following Fountain Creek, continues southward from Colorado Springs, the mountains recede to the west; consequently, the city of Pueblo on the Arkansas River is out on the plains about 30 miles from the foothills. At Pueblo the Arkansas drainage extends from Palmer Lake on the north to Trinidad on the south, a distance of almost 150 miles. Westward from Pueblo, however, the valley narrows until the stream is forced into a sheer canyon named the Royal Gorge. (Formerly it was called the Grand Canyon of the Arkansas.) West of the Gorge the rails follow the stream quite closely along its route through a valley bounded by rounded hills. At Pleasanton the river is deflected northward by the northern end of the mighty Sangre de Cristo Range, remaining in a slowly narrowing valley as far as Salida. Here, where the South Arkansas joins the main stream, there is a large open area in which the city is laid out.

As is the case north of Colorado Springs, the AT&SF track is paired with the D&RGW's as far as Bragdon, with crossovers located at Fountain, allowing individual trackage into Pueblo Union Depot. Previously, the C&S track from Denver had paralleled the other two between Fountain and Pueblo, and the CRI&P had operated into Pueblo over D&RGW rails. West of Pueblo the AT&SF and D&RGW ran on opposite banks of the Arkansas as far as Cañon City where the AT&SF had some short branches to coal mines south of Florence. (The AT&SF now uses D&RGW track to Clelland.) The D&RGW also had branches into the same area, serving mines at Coal Banks, Canfield, Oak Creek, Chandler and Fremont. A long branch ran through rugged Grape Creek Canyon to Westcliffe and when this narrow-gauge line was washed out in 1889 it remained so, having been too difficult to repair. Service to that terminus was not restored until the standard-gauge branch from Texas Creek was constructed in 1901. Another branch was the short and steep one from Howard to the marble quarry at Calcite, high on the east slope of the Sangre de Cristo mountains.

At Colorado Springs the D&RGW was connected with the CRI&P; the Colorado Springs & Cripple District; the Colorado Midland (later, the Midland Terminal); and the C&S. Pueblo was quite a railroad center, being served by the AT&SF; C&S; Missouri Pacific; and the Colorado (formerly the Colorado-Kansas). At Beaver the Beaver, Penrose & Northern ran its uncertain rails off to the north, while the narrow gauge Florence & Cripple Creek connected at both Florence and Cañon City.

The D&RGW can claim a number of unusual features

The D&RG's track through the Royal Gorge — narrowest part of what was called the "Grand Canyon of the Arkansas River" at the time this engraving was made — was laid on a bridge suspended from two iron girders spanning the narrow chasm.

concerning its various lines, and that up the Arkansas Valley is one which certainly qualifies for distinction. Between Pueblo and Cañon City the gradient is .5 to .9-percent for 41 miles; to Buena Vista it is 80 miles of .9 to 1.4-percent grade; while the last 41 miles to Tennessee Pass are on a 1.4 to 1.5-percent incline. In the 162 miles of water-course continuous grade, the railroad rises 5600-feet above Pueblo to an elevation of 10,200-feet at Tennessee Pass.

In June of 1921, Pueblo was struck by an unprecedented flood which made a shambles of all railroad facilities near the depot, where the debris-laden waters surged 10 feet deep over the rails. Every locomotive was immobilized by mud; almost 500 cars were damaged; and 35 miles of track were rendered unfit for operation. Equipment from seven other railroads was used for almost an entire month to restore normal service, although the full damage was not repaired until the end of the year.

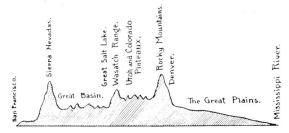

PROFILE of WESTERN UNITED STATES thru DENVER

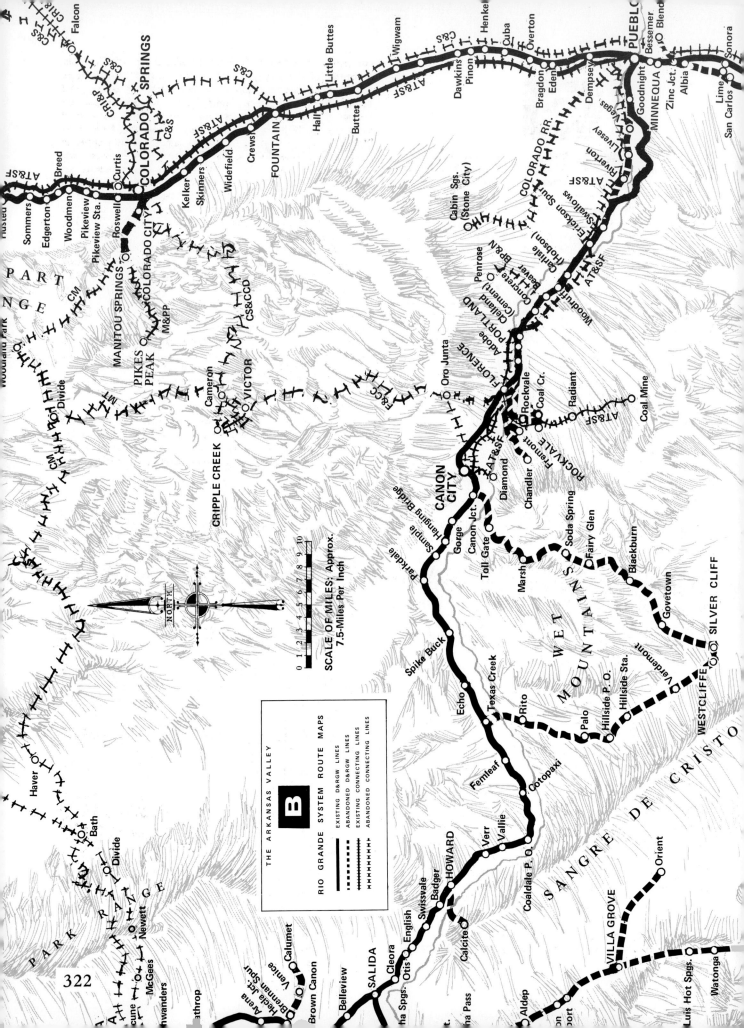

THE ARKANSAS VALLEY

B

RIO GRANDE SYSTEM ROUTE MAPS

EXISTING D&RGW LINES
ABANDONED D&RGW LINES
EXISTING CONNECTING LINES
ABANDONED CONNECTING LINES

SCALE OF MILES: Approx.
7.5 Miles Per Inch

0 1 2 3 4 5 6 7 8 9 10

NORTH

322

THE SOUTHERN COAL FIELDS

It has been estimated that half of Colorado's area, comprising practically all its non-mountainous regions, is underlain with coal. Somewhat more than half of the known deposits have never been worked, however, due to their great depth beneath the surface. Although coal has been mined at many locations in the state, the most extensively mined region is that lying between Walsenburg and Trinidad which is but part of a vast field of excellent coal.

When the railroad was built southward out of Pueblo in 1876 its destination was intended to be Mexico City, but it was prevented from going beyond Trinidad by the AT&SF which had occupied the only practical route into New Mexico. Ordinarily such a blockade would have spelled disaster, but to the tiny D&RG it was perhaps an unsuspected blessing; this extension had been built along the eastern edge of a coal outcropping which was to supply the railroad with considerable traffic for an entire century.

All of this section, which rises gradually toward the New Mexico border, is drained by a great many small streams flowing northeast into the Arkansas River. Consequently, the D&RGW's original line south of Pueblo was one of sawtooth profile combined with successions of sharp curves to minimize construction costs. At first its only competitor was the AT&SF which passed through Trinidad en-route (eventually) to the Pacific Coast. This virtual monopoly ended in 1888 when corporate predecessors of today's C&S built into Trinidad from the south, and by virtue of a trackage agreement with the D&RG, connected with previously built track between Pueblo and Denver. In 1895 these new competitors built their own line between Trinidad and Walsenburg. By 1911 the roller-coaster railroad between Walsenburg and Pueblo had become an operating impossibility and the two railroads (D&RG and C&S) joined in the construction of an admirable double-track line between those two points. In 1936 the D&RGW dismantled its own line between Walsenburg and Trinidad, operating over the C&S instead.

Branches were numerous. A short one ran to a zinc smelter (Blende) to the southeast of Pueblo, while another served a powder plant south of Boaz. All of the others served coal mines. The longest of these curled around the hills northwest of Walsenburg to Alamo Number 1 mine, with a spur to the New Pacific mine. Another ran to Rouse and Santa Clara, and one climbed up south of Trinidad to Engleville. The mine at Bon Carbo and the coke plant at Cokedale were reached via AT&SF track between Trinidad and Jansen, and Colorado & Wyoming track from Jansen to Longsdale. In addition, the D&RG operated the Hezron branch for the C&W.

An intended main-line had been built west of Walsenburg over Veta Pass, a low point between the Sangre de Cristo and Culebra ranges, to reach the San Luis Valley and the Rio Grande. Being too steep and curved for standard-gauge operation, this line was abandoned, having been

Dump Mountain guards the eastern approach to Veta Pass— 9393 feet above sea level—highest railroad location in the United States at the time the Denver & Rio Grande laid its rails across it in 1877, from La Veta to Alamosa.

323

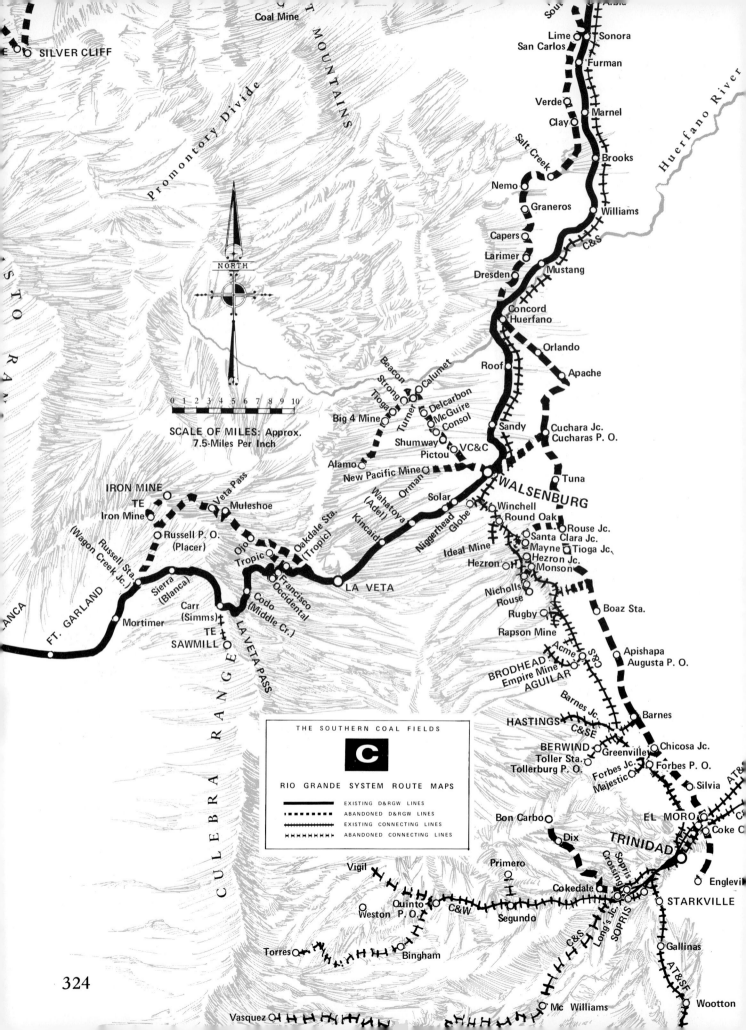

SILVER CLIFF

Coal Mine

WET MOUNTAINS

Promontory Divide

Huerfano River

NORTH

0 1 2 3 4 5 6 7 8 9 10
SCALE OF MILES: Approx.
7.5-Miles Per Inch

South Pueblo

Lime
San Carlos
Sonora
Furman
Verde
Marnel
Clay
Brooks
Salt Creek
Nemo
Graneros
Williams
Capers
C&S
Larimer
Mustang
Dresden
Concord
Huerfano
Orlando
Apache
Roof
Sandy
Cuchara Jc.
Cucharas P. O.

Beacon
Calumet
Strong
Delcarbon
Tioga
Turner
McGuire
Big 4 Mine
Consol
Shumway
VC&C
Pictou
Alamo
New Pacific Mine
Tuna
WALSENBURG

IRON MINE
TE
Iron Mine
Veta Pass
Muleshoe
Wahatoya
(Adel)
Orman
Solar
Winchell
Round Oak
Russell P. O.
(Placer)
Ojo
Oakdale Sta.
(Tropic)
Kincaid
Niggerhead
Globe
Rouse Jc.
(Wagon Creek Jc.)
Russell Sta.
Tropic
Santa Clara Jc.
Mayne
Tioga Jc.
Sierra
(Blanca)
Francisco
Occidental
LA VETA
Ideal Mine
Hezron Jc.
Hezron
Monson
FT. GARLAND
Mortimer
Carr
(Simms)
Codo
(Middle Cr.)
Nicholls
Rouse
Boaz Sta.
TE
SAWMILL
Rugby
Rapson Mine
Apishapa
Augusta P. O.
BLANCA
Acme
C&S
CULEBRA RANGE
LA VETA PASS
BRODHEAD
Empire Mine
AGUILAR
Barnes Jc.
Barnes
HASTINGS
C&SE
Chicosa Jc.
BERWIND
Greenville
Toller Sta.
Tollerburg P. O.
Forbes Jc.
Forbes P. O.
Majestic
Silvia
AT&
Bon Carbo
EL MORO
Coke O
Dix
TRINIDAD
Vigil
Primero
Sopris Crossing
Cokedale
Englevil
Quinto
P. O.
C&W
Long's Jc.
STARKVILLE
Weston P. O.
Segundo
SOPRIS
C&S
Torres
Bingham
Gallinas
AT&SF
Mc Williams
Wootton
Vasquez

THE SOUTHERN COAL FIELDS

C

RIO GRANDE SYSTEM ROUTE MAPS

EXISTING D&RGW LINES
ABANDONED D&RGW LINES
EXISTING CONNECTING LINES
ABANDONED CONNECTING LINES

replaced by a more suitable one built over La Veta Pass to the south in 1899.

Besides the larger carriers mentioned previously, the only other railroads in the area were the Colorado & Southeastern, which connected at Barnes, the narrow-gauge Bald Mountain, which transferred coal at Occidental, and the two pieces of the Trinchera Estate's railroad, joining at Placer (narrow-gauge) and Carr (standard-gauge). And, most important, the network of standard-gauge trackage owned by the CF&I Steel Corporation (formerly Colorado Fuel & Iron Corporation), which served its great steel mill—connected with the D&RGW at Minnequa. In earlier times, this gigantic plant had an internal narrow-gauge system, also, on which 16 tiny steam locomotives operated.

CREST OF THE CONTINENT

This mountainous region, bisected diagonally from northeast to southwest by the ridge forming the Continental Divide, includes both of the D&RG's trans-mountain routes. The ex-D&SL line passes through the six-mile Moffat Tunnel, under the Divide, while the Royal Gorge route burrows through it by means of a short tunnel under Tennessee Pass.

The Divide itself is quite high and is studded with several peaks above the 14,000-foot mark; rarely does it dip below 11,000-feet. Consequently, every one of the railroad lines which crossed it was forced to do so at exceptional altitudes. The original D&SL line over Rollins Pass attained 11,660-feet, which the Moffat Tunnel reduced to 9240-feet. The Colorado & Southern's narrow-gauge tracks crossed Boreas Pass at 11,320-feet. The original narrow-gauge line of the railroad ascended to 10,430-feet at Tennessee Pass; later tunnels were bored beneath it at 10,220-feet. West of Leadville the CM's Hagerman Tunnel reached 11,530-feet, and its Busk-Ivanhoe Tunnel attained 10,950-feet at its west portal. All of these lines were difficult to operate, but perhaps the D&RGW's Tennessee Pass line was somewhat less of a problem than the others; at least it was not regularly blocked with snow every winter.

The eastern portion of this area contains the headwaters of the South Platte River into which drain numberless tributaries. The Moffat Tunnel Route follows one of these, South Boulder Creek, up an unrelenting two-percent grade through steep-walled rocky canyons to the tunnel. Emerging from the west portal, it follows the Fraser River into the high open basin of Middle Park which is surrounded by tall peaks. Spectacular and narrow gorges accent the course of the Colorado River which the tracks parallel through Byers and Gore canyons, downgrade all the way. The former D&SL line over the Great Divide had diverged at East Portal, climbing the hillside to the north in a series of hairpin loops. On the west side of the summit the track curled around a hill in an over-and-under loop and had come down to the west portal from the north.

The main-line from Pueblo, ascending the Arkansas River's steep gradient, found a much different situation

Mount Democrat towers 3000 feet above the great hairpin loop in the valley at the southern foot of Fremont Pass *in this early-day view. Part of the Mosquito Range, this pass tops the Continental Divide at 11,320 feet.*

RUSS COLLMAN

This quartet of General Motors GP40-model units, numbers 3077, 3072, 3066, 3073 — whose diesel engines produced 12,000 horsepower — provide a striking contrast to the husky 4-8-2 — Number 1505 — in the photograph below. Number 1505 was assisted by a three-cylinder 4-8-2 — Number 1600 — as they highballed the east-bound "Scenic Limited" over Tennessee Pass nearly a half-century before the scene above was recorded. The diesel-electric units, hauling a long west-bound freight train, were approaching the Tennessee Pass Tunnel's eastern portal — at 10,221 feet above sea level. The steam-powered passenger train had just emerged from the bore beneath the Continental Divide and was on its way toward Pueblo and Denver via the Royal Gorge route.

GEORGE BEAM

326

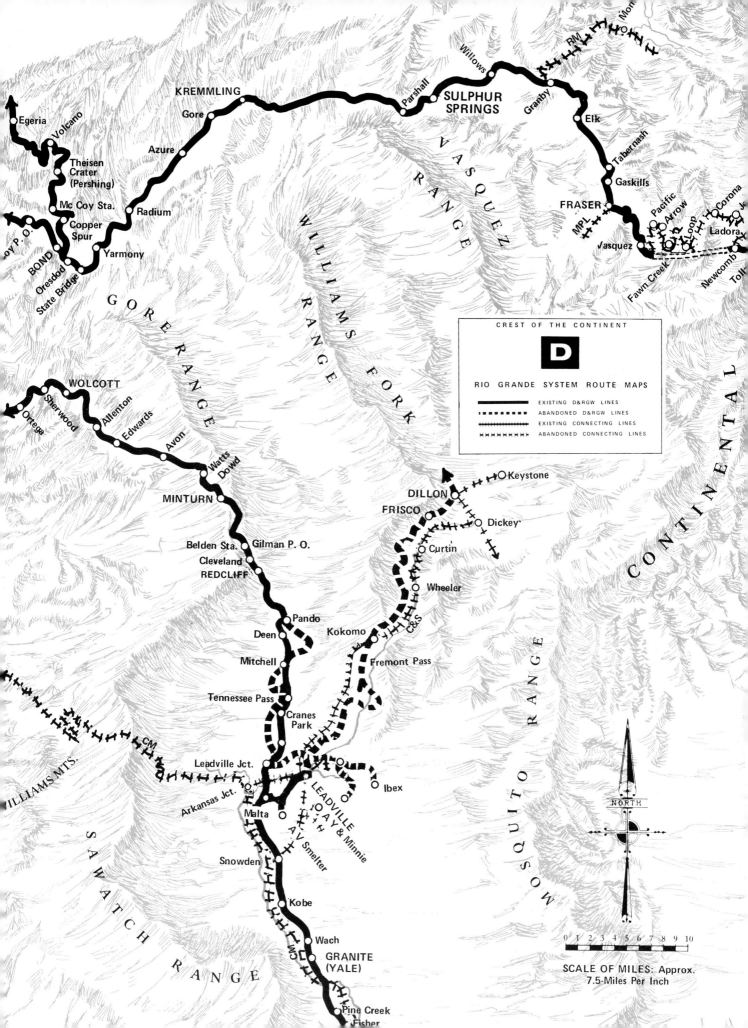

Egeria

Volcano

Theisen Crater (Pershing)

KREMMLING

Gore

Azure

Mc Coy Sta.

Radium

Copper Spur

Coy P.O.

Yarmony

BOND

Oresdod

State Bridge

WILLIAMS FORK RANGE

GORE RANGE

WOLCOTT

Sherwood

Ortega

Allenton

Edwards

Avon

Watts

Dowd

MINTURN

Belden Sta.

Gilman P. O.

Cleveland

REDCLIFF

Pando

Deen

Mitchell

Tennessee Pass

Cranes Park

Leadville Jct.

Arkansas Jct.

Malta

Snowden

Kobe

Wach

GRANITE (YALE)

Pine Creek

Fisher

SAWATCH RANGE

WILLIAMS MTS.

CM

Willows

Parshall

SULPHUR SPRINGS

Granby

Elk

Tabernash

Gaskills

FRASER

Pacific

Arrow

MPL

Vasquez

Fawn Creek

Loop

Ladora

Corona

Newcomb

Toll

VASQUEZ RANGE

RM

Mon

CONTINENTAL

Keystone

DILLON

FRISCO

Dickey

Curtin

Wheeler

C&S

Kokomo

Fremont Pass

Ibex

LEADVILLE

O A Y & Minnie

A V Smelter

MOSQUITO RANGE

CREST OF THE CONTINENT

D

RIO GRANDE SYSTEM ROUTE MAPS

EXISTING D&RGW LINES

ABANDONED D&RGW LINES

EXISTING CONNECTING LINES

ABANDONED CONNECTING LINES

NORTH

0 1 2 3 4 5 6 7 8 9 10

SCALE OF MILES: Approx.
7.5-Miles Per Inch

on the west side of Tennessee Pass. Here the downhill grade of the Eagle River is as high as 3.3-percent, with little reduction until it reaches Minturn, and the railroad was forced to accept this steep profile because of the extremely narrow canyon between Pando and Rex. The original N-G line had departed from the present alignment at Keeldar, had crossed over the Pass, and had looped to the west then to the east of the S-G line, rejoining it at Pando. The D&RG's one principal branch had gone over Fremont Pass then desended Ten Mile Creek to Dillon, at which point it was 313 track-miles from Denver, but only 60 miles away on the map.

Leadville, with all of its complicated trackage strewn across the steep hillsides east of the town, was not on the

DELL A. MCCOY

The six-mile-long Moffat Tunnel penetrates the mountain range forming the Continental Divide directly beneath the peak in the center background. In the foreground a freight train begins the long descent to Denver.

main-line, but on a loop which circled from Malta through Leadville to Leadville Junction. Short branches emanated from this once oppulous and industrious city to essentially every mine in the district. One such branch served the rich Ibex mines, at 11,600-feet. The lush traffic generated here was not without competitors, however, since both the CM and the C&S (and its corporate ancestors) served the town and its local versions of King Solomon's mines.

Only two other railroads had connected with the D&SL's trackage. The Middle Park Lumber Company operated a few miles of track into the woods south of Fraser, and the Rocky Mountain railroad, also a lumber carrier, had joined at Granby. Both of these had vanished long before the D&RGW acquired the D&SL track, however.

Denver & Rio Grande Railroad.

Mountain Time (105th Mer.) the Standard, furnished by A. B. Ingols, Jeweler, 1614 Larimer St., Denver

EAGLE RIVER BRANCH.

WEST.					EAST.	
No. 45. Fr & Pass. S. E.	No. 43. Glenw'od Express. D	Miles	STATIONS.	Miles	No. 44. Denver Express. D	No. 46. Fr & Pass. S. E.
*	7 30	....	Lv..........Denver..........Ar	342.0	7 00	*
*	12 15	119.6	..........Pueblo	224.4	1 55	*
8 45	7 40	277.4	N..........Leadville.....	74.4	7 05	4 20
8 57	7 48	274.9	N..........Eiler..........	71.9	6 55	4 07
ar 9 10		272.5	N..........Malta	69.5	le 6 45	le 3 55
le 9 45	le 8 00				ar	ar 3 40
		255.2	..........Ryan	66 8		† 3 25
† 10 17	† 8 20	278.8	..........Keddar..........	63.2	† 6 23	† 3 07
† 10 31	† 8 28	281.5	..........Crane Park........	60.5	† 6 14	† 2 50
ar 10 42	ar 8 35	283.4	D..........Tenn. Pass.....	58.6	le 6 07	le 2 40
le 11 10	le				ar	ar 2 15
† 11 32	† 8 53	287.5	..........Mitchell..........	54.5	† 5 48	† 1 50
† 12 10	† 9 17	294.1	..........Eagle Park..........	47.9	† 5 28	† 1 12
12 40	ar 9 35				le 5 10	Le 1 00
1 15	le 9 40	299.5	D..........Red Cliff..........	42.5	ar 5 05	†Ar 12 30
† 1 30	† 9 53	302.9	..........Rock Creek..........	39.1	† 4 52	† 12 15
1 55	* 10 17	308.1	D..........Minturn..........	33.9	* 4 32	† 11 48
2 55	† 10 51	320.5	..........Allenton..........	21.5	† 3 55	† 10 51
3 33	† 11 10	827.6	..........Sherwood..........	14.4	† 3 33	† 10 13
4 07	† 11 30	335.1	..........Eagle River..........	6.9	† 3 12	* 9 40
4 40	11 53	342.0	D..........Gypsum..........	6.3	† 2 52	* 3 10
5 10	12 12	348.3	..........Dotsero..........	19.2	† 2 32	* 8 32
6 30	4 00	357.5	..........Glenwood Springs..........		1 45	7 10
† 5 45	† 12 32	357.0	..........Shoshone..........	10.5	† 2 12	† 7 52
6 15	† 12 52	364.0	..........Sulphur Springs..........	3.5	† 1 53	† 7 25

DELL A. MCCOY

Six older model GM General Purpose diesel-electric units coast downgrade past Redcliff in Eagle River Canyon —

after having helped an east-bound freight train up the three-percent grade between Minturn and Tennessee Pass.

HEART OF THE ROCKIES

This interior mountainous region of Colorado is divided into three principal areas by the Continental Divide and the Sangre de Cristo Range of mountains. The northeastern sector is drained by the Arkansas River, flowing from northwest to southeast in a wide valley which narrows considerably downstream from Salida. Streams in the southeast sector are tributaries of the Rio Grande. The remaining sector (western) consists of a vast basin draining into the Gunnison River which feeds the Colorado River at Grand Junction. The chain of high mountains formed by the Collegiate, Saguache and Sangre de Cristo ranges includes several peaks above 14,000-feet, while the passes across them are at 11,000 to 12,000-foot elevation. Consequently, railroad operation was very difficult; hence, when local industry (primarily mining) declined and highways were built to the remaining towns, the railroads pulled up their tracks. Today only the D&RGW serves the area with its line up the Arkansas from Pueblo, and a branch to the limestone quarry at Monarch.

Prior to 1890, this had been exclusively a narrow-gauge empire, with the D&RG and Denver, South Park & Pacific systems operating a multitude of trains into every point of consequence. First, the DSP&P trackage (later owned by the C&S) was blocked by a cave-in of Alpine Tunnel, the dismembered pieces having been operated by the D&RG for the C&S. The D&RG three-railed its line along the Arkansas, later made it standard-gauge. One by one, the branches folded for lack of traffic until today only the branch to the CF&I Steel Corporation limestone quarry at Monarch remains. At one time Salida was the junction point of the "Narrow-Gauge Circle," a side trip of immense fascination and interest to the tourist. This remarkably scenic excursion took the traveler westward to Ridgway, south over the Rio Grande Southern to Durango, thence east along the New Mexico border to Antonito, and finally northward through Alamosa to Salida.

The standard-gauge main-line north of Salida is centered in a wide valley whose western rim is formed by a row of peaks rising well over a mile above the tracks. But the narrow-gauge lines were entirely different in character. They climbed up four-percent grades to cross Poncha Pass to the iron mines at Orient, and the San Luis Valley. Likewise, one line—since converted to standard-gauge—reached Monarch, negotiating a double-switchback in the process. The narrow-gauge main-line wriggled over Marshall Pass to Gunnison where it joined coal-producing branches from Baldwin (formerly C&S), Crested Butte, Anthracite and Floresta. Beyond Gunnison the main-line continued down the Gunnison River toward the Black Canyon. At Aberdeen Junction a branch once went to a granite quarry, while another diverged at Lake Junction to reach the mining

This old-time engraving shows the west side of Marshall Pass — the highest point reached by the Denver & Rio Grande on its narrow-gauge main-line between Denver and Salt Lake City — 10,856 feet above sea level.

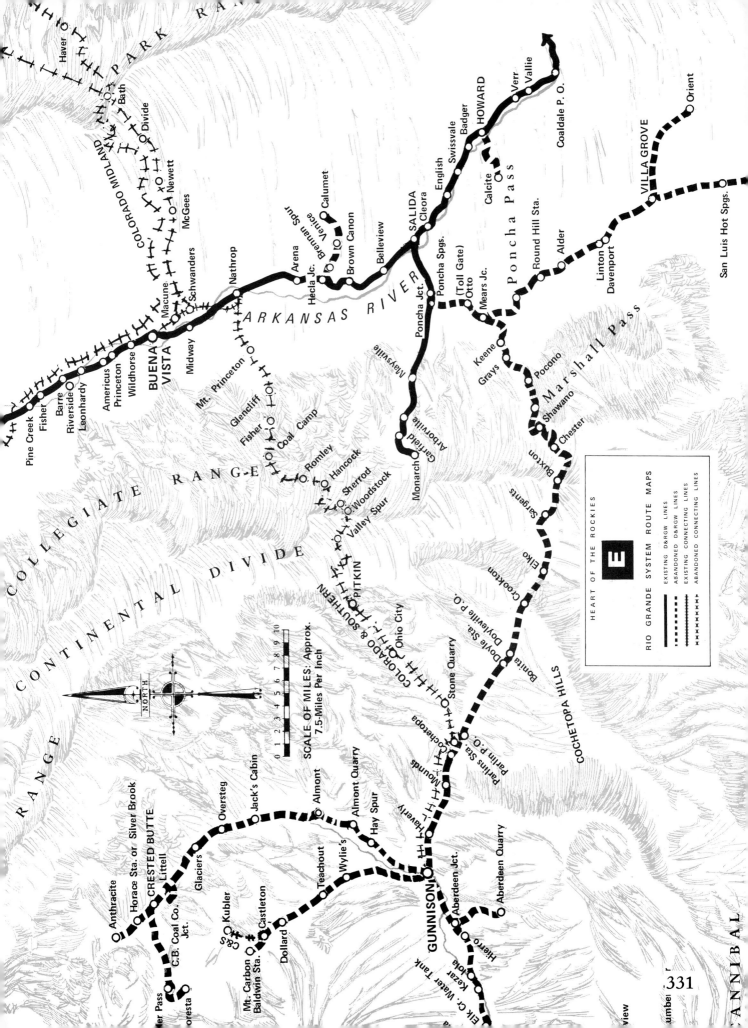

THOR PARK RANGE

Haver
Bath
Divide
Newett
McGees
Schwanders
Nathrop
Macune
Midway
Wildhorse
Princeton
Americus
Leonhardy
Riverside
Barre
Fisher
Pine Creek
BUENA VISTA

COLORADO MIDLAND

Arena
Hecla Jc.
Brennan Spur
Venice
Calumet
Brown Canon
Belleview

ARKANSAS RIVER

SALIDA
Cleora
English
Swissvale
Badger
HOWARD
Verr
Vallie
Coaldale P. O.
Poncha Pass
VILLA GROVE
Orient
San Luis Hot Spgs.

Poncha Jct.
Poncha Spgs.
(Toll Gate)
Otto
Mears Jc.
Calcite
Round Hill Sta.
Alder
Linton
Davenport

Mt. Princeton
Glencliff
Fisher
Coal Camp
Romley
Hancock
Sherrod
Woodstock
Valley Spur

COLLEGIATE RANGE

Maysville
Garfield
Arborville
Monarch

Keene
Grays
Pocono
Shawano
Chester
Buxton

Marshall Pass

CONTINENTAL DIVIDE

PITKIN
Ohio City
Stone Quarry
Doyleville P. O.
Doyle Sta.
Bonita
Elko
Crookton

COLORADO & SOUTHERN

RANGE

NORTH

SCALE OF MILES: Approx.
7.5-Miles Per Inch
0 1 2 3 4 5 6 7 8 9 10

COCHETOPA HILLS

HEART OF THE ROCKIES

RIO GRANDE SYSTEM ROUTE MAPS

EXISTING D&RGW LINES
ABANDONED D&RGW LINES
EXISTING CONNECTING LINES
ABANDONED CONNECTING LINES

Oversteg
Jack's Cabin
Almont
Almont Quarry
Hay Spur
Wylie's
Teachout

Parlins P. O.
Parlins Sta.
Cochetopa
Mounds
Haverly
Sargents

CRESTED BUTTE
Horace Sta. or Silver Brook
Littell
Glaciers
Anthracite
C.B. Coal Co.
Jct.
Kubler
Castleton
Dollard
Mt. Carbon
Baldwin Sta.

GUNNISON
Aberdeen Jct.
Aberdeen Quarry
Hierro
Iola
Kezar
Elk Cr. Water Tank

ANNIBAL

331

An early view of Marshall Pass, looking southward across the long snowshed which covered the D&RG's track and turntable at this point. The U.S. Geological Survey benchmark shows 10,855.903 feet elevation for this pass.

town of Lake City. The South Park Division of the C&S had come down from Alpine Tunnel to Parlin, whence it had paralleled the D&RG into Gunnison.

A steep D&RG branch went up to Calumet north of Salida where another early iron mine was located. The CM dipped into the area for only a short distance, descending to Buena Vista from Trout Creek Pass (also used by the C&S) and paralleled the D&RG up the Arkansas River into Leadville.

Today's traveler, speeding along the highway at mile-a-minute pace, finds it difficult to discern traces of former populous towns, the busy industries and vanished roadbed, and he finds it even more difficult to believe that any previous civilized activity ever existed, so rapidly has time erased man's comparatively transient work.

THE SAN LUIS VALLEY

The headwaters of the Rio Grande drain a great wide, almost-level, basin stretching 100 miles north to south and almost as far east to west. There are hardly any natural impediments to railroad routes until the foothills of the surrounding mountains are reached, and altitudes vary only gradually within a range of about 1000-feet. To the east this upland basin is rimmed by the Sangre de Cristo and Culebra ranges, both of which have peaks well above 14,000-feet. Northwestward and southwestward the Continental Divide encloses the farthest sources of the Rio Grande, limiting the basin in these directions. Only to the south is there a natural outlet for the river which has cut a deepening canyon in its long journey to the sea.

Taking advantage of this untypical mountain terrain, the D&RG was able to construct the longest stretches of tangent track in its system, radiating from Alamosa to Fort Garland, Torres, Antonito and Villa Grove. Before it was dismantled, the 53 miles of narrow-gauge track from

Alamosa Junction to the curve just south of Villa Grove had comprised the fifth-longest stretch of straight track in the United States, a distinction which could hardly be expected of either the D&RG or its narrow-gauge trackage.

The railroad entered the basin from Veta Pass, but replaced this route with a lower-grade line several miles to the south at La Veta Pass. A second line came in from the north over Poncha Pass to tap the iron mines at Orient; the Villa Grove-Alamosa segment having been constructed when the track east from Alamosa was converted to standard-gauge. The narrow-gauge main-line went south Alamosa to Antonito, splitting there to reach Santa Fé and Durango. One other line followed the Rio Grande upstream through a narrowing valley (beyond Del Norte) to North Creede. During years of full-scale operations the standard-gauge (North Creede to La Veta Pass) handled outbound lumber, livestock and agricultural products, while the narrow-gauge line (Antonito to Poncha Pass) was kept busy with considerable traffic in minerals. The construction of good highways parallel to the tracks, and the general reduction of all varieties of traffic otherwise, caused the removal of the line over Poncha Pass. And today there is even some doubt that all remaining trackage in the "Valley" will be self-supporting for very many years longer, so great has been the diversion of remaining traffic to highway transportation.

In this section there was only one branch, which went from Moffat over to a mine and mill at Cottonwood located on the lower slopes of the Sangre de Cristos. However, there were two other railroads connecting with the D&RG. One of these was the ill-fated San Luis Southern, a remnant of which still exists at Blanca as the Southern San Luis Valley. The other one is the relatively healthy San Luis Central, running north from Sugar Junction to Center. Both of these railroads have always been standard gauge, having been constructed after the D&RG had changed its track gauge.

The line to Antonito had been three-rail for many years, providing an interesting operation with cars of both gauges. Narrow-gauge locomotives hauled both standard-gauge and narrow-gauge cars, the standard-gauge ones being coupled between two idler-cars which match couplers with

Sierra Blanca, at an elevation of 14,363 feet, was considered to be Colorado's loftiest peak for many years. Overlooking the vast San Luis Valley, this jagged mountain is at the southern edge of the Sangre de Cristo Range.

Wagon Wheel Gap, gateway to the vast headwaters basin of the Rio Grande del Norte — the Great River of the North. This narrow gap in the canyon is on the Creede Branch of the Denver & Rio Grande.

333

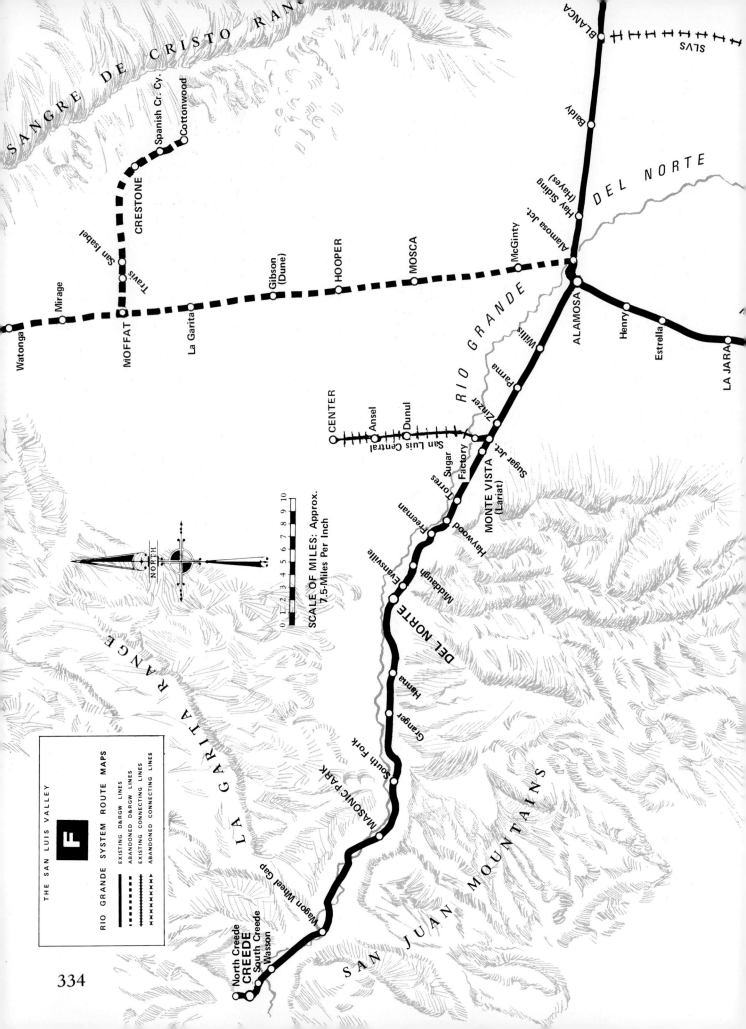

THE SAN LUIS VALLEY

RIO GRANDE SYSTEM ROUTE MAPS

EXISTING D&RGW LINES
ABANDONED D&RGW LINES
EXISTING CONNECTING LINES
ABANDONED CONNECTING LINES

SCALE OF MILES: Approx.
7.5-Miles Per Inch

0 1 2 3 4 5 6 7 8 9 10

F

NORTH

SANGRE DE CRISTO RANGE

BLANCA

SLVS

DEL NORTE

Baldy

Hay Siding (Hayes)

Alamosa Jct.

ALAMOSA

Henry

Estrella

LA JARA

Spanish Cr. Cy.

Cottonwood

CRESTONE

San Isabel

Travis

Mirage

Watonga

MOFFAT

La Garita

Gibson (Dune)

HOOPER

MOSCA

McGinty

RIO GRANDE

Willis

Parma

Zinzer

Sugar Jct.

CENTER

Ansel

Dunul

San Luis Central

Sugar Factory

Torres

MONTE VISTA (Lariat)

Haywood

Freeman

Evansville

Middaugh

DEL NORTE

Hanna

Granger

South Fork

MASONIC PARK

Wagon Wheel Gap

SAN JUAN MOUNTAINS

North Creede

CREEDE

South Creede

Wasson

LA GARITA RANGE

334

cars of either gauge. During the winter or whenever the narrow-gauge line was not operating, standard-gauge locomotives handled the traffic, usually all standard-gauge cars.

It was in this area that the D&RGW operated its last S-G steam locomotive. This occurred on December 26, 1956, when the 1151 made a trip from Alamosa to South Fork for a few cars of freight.

At Toltec Gorge — on the D&RG narrow-gauge line between Alamosa and Durango — the rails were more than one-thousand feet above the tumbling waters of the Los Pinos River. This was part of the long climb from Antonito to Cumbres Pass, which is at 10,015 feet above sea level.

THE LONELY PINE FORESTS

West of the Rio Grande del Norte, where the river crosses the Colorado-New Mexico border, lies a virtually uninhabited region characterized by extensive forests of ponderosa pine which grow prolifically in the warm, dry climate. Though the Continental Divide separates this section into two areas, one drained by the Rio Grande, the other by the San Juan River, the overall topography is much the same in both. The Divide itself is much lower than the higher peaks on either side of it and it intersected D&RGW tracks at the relatively insignificant altitude of 7730-feet, a few miles west of Chama. Timberline here is much higher than in the northern mountains and it is an uncommon mountain which thrusts its bare summit above the trees covering its lower slopes.

Names on the maps of this territory rarely designate organized towns; more likely they locate solitary outposts of civilization: section houses, water tanks, sidings, lumber mills, general stores, vanished stations, road crossings or the decayed remains of a once prosperous village. Yet this is not so strange. The railroads were built through this unpopulated country to provide freight and passenger transportation for the lumber industry (which developed alongside the mining industry) and the cities which grew with them. There was never much evidence of civilized activity, except in those towns which became big enough to become permanent, and the entire region is very much as it was before the arrival of the railroad. Like many other examples in Colorado, an era of human endeavor came, flourished briefly, then departed, leaving scant trace of its ephemeral existence.

Originally it had been the D&RG's intention to build south from Alamosa to reach Santa Fé, then a commercial center of some importance, and it had planned to build southwestward into the San Juan mining district. En route to both destinations it developed a considerable traffic in lumber produced at trackside mills, as well as that delivered in car-load lots by connecting lines. One of these railroads was the Tierra Amarilla Southern which ran down the Chama River from the end of the Chama lumber spur to Tierra Amarilla. Two others were the Rio Grande & Pagosa Springs and the Rio Grande & Southwestern, operating as a coordinated system north and south of Lumberton. These lines were taken up when the big timber was logged-out of their operating territories. Two other factors contributed to the demise of the lumber industry: the decline of the mining industry, and the availability of Oregon and Washington lumber at Denver.

West of Antonito the tracks, beginning a long climb of 1.4-percent grade, ascend sagebrush covered slopes to attain the tops of lava-capped mesas, meandering over the open landscape in continuous curves. Winding in and out of every side canyon north of the Los Pinos River, the line finally surmounts Cumbres Pass, then drops precipitously down a four-percent grade to Chama. Incidentally, this grade, with its three-locomotive freight trains, provided the United States with their last look at steam-operated main-line narrow-gauge railroading — substantially as it was 40 years ago. This is now the Cumbres & Toltec Scenic Railroad, owned jointly by the States of Colorado and New Mexico.

335

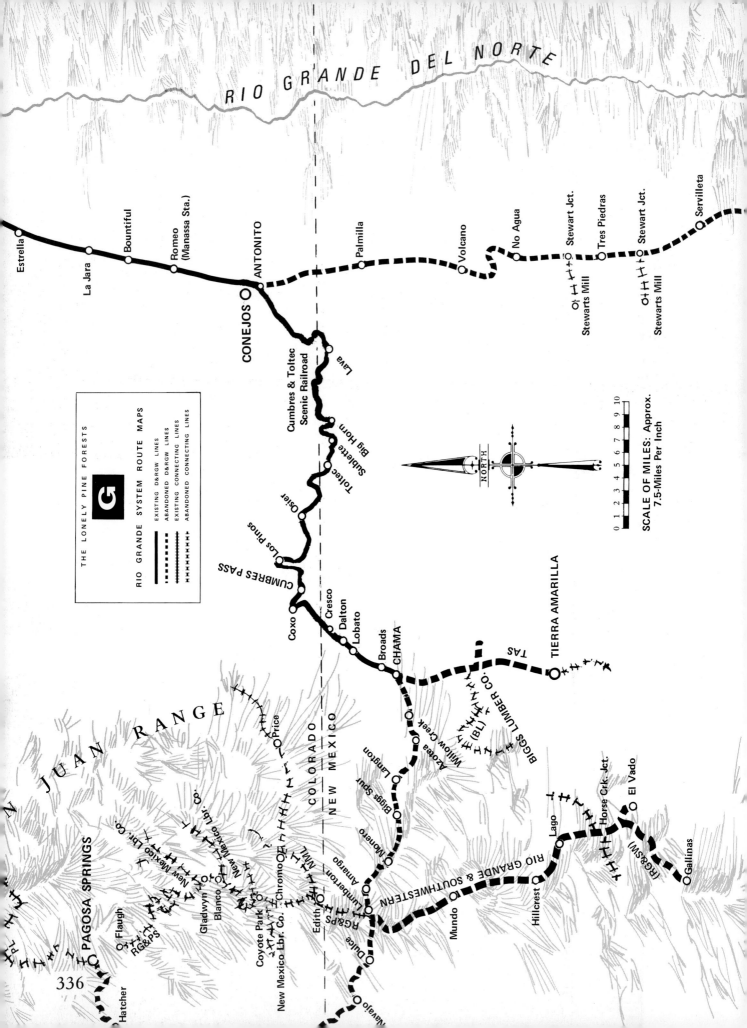

RIO GRANDE DEL NORTE

Estrella
La Jara
Bountiful
Romeo (Manassa Sta.)
ANTONITO
CONEJOS
Palmilla
Volcano
No Agua
Stewart Jct.
Stewarts Mill
Tres Piedras
Stewart Jct.
Stewarts Mill
Servilleta

Lava
Cumbres & Toltec Scenic Railroad
Sublette
Big Horn
Toltec
Osier
Los Pinos
CUMBRES PASS
Coxo
Cresco
Dalton
Lobato
Broads
CHAMA
TAS
TIERRA AMARILLA

BIGGS LUMBER CO. (BL)

SAN JUAN RANGE

Price
COLORADO
NEW MEXICO

Azotea
Willow Creek
Biggs Spur
Lagunton
Monero

RIO GRANDE & SOUTHWESTERN

Lago
Horse Crk. Jct.
El Vado
(RG&SW)
Gallinas

PAGOSA SPRINGS
Flaugh
RG&PS
Hatcher
Gladwyn
Blanco
New Mexico Lbr. Co.
New Mexico Lbr:
Coyote Park
NML
Chromo
NML
Edith
Amargo
Lumberton
RG&PS
Dulce
Navajo
Mundo
Hillcrest

THE LONELY PINE FORESTS

G

RIO GRANDE SYSTEM ROUTE MAPS

EXISTING D&RGW LINES
ABANDONED D&RGW LINES
EXISTING CONNECTING LINES
ABANDONED CONNECTING LINES

NORTH

SCALE OF MILES: Approx.
7.5-Miles Per Inch
0 1 2 3 4 5 6 7 8 9 10

336

Number 481 — having departed Alamosa at dawn with a long train of narrow-gauge freight cars, and assisted by a sister 2-8-2 — attained the summit of Cumbres Pass near sundown. The helper engine was cut off the train here to drift downgrade light — a standard practice.

The combined efforts of two of the D&RGW's outside-frame 2-8-2's were required to boost 25 freight cars up the four-percent grade on the west side of Cumbres Pass. This scene was photographed from the top of the pass and is directed southward toward Chama, New Mexico, about 14 miles away.

This little picture shows the D&RGW's famous Phantom Curve as viewed from the east. This scene is east of Cumbres Pass on the Alamosa-Durango narrow-gauge line.

ESPANOLA BRANCH.					
SOUTH.					**NORTH.**
No. 53, Frt & Pass S. E.	Miles	STATIONS.		Miles	No. 54, Frt & Pass S. E.
8 15	......	Lv..........Denver..........Ar		370.1	6 40
7 25	251.1	..........Alamosa..........		120.0	6 15
ar 9 00	278.8	D..........Antonito..........		91.3	lv 5 00
lv 9 15					ar 4 45
9 50	290.2	..........Palmilla..........		79.9	† 4 05
10 12	297.1	..........Volcano..........		73.0	† 3 42
10 45	306.3	..........No Agua..........		63.8	† 3 10
11 05	313.5	D..........Tres Piedras..........		56.6	* 2 45
ar 11 55	323.0	..........Serviletta..........		47.1	‡lv 2 05
lv 12 30					‡ar 1 48
1 07	335.0	..........Caliente..........		35.1	1 07
1 40	343.5	D..........Barranca..........		26.6	12 30
1 52	346.5	..........Comanche..........		23.6	† 12 12
2 15	351.0	D..........Embudo..........		19.1	* 11 55
2 40	359.1	..........Alcalde..........		11.0	† 11 22
2 59	365.2	..........Chamita..........		4.9	† 11 02
3 15	370.1	..........Espanola..........		......	10 45
5 45	408.4	..........Santa Fe..........			8 15

☞ See page 5 for explanation of terms.
Mountain Time (105th Mer.) the Standard, furnished by A. B. Ingols, Jeweler, 1614 Larimer St., Denver.

South of Antonito, the branch to Santa Fe´was built well to the west of the Cañon of the Rio Grande del Norte to avoid extremely difficult construction and to tap what little lumber business there was (Stewart Lumber spur).

The only other railroad in the area was the San Luis Valley Southern which built south from Blanca to Jarosa at the Colorado - New Mexico border. This railroad had intended to continue southward to Taos, New Mexico; however, this never materialized, and in time the line folded due to lack of traffic.

THE RIO GRANDE VALLEY

In its long course from sources in Colorado to the Gulf of Mexico, the Rio Grande flows through high mountain valleys, across a level upland plain (the San Luis Valley), then heads directly southward at Alamosa. As it approaches the New Mexico border, the river sinks below the surface of the ground, forming an ever-deepening canyon in the great lava sheets which cover much of this area. Close to the river, vegetation is scant, but the farther hills and the distant mountains are covered with dense forests of pine. At Embudo the river emerges from the confines of its long and deep gorge and flows through a valley which widens rapidly to the south. In the small area between Española and Embudo there is located an unusual phenomenon of nature. Here, temperate climate fruits—apples, cherries and pears—grow along-side produce requiring a hot climate—apricots, melons and peppers—an unusual situation resulting from the high altitude (5600 feet) and a long warm growing season.

The entire country south of Antonito is very old. Buildings erected by the Spaniards date back to 1600, and Indian dwellings have been inhabited as far back as 1100. Even the ground itself reflects this great age, being divided into land grants given to the early Spanish settlers, or pueblos belonging to the original Indian tribes. The passage of time has shown hardly any effect upon this ancient

valley, and except for Los Alamos, Santa Fe´and paved roads, the valley remains much as it was ten centuries ago. And even though railroads penetrated the area, time has erased all but one.

The Denver & Rio Grande's route to Santa Fe´stayed west of the river to avoid its deep canyon, thus creating the problem of reaching Santa Fe´, which was high above the river to the east. The only answer lay in a four-percent descent down Comanche Canyon to Embudo on the river's banks, along which the track was laid to Española. Here the D&RG was prohibited from building farther south because of its agreement terminating the dispute with the AT&SF over Raton Pass and Royal Gorge construction rights. But all was not lost; hardly had the D&RG arrived at its end of track when a group of local citizens built the

Embudo, New Mexico, was an isolated station at the southern end of the long, deep Cañon of the Rio Grande del Norte. This was on the narrow-gauge Santa Fe´Branch of the D&RG.

338

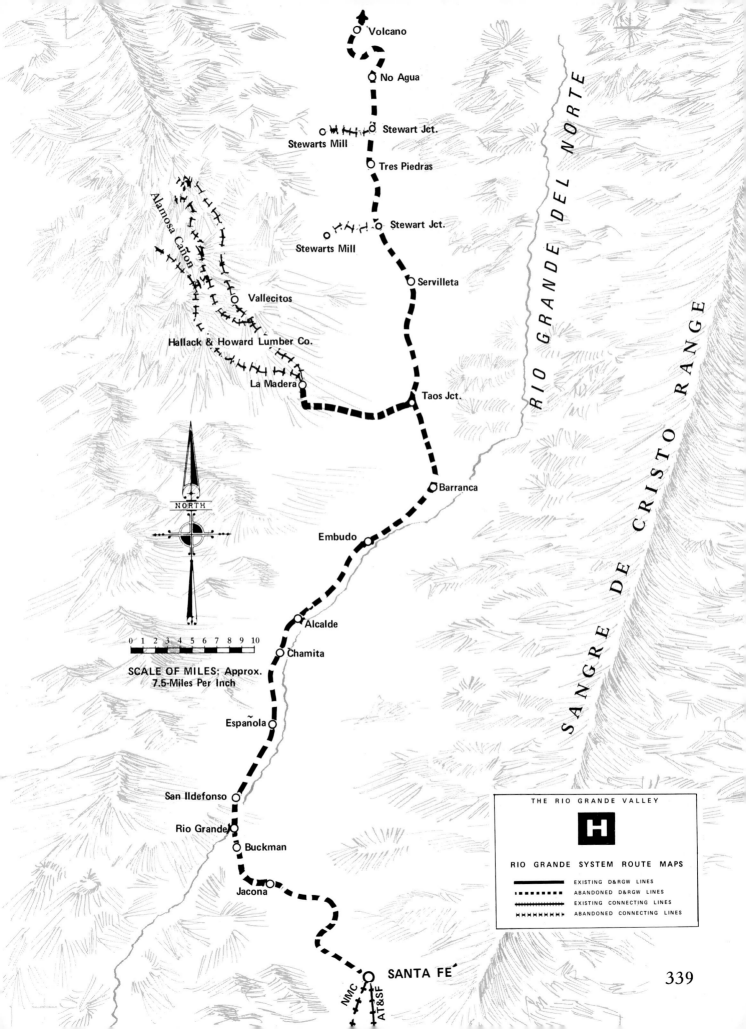

Volcano

No Agua

Stewart Jct.
Stewarts Mill

Tres Piedras

Stewart Jct.
Stewarts Mill

Servilleta

Alamosa Cañon

Vallecitos

Hallack & Howard Lumber Co.

La Madera

Taos Jct.

Barranca

Embudo

Alcalde

Chamita

Española

San Ildefonso

Rio Grande

Buckman

Jacona

NORTH

0 1 2 3 4 5 6 7 8 9 10

SCALE OF MILES; Approx.
7.5-Miles Per Inch

RIO GRANDE DEL NORTE

SANGRE DE CRISTO RANGE

SANTA FE

NMC

AT&SF

THE RIO GRANDE VALLEY

H

RIO GRANDE SYSTEM ROUTE MAPS

———————— EXISTING D&RGW LINES
- - - - - - - ABANDONED D&RGW LINES
++++++++++ EXISTING CONNECTING LINES
╫╫╫╫╫╫╫╫ ABANDONED CONNECTING LINES

Texas, Santa Fe' & Northern from Santa Fe' to Española. This latter company—which came no closer to Texas than Santa Fe's city limits—failed to pay its debts, and was reorganized as the Santa Fe' Southern, which likewise did no better with either finances or a southward extension. The D&RG, not too happy with this uncertain connection, traded some of its Rio Grande Southern bonds for the railroad, calling it the Rio Grande & Santa Fe until it was absorbed by the D&RG.

The line had only one branch, which went from Taos Junction through Ojo Caliente, an old spa, to La Madera where it connected with the Hallack & Howard Lumber Company line. At Santa Fe', D&RG rails met those of the long-gone New Mexico Central and the Santa Fe'Branch of the AT&SF. There was no interchange of cars, however, because of the difference in gauges. Oddly enough, there was a completely disconnected railroad in the area which provided some traffic for the D&RG. It was the Santa Barbara Pole & Tie Company, a subsidiary of the AT&SF, which produced poles and ties for its parent. It operated several miles of track in the forests of the Santa Barbara Grant, and floated the finished lumber down to the D&RG near Embudo where it was loaded for shipment. Its Shay locomotive and cars were hauled overland to the operation some 25 miles east of Embudo, and when operations ceased everything was hauled out in the same manner.

THE NORTHERN COAL FIELDS

This section of northwestern Colorado contains the White River Plateau from whose heights streams run in every direction of the compass, although all of them eventually pour their waters into the Colorado River. The periphery of this great up-lift is underlain with coal which has been mined in a great many locations, much of it travelling over the Craig Branch to points of combustion. The general topography of the country through which the railroad operates is quite varied, ranging from deep canyons to heavily timbered mountains and wide expanses of open plain. At Steamboat Springs the Continental Divide is only eight miles east of the track, yet it is only 4000-feet above the city's 6700-foot elevation, and there are no great peaks which are so typical of the Divide elsewhere.

All D&RGW trackage in this region was acquired through the merger of other companies. The earliest one was the Denver, Northwestern & Pacific, which operated as far as Steamboat Springs. This company was succeeded

The jagged buttes in the background of this photograph mark the location of Phippsburg, Colorado, in the arid northwest corner of the state. Here solid trains of coal are

DELL A. MC COY

assembled for movement to electric generating plants near Denver. This was formerly D&SL trackage and is now on the Craig Branch of the D&RGW.

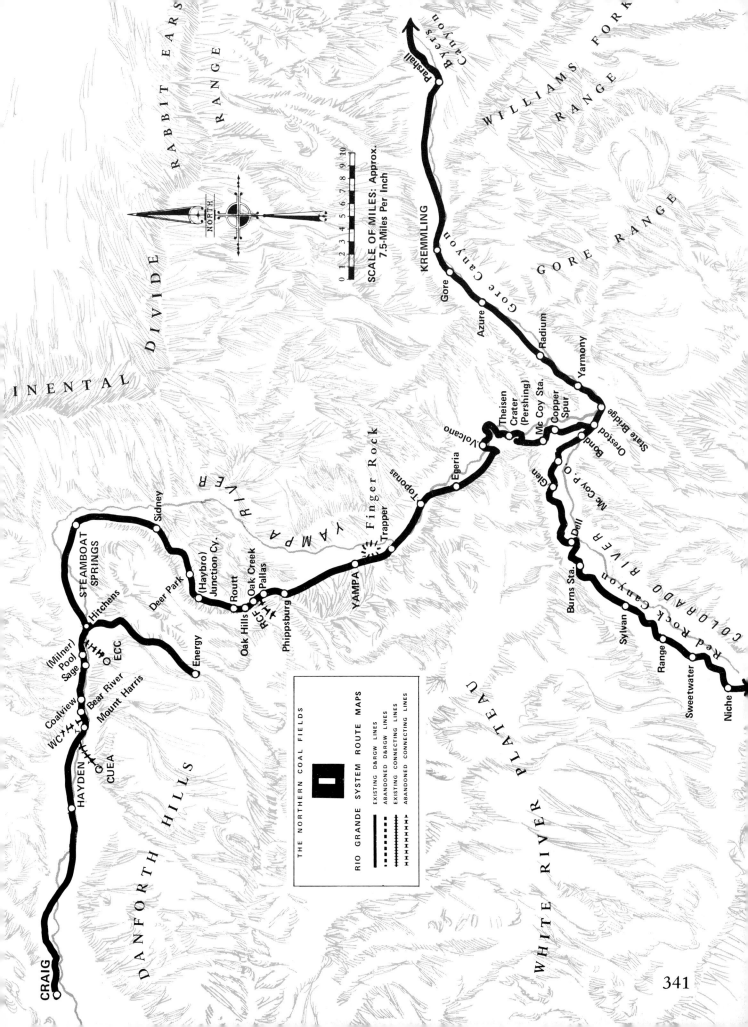

CRAIG

STEAMBOAT SPRINGS

Hirchens

(Milner)
Pool
Sage
ECC
Coalview
Bear River
Mount Harris
WC
CUEA
HAYDEN

Energy

Sidney

Deer Park

(Haybro)
Junction Cy.
Routt
Oak Hills
Oak Creek
RCC
Pallas
Phippsburg

YAMPA

Trapper

Finger Rock

Toponas

Egeria

Volcano

Theisen
Crater
(Pershing)
Mc Coy Sta.
Copper
Spur

Glen

Yarmony

Radium

Azure

Gore

KREMMLING

Parshall

Byers Canyon

Gore Canyon

State Bridge
Orestod
Bond

Mc Coy P.O.

Dell

Burns Sta.

Sylvan

Range

Sweetwater

Niche

CONTINENTAL DIVIDE

RABBIT EARS RANGE

WILLIAMS FORK RANGE

GORE RANGE

YAMPA RIVER

DANFORTH HILLS

WHITE RIVER PLATEAU

COLORADO RIVER

Red Rock Canyon

SCALE OF MILES: Approx.
7.5-Miles Per Inch

0 1 2 3 4 5 6 7 8 9 10

NORTH

THE NORTHERN COAL FIELDS

RIO GRANDE SYSTEM ROUTE MAPS

EXISTING D&RGW LINES
ABANDONED D&RGW LINES
EXISTING CONNECTING LINES
ABANDONED CONNECTING LINES

341

RUSS COLLMAN

Led by two General Motors F9-model diesel-electrics, the four-car "Rio Grande Zephyr" was rolling eastward in this view looking down into the rocky canyon of the Colorado River near the mid-point of the Dotsero Cutoff.

The view above shows the Routt County Fuel Company's loading facilities at Oak Creek, Colorado, on what was the Denver & Salt Lake main-line. Coal was supplied to these facilities by a cable-tramway which ran up the hillside to mine trackage. Other Oak Creek mine buildings are shown below. The upper one was the Yampa Valley Coal Company tipple, while the lower one shows an overall view of the Moffat Coal Company structures. All of these photos are from the D&SL's booklet, "The Yampa Coal Field," published in 1914.

by the Denver & Salt Lake, which pushed the track as far as Craig, hoping (as did the DNW&P) to continue westward to Salt Lake City. Its successor also was unable to go any farther and in time became controlled by the D&RGW, which absorbed it in 1947. Even the Cutoff between the D&SL at Orestod and the D&RGW at Dotsero had been a separate company (D&SLW), likewise merged in 1947.

West of Kremmling the rails follow the Colorado River downgrade through a continuous series of rocky canyons all of the way to Dotsero where the Eagle River joins the Colorado and the Cutoff connects with the original main-line. North of Orestod the track winds in and out of wide and deep canyons in its ascent to Toponas whence it follows the Yampa River and its tributaries down to Craig. The railroad is well confined by close hills as far as Steamboat Springs, but beyond that city the horizon recedes to considerable distances.

At first, practically the only traffic on the long line was coal destined for Denver; later came lumber, feed and livestock. Now it is essentially all coal again to be consumed in Denver's giant electric-generating stations — all of the passenger traffic and much of the freight traffic having been diverted to improved public highways. The construction of the Moffat Tunnel, completed in 1927, eliminated the difficult and uncertain operations over Rollins Pass, and paved the way for the construction of the Dotsero Cutoff which shortened the Denver-Salt Lake City route by 175 miles, making the D&RGW competitive with other railroads for long-haul through traffic. Through service began over the "Moffat Tunnel Route" in 1934, and in 1947 the track between Orestod and Craig became a long branch from the new main-line.

Until fairly recent times there were no branches between Orestod and Craig; nevertheless some of the coal companies

DELL A. MCCOY

The upper level of the long loop into narrow Rock Creek Canyon is perched on ledges far above the stream and connected by steel deck-trestles. The D&RGW passenger train is running downgrade toward Orestod.

As shown in this old-time view of the Juniper Coal Company's loading facilities at Oak Creek, coal was being shipped in wooden box-cars belonging to the Southern Pacific and Great Northern railroads.

"THE YAMPA COAL FIELD"

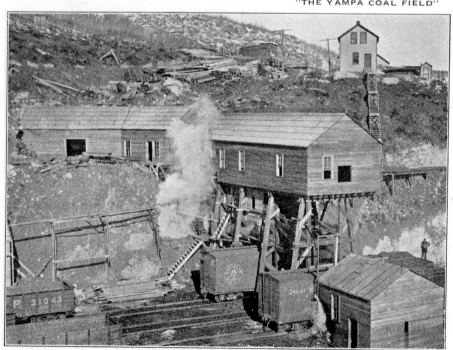

MOFFAT TUNNEL ROUTE

The Colorado River — originally called the Grand River in Colorado — wound through nearly 20 miles of colorful, deep canyon east of Glenwood Springs. This scene shows the original narrow-gauge trackage along the south side of the gorge — later known as Glenwood Canyon. Today this is the heavy-duty main-line of the D&RGW.

operated short spurs between their mines and the tipples adjacent to the railroad. A recently-built branch now runs south from Milner to a new large coal mine at Energy, and the D&RGW operates the spur which serves the Colorado-Ute Electric Association power plant south of Hayden. Although the coal is but of average quality for Colorado, it is readily available, can be mined cheaply and is easily transported to Denver, where it has entirely displaced the somewhat better Trinidad coal which rarely moves north of Pueblo.

THE COLORADO RIVER BASIN

Prior to 1921 Colorado's boundaries included two major rivers with very nearly the same name, the Rio Grande (Great River to the Spanish-speaking citizens) and the Grand River of the State's northwestern quadrant. This somewhat confusing situation was remedied by Congress when it renamed the Grand River, "Colorado," and thereby avoided any possible conflict with Mexico—which would have been uncooperative in the renaming of its border river. (Previously, the Colorado River began at the confluence of the Green and Grand rivers in southeast Utah.)

With the Continental Divide at the southeast corner of this section and the Grand Mesa in the southwest corner, the predominant drainage is northward and westward. The principal streams originate quite high on the mountains, frequently just below timberline at 11,000-feet, and flow through valleys which often become canyons for short distances. This difficult topography forced the railroad lines to follow the streams to their destinations, and only one (Colorado Midland) chose to force a direct trans-mountain passage.

Lured by the fabulous wealth of Aspen's multiplicity of silver mines, but deterred by the gigantic peaks which separated it from Leadville, the D&RG built hastily down the Eagle River, laying narrow-gauge rails on standard-gauge ties, Between Dotsero and Glenwood Springs it blasted a

345

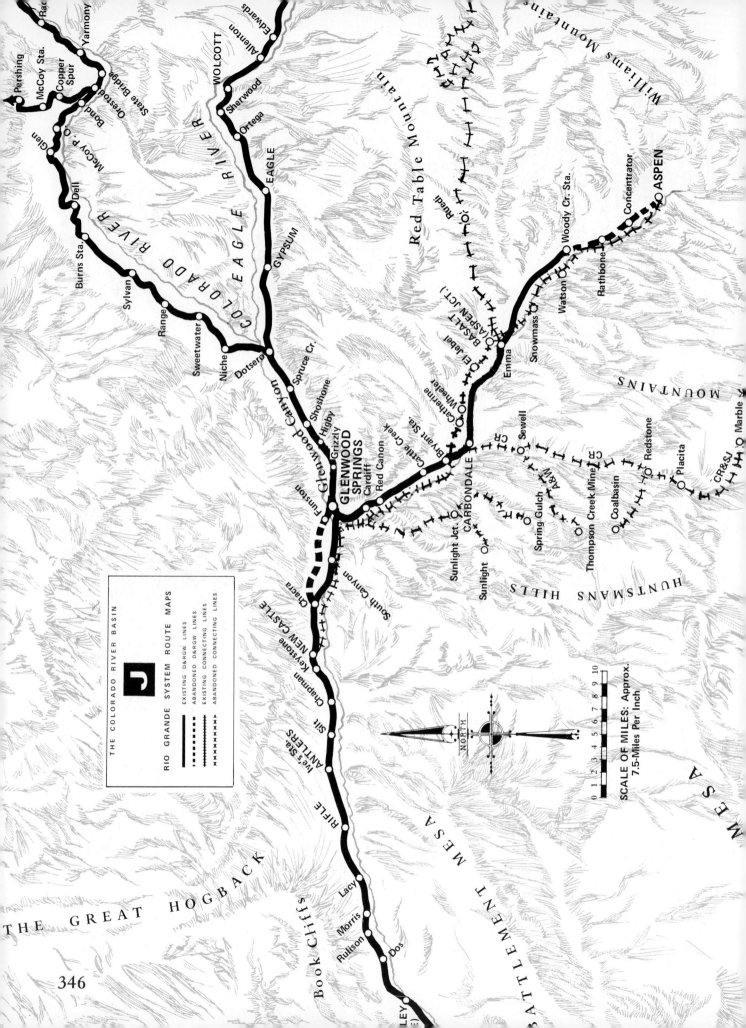

346

WILLIAM H. JACKSON

Through the beautiful Glenwood Canyon, the Denver & Rio Grande's original rails were laid to three-foot narrow-gauge on standard-gauge cross-ties in anticipation of an imminent gauge conversion.

Prior to the turn of the century, Glenwood Springs became a popular spa for well-to-do tourists visiting the Rocky Mountains. This lithograph shows how the Hotel Colorado,

Hot Springs Pool and Bath House looked from the D&RG depot grounds across the Colorado River. Glenwood Springs is at the western end of Glenwood Canyon.

347

shelf along the south wall of the deep and narrow canyon, thence it ascended the open valley of the Roaring Fork to Aspen. Aspen was only a bit more than 25 map-miles from Leadville, yet it was 130 miles by railroad, so formidable was this mountain barrier. Though this was a roundabout route to Aspen, the D&RG had a second motive for its choice; it could continue down the Colorado from Glenwood Springs to meet the Rio Grande Western at Grand Junction, thus providing a new main-line which could be converted easily to standard gauge. This was done shortly after the N-G rails had reached Aspen, and the D&RG together with the RGW initiated S-G service between Denver and Ogden. Considerably longer than the Union Pacific's line connecting the two cities, the D&RG-RGW's route at least allowed it to serve them as did other principal railroads.

In 1934, another change was made in the D&RGW's main-line routing; the Dotsero Cutoff completed the link along the Colorado River between the Denver & Salt Lake and the D&RGW, creating a much shorter and highly competitive transcontinental route.

The D&RG had one rival for the Aspen business, the mountain-hurdling Colorado Midland, which paralleled its rails between Aspen and New Castle, but after a fitful existence, the latter carrier disappeared following World War I. In time Aspen's burgeoning traffic dwindled to nothing, but the Aspen Branch managed to subsist on agriculture and livestock. Today, iron ore and coal are important.

Other railroads once contributed to the prosperity of the Aspen Branch. First, the narrow-gauge Aspen & Western delivered some poor coal to the D&RG at Carbondale. This N-G line was quickly abandoned, being replaced by a N-G extension of the Crystal River railroad which obligingly extended its S-G track to Redstone where a battery of coke ovens was installed. It also served a coal mine at Placita, farther up the river. At a later date, the Crystal River & San Juan built from Placita to Marble, where a giant marble-finishing mill was erected. The Colorado-Yule Marble Company operated an extremely steep electric line up to a deposit of white marble of incomparable quality. Still another S-G line, the Treasury Mountain, built a short line to a similar deposit, but of inferior quality. In time, the marble business decayed; it could not compete with stone from Georgia and Vermont, and eventually all of this trackage, including the N-G line to Coal Basin, was removed, leaving the D&RGW as the sole surviving railroad.

COLORADO FRUIT COUNTRY

South of Grand Mesa—which lies across the northern boundary of this section—is a fair land of spacious valleys and mild climate, renowned for its production of fruit. At the extreme southern end of this section the great peaks jutting westward from the Continental Divide's elbow are arrayed in a massive wall, piercing the clouds at 14,000-feet. Thus protected from the elements, and watered by the Gunnison River and its multiple tributaries, the entire

From this point — looking westward along the Gunnison River near Cebolla — the Denver & Rio Grande entered the mesa-lands of western Colorado. Ahead lie the famous Black Canyon of the Gunnison.

region is eminently suited to agriculture, particularly the growing of fruit.

Much of the country, however, is still relatively primitive. The Grand Mesa, the deep canyon of the Gunnison, the West Elk Mountains and Trident Mesa are essentially devoid of permanent habitation. On the other hand, not all of the area's commercial acitivity has been agricultural. Lake City and Ouray were surrounded by veritable treasuries of silver ore which was mined in staggering quantities, while Bowie, Somerset and Oliver still produce considerable tonnages of excellent coal.

The railroad entered the region by coming down the Gunnison, headed for Grand Junction. After following the river into the upper portion of the Black Canyon, it found the lower canyon impractical and emerged from the gorge at Cimarron, whence it climbed a four-percent grade over Cerro Summit to reach the Uncompahgre River at Montrose. This detour from the original route enabled the tracks to follow the Uncompahgre down a wide valley to its junction with the Gunnison at Delta. For almost a decade this was the D&RG's main-line between Denver and Salt Lake City, later becoming part of the famous Narrow-Gauge Circle.

Three long branches were built. The first one joined at Montrose and proceeded up the Uncompaghre to Ouray, then the center of a booming silver and gold mining district. A few years later the Rio Grande Southern, which became a D&RG subsidiary, started construction at Ridgway, intending to reach Telluride by the long way. Next came the Lake City Branch, which diverged a few miles west of Sapinero at an interesting junction deep within the Gunnison's canyon. Emerging from the canyon, this line ran southward to the city of fabled silver production. The third branch was constructed up the North Fork of the Gunnison to reach the coal deposits at Somerset. Though built narrow-gauge, the line was quickly converted to standard gauge.

In time, the silver mines became depleted or uneconomical to operate; Lake City and Ouray wasted away. The Lake City Branch was sold to a local man who operated it as the San Cristobal railroad, using a "Galloping Goose" built for him by the RGS, but he abandoned the enterprise after a year or so. The Ouray Branch remained in service until the RGS gave up, at which time the Ridgway-Ouray segment was removed and the Montrose-Ridgway

For half-a-century the Denver & Rio Grande used the Curecanti Needle for their trade-mark. This sheer rocky spire was in the depths of the Black Canyon of the Gunnison River — along the original main-line of the railroad.

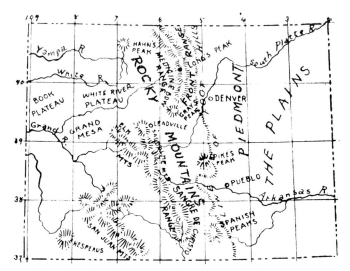

MAP OF COLORADO — SHOWING THE PRINCIPAL MOUNTAIN RANGES AND PHYSICAL FEATURES

portion converted to standard-gauge. The improved highway between Gunnison and Montrose handled all of the traffic between the towns; hence the track was taken up. The remaining lines now carry a considerable tonnage of metallurgical coal billed to steel mills in Utah, as well as the local agricultural and merchandise traffic. While there is a current revival of silver mining in the Ouray-Telluride-Silverton area, it would be expecting too much to see rails in Ouray once again, since the ore and concentrates are being trucked to Ridgway and Montrose for loading there.

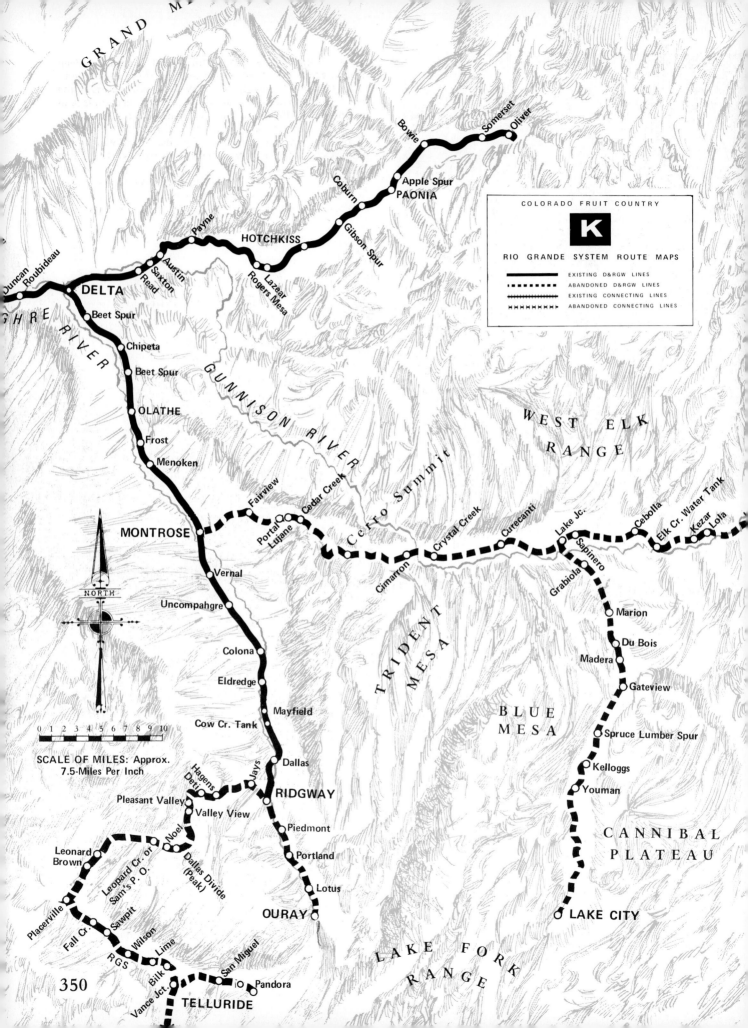

GRAND M...

Duncan
Roubideau
GHRE
RIVER

Oliver
Somerset
Bowie
Apple Spur
Coburn
PAONIA
Gibson Spur
Payne
HOTCHKISS
Austin
Saxton
Read
DELTA
Lazear
Rogers Mesa

Beet Spur
Chipeta
Beet Spur
OLATHE
Frost
Menoken

GUNNISON RIVER

WEST ELK
RANGE

COLORADO FRUIT COUNTRY

K

RIO GRANDE SYSTEM ROUTE MAPS

EXISTING D&RGW LINES
ABANDONED D&RGW LINES
EXISTING CONNECTING LINES
ABANDONED CONNECTING LINES

Fairview
Cedar Creek
Portal
Lujane
Cerro Summit
Crystal Creek
Curecanti
Lake Jc.
Cebolla
Elk Cr. Water Tank
Kezar
Lola
MONTROSE
Cimarron
Sapinero
Grabiola

NORTH

Vernal
Uncompahgre

Marion
Du Bois
Madera
Gateview

Colona
Eldredge

TRIDENT
MESA

BLUE
MESA

Mayfield
Cow Cr. Tank

0 1 2 3 4 5 6 7 8 9 10

SCALE OF MILES: Approx.
7.5-Miles Per Inch

Dallas

Hagens
Deti
Jays
RIDGWAY

Spruce Lumber Spur

Kelloggs
Youman

Pleasant Valley
Valley View
Piedmont
Noel
Dallas Divide
(Peak)
Portland

CANNIBAL
PLATEAU

Leonard
Brown
Leopard Cr. or
Sam's P. O.
Sawpit
Lotus

Placerville
Fall Cr.
Wilson
Lime
RGS
OURAY

LAKE CITY

Bilk
San Miguel
io Pandora
Vance Jct.
TELLURIDE

LAKE FORK
RANGE

350

At the southern end of the Cañon of the Rio de Las Animas — a short distance above Rockwood — the D&RG located its narrow-gauge line on a shelf hewn into the face of a vertical cliff, hundreds of feet above the stream.

THE SOUTHWESTERN MOUNTAINS

Southwestern Colorado — the San Juan Country — has long been famous for its majestic lofty mountains as well as for the unbelievable mineral wealth embedded within their very rocks. Peak after peak towers well above 14,000-feet and it is a rare pass indeed which is as low as 11,000-feet. Strangely enough, these massive mountain groups are not part of the Continental Divide; all are west of it, standing rather alone, though separated distinctly by relatively narrow valleys.

The streams of the southern portion of this section drain southward into the San Juan River; those in the northern half drain into the Dolores or Uncompahgre. But all of them are part of the Colorado River's vast basin, joining the main stream at widely separated locations. The Animas in its southward course flows through a deep canyon almost 50 miles long before it breaks free from its rocky confinement near Durango. The Uncompahgre escapes at Ridgway after being a turbulent mountain stream for relatively few miles, while the San Miguel is forced to remain within precipitous walls for long distances. Only the Dolores has a

valley of appreciable dimensions and it becomes a deep canyon soon after it leaves this section. These stream beds, such as they are, provided the only avenues of access to the area by rail, and construction was most circuitous and expensive. Yet the traffic was worth the effort.

D&RG rails, advancing cross-country along the New Mexico border, first reached Durango, and with scant hesitation pushed up the Animas toward Silverton. Then down from the north came a branch to Ouray. Continuing beyond the D&RG's railheads, the Silverton Railroad hurdled Sheridan Pass, hoping to connect with the D&RG at Ouray. It stopped six miles short, however, unable to

A highly exaggerated rendition of the Cañon of the Rio de Las Animas and the Needle Mountains — looking south from the mining town of Silverton, Colorado.

351

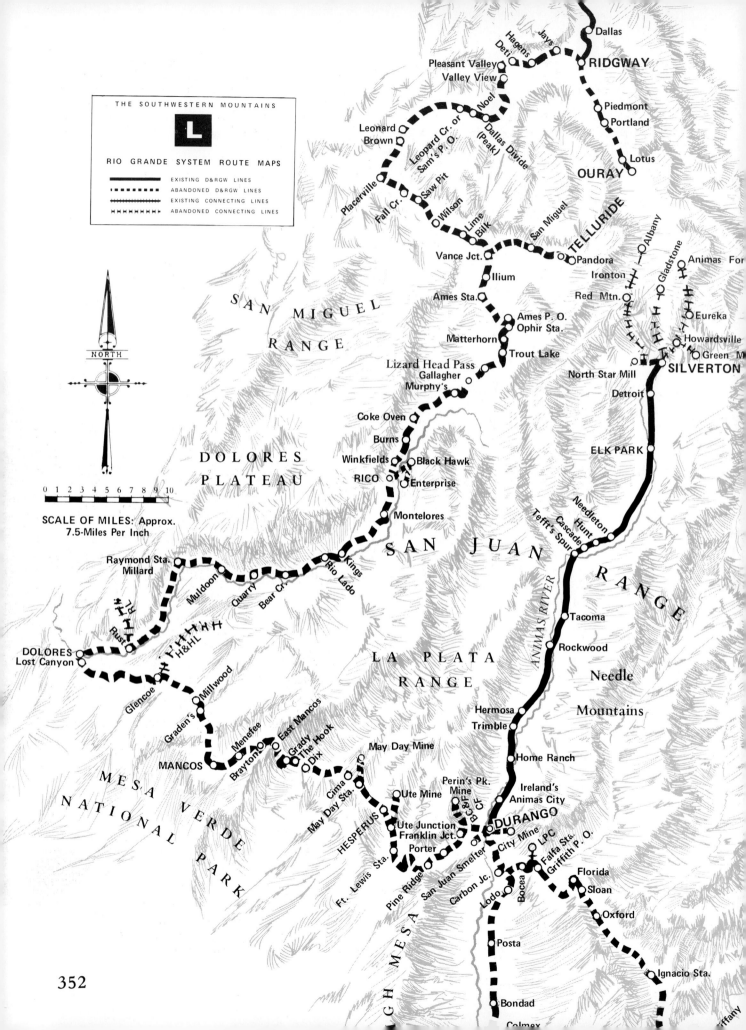

THE SOUTHWESTERN MOUNTAINS

L

RIO GRANDE SYSTEM ROUTE MAPS

EXISTING D&RGW LINES
ABANDONED D&RGW LINES
EXISTING CONNECTING LINES
ABANDONED CONNECTING LINES

NORTH

0 1 2 3 4 5 6 7 8 9 10

SCALE OF MILES: Approx.
7.5-Miles Per Inch

Dallas

Hagens
Jays
Deti.

RIDGWAY

Pleasant Valley
Valley View
Noel

Leopard Cr. or
Sam's P. O.
Dallas Divide
(Peak)

Piedmont
Portland

Lotus

OURAY

Leonard
Brown

Placerville

Fall Cr.
Saw Pit
Wilson
Lime
Bilk

San Miguel

TELLURIDE

Albany
Gladstone
Animas For

Vance Jct.

Ilium

Pandora
Ironton

Red Mtn.

Eureka

Ames Sta.

Ames P. O.
Ophir Sta.
Matterhorn
Trout Lake

Howardsville
Green M

SAN MIGUEL

RANGE

Lizard Head Pass
Gallagher
Murphy's

North Star Mill

SILVERTON

DOLORES
PLATEAU

Coke Oven

Burns

Winkfields
RICO
Enterprise

Black Hawk

Detroit

ELK PARK

Montelores

Raymond Sta.
Millard

Muldoon
Quarry
Bear Cr.
Rio Lado
Kings

SAN JUAN

Needleton
Hunt
Tefft's Spur
Cascade

RANGE

Rust

LA PLATA
RANGE

Tacoma

Rockwood

Needle

DOLORES
Lost Canyon

H&HL

Glencoe
Millwood
Graden's

Hermosa
Trimble

Mountains

ANIMAS RIVER

Menefee
Brayton
East Mancos
Grady
The Hook
Dix

May Day Mine

Home Ranch

MANCOS

Cima
May Day Sta.

Ute Mine

Perin's Pk.
Mine

Ireland's
Animas City

HESPERUS

Ute Junction
Franklin Jct.
Porter

BC&F

DURANGO

MESA

VERDE

Ft. Lewis Sta.

Pine Ridge
San Juan Smelter

City Mine
LPC

Florida

NATIONAL

PARK

Carbon Jc.

Bocea
Lodo

Falfa Sta.
Griffith P. O.

Sloan

Oxford

Posta

Ignacio Sta.

Bondad

Colmex

Tiffany

352

proceed farther because of the insurmountable difficulties involved in the vertical-walled canyon which lay ahead. Next, the Silverton Northern built up Animas Canyon to about as far as railroad tracks could go, and the Silverton, Gladstone & Northerly did likewise shortly thereafter up Cement Creek. These three lines and the Silverton Branch served a great complex of mines and mills which poured out seemingly endless carloads of ore, concentrates, lead ingots, silver bars and gold bricks.

Meanwhile, the Rio Grande Southern, with D&RG financial backing, had tapped another outlet by building into Telluride from Ridgway, then went southwest to serve Rico, still another source of mineral traffic. The lower portion of the RGS was built west from Durango, throwing out branches to coal mines en route, and after an inordinate amount of up-and-down ridge-hopping, reached the lumber town of Dolores. It was then a simple matter to connect the two segments by a track up the Dolores River. The entire line was one of great scenic beauty,

particularly between Placerville and Lizard Head Pass. Besides being very close to the high peaks, the track contained much three-percent grade and was supported in many places by extremely high wooden trestles which scared many a faint-hearted passenger. At Ophir a long tight loop climbed the mountainside on a continuous series of these uncertain structures.

The decline in silver mining eventually resulted in the abandonment of the three Silverton roads and the RGS, although it hung on for many years with the help of lumber fed to it at Dolores (New Mexico and Montezuma Lumber Company lines) and Glencoe (Hallack & Howard Company line, transferred from La Madera), plus coal from mines west of Durango.

Today the D&RGW's Silverton Branch is enjoying a veritable rush each summer as thousands of tourists ride its two-section narrow-gauge trains, last of their kind, up the spectacular Rio de Las Animas Canyon to Silverton.

DELL A. MCCOY

Just south of Tacoma, Colorado—on the Silverton Branch of the D&RGW—the railroad crosses the Rio de Las Animas on a high trestle to attain a better location on the east bank of the tumbling mountain stream.

353

After the White Man had conquered the native Indians, who had inhabited this land long prior to the arrival of Columbus, he banished those remaining alive to so-called "reservations." One such area was in northeastern Utah; others were in southwestern Colorado and northwestern New Mexico. The land to which the Indians were sent was about as far from civilization as possible and barely more hospitable than a desert. One of the Indians' "privileges" was that of being allowed to ride the D&RG at Federal expense, which they did occasionally, more for the thrill of letting the iron horse do the work than for any particular purpose.

This section includes one of these reservations as well as the more wooded, fertile and moist land which had been the Indians' home territory. There are no high peaks; instead the hills are rounded and their slopes gentle. Forests of ponderosa pine cover the hills and fill the canyons of the northern portion, but in the southern portion the heat-loving piñon testifies to the lack of rainfall. Though the ground surface is flatter, it is deeply gouged by canyons rimmed with tremendous thicknesses of sandstone or lava. There are many streams, but none except the San Juan River (into which everything drains) are of appreciable size. The forests in the northeastern quadrant still provide considerable lumber, but the superior coal formerly mined west of Durango is hardly touched any more. Natural gas has been discovered near Farmington; otherwise the southeastern corner remains a veritable terra incognita to the White Man.

Anxious to participate in the riches of Silverton, the D&RG built its line cross-drainage, down into each valley and up over the intervening hills. It was indeed a rollercoaster profile, abounding in sharp curves and steep pitches which hampered any sort of efficient operation. West of Lumberton, where the track followed the Navajo and San Juan rivers for a short distance, the line was at the bottom of a tortuous canyon overhung with monstrous

Much of the Denver & Rio Grande's territory had been Ute Indian land only a short time before they pushed trackage into western Colorado. Indian tepees were often within sight of passing trains during the early days.

cliffs which sometimes broke off, depositing house-size chunks upon the track with catastrophic consequences.

Lumber was the principal commodity originated along this lonely stretch of railroad, produced by sawmills located close to the track. A considerable amount came down the Pagosa Springs Branch, which had been built in cooperation with a lumber company. Known as the Rio Grande, Pagosa & Northern, the branch was later acquired and absorbed by the D&RG. When the lumber industry in the area declined and trucks hauled what was left, the tracks were removed. A coal company built a spur from La Plata Junction east of Durango; it lasted only a year due to poor coal.

In 1905 the D&RG decided that it would be a good idea to build a branch from Durango south along the Animas River through an agricultural area to Farmington. Instead of being narrow-gauge, like all of the other trackage in Durango, this one was standard-gauge, perhaps because the railroad was hoping that the AT&SF or Southern Pacific would build a similar branch to connect with it, thus providing an outlet for the coal mined west of Durango. Neither company responded to the overture, and this isolated piece of standard-gauge railroad operated thus for 18 years, finally being converted to narrow-gauge. Locomotives were brought in on narrow-gauge cars and re-erected at Durango, while the cars merely received standard-gauge trucks. Pipe and gas-well supplies provided a large amount of traffic in recent years, but this has tapered down to only a trickle, now that the field has been thoroughly developed.

Durango was the terminus for two short spurs. One of them served the City Coal Mine to the east of the city, while the other one went to the big San Juan smelter across the Animas River from the railroad terminal.

Indian life in the ancient pueblo of San Juan — near Española, New Mexico, was hardly affected by the coming of the Denver & Rio Grande to the area. This scene shows Pueblo Indians at one of their irrigation canals.

354

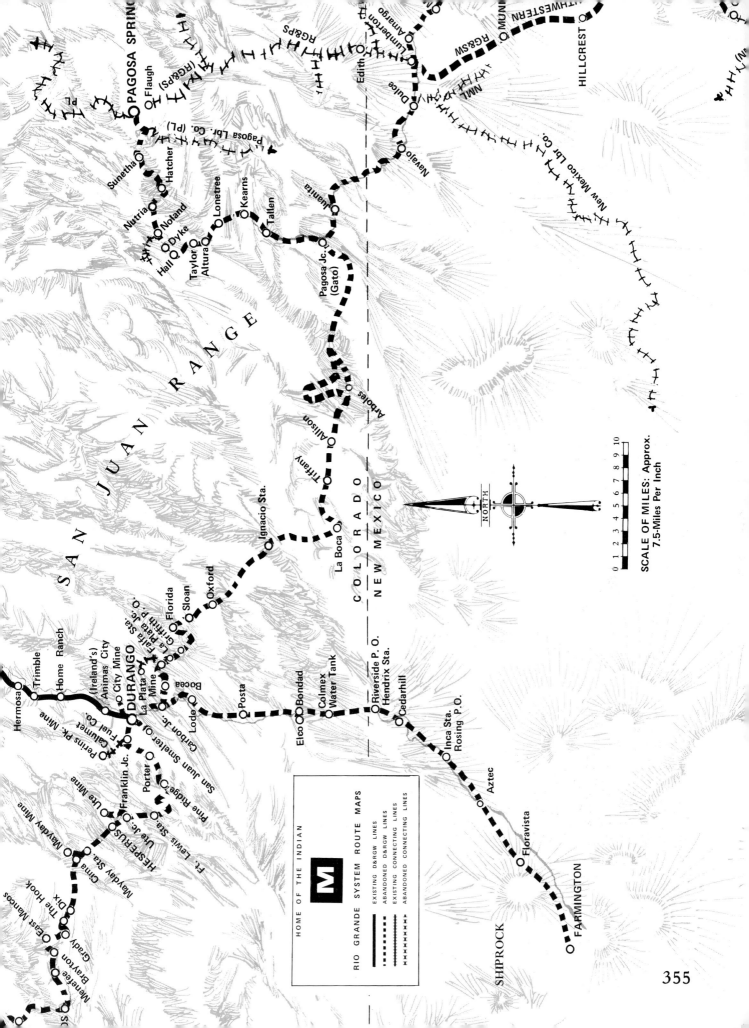

PAGOSA SPRINGS

Flaugh

(RG&PS)

Pagosa Lbr. Co. (PL)

Hatcher

Sunetha

Nutria

Noland

Hall Dyke

Lonetree

Taylor

Altura

Kearns

Tallen

SAN JUAN RANGE

Pagosa Jc. (Gato)

Juanita

Edith

Dulce

Navajo

Lumberton

Amargo

RG&PS

RG&SW

NML

NORTHWESTERN

HILLCREST

New Mexico Lbr. Co.

Allison

Tiffany

Arboles

Ignacio Sta.

La Boca

COLORADO

NEW MEXICO

Trimble

Home Ranch

Hermosa

(Ireland's)

Animas City

City Mine

Perins Pk. Mine

Calumet Fuel Co.

DURANGO

La Plata Mine

La Plata Sta.

Griffith P. O.

Oco

Florida

Sloan

Oxford

Franklin Jc.

Porter

Pine Ridge

San Juan Smelter (J)

Carbon Jc.

Lode

Bocea

Posta

Elco

Bondad

Colmex

Water Tank

Riverside P. O.

Hendrix Sta.

Cedarhill

Ute Mine

Ft. Lewis Sta.

Ute Jc.

HESPERUS

Mayday Sta.

Cima

Mayday Mine

Dix

The Hook

East Manos

Grady

Brayton

Menefee

Inca Sta.

Rosing P. O.

Aztec

SHIPROCK

Floravista

FARMINGTON

SCALE OF MILES: Approx.
7.5-Miles Per Inch

0 1 2 3 4 5 6 7 8 9 10

355

This red sandstone rock formation — called Dodges Bluff — rises vertically above the Colorado River and the RGW's *new standard-gauge line. This view is typical of the scenery in Ruby Canyon along the Colorado-Utah border.*

LAND OF ROCKY CANYONS

In some far distant era, western Colorado and eastern Utah had been the bed of an ancient sea. Hundreds of feet of sediment were deposited on its bottom, and in a subsequent upheaval of the Earth's crust, this ocean's floor became a vast plain of dry land. Still later, molten rock flowed over this plain forming a hard thick surface. As the lava cooled, it cracked and streams formed in the fissures, enlarging them into gullies. Over the span of more years than a man can count, rain and snow, heat and cold eroded the once flat surface of the ground, forming the canyons, cliffs and mesas which characterize this area today.

Throughout this entire region there are no other practical routes for travel, and a railroad in particular is obligated to follow the rivers quite closely, for they flow along the easiest gradients at the lowest altitudes. To the traveler the horizon is usually upward and close at hand, entirely different from the wide vistas of the Great Plains of Kansas where the indistinct horizon is always outward and far away. Trees are rare, and even along the streams, vegetation of any kind is relatively sparse. Agriculture is possible only in those areas where water can be diverted from the streams and conducted to fields and orchards by open ditch or pipeline.

The D&RG first entered the region by building down the Gunnison River from Delta. As could be expected, much of this route was in a canyon, emerging from it slightly south of Grand Junction which was situated in a large open valley. Proceeding northwestward the track encountered few obstacles to a long tangent ending close to the Utah-Colorado border. Here the topography changed abruptly, and locating engineers chose to place the line several miles north of the Grand (Colorado) River to avoid its long and deep canyon. After but a few years of operation as a narrow-gauge line linking Denver and Ogden, the railroad was reconstructed with a standard-gauge line down the Colorado River from Glenwood Springs to Grand Junction. It too passed through a long canyon between De Beque and

356

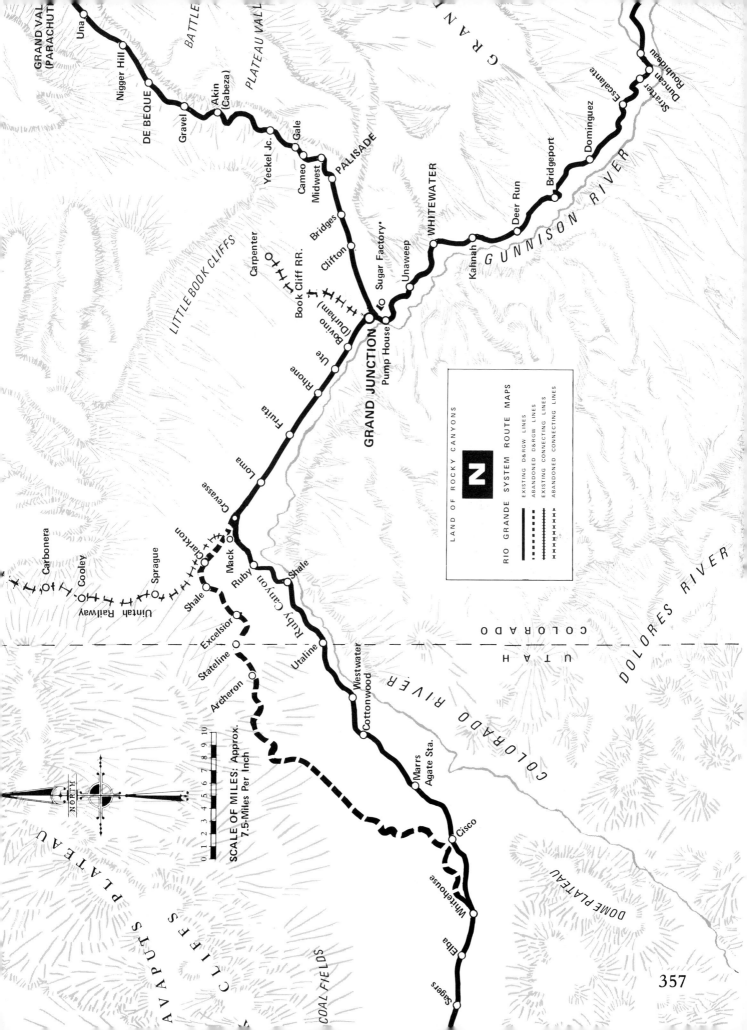

GRAND VAL
(PARACHUTE)

Una

Nigger Hill

DE BEQUE

Gravel

Akin
(Cabeza)

BATTLE

PLATEAU VALLEY

Yeckel Jc.

Gale

Cameo

Midwest

PALISADE

Bridges

Clifton

Carpenter

LITTLE BOOK CLIFFS

Book Cliff RR.

Sugar Factory

Unaweep

WHITEWATER

GRAN

GRAN

Escalante

Strater
Duncan
Roubideau

Dominguez

Bridgeport

Deer Run

Kahnah

GUNNISON RIVER

Bovino
(Durham)

Ute

Rhone

Fruita

Loma

GRAND JUNCTION

Pump House

Crevasse

Carbonera

Cooley

Sprague

Clarkton

Uintah Railway

Shale

Mack

Ruby

Shale

Ruby Canyon

Excelsior

Stateline

Archeron

Utaline

Westwater

Cottonwood

Marrs
Agate Sta.

Cisco

Whitehouse

Elba

Sagers

COLORADO

UTAH

DOLORES RIVER

COLORADO RIVER

DOME PLATEAU

COAL FIELDS

CLIFFS

AVAPULT PLATEAU

LAND OF ROCKY CANYONS

RIO GRANDE SYSTEM ROUTE MAPS

N

EXISTING D&RGW LINES
ABANDONED D&RGW LINES
EXISTING CONNECTING LINES
ABANDONED CONNECTING LINES

NORTH

SCALE OF MILES: Approx.
7.5 Miles Per Inch

0 1 2 3 4 5 6 7 8 9 10

357

"AMERICA'S WONDERLANDS"

The Colorado - Utah border intersected the Rio Grande Western's main-line at the western end of Ruby Canyon.

This one-car special train accommodated camera-men who photographed the spectacular scenery along the new line.

Palisade. West of Grand Junction, however, the narrow-gauge trackage was converted to standard-gauge only as far as Crevasse, Colorado, whence a new standard-gauge track was built through the very canyon which had been avoided earlier. The new trackage left the gorge at Westwater, Utah, and rejoined the original alignment at Whitehouse, Utah. Several years later the narrow-gauge track to Delta, Colorado, was converted, and all lines remain in service today.

Except for a little coal, the entire region has few developed natural resources; however, around Grand Junction peach orchards are to be found in great profusion, the city itself being more of a distribution center than anything else.

The D&RGW had no branches in this section, although some other railroads did connect with it. The Colorado Midland operated into Grand Junction, sharing Rio Grande Junction track with the D&RG west of Rifle. The Rio Grande Western—later acquired by, and merged with, the D&RG—connected with both the CM and D&RG at Grand Junction, and hauled their cars through to Ogden. The narrow-gauge Little Book Cliff brought down coal from a mine north of Grand Junction, while the all-electric Grand River Valley interurban line served the farming area between Grand Junction and Fruita. At one time, sugar

beets were grown near Grand Junction, and a short spur was built southeast of town to serve a sugar factory. All of these other railroads have disappeared, leaving just the D&RGW, which has improved its facilities by the construction of a large classification yard to the east of Grand Junction.

At Mack, the Uintah Railway—famous for its 80° curves and 7½-percent grades—connected with the D&RG, hauling gilsonite until a pipeline replaced the little railroad.

THE EASTERN UTAH DESERT

To the passenger aboard the California Zephyr who had never seen the Sahara Desert, eastern Utah as viewed from the Vista Dome was perhaps a very reasonable facsimile. The seemingly endless Book Cliffs to the north and the equally barren dry valleys to the south make him wonder if rain ever had fallen upon this baked earth.

Twelve-thousand engine-horsepower—represented by diesel-electric units numbered 3002, 3043, 3050 and 5319—was employed on this freight train departing Green River for *Salt Lake City. The emptiness of the eastern Utah desert is relieved only by the stratified Book Cliffs, which rise in the distance, north of the railroad.*

But it does rain occasionally, while snow is not altogether unknown, and the vivid-hued waxy cactus blossoms of spring rival ordinary flowers for sheer beauty. Like the western portion of the previous section, this is a country of great cliffs, deep canyons and high plateaus. In this virtually treeless and waterless land, any permanent source of water creates an oasis. Even the names of stations are most suggestive of the immediate surroundings: Thompson's Spring, Vista, Solitude, Green River, Desert, Sphinx, Cliff, Grassy Trail, Verde and Mounds. The population of

the 15 D&RGW "stations" in this section is so small that the number of passengers on a single "California Zephyr" frequently outnumbered their cumulative total.

A question could easily be raised regarding the railroad's past judgment in building a railroad through such an unpeopled, unproductive and resourceless territory. The reason is relatively simple. Having crossed the Rockies in Colorado and having developed a network of supporting lines there, the management next sought to attain another of its original corporate objectives: a through line

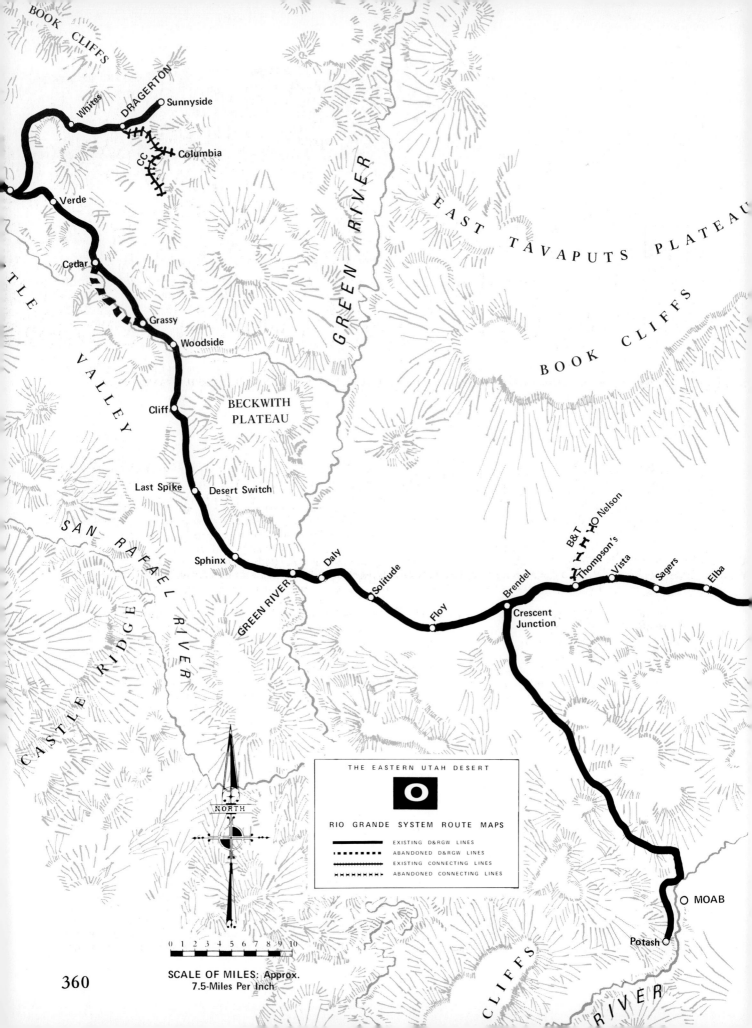

BOOK CLIFFS

DRAGERTON

Whites

Sunnyside

Columbia

CC

Verde

Cedar

GREEN RIVER

EAST TAVAPUTS PLATEAU

Grassy

Woodside

BOOK CLIFFS

Cliff

BECKWITH PLATEAU

TLE VALLEY

Last Spike

Desert Switch

SAN RAFAEL RIVER

Sphinx

Daly

Solitude

Floy

Brendel

B&T

Nelson

Thompson's

Vista

Sagers

Elba

GREEN RIVER

Crescent Junction

CASTLE RIDGE

NORTH

MOAB

THE EASTERN UTAH DESERT

RIO GRANDE SYSTEM ROUTE MAPS

EXISTING D&RGW LINES
ABANDONED D&RGW LINES
EXISTING CONNECTING LINES
ABANDONED CONNECTING LINES

Potash

360

0 1 2 3 4 5 6 7 8 9 10

SCALE OF MILES: Approx.
7.5-Miles Per Inch

CLIFFS

RIVER

connecting Denver with Ogden. At a relatively early date, the D&RG's management organized a Utah subsidiary and proceeded to assemble a small self-sufficient system in the Salt Lake valley, right in the midst of a Union Pacific kingdom. Completely logical, the two systems built toward each other, the rails meeting at Desert Switch, out in the middle of as much nothingness as one could imagine.

Construction was hasty, the narrow-gauge rails having been spiked to ties which were laid on bare ground. Only a few years afterward, the entire railroad was converted to standard gauge, and considerable relocation and reconstruction were required to produce a satisfactory S-G profile and alignment.

There is only one river of any consequence, the Green, which traverses the section from north to south. The railroad crosses it (at Green River) where it escapes the confines of lengthy canyons for a rare and brief distance. The Green's major tributary is the Price which the track follows upstream to the summit of the Wasatch Mountains. Although the route could have gone up the Green to the mouth of the Price, it was located south of the Beckwith Plateau, meeting the Price at Woodside to avoid the difficulties involved through two long canyons. Even after attaining the banks of the Price, the tracks detour between Cedar and Grassy Trail to avoid another deep and winding arroyo.

The D&RGW has two branches in this section. The first runs northeast from Mounds to Sunnyside where a considerable tonnage of excellent coal is originated. The other one, constructed only recently, goes south from Cresent Junction to a large potash deposit near Moab. This branch is quite spectacular as it descends to the bottom of the Colorado River's precipitous gorge.

The Ballard & Thompson railroad, running north from Thompson's to a coal mine at Sego, was operated for several years, then abandoned. A still prosperous one is the Carbon County which delivers coal near Sunnyside.

THE GREAT SALT LAKE BASIN

The site of Salt Lake City, located in the southeast part of the Great Salt Lake Basin, is the center of an extremely varied country. Northwest of the city lies the Great Salt Lake itself, surrounded by flat expanses of near-desert with irregular masses of steep barren hills. Utah Lake and a range of mountains are to the southwest. Both the north and south ends of this range are productive of silver and copper minerals. To the east of the Ogden - Salt Lake City - Provo contour, the impressive Wasatch Range rises abruptly, reaching an elevation of 12,000 feet above sea level only eight miles away from the rails at the 4500-foot mark. This huge upthrust block of mountains is sliced by narrow canyons giving access to the moister and wooded country to the east, which has yielded ore, coal, timber and hay.

All rivers flow westward and northward into the Great Salt Lake, a true inland sea and the second-largest body of water in the nation. The gradeless streams of the desert are often intermittent, while those of the mountains have succeeded in cutting deep steeply-sloped canyons through the mighty Wasatch Range.

West of Green River, Utah, the rails skirted the southwestern flanks of the spectacular Beckwith Plateau.

The D&RGW's initial trackage in the basin was a pair of acquired narrow-gauge lines — the Bingham Canon & Camp Floyd and the Wasatch & Jordan Valley — running from Sandy to the mining camps of Bingham and Alta. Construction from Sandy to Provo linked these two railroads with a third acquired line — the Utah & Pleasant Valley — which ran to some coal mines near Scofield. Later, the line to Ogden was built, despite vigorous opposition of the Union Pacific. Many branches were added by both construction and acquisition, giving access to essentially every source of revenue in the area.

Going south from Ogden, where connections are made with the Union Pacific and Southern Pacific, the track hugs the western foot of the mountains. Short branches toward the lake shore served a sugar factory (Ogden), canning plants (Hooper, Farnsworth), an amusement park (Lake Park), stockyards (Stockyards) and a smelter (Copper Plant) along the line to Salt Lake City. There the Union Pacific and Western Pacific provide connections today. In the late 1880's there was a network of narrow-gauge track owned by the Salt Lake & Fort Douglas, which served the fort, a quarry, a brick-works and a penitentiary. Over one leg of this network ran the Salt Lake & Eastern, which ascended an extremely steep gradient in Parley's Canyon to cross the divide into Park City. After these two lines came under RGW control — through the Utah Central — the Park City Branch was extensively rebuilt during its standard-gauge conversion, so that the lead-silver ores and concentrates could be handled more economically.

Like the Park City Branch, the one to Alta ascended a narrow, deep canyon to a silver mining district; however, it was operated only briefly before its ore ran out. The Bingham Branch at first served some small gold and silver mines which eventually were developed into the world's largest copper mine. A considerable amount of spur trackage was built to serve the mills and mines around Bingham, and a branch was built north from Welby to reach the giant copper smelters at Garfield, which also was served by the Bingham & Garfield railroad, recently replaced by an electrified line.

Still staying close to the mountains, the D&RGW parallels UP rails to Springville, skirting Utah Lake near Geneva. From Provo a longer branch ran up another typical canyon to Heber, and a short one (ex Salt Lake & Utah track) goes to Orem. Electric interurban lines (Salt Lake & Utah, and Bamberger) once paralleled all of the way from Provo to Ogden, connecting with other such lines to Saltair (Salt Lake, Garfield & Western), Huntsville (Utah, Logan & Idaho), Utah Hot Springs (Ogden & Northwestern), and Payson, Idaho (Utah-Idaho Central).

This fanciful gravity-operated vehicle — purportedly used on the branch to Alta, Utah — was not listed in the Denver & Rio Grande's equipment roster.

The RGW's new standard-gauge line through Ruby Canyon was located along the Colorado River where gigantic blocks of red sandstone had fallen from the precipitous cliffs.

The Great Salt Lake in Utah is an inland sea located in a huge closed basin surrounded by mountains. This is the second-largest body of water in the United States — and one of the most saline bodies of water in the world.

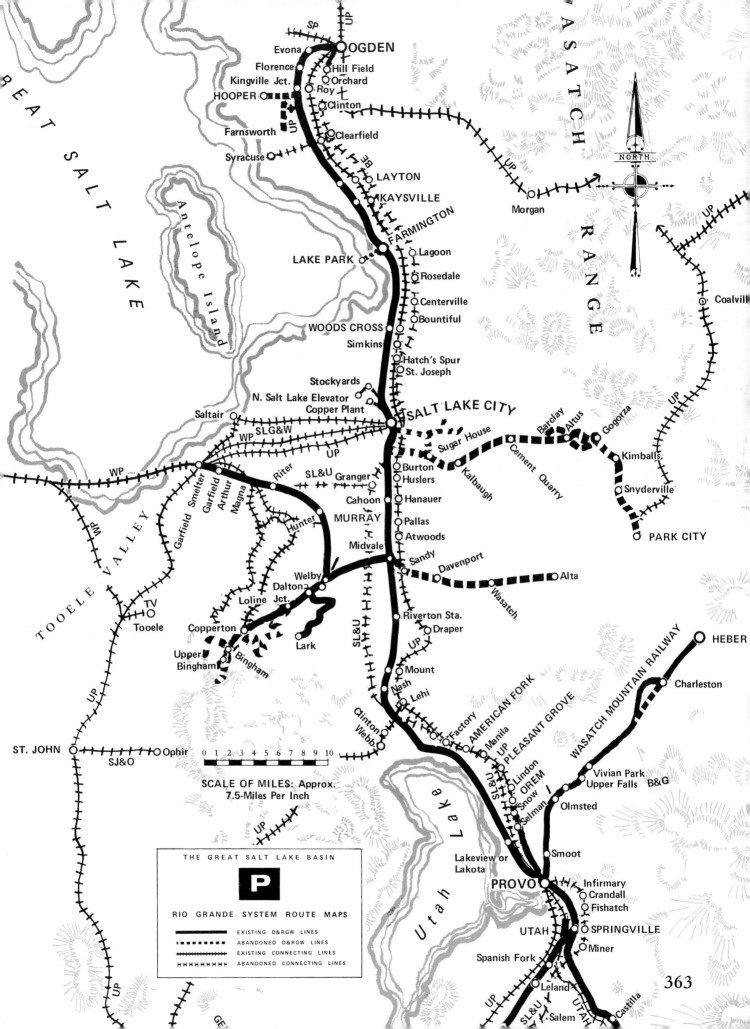

GREAT SALT LAKE

Antelope Island

WASATCH RANGE

NORTH

SP
UP
Evona
Florence
Hill Field
Orchard
Kingville Jct.
Roy
HOOPER
Clinton
Farnsworth
UP
Clearfield
Syracuse
BE
LAYTON
KAYSVILLE
FARMINGTON
LAKE PARK
Lagoon
Rosedale
Centerville
Bountiful
WOODS CROSS
Simkins
Hatch's Spur
St. Joseph
Stockyards
N. Salt Lake Elevator
Copper Plant
SALT LAKE CITY
Saltair
SLG&W
WP
UP
Sugar House
Barclay
Altus
Gogorza
UP
Kimballs
Snyderville
PARK CITY
Cement Quarry
Burton
Huslers
Hanauer
Kalbaugh
Riter
SL&U
Granger
Cahoon
MURRAY
Pallas
Atwoods
Midvale
Sandy
Davenport
Alta
Wasatch
Garfield Smelter
Garfield
Arthur
Magna
Hunter
Welby
Dalton
Loline
Jct.
Copperton
Lark
Riverton Sta.
Draper
UP
TOOELE VALLEY
TV
Tooele
Upper
Bingham
Bingham
Mount
Nash
Lehi
SL&U
ST. JOHN
SJ&O
Ophir
Clinton
Webb
Factory
AMERICAN FORK
Manila
PLEASANT GROVE
UP
Lindon
OREM
Snow
Selman
WASATCH MOUNTAIN RAILWAY
HEBER
Charleston
Vivian Park
Upper Falls
B&G
Olmsted
Smoot

SCALE OF MILES: Approx.
7.5-Miles Per Inch
0 1 2 3 4 5 6 7 8 9 10

UP

Utah Lake

Lakeview or
Lakota
PROVO
Infirmary
Crandall
Fishatch
UTAH
SPRINGVILLE
Miner
Spanish Fork
SL&U
UTAH
Leland
Salem
Castilla

THE GREAT SALT LAKE BASIN

P

RIO GRANDE SYSTEM ROUTE MAPS

	EXISTING D&RGW LINES
	ABANDONED D&RGW LINES
	EXISTING CONNECTING LINES
	ABANDONED CONNECTING LINES

363

© F.H.LEIB.

Two pair of ex-Rio Grande Western 2-8-0's and 4-6-0s, plus a 2-6-0 rear-end pusher, were needed to boost this 12- car passenger train up the four-percent grade on the west side of Soldier Summit.

THE UTAH COAL FIELDS

Utah, like Colorado, is most fortunate in possessing a tremendous reserve of high-quality coal, and the railroad is equally fortunate in operating the natural routes for its trackage close to these deposits. Almost all of this coal is mined east of the Wasatch range, which runs north-and-south through the center of this section. The western portion of the section is quite different though, being an easterly extension of Utah's western desert, and known primarily for its mineral deposits which still provide some traffic.

The eastern slope of the Wasatch range drains into the Colorado River through the Price, a major tributary. The northwest corner belongs to the Great Salt Lake drainage system, while southwest quadrant streams flow into the Sevier River, which empties into land-locked Sevier Lake.

A corporate ancestor of the D&RGW provided its entry into the section by acquiring a narrow-gauge coal-hauling railroad—the Utah & Pleasant Valley—which ran from Provo to mines near Scofield. Its track, crossing the Wasatch by means of a curious configuration of switch-backs, was soon replaced by a more favorable, though longer, route over Soldier Summit. Then to connect the Utah and Colorado lines, track was laid hurriedly down the Price River to Desert Switch where the Last Spike was driven in 1883.

Coal was everywhere along the river and it was found in numerous side canyons also. Except for the Scofield and Sunnyside branches the Rio Grande Western adhered to main-line haulage, while other railroads or coal companies constructed branches on which the coal originated. Three such companies were the Castle Valley, Southern Utah and

Castle Gate, Utah, was a spectacular gap in the Wasatch Range, sliced through a narrow wall of hard basalt rock by the Price River. West of Castle Gate the railroad climbed to the top of the range at Soldier Summit, 7465 feet elevation.

Locomotives of the Utah Railway were rarely seen most of their journeys between Castle Gate and Provo, having been scheduled for night-time passage. In this scene at Soldier Summit, a pair of ALCO RSD4-model units—numbered 300 and 305—begin the tortuous descent to their western terminal. This scene was photographed during the longest day of the year

DELL A. McCOY

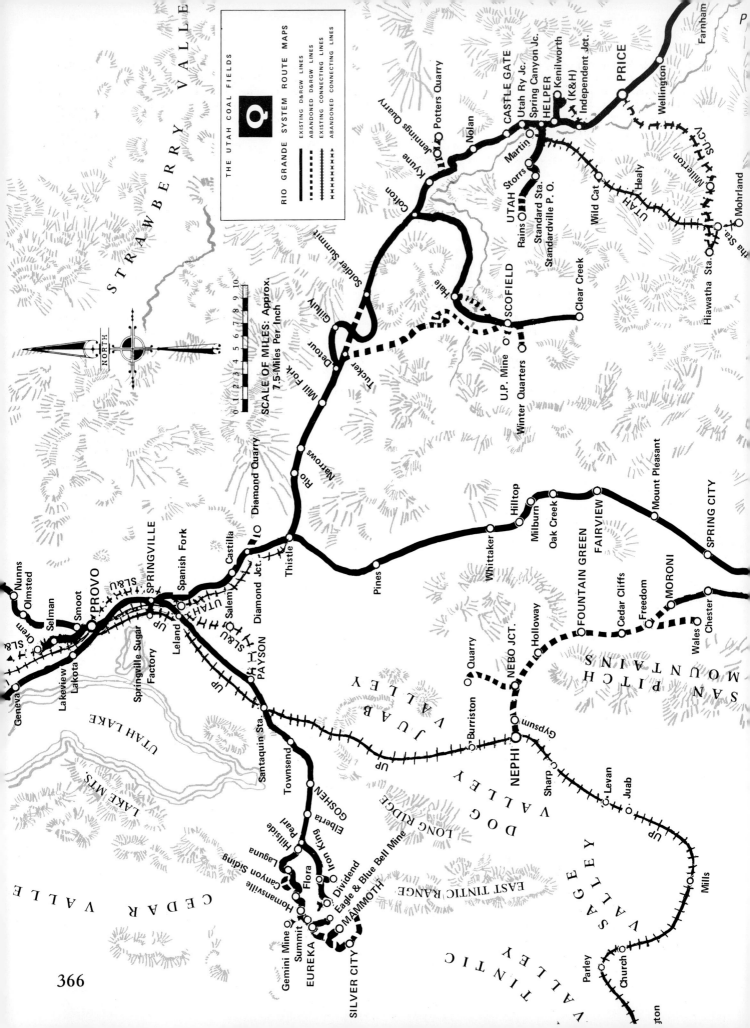

Kenilworth & Helper railroads, the D&RG operating them for a few years with equipment owned by those railroads. The K&H track was so steep — 6.1-percent — that the D&RG later constructed its own branch to Kenilworth. The Southern Utah was eventually abandoned, its mines being served by the Utah Railway. The present branch (with 4.4-percent grades) in Spring Canyon was paid for by three coal companies; the D&RG acquiring their interests subsequently.

South of Springville, the main-line follows the Spanish Fork River up its canyon to Thistle, thence up Soldier Creek to Soldier Summit. The original line from Detour to the summit was on a four-percent grade, this being reduced to two-percent in later years by a longer line. At one time there had been a sizable terminal at the summit; it was returned to Helper when it proved to be impractical. The descent along the Price River was not easy; sharp curves came one after the other, and there were 2.4-percent grades between Kyune and Castle Gate. Two short branches went to stone quarries; one from Kyune to Potters Quarry, the other being north of Thistle at the mouth of Diamond Creek.

Thistle was not only the helper terminal at the west foot of the Soldier Summit grade, but also the junction of the long branch which diverges southward to Marysvale. This branch first surmounts a low divide then begins a long descent into the wide valley of the San Pitch River. Another long branch diverges southwestward at Springville, curving around the southern end of Utah Lake to reach the silver mines in the Tintic range. A later acquisition in this area was the Goshen Valley railroad, operated by the D&RGW for its owners. A very early railroad was the N-G line between Nephi on the Union Pacific to Manti on the RGW. Although it had branches to quarries and coal mines, its traffic was not substantial, having been purchased primarily to keep the UP out of the D&RG's domain.

The Utah Railway, successor to the Castle Valley, was operated by the D&RG for a few years; afterward it built its own track between Provo and Thistle adjacent to D&RG rails. This segment has been operated as joint double track, with Utah Railway trains using D&RGW track between Castle Gate and Thistle.

THE SEVIER RIVER VALLEY

There is no question that Utah is an unusual state. It possesses the nation's only major east-west mountain range (the Uintahs), an inland sea (the Great Salt Lake), and rivers whose waters never reach the ocean. One of these streams is the Sevier River which has the additional distinction of flowing first northward for a long distance, then southward, emptying into a lake with no outlet.

The clue to this strange behavior is to be found in the local topography, which is tilted from southeast to north-west, causing the river to flow north onto a flat basin where the drainage is to the south. The southern extremities of the Wasatch range spread out across the eastern and southern portions of this section, while the Sevier Desert occupies the northern and western portions. As is the case with other sections in Utah, the mountains are creased with deep narrow valleys and the desert is punctuated with irregular groups of steep bare ridges.

The first railroad to enter this section was the San Pete Valley which climbed a ridge east of Nephi to tap a coal mine at Wales, later extending its line to a quarry near Manti. The Rio Grande Western, building south from Thistle intersected this line at Manti, and when the RGW's narrow-gauge track was converted to standard-gauge, the SPV did likewise. In time it became part of the D&RG's system, but was partially dismantled when its traffic declined.

South of Manti, where the San Pitch joins the Sevier, the valley is very broad, supporting considerable agriculture. Here sugar beets are grown and a short branch serves the sugar mill at Gunnison. South of Gunnison the rails slope upward through Salina (where the Nioche Branch once connected), following the Sevier River to a terminal at Marysvale. The remainder of the branch to Marysvale has been marked with disappointment. The gold deposits of the area never produced very much ore and any hopes of extension toward southern California were eclipsed by a collapse of the D&RG's financial structure. Passenger trains on the line disappeared after the highway parallel to the track was improved, but considerable freight traffic is generated by plaster-board plants and sugar mills.

The only branch from this line was the one to Nioche, a piece of track noted for its unfortunate history. It was intended originally to be a shortcut between Farnham on the main-line and Milford on the present Union Pacific. This scheme came to prompt grief when the UP obtained control of the railroad extending to the Pacific Coast. The branch was hardly suited to main-line operations any-how, being on a continuous 2.5-percent grade in a narrow rocky canyon. Washed out soon after construction, it served a coal mine for only a year or so. Reconstruction continued spasmodically over a long span of years, still without train service, until the shortages of World War II required the removal of its rails and fastenings for use elsewhere.

The Sevier River Valley of Utah was most suitable for the growing of sugar beets, and huge factories were constructed in the area to extract and refine the sugar. This 1912 view shows the refinery at Elsinore, Utah, on the D&RG's Marysvale Branch, 177 miles south of Salt Lake City.

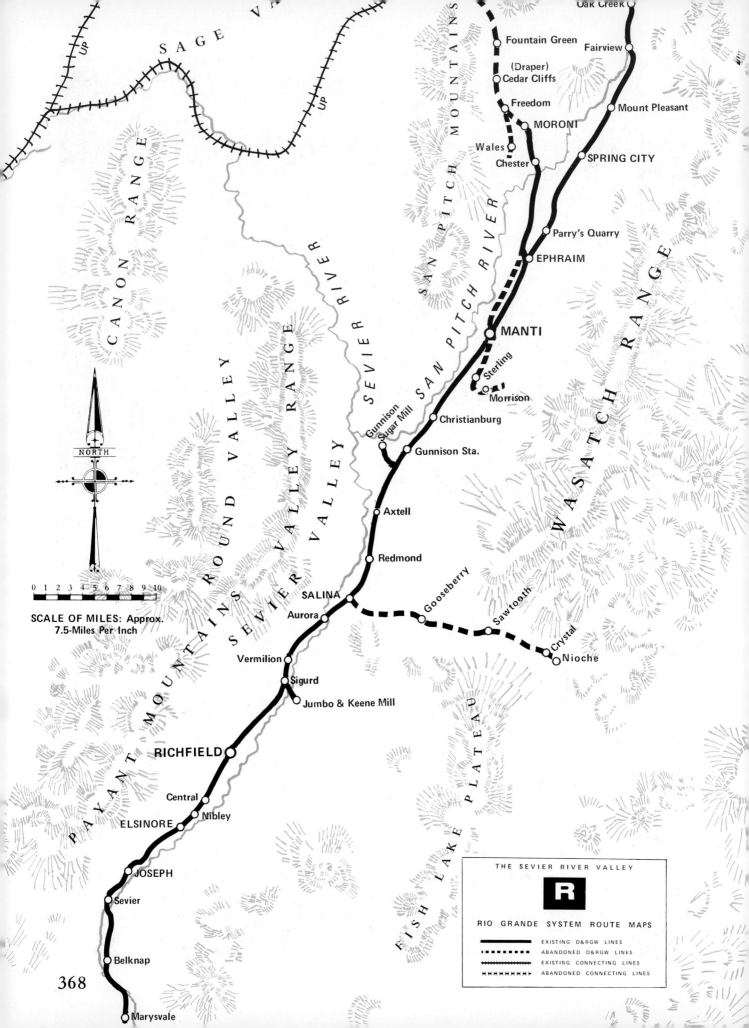

SAGE VALLEY

UP

UP

CANON RANGE

ROUND VALLEY

SEVIER VALLEY RANGE

SEVIER VALLEY

SEVIER RIVER

SAN PITCH MOUNTAINS

SAN PITCH RIVER

WASATCH RANGE

PAVANT MOUNTAINS

FISH LAKE PLATEAU

NORTH

0 1 2 3 4 5 6 7 8 9 10

SCALE OF MILES: Approx.
7.5-Miles Per Inch

Oak Creek

Fountain Green

Fairview

(Draper)
Cedar Cliffs

Freedom

Mount Pleasant

MORONI

Wales

SPRING CITY

Chester

Parry's Quarry

EPHRAIM

MANTI

Sterling

Morrison

Gunnison
Sugar Mill

Christianburg

Gunnison Sta.

Axtell

Redmond

Gooseberry

Salina

Sawtooth

Aurora

Crystal

Vermilion

Nioche

Sigurd

Jumbo & Keene Mill

RICHFIELD

Central

Nibley

ELSINORE

JOSEPH

Sevier

Belknap

368

Marysvale

THE SEVIER RIVER VALLEY

R

RIO GRANDE SYSTEM ROUTE MAPS

EXISTING D&RGW LINES

ABANDONED D&RGW LINES

EXISTING CONNECTING LINES

ABANDONED CONNECTING LINES

From the rocky slopes above Eureka, Utah, Mount Nebo's snowy slopes can be seen to the southeast, 20 miles distant. Part of the Wasatch Range, Mount Nebo is one of the last great, magnificent peaks one sees west-bound en route to Salt Lake City on the D&RGW.

Ogden, Utah — junction of the Union Pacific, Central Pacific (later Southern Pacific), Utah Northern and Rio Grande Western (later Denver & Rio Grande Western) railroads — was the major transportation center between Denver and the Pacific Coast.

Railroad Profiles

These Profiles of the entire Rio Grande System, reproduced here for the first time, show names, gradients, elevations and distances as they were in 1920—with subsequent additions from contemporary information. Some profiles of abandoned original trackage were not available, however. They were obtained by plotting the routes on topographic maps, then deriving the altitudes from contours along the lines.

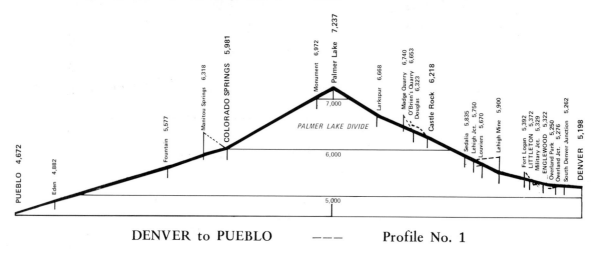

DENVER to PUEBLO   ----   Profile No. 1

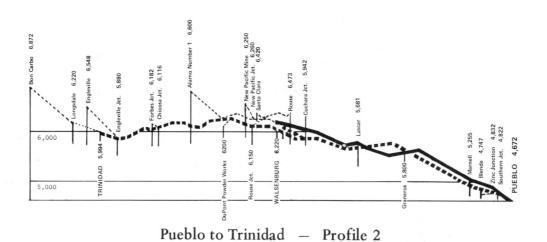

Pueblo to Trinidad — Profile 2

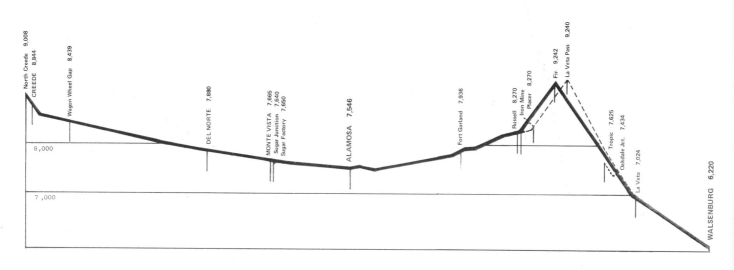

Walsenburg to Creede   —   Profile 3

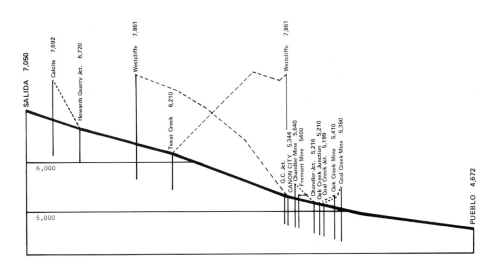

Pueblo to Salida — Profile 4

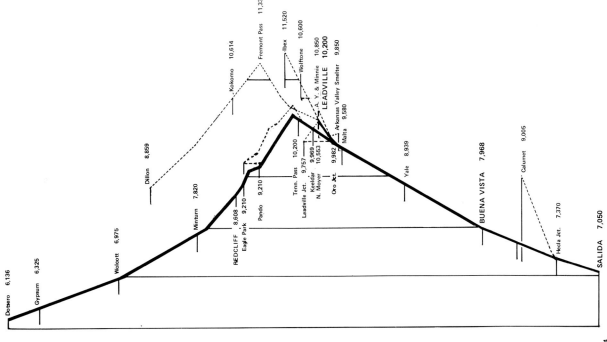

Salida to Dotsero — Profile 5

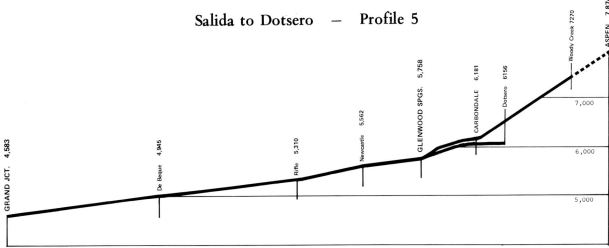

Dotsero to Grand Junction — Profile 6

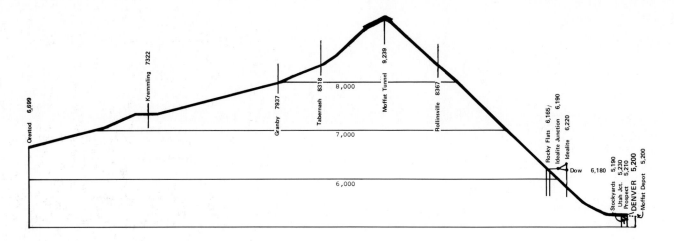

Denver to Orestod — Profile 7

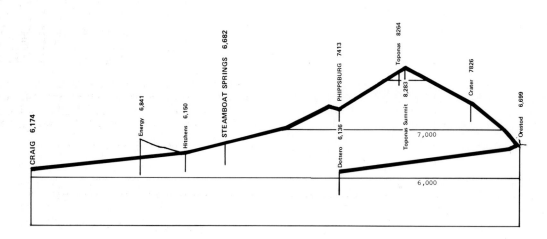

Orestod to Craig — Profile 8

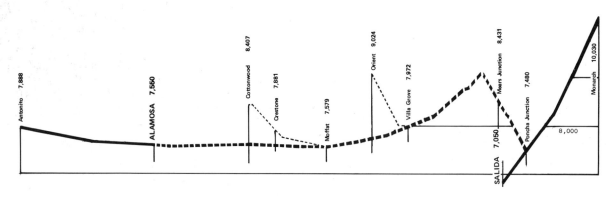

Salida to Antonito — Profile 9

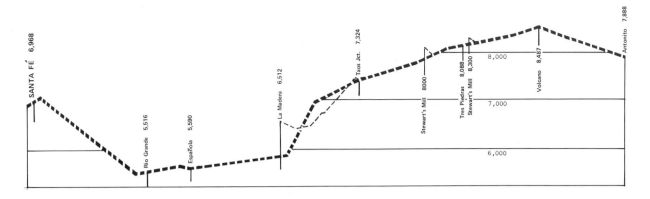

Antonito to Santa Fé   —   Profile 10

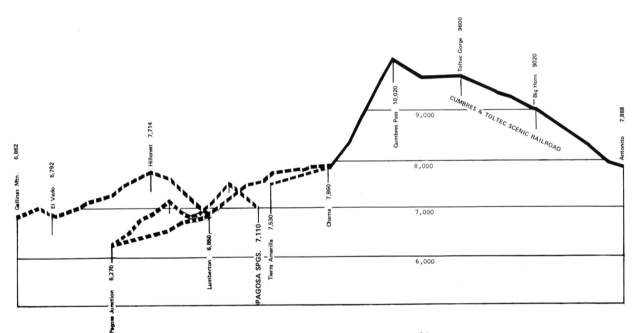

Antonito to Pagosa Junction   —   Profile 11

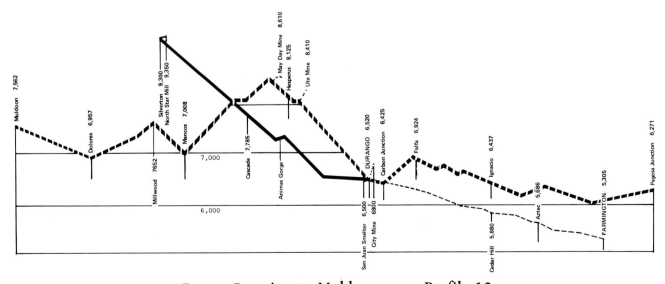

Pagosa Junction to Muldoon   —   Profile 12

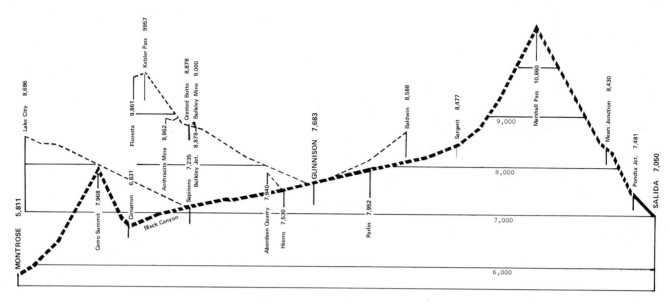

Salida to Montrose   —   Profile 13

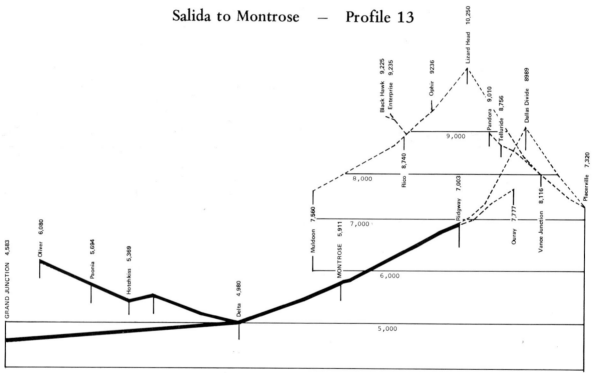

Muldoon to Grand Junction   —   Profile 14

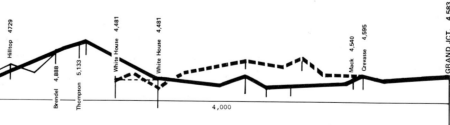

Grand Junction to Green River   —   Profile 15

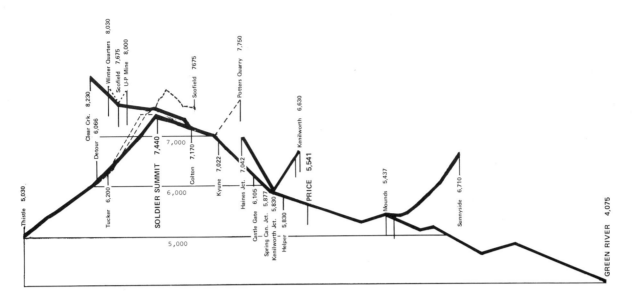

Green River to Thistle — Profile 16

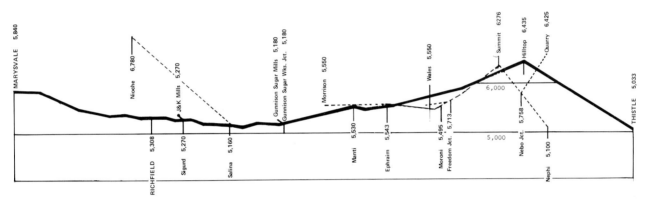

Thistle to Marysvale — Profile 17

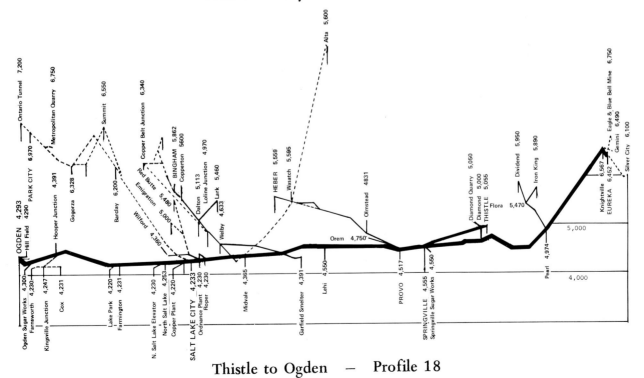

Thistle to Ogden — Profile 18

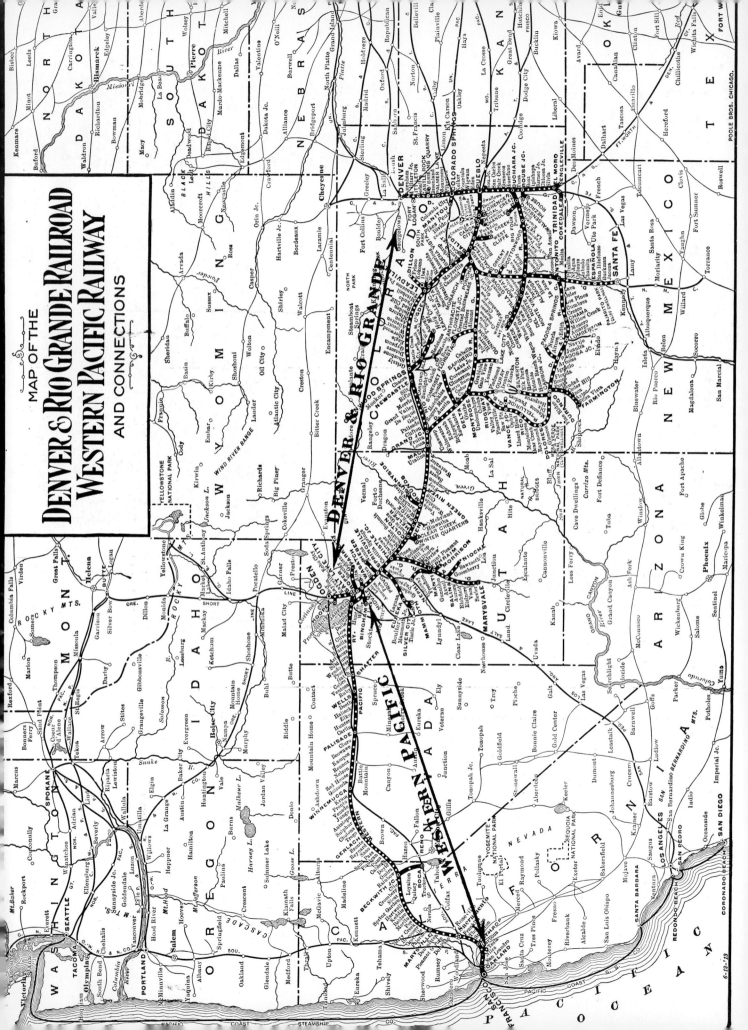

MAP OF THE
DENVER & RIO GRANDE RAILROAD
WESTERN PACIFIC RAILWAY
AND CONNECTIONS

Denver & Rio Grande, and Western Pacific
Time-Table Excerpts

Over the span of a century, covers of the Rio Grande System public time-tables have reflected manifold aspects of the various affiliated railroads; their corporate relationships, traffic routing, trackside scenery, and advertising slogans. The earliest ones confined their advertising to points of local interest, and by 1886, the D&RG claimed that it was the "Scenic Line of the World" and implied that its narrow-gauge main-line stretched "across the continent." Consolidation with the Rio Grande Western introduced the term, "system," and the completion of Western Pacific provided an opportunity to exploit the West Coast, although the Western Pacific's time-table ignored both the D&RG and Colorado. Later, the acquisition of the Denver & Salt Lake

introduced a much shorter route of exceptional scenic attraction. The recent elimination of nearly all passenger service on the D&RGW was expressed by a tiny time-card—printed in 1970—showing only one narrow-gauge steam-powered train (operating on the Silverton Branch) and the luxurious "Rio Grande Zephyr" running between Denver and Ogden.

Excerpts from several Rio Grande System public time-tables are reproduced on the following pages—377 through 384—and on the last page of the Index—page 414. Beginning on page 385, a Denver & Rio Grande employees' time-table of 1881 is printed in full.

DENVER AND RIO GRANDE WESTERN PACIFIC

The Great Salt Lake Route

CURECANTI NEEDLE
Marshall Pass Line between Salida and Grand Junction

DENVER AND RIO GRA WESTE PACI

A. S. HUGHES,
GEN. TRAFFIC MANAGER,
DENVER, COLO.

ASST. PASS'R TRAF.
SAN FRANCISCO, CAL.

J. M. JOHNSON,
Vice-President.

Rio Grande TIME TABLES

ROYAL GORGE ROUTE

Royal Gorge of the Arkansas River

DENVER & RIO GRANDE WESTERN RAILROAD

ISSUED JUNE 8, 1947

Rio Grande TIME TABLES

MOFFAT TUNNEL ROUTE

Gore Canyon of the Colorado River

DENVER & RIO GRANDE WESTERN RAILROAD

ISSUED JUNE 8, 1947

DENVER AND RIO GRANDE WESTERN

The ROYAL GORGE Route

"The Scenic Line of the World"

FALL—WINTER—1931-1932

DENVER R WESTE

"The Scenic L of the

FALL—WINTER

Great Salt Lake Route

RIO GRANDE GREAT SALT LAKE ROUTE WESTERN RAILWAY

Rio Grande Western Railway

A SPLENDIDLY EQUIPPED STANDARD GAUGE RAILWAY THROUGH THE

ROCKY MOUNTAINS

AND THE MOST MAGNIFICENT SCENERY IN AMERICA.

D. C. DODGE,
2d Vice-Pres't. and Gen'l Manager,

S. H. BABCOCK,
Traffic Manager,

F. A. WADLEIGH, Gen'l Passenger Agent,

SALT LAKE CITY, UTAH.

POOLE BROS., CHICAGO.

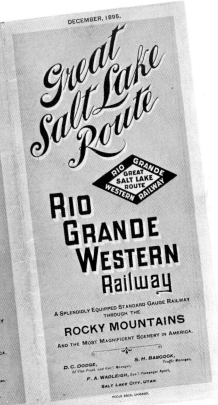

Great Salt Lake Route

RIO GRANDE GREAT SALT LAKE ROUTE WESTERN RAILWAY

Rio Grande Western Railway

A SPLENDIDLY EQUIPPED STANDARD GAUGE RAILWAY THROUGH THE

ROCKY MOUNTAINS

AND THE MOST MAGNIFICENT SCENERY IN AMERICA.

D. C. DODGE,
2d Vice-Pres't. and Gen'l Manager,

S. H. BABCOCK,
Traffic Manager,

F. A. WADLEIGH, Gen'l Passenger Agent,

SALT LAKE CITY, UTAH.

POOLE BROS., CHICAGO.

DENVER & RIO GRANDE WESTERN

SCHEDULE OF TRAINS — Table No. 1

Denver, Colorado Springs, Pueblo, Cañon City, Salida, Glenwood Springs, Grand Junction, Salt Lake City, Ogden, Oakland and San Francisco

---

WESTBOUND

(Mountain Time on Denver & Rio Grande Western; Pacific Time on Western Pacific)

Train columns: **1** Scenic Limited · **3** Salt Lake–San Francisco Express · **15** Colorado–New Mexico Express · **9** Colo. Spg.–Pueblo & Eastern Express

Miles from Denver	Station	Elevation
0.0	Lv DENVER	5280
10.5	Ar Littleton	5372
13.5	Ar Wolhurst	5419
17.3	Ar Acequia	5533
20.7	Ar Louviers	5675
24.5	Ar Sedalia	5835
32.5	Ar Castle Rock	6218
42.9	Ar Larkspur	6668
46.9	Ar Greenland	6919
52.2	Ar PALMER LAKE	7237
55.9	Ar Monument	6972
61.9	Ar Husted	6596
70.3	Ar Pikeview	6199
74.9	Ar COLORADO SPGS., U.S.M.D	5989
74.9	Lv Colorado Springs	5989
77.0	Ar Colorado City	6000
80.1	Ar MANITOU	6318
80.1	Lv MANITOU	6318
77.0	Lv Colorado City	6000
74.9	Ar Colorado Springs	5989
74.9	Lv COLORADO SPRINGS, U.S.M.D	5989
87.9	Ar Fountain	5577
93.4	Ar Buttes	5386
99.0	Ar Henkel	5232
105.3	Ar Pinon	5038
111.5	Ar Eden	4882
117.7	Ar 8th St., Pueblo	4667
119.4	Ar PUEBLO, U.S.M.	4668
119.4	Ar PUEBLO	4668
134.6	Ar Swallows	4887
139.6	Ar Carlile	4952
144.4	Ar Concrete	5023
145.8	Ar Portland	5051
151.9	Ar Florence	5199
160.0	Ar CAÑON CITY, U.S.M.	5344
160.0	Ar CAÑON CITY	5344
164.3	Ar Royal Gorge	5494
	Grand Cañon of the Arkansas	
167.8	Ar Sample	5800
171.2	Ar Parkdale	5800
184.1	Ar Texas Creek	6210
191.7	Ar Cotopaxi	6385
195.7	Ar Pleasanton	6481
198.1	Ar Vallie	6534
203.4	Ar Howard	6718
215.1	Lv SALIDA, U.S.M.	7050
215.1	Lv SALIDA	7050
222.2	Ar Brown's Cañon	7324
232.8	Ar Nathrop	7696
240.3	Ar Buena Vista	7968
248.0	Ar Granite	8374
257.3	Ar Riverside	8943
271.0	Ar Malta	9580
271.0	Lv Malta	9580
275.8	Lv LEADVILLE	10200
271.0	Ar Malta	10200
271.0	Ar Malta	9580
281.0	Ar Tennessee Pass	10240
288.7	Ar Pando	9608
293.9	Ar Red Cliff	8608
	Eagle River Cañon	8304
296.1	Ar Belden	8304
302.0	Lv Minturn	7825
302.0	Lv Minturn	7825
308.0	Ar Avon	7465
319.1	Ar Wolcott	6975
329.0	Ar Eagle	6598
335.8	Ar Gypsum	6325

DENVER — Scenic gateway to twelve National Parks and thirty-two National Monuments. Denver affords a vision of 200 miles of the Rocky Mountains, extending from Long's Peak to Pikes Peak.

Colorado Springs — Colorado Springs and the Pikes Peak region offer many varied attractions. Crowded within this region are perhaps more wonders than are found in any like area on the globe. Those who tarry a while, will be amply repaid with new sights and scenes.

Manitou Springs — "The Saratoga of the West," at the entrance to the Garden of the Gods, with its other wonders, such as Crystal Park, the Cave of the Winds, etc., its hotels and cottages and its new bath house perhaps the finest in the United States, is one of the resort places of the world. Here the ascent of Pikes Peak, 14,110 feet, is made by cog road or auto.

EASTBOUND

(Mountain Time on Denver & Rio Grande Western; Pacific Time on Western Pacific)

Train columns: **512** Marysvale Passenger · **18** Price Passenger · **2** Scenic Limited · **4** Denver and Eastern Express · **9** Colo.Spg.–Pueblo & Eastern Express · **16** Colorado–New Mexico Express

Miles from Ogden	Station
0.0	Lv OGDEN, U.S.M.
7.4	Lv Roy
14.8	Lv Layton
17.5	Lv Kaysville
21.4	Lv Farmington
28.4	Lv Woods Cross
31.1	Lv North Salt Lake
36.9	Ar SALT LAKE CITY, U.S.M.
	Western Pacific R. R. (Pacific Time)
0.6	Lv SAN FRANCISCO
93.8	Lv Oakland
138.6	Lv Stockton
178.8	Lv Sacramento
205.1	Lv Marysville
362.9	Lv Oroville
532.3	Lv Portola
927.5	Ar SALT LAKE CITY, U.S.M.
	(Mountain Time)
927.5	Ar SALT LAKE CITY
	Denver & Rio Grande Western
36.9	Lv SALT LAKE CITY
39.5	Lv Roper
43.6	Lv Murray
47.5	Ar Midvale
53.4	Ar Riverton
56.5	Ar Olivers
59.2	Ar Nash
61.8	Lv Mesa
65.0	Ar Lehi
68.3	Ar American Fork
72.0	Ar PROVO, U.S.M.
80.8	Ar Geneva
80.8	Ar Springville
98.4	Ar Castilla
102.1	Ar Thistle
113.2	Ar Mill Fork
122.0	Ar Gilluly
126.5	Ar Soldier Summit, U.S.M.
131.5	Ar Colton
143.7	Ar Kyune
152.7	Ar Castle Gate
154.1	Ar Utah Railway Jct.
156.5	Lv Helper
163.9	Ar PRICE, U.S.M.
169.5	Lv Wellington
179.8	Lv Mounds
202.4	Lv Woodside
227.8	Lv Green River
254.9	Lv Thompson
278.6	Lv Cisco
294.6	Lv Westwater
314.1	Lv Loma
317.4	Lv Mack, Colo.
322.5	Lv Fruita
332.4	Ar GRAND JUNC., U.S.M.
332.4	Ar GRAND JUNC.
339.3	Lv Clifton
344.9	Lv Palisade
349.5	Lv Gale
365.3	Lv DeBeque
373.2	Lv Una
378.0	Lv Grand Valley
390.5	Lv Lacy
395.3	Lv Rifle
402.5	Lv Silt
409.3	Lv New Castle

MOUNTAIN TROUT EVERY DAY — DINING CAR

Visit the Mesa Verde National Park (Open May to November) — The transcontinental traveler will do well to visit the Mesa Verde National Park, the homeland of the Cliff Dwellers in Southwestern Colorado, Uncle Sam's only archaeological preserve.

PROVO — Provo, just back from the shore of Utah Lake, at the base of the Wasatch Range, is dominated by lofty Mount Timpanogos, a mountain 11,957 feet in altitude, and is scaled annually by hundreds of hikers. On the road to the summit of the peak is Timpanogos Cave National Monument, containing a recently discovered cave, some 700 feet long.

ONE HOUR AND FORTY-FIVE MINUTES BETWEEN TRAINS — For Sight-seeing Salt Lake City — An excellent opportunity is afforded passengers en route to San Francisco to visit the principal points of interest in Salt Lake City between the arrival of Rio Grande No. 1, 12.55 Noon (Mt. Time) and the departure of Western Pacific No. 1, 1.40 P.M. Much of the history and romance of the West is centered about Salt Lake City. One should visit Temple Square, containing the principal buildings of the Mormon Churches and hear the famous Tabernacle Organ. The Great Salt Lake and many other attractions offer profitable pastimes.

GUIDEBOOK of the WESTERN UNITED STATES — A Government publication entitled The Denver & Rio Grande Western Route, gotten out by the United States Geological Survey in recognition of the surpassing scenic attractions as seen from the car windows along the Denver & Rio Grande Western. The price of the book is $1.00 per copy, and may be secured from the Superintendent of Documents, Washington, D. C., or—

F. A. WADLEIGH, Passenger Traffic Manager, Denver Rio Grande Western System, Denver, Colorado.

Denver & Rio Grande Western — SCENIC LINE OF THE WORLD

Western Pacific R. R.

Denver & Rio Grande Western

Timetable — principal stations (selected):

Shoshone — Cañon of Colorado River — GLENWOOD SPRINGS, U.S.M. — Carbondale — ASPEN — New Castle — Silt — Rifle — Grand Valley — Una — Gale — De Beque — Palisade — Clifton — GRAND JUNC., U.S.M. — Fruita — Loma — Mack — Westwater, Utah — Cisco — Thompson — Green River — Woodside — Mounds — Wellington — PRICE, U.S.M. — Helper — Utah Railway Jct. — Castle Gate — Kyune — Colton — Soldier Summit, U.S.M. — Scenic — Gilluly — Mill Fork — Thistle — Castilla — Springville — PROVO — Geneva — American Fork — Lehi — Mesa — Nash — Olivers — Riverton — Midvale — Murray — Roper — SALT LAKE CITY, U.S.M.

Western Pacific R. R. (Mountain Time / Pacific Time): Lv SALT LAKE CITY — Winnemucca — Portola — Oroville — Marysville — Sacramento — Stockton — Oakland — Ar SAN FRANCISCO

Denver & Rio Grande Western: Lv SALT LAKE CITY — North Salt Lake — Woods Cross — Farmington — Kaysville — Layton — Roy — Ar OGDEN, U.S.M.

Eastern portion stations (selected):

Ar GLENWOOD SPGS., U.S.M. — Lv GLENWOOD SPRINGS — Carbondale — ASPEN — Cañon of Colorado River — Shoshone — Gypsum — Eagle — Wolcott — Avon — Minturn — Belden — Eagle River Cañon — Red Cliff — Pando — Tennessee Pass — Malta — LEADVILLE — Granite — Riverside — Buena Vista — Nathrop — Brown's Cañon — SALIDA, U.S.M. — Howard — Vallie — Pleasanton — Cotopaxi — Texas Creek — Parkdale — Sample — Grand Cañon of the Arkansas — Royal Gorge — CAÑON CITY, U.S.M. — Florence — Portland — Concrete — Carlile — Swallows — PUEBLO, U.S.M. — 8th St., Pueblo — Eden — Pinon — Wigwam — Buttes — Fountain — COLORADO SPGS., U.S.M. — MANITOU — Colorado City — COLORADO SPRINGS — Pikeview — Husted — Monument — PALMER LAKE — Greenland — Larkspur — Castle Rock — Sedalia — Gann — Acequia — Struby — Littleton — DENVER

13   14

381

WESTERN PACIFIC

SCHEDULE OF TRAINS

Denver, Colorado Springs, Pueblo, Grand Junction, Salt Lake City, Ogden, Wells, Elko, Winnemucca, Doyle, Portola, Oroville, Marysville, Sacramento, Stockton, Oakland and San Francisco

Table No. 2

WESTBOUND

(Pacific Time on Western Pacific; Mountain Time on Denver & Rio Grande Western)

Miles	Station	Elevation	1 Scenic Limited	3 Pacific Express
	Denver & Rio Grande Western			
0.0	Lv DENVER (M.T.)	5280	*8.15 am	*2.40 pm
74.9	Lv COLORADO SPRGS.	5989	11.05	5.30 pm
119.4	Lv PUEBLO	4668	12.35 pm	7.05
215.1	Lv Salida	7050	4.40	11.05
275.8	Lv Leadville	10200	*6.35	
360.1	Lv GLENWOOD SPRGS.	5758	10.57	5.22 am
449.6	Lv Grand Junction	4583	2.10	8.55
701.2	Lv Provo	4512	11.40 am	6.55
745.1	Ar SALT LAKE CITY	4224	12.55 pm	8.20
0.0	Lv OGDEN	4293	6.45	3.05 pm
36.9	Ar SALT LAKE CITY	4224	7.55	4.25
	Western Pacific R.R.		1	3
	(Mountain Time)			
0.0	Lv SALT LAKE CITY U.S.M.	4224	*2.40	*11.00
	(Pacific Time)			
0.0	Lv SALT LAKE CITY	4224	1.40	10.00
14.4	Lv Garfield { Great Salt Lake }	4230	y	10.32
19.7	Lv Lago	4203	y	f10.44
30.5	Lv Burmester	4218	2.38	f11.10
30.5	Lv Ellerbeck	4220	f	f11.17
41.8	Lv Timpie	4219	y	11.31
49.1	Lv Delle	4269	y	11.45
61.3	Lv Low	4602	y	f12.10
73.0	Lv Clive	4282	y	f12.30
82.0	Lv Knolls	4230	y	f12.47
92.3	Lv Barro } Salt Beds	4220	y	1.05 am
112.3	Lv Saldure } Salt Beds	4218	y	1.43
121.2	Lv WENDOVER	4237	5.00	2.10
138.9	Lv Pilot	5123	y	2.45
144.2	Lv Proctor	5385	y	2.58
154.1	Lv Silver Zone	5819	y	3.25
161.7	Lv SHAFTER	5553	6.30	3.40
174.5	Lv Jasper	5876	y	4.05
189.0	Lv Ventosa	5602	y	4.26
194.1	Lv Tobar	5681	y	4.36
203.9	Lv Boaz	5786	y	4.53
210.2	Lv WELLS	5674	7.45	5.03
218.9	Lv Starr	5786	y	5.16
228.0	Lv Deeth	5506	y	5.34
239.4	Lv Halleck	5344	y	5.53
244.2	Lv Elburz	5235	y	6.00
254.4	Lv Pardo	5196	y	6.17
262.1	Lv ELKO	5119	9.00	6.45
270.9	Lv Hunter	5059	y	6.45
283.1	Lv Carlin	4899	9.35	7.35
291.7	Lv PALISADE	4852	f9.50	7.51
300.3	Lv Cluro	4764	y	8.07
308.3	Lv Beowawe	4696	y	8.22
317.5	Lv Dunphy	4628	y	8.35
326.7	Lv Kampos	4562	y	8.50
337.0	Lv Rennox	4509	y	9.05
352.3	Lv Ellison	4433	y	9.27
365.6	Lv Red House	4387	y	9.47
379.1	Lv Golconda	4344	y	10.07
387.0	Lv Bliss	4329	y	10.22
395.2	Lv WINNEMUCCA	4277	12.30 am	10.50
401.9	Lv Krum	4299	y	f11.02
413.0	Lv Pronto	4238	y	f11.23
430.9	Lv Jungo	4165	y	11.54
439.7	Lv Antelope	4507	y	f12.15
452.2	Lv Sulphur	4044	y	f12.35
456.7	Lv Ronda	4025	y	f12.42
476.0	Lv Trego	3912	y	f1.15

SIGHTSEEING — SALT LAKE CITY

Zion, the city of Saints, capital of Utah, founded in 1847 by the Mormon pioneers who had trudged overland from Illinois, is a center of business enterprise, natural beauty and historic interest. It is notably well laid out, with wide, straight streets, shaded by poplars, catalpas and other deciduous trees, and bordered by running mountain water. Within the city what is usually first inspected by the visitor is Temple Square, containing the chief Mormon buildings—the Temple, Tabernacle and Assembly Hall. Adjacent to the Square are the Beehive and Lion Houses, formerly the headquarters of Brigham Young, and the new Administration Building. The State Capitol Building, built of Utah granite and marble at a cost of $2,500,000, stands on an eminence at the head of State Street, overlooking the city, and contains a museum of natural resources that is well worth visiting. Fort Douglas, U. S. Military Post, is located on the bench of the Wasatch Mountains, three miles east of the city, and can be reached by auto or electric car.

The one hour and forty-five minute interval between the arrival of RioGrande No. 1, 12 55 Noon (Mountain Time), and departure of Western Pacific No. 1, 1 40 P. M. (Pacific Time), affords the through traveler an opportunity to visit the principal places of interest in Salt Lake City and enjoy the stop to the fullest extent.

EASTBOUND

(Pacific Time on Western Pacific; Mountain Time on Denver & Rio Grande Western)

(Pacific Time)

Miles	Station	2 Scenic Limited	4 Pacific Express
0.0	Lv SAN FRANCISCO (Union Ferry Station)	*9.20 am	*7.20 pm
3.5	Lv Western Pacific Mole.	9.50 am	7.55 pm
6.6	Lv OAKLAND, U.S.M. (3d & Washington Sts.)	10.00 am	8.10 pm
9.7	Lv Oakland (Fruitvale Sta)	x	8.20
13.4	Lv Oakland (Elmhurst Sta)	x	8.32
14.8	Lv SAN LEANDRO	x	8.41
20.4	Lv HAYWARD	x	8.50
26.6	Lv Decoto	x	8.57
29.7	Lv NILES	10.42	9.10
36.0	Lv Sunol	x	9.19
41.5	Lv PLEASANTON	x	9.30
47.6	Lv LIVERMORE	x	9.47
56.5	Lv ALTAMONT	x	10.00
62.9	Lv Midway	x	10.14
71.8	Ar CARBONA	x	10.18
73.9	Lv Lyoth	x	10.23
82.0	Lv Nilegarden	x	10.33
83.8	Lv LATHROP	x	10.35
93.8	Lv STOCKTON, U.S.M.	12.35	11.00
104.8	Lv Kingdon	x	f11.28
109.5	Lv Brack	1.08	11.35
113.9	Lv Thornton	x	f11.43
118.9	Lv Glannvale	x	f11.51
124.7	Lv Franklin	x	f12.01
136.3	Lv Jeffery Shops	x	f12.25
138.6	Lv SACRAMENTO, U.S.M.	2.00 pm	12.50
143.9	Lv Del Paso	x	1.16
150.6	Lv Counsman	x	1.30
156.1	Lv PLEASANT GROVE	x	1.55
172.5	Lv Arboga	3.10	2.15
178.8	Lv Tambo	x	2.27
185.8	Lv MARYSVILLE	x	2.39
192.9	Lv Craig	x	2.50
199.4	Lv Palermo	x	3.05
205.1	Ar OROVILLE, U.S.M.	3.55	3.15
205.1	Lv OROVILLE, U.S.M.	4.05	3.34
212.7	Lv Bidwell	x	3.45
217.5	Lv Bloomer	x	3.55
221.4	Lv Las Plumas	f4.37	f4.03
224.3	Lv Berry Creek	x	4.13
228.6	Lv Blinzig	x	
232.0	Lv Intake	x	
235.2	Lv Poe	x	
239.0	Lv Pulga	x	4.29
241.0	Lv Mayaro	x	4.45
243.7	Lv Cresta	x	
249.1	Lv Rock Creek	x	4.59
253.1	Lv Tobin	x	
255.8	Lv Camp Rodgers	x	5.28
259.9	Lv Belden	x	
262.0	Lv Howells	x	5.50
264.6	Lv Rich	x	6.00
270.3	Lv Virgilia	x	6.09
273.0	Lv Gray's Flat	x	6.25
273.7	Lv Twain	x	
277.5	Lv Paxton	f	6.35
281.8	Lv Keddie	7.04	6.55
287.8	Ar Quincy Junction	x	7.10
296.6	Lv Spring Garden	7.40	7.40
301.6	Lv Sloat	x	8.05
303.4	Lv Cromberg	x	8.17
309.3	Ar Feather River Inn	x	
310.3	Ar Blairsden	8.40	8.48 am

(Grand Cañon of the Feather River)

HELP PREVENT FOREST FIRES

Do not throw lighted cigars or cigarettes out of CAR WINDOWS

15   16

WESTERN PACIFIC

LOYALTON BRANCH

Mixed Trains — Tues., Thur. and Sat.

418	416			415
4.10	10.30	Lv......BECKWITH....Ar	3.50	
4.20	11.30	Lv......Hawley.....Lv	3.30	
		Ar.....LOYALTON...Lv	2.30	

RENO BRANCH

202	204	Mls		201	203
*5.10	*10.35	341	Lv..RENO JCT..Ar	*10.15	*4.50
f5.20	f10.45	344	Lv...Plumas...Lv	f10.05	f4.40
f5.36	f11.01	351	Lv...Peavine...Lv	f 9.48	f4.23
f5.50	f11.17	357	Lv..Copperfield..Lv	f 9.25	f4.07
f5.57	f11.23	360	Lv..Anderson..Lv	f 9.25	f4.00
6.40	12.05	374	Ar....RENO....Lv	8.45	3.25

Main Line				1	3
	3951	489.2	Lv Gerlach......	3.05 am	1.50 pm
	3854	503.5	Lv Bronte......	y...	2.17
	3891	511.3	Lv Reynard.....	y...	2.33
	4198	534.0	Lv Sand Pass....	y...	f2.55
	3995	543.6	Lv Flanigan.....	y...	3.09
	3999	549.9	Lv Calneva.....	x...	f3.31
	4112	556.0	Ar Hackstaff....	x...	f3.51
	4266	564.6	Lv Doyle......	x...	4.09
	4351	569.3	Lv Omira......	x...	4.21
	4452	572.0	Lv Constantia...	x...	4.28
	4574	575.4	Lv Red Rock....	x...	4.35
	4814	581.5	Lv Scotts......	x...	4.48
		585.8	Lv Reno Junction..		5.08
		587.9	Lv Chilcoot.....		5.18
		599.4	Lv Hawley.....		5.40
		601.0	Lv Calpine Jct...		5.43
	4632	606.1	Lv PORTOLA, U.S.M.	6.30 am	f5.45
	4581	613.9	Lv Clio.......	x...	6.25
	4410	617.2	Lv Blairsden....	x...	6.35
	4411	619.5	Lv Feather River Inn	6.53 am	6.36
	4115	624.1	Lv Cromberg....	x...	6.59
	202	625.9	Lv Sloat......	x...	7.12
	202	630.9	Lv Spring Garden..	x...	7.40
	102	639.7	Lv Quincy Jct...	7.40 am	8.01
	84	646.5	Lv Keddie.....	x...	8.06
	3223	650.0	Lv Paxton.....	8.06 am	8.11
	3080	653.8	Lv Twain......	x...	8.20
	2845	654.5	Lv Gray's Flat...	x...	8.32
	2848	657.2	Lv Virgilia....	x...	f8.43
	2751	662.9	Lv Rich......	x...	f8.58
	2500	665.0	Lv Howells.....	x...	9.10
	2312	667.6	Lv Belden.....	x...	9.20
	2306	671.7	Lv Camp Rodgers..	x...	
	2050	674.4	Lv Tobin......	x...	f9.40
	2006	678.4	Lv Cresta.....	x...	
	1805	683.8	Lv Mayaro.....	x...	f10.06
	1579	686.5	Lv Pulga......	x...	
	1450	688.8	Lv Poe.......	x...	10.22
	1380	692.3	Lv Intake.....	x...	10.34
	1204	695.6	Lv Rock Creek....	x...	
	1035	698.7	Lv Blinzig.....	x...	10.50
	890	703.1	Lv Berry Creek...	x...	11.03
	560	706.1	Lv Las Plumas...	x...	11.12
	415	710.0	Lv Bloomer.....	x...	11.55
	331	714.8	Lv Bidwell.....	x...	f11.55
	202	722.3	Ar OROVILLE, U.S.M.	10.45 am	12.05 pm
	202	722.3	Lv OROVILLE.....	10.55 am	12.16
	202	728.1	Lv Palermo.....	x...	12.26
	102	734.6	Lv Craig......	x...	12.31
	81	741.7	Lv Tambo.....	x...	12.37
	84	748.7	Lv MARYSVILLE...	11.36 am	12.52
	64	755.1	Lv Arboga.....	x...	1.02
	46	771.4	Lv Pleasant Grove..	x...	f1.31
	36	778.9	Lv Counsman....	x...	1.40
	23	788.9	Lv SACRAMENTO, U.S.M.	12.40 pm	1.51
	23	791.2	Lv Jeffery Shops..	x...	2.05
	23	802.8	Lv Franklin....	x...	2.24
	19	808.9	Lv Glannvale....	x...	2.35
	17	813.9	Lv Thornton....	x...	2.44
	24	818.0	Lv Brack......	x...	3.05
	24	822.7	Lv Kingdon....	x...	3.13
	21	833.7	Lv STOCKTON, U.S.M.	2.10 pm	3.23
	23	843.7	Lv LATHROP....	x...	3.50
	23	853.6	Lv Nilegarden...	x...	4.13
	102	855.7	Lv Lyoth......	x...	4.31
	135	864.6	Lv CARBONA....	x...	4.55
	479	871.0	Lv Midway.....	x...	5.10
	750	879.9	Lv ALTAMONT...	x...	5.28
	476	885.0	Lv LIVERMORE...	x...	5.35
	340	891.5	Lv PLEASANTON..	x...	5.47
	252	897.8	Lv Sunol......	x...	6.01
	61	900.9	Lv Niles......	4.11 pm	6.06
	94	907.1	Lv Decoto.....	x...	6.18
	42	912.9	Lv HAYWARD....	x...	6.28
	21	914.1	Lv SAN LEANDRO..	x...	6.32
	32	917.6	Lv Oakland (Elmhurst Sta.)	x...	6.43
	11	920.9	Ar Oakland (Fruitvale Sta.)	5.05 pm	7.00
	6	924.0	Ar Western Pacific Mole (3d & Washington Sts)	5.15	7.15 am
		927.5	Ar SAN FRANCISCO (Union Ferry Station)	5.45	7.45 am

Main Line (continued, page 18)

	Mls	Station	2	4
	313.6	Lv Clio.......	x...	8.58 am
	321.4	Lv PORTOLA, U.S.M.	9.20 pm	9.30
	326.0	Lv Calpine Jct...	x...	9.44
	329.6	Lv Hawley.....	x...	9.52
	339.6	Lv Chilcoot.....	x...	10.16
	341.7	Lv Reno Junction..	x...	10.32
	346.0	Lv Scotts.....	x...	f10.40
	351.7	Lv Red Rock....	x...	f10.53
	355.5	Lv Constantia...	x...	f10.59
	358.2	Lv Omira......	x...	f11.06
	362.9	Ar Doyle......	x...	11.17
	371.5	Lv Hackstaff....	x...	f11.32
	377.6	Lv Calneva.....	x...	f11.42
	383.9	Lv Flanigan....	x...	f11.52
	393.6	Lv Sand Pass....	y...	f12.12 pm
	416.4	Lv Reynard....	y...	f12.58
	424.0	Lv Bronte.....	12.55 am	1.50
	438.3	Ar Gerlach.....	y...	2.22
	470.8	Lv Trego......	y...	2.55
	474.6	Lv Ronda......	y...	3.02
	487.8	Lv Sulphur....	y...	3.25
	496.6	Lv Antelope....	y...	3.40
	514.5	Lv Jungo......	y...	4.10
	525.0	Lv Pronto.....	y...	4.30
	532.3	Lv Krum......	3.50 am	4.50
	540.3	Lv WINNEMUCCA..	y...	5.20
	548.4	Lv Bliss......	y...	5.44
	561.9	Lv Golconda....	y...	6.05
	575.2	Lv Red House....	y...	6.30
	590.5	Lv Rennox.....	y...	6.45
	600.8	Lv Kampos.....	y...	7.00
	610.0	Lv Dunphy.....	y...	7.15
	619.2	Lv Beowawe....	y...	7.30
	627.1	Lv Churo......	f 6.29 am	7.48
	635.8	Lv PALISADE....	f 6.44 am	8.05
	644.4	Lv Carlin.....	y...	8.30
	656.6	Lv Hunter.....	7.40 am	8.55
	665.4	Lv ELKO......	y...	9.12
	673.1	Lv Pardo......	y...	9.30
	683.3	Lv Elburz.....	y...	9.37
	688.1	Lv Halleck....	y...	9.59
	699.5	Lv Deeth......	y...	10.15
	717.3	Lv Starr......	9.09 am	10.30
	723.6	Lv WELLS......	y...	10.42
	733.4	Lv Boaz.......	y...	11.00
	738.5	Lv Tobar......	y...	11.08
	752.8	Lv Ventosa.....	y...	11.42
	765.8	Lv Jasper.....	10.30 am	11.55
	772.1	Lv SHAFTER, U.S.M.	y...	12.10 am
	783.3	Lv Silver Zone...	y...	12.35 am
	788.6	Lv Proctor.....	y...	12.47 am
	806.3	Lv Pilot......	11.50 am	1.25
	835.1	Lv WENDOVER {Salt Beds}	y...	1.43
	835.1	Lv Salduro {Great Salt Lake}	y...	2.17
	845.4	Lv Barro......	y...	2.35
	854.4	Lv Knolls.....	y...	2.52
	866.1	Lv Clive......	y...	3.15
	871.9	Lv Low.......	y...	3.37
	878.3	Lv Delle......	y...	3.50
	885.7	Lv Timpie.....	y...	4.03
	893.0	Lv Ellerbeck....	y...	4.20
	896.7	Lv Burmester {Great Salt Lake}	2.13 pm	4.35
	907.7	Lv Lago.......	y...	4.48
	913.1	Lv Garfield....	3.30 pm	5.30
	927.5	Ar SALT LAKE CITY (Pacific Time) U.S.M.	4.30 pm	6.30

Denver & Rio Grande Western (Mountain Time)

	Mls	Station	3	1
	0.0	Lv SALT LAKE CITY	8.35 am	*1.10 pm
	36.9	Ar OGDEN......	9.45 am	2.10 pm
			2	4
	36.9	Lv SALT LAKE CITY	4.45 pm	*8.10 am
	80.8	Lv Provo......	6.00 pm	9.27 am
	332.4	Lv Grand Junction..	3.20 am	3.15 pm
	422.3	Ar GLENWOOD SPRGS.	6.22 am	10.26 pm
	515.7	Lv Leadville.....	10.30	
	566.8	Lv Salida......	12.55 pm	5.10 am
	662.6	Ar PUEBLO.....	4.45	8.35 am
	707.1	Ar COLORADO SPRGS.	5.55	10.10 am
	782.2	Ar DENVER.....	8.30	12.45 pm

San Francisco, Cal.: Baggage checked from hotels or residences by Union Transfer Co. Oakland, Cal.: Baggage checked from hotels or residences by United Transfer Co.

CALPINE BRANCH

314 Mixed	Station	313 Mixed
R 10.15am	Lv CALPINE JUNCTION. Ar	3.15pm
11.30am	Ar.... CALPINE....Lv	R 2.00pm

SAN JOSE BRANCH

102 Motor	Station	101 Motor
*4.15pm	Lv.... NILES....Ar	*10.30am
f 4.27pm	Ar..Irvington..Lv	f10.13am
f 4.36pm	Ar..Warm Springs..Lv	f10.04am
f 4.46pm	Ar..Milpitas..Lv	f 9.54am
f 4.55pm	Ar..Berryessa..Lv	f 9.47am
5.05pm	Ar..East San Jose..Lv	9.40am
	SAN JOSE	

Grand Cañon of the Feather River

*Daily. †Daily except Sunday. R Mon. Wed. and Fri. x Stops to take revenue passengers for or leave from Salt Lake City and east. y Stops to take revenue passengers for or leave from Pueblo, Colo., and east. f Stops on signal. §Lunch. The above trains stop only at stations where time is given or shown as flag stop. U.S.M.—Mail boxes are located on station platform.

Denver and Rio Grande RAILWAY

Over One Thousand Miles in operation, through the
MOST SUBLIME AND INTERESTING
Mountain and Valley Scenery
IN THE WORLD.
A continual delight to the Tourist and the Student.

DENVER AND RIO GRANDE

RAILWAY.

TIME TABLE No. 13,

To take Effect Sunday, Nov. 13th, 1881,

AT 12:01 A. M.

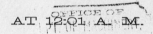

FOR USE AND GUIDANCE OF EMPLOYES ONLY.

Conductors and Engineers must have a copy of the BOOK OF RULES in their possession at all times.

DESTROY ALL TIME TABLES OF PREVIOUS DATE.

M. C. KIMBERLY, Supt. 1st Div. and Branches.
PUEBLO.

W. H. BANCROFT, Supt. 2d Div. and Branches.
ALAMOSA.

R. M. RIDGWAY, Supt. San Juan Div.
ANTONITO.

G. W. CUSHING, Gen'l Superintendent.
DENVER.

D. C. DODGE, Gen'l Manager,
DENVER.

NEWS PRINTING CO., DENVER

First Division—Denver Section—Southward Trains.

SECOND CLASS.				Telegraph, Water and Coaling Stations.	TIME TABLE No. 13. Nov. 13, 1881. STATIONS AND Passing Places.	Distances from Denver.	FIRST CLASS.		
No. 27. Stone.	No. 25.	No. 23.	No. 21. Freight and Emigrant.				No. 1. Leadville Express.	No. 3. Gunnison Express.	No. 5. Durango Express.
†6 35 Am	3 05 Pm	5 15 Am	9 00 Pm	N W	Dep Denver. Dep		8 00 Am	*7 30 Pm	3 00 Pm
6 50	3 20	5 30	9 15	N W C	" Burnham. "	2.2	8 15	7 45	3 15
6 59	3 35	5 42	9 30		" N. O. Crossing. "	4.	8 22	7 51	3 21
7 24	4 00	6 04	9 55		" Petersburg. "	8.	8 30	8 00	3 32
7 40	4 17	6 20	10 14	D W	" Littleton. "	10.6	8 37	8 07	3 40
8 20	4 58	7 12	11 00		" Acequia. "	17.5	8 55	8 28	3 58
9 05	5 40	8 05	11 50 Pm	D	" Sedalia. "	24.7	9 20	8 53	4 18
9 35	6 07	8 35	12 20 Am	W	" Mill No. 2. "	29.1	9 35	9 07	4 30
10 00	6 30	9 03	12 46	N	" Castle Rock. "	32.8	9 47	9 17	4 42
10 45	6 50	9 22	1 03		" Douglas. "	35.4	9 55	9 27	4 48
11 31 Am	7 13	9 45	1 25		" Glade. "	38.6	10 07	•9 38	4 59
12 30 Pm	7 50	10 22	1 57	D W C	" Larkspur. "	43.3	10 22	9 52	5 12
1 00	8 20	10 55	2 23		" Greenland. "	47.1	10 34	10 05	5 23
1 35	9 00	11 45 Am	3 00	N W C	" Divide. "	52.4	10 50	10 20	5 40 Ar 6 00 Dep
2 00	9 19	12 10 Pm	3 24	D	" Monument. "	56.	11 00	10 30	6 10
2 15	9 30	12 25	3 40	W	" Borsts. "	58.4	11 05	10 35	6 16
2 37	9 47	12 43	4 05	N	" Husted's. "	62.	11 14	10 43	6 25
3 08	10 13	1 08	4 44	W	" Edgerton. "	67.	11 25	10 55	6 40
4 00 Pm	10 55	1 50	5 55	N W C	Ar Colo. Springs. Ar	75.2	11 45	11 15	7 05
	11 20 Pm	2 15	6 10	N W C	Dep Colo. Springs. Dep	75.2	11 50 Am	11 20	7 10
	12 10 Am	3 08	6 53		" Widefield. "	84.	12 10 Pm	11 39	7 32
	12 35	3 33	7 10		" Fountain. "	88.6	12 20	11 48 Pm	7 43
	1 20	4 00	7 35	N W	" Little Butte. "	94.3	12 34	12 02 Am	7 55
	2 00	4 25	8 00		" Wigwam. "	100.	12 45	12 13	8 10
	2 34	4 53	8 26	D W	" Pinon. "	105.8	12 59	12 25	8 23
	3 10	5 22	8 54		" Cactus. "	112.	1 13	12 37	8 39
	3 45	5 47	9 19		" Nada. "	117.5	1 25	12 48	8 53
	4 00 Am	6 00 Pm	9 30 Am	N W C	Ar South Pueblo. Ar	119.6	1 30 Pm	12 55 Am	9 00 Pm
(9.05)	(12.55)	(12.45)	(12.30)		(119.6)		(5.30)	(5.25)	(6.00)

All trains leave terminal Stations daily.

No train or engine must leave Denver without the Conductor or Engineer inquiring at the Telegraph office for orders.

The double track will be in use for all trains between Holladay street, Denver, and Burnham, during the continuance of this Time Table.

Passengers will not be carried on freight trains on the first division, Denver to Leadville, except on emigrant train No. 21 between Denver and Arkansas, and on No. 24 between Pueblo and Denver.

*NOTE.—Nos. 3 and 28 will meet on double track between Denver and Burnham.

First Division—Denver Section—Northward Trains.

FIRST CLASS.			LENGTH OF SIDINGS—FEET.	TIME TABLE. No. 13. Nov. 13, 1881. STATIONS AND Passing Places.	DISTANCES BETWEEN STATIONS.	SECOND CLASS.					
No. 6. Denver Passenger.	No. 4. Eastern Express.	No. 2. Denver Express.				No. 22.	No. 24.	No. 26.	No. 28. Stone.		
12 30 Pm	6 55 Am	8 00 Pm		Ar Denver. Ar		4 45 Pm	12 35 Am	7 25 Am	7 50 Pm		
12 15	6 40 †	7 45		Dep Burnham. Dep	2.2	4 30	12 20	7 10	7 35 *		
12 09 Pm	6 35	7 40		" N. O. Crossing "	1.8	4 20	12 10 Am	6 59	7 25		
11 59 Am	6 25	7 30		" Petersburg. "	5.8	4 00	11 50 Pm	6 37	7 05		
11 52	6 20	7 23		" Littleton. "	2.6	3 40	11 35	6 20	6 52		
11 32	6 05	7 07		" Acequia. "	6.9	2 58	11 00	5 47	6 17		
11 15	5 48	6 49		" Sedalia. "	7.2	2 17	10 12	5 11	5 40		
11 03	5 38	6 38		" Mill No. 2. "	4.4	1 50	9 42	4 50	5 09		
10 53	5 30	6 30		" Castle Rock. "	3.7	1 31	9 17	4 32	4 42		
10 45	5 24	6 23		" Douglas. "	2.6	1 16	9 07	4 21	3 45		
10 35	5 17	6 15		" Glade. "	3.2	12 56	8 55	4 05	3 20		
10 22	5 06	6 03		" Larkspur. "	4.7	12 30	8 37	34 8	2 45		
10 11	4 57	5 53		" Greenland. "	3.8	12 11 Pm	8 20	3 25	2 15		
9 55	4 45	5 40		" Divide. "	5.3	11 45 Am	7 50	3 00	1 35		
9 44	4 30	5 28		" Monument. "	3.6	11 00	7 20	2 30	12 50		
9 35	4 20	5 19		" Borsts. "	2.4	10 35	6 59	2 05	12 25		
9 23	4 05	5 06		" Husted's. "	3.6	9 59	6 25	1 35	12 01 Pm		
9 05	3 46	4 47		" Edgerton. "	5.	9 05	5 41	12 45 Am	11 25 Am		
8 30	3 10	4 15		Dep Colo. Springs. Dep	8.2	8 00	4 25	11 30 Pm	10 10 Am		
8 25	3 05	4 10		Ar Colo. Springs. Ar		7 45	4 05	10 45			
8 02	2 42	3 46		Dep Widefield. Dep	8.8	6 53	3 08	9 50			
7 50	2 30	3 33		" Fountain "	4.6	6 25	2 28	9 22			
7 35	2 15	3 18		" Little Butte. "	5.7	5 53	1 36	8 46			
7 20	2 00	3 03		" Wigwam. "	5.7	5 20	12 45	8 10			
7 05	1 46	2 47		" Pinon. "	5.8	4 49	12 07 Pm	7 34			
6 47	1 30	2 32		" Cactus. "	6.2	4 15	11 25 Am	6 53			
6 32	1 15	2 17		" Nada. "	5.5	3 45	10 45	6 17			
6 25 Am	1 10 Am	2 10 Pm		Dep South Pueblo. Dep	2.1	3 30 Am	10 30 Am	6 00 Pm			
(6.05)	(5.30)	(5.50)		(119.6)		(13.15)	(14.05)	(13.25)	(9.40)		

All trains leave terminal Stations daily.

No train or engine must leave South Pueblo without the Conductor or Engineer inquiring at the Dispatcher's office for orders.

On the double track trains will use the right hand track.

Trains which by the Time Table should pass at Burnham will pass on the double track.

† Nos. 4 and 27 will meet on double track between Burnham and Denver.

First Division—Leadville Section—Westward Trains.

SECOND CLASS					TELEGRAPH, WATER AND COALING STATIONS.	TIME TABLE No. 13. Nov. 13, 1881. STATIONS AND Passing Places.	DISTANCES FROM DENVER.	FIRST CLASS			
No. 73.	No. 25.	No. 23.	No. 21. Freight and Emigrant.	No. 15.				No. 1. Leadville Express.	No. 3. Gunnison Express.	No. 71. Silver Cliff Passenger.	No. 55. Blue River Accom.
	3 05 Pm	5 30 Am	9 00 Pm		NWC	Dep Denver Dep		8 00 Am	7 30 Pm		
	6 30 Am	7 00 Pm	10 30 Am		NWC	Dep South Pueblo. Dep	119.6	2 05 Pm	1 25 Am		
	6 55	7 24	10 58			" Goodnight. "	124.2	2 17	1 36		
	7 24	7 49	11 31 Am			" Meadows. "	129.5	2 30	1 48		
	7 56	8 20	12 06 PM			" Swallows. "	155.6	2 45	2 02		
	8 22	8 45	12 40 Pm			" Carlile Springs. "	140.	2 59	2 14		
	8 45	9 00	1 00		N	" Beaver Creek. "	143.	3 06	2 22		
	8 50	9 05	1 04			" Thompson. "	143.6	3 09	2 25		
	9 45	9 52	2 00		D W	" Labran. "	152.	3 30	2 43		
	10 00	9 57	2 15			" Florence. "	152.4	3 32	2 46		
	11 00	10 45	3 00		NWC	Ar Canon City. Ar	160.6	3 55	3 05		
6 00 Am	11 40	12 00	3 30	7 15 Am	NWC	Dep Canon City. Dep	160.6	4 00	3 10	4 10 Pm	
Ar 6 10 Am	11 55 Am	12 10 Am	3 42	7 25		" Grape Creek Junc. "	162.4	4 05	3 14	Ar 4 20 Pm	
	12 50 Pm	1 10	4 40	8 07	D W	" Park Dale. "	170.7	4 40	3 42		
	1 28	1 52	5 15	8 38		" Spike Buck. "	176.3	4 57	4 00		
	2 28	2 57	6 10	9 25	N C	" Texas Creek. "	185.5	5 25	4 28		
	3 15	3 43	6 55	10 05	D W	" Cotopaxi. "	192.7	5 46	4 52		
	3 55	4 22	7 30	10 40	DWC	" Vallie. "	199.2	6 05	5 12		
	4 30	4 57	8 20	11 08	D	" Howards. "	204.5	6 20	5 28		
	4 43	5 10	8 35	11 20 Am	W	" Badger. "	206.8	6 26	5 35		
	5 30	6 00	9 26	12 03 Pm		" Cleora. "	214.6	6 49	6 00		
	5 45	6 20	9 40	12 15 Pm	NWC	Ar Salida. Ar	216.5	6 55	6 05		
	6 10	7 10	10 15		NWG	Dep Salida Dep	216.5	7 20	6 15		
	7 01	8 15	11 05 Pm		D	" Brown's Canon. "	223.6	7 42	6 32		
	7 15	8 35	11 20 Pm			" Hecla. "	225.7	7 48	6 38		
	8 15	9 35	12 15 Am		NW	" Nathrop. "	234.3	8 15	7 00		
	8 50	10 10	12 45			" Midway. "	239.1	8 33	7 12		
	9 10	10 30	1 00		NWC	Ar Buena Vista. Ar	241.8	8 45	7 20		
	9 35	10 45	1 15		NWC	Dep Buena Vista. Dep	241.8	8 55	7 40		
	9 45	11 00	1 25			" Boulder Siding. "	243.	9 00	7 45		
	10 02	11 20	1 42			" Americus. "	245.7	9 08	7 52		
	10 25	11 50 Am	2 10		D	" Riverside. "	249.6	9 20	8 05		
	11 02	12 35 Pm	2 50			" Pine Creek. "	255.4	9 37	8 25		
	11 25	1 00	3 15		D	" Granite. "	258.8	9 48	8 35		
	11 40 Pm	1 20	3 30			" Twin Lakes. "	261.1	9 55	8 40		
	12 05 Am	1 53	3 55		D	" Haydens. "	264.8	10 05	8 50		
	12 50	2 43	4 35			" Crystal Lake. "	270.3	10 22	9 08		
	1 07	3 00	4 50		NWC	" Malta. "	272.4	10 30	9 15		2 30 PM
	1 27	3 20	5 15			" Eiler. "	274.8	10 45	9 30		2 45
	1 45 Am	3 35 Pm	5 30 Am		NWC	Ar Leadville. Ar	277.4	10 55 Pm	9 40 Am		3 00 PM
(.10)	(19.15)	(20.20)	(19.00)	(5.00)		(157.8)		(8.50)	(8.15)	(.10)	(.30)

All trains leave terminal Stations daily.

No train or engine must leave South Pueblo without the Conductor or Engineer inquiring at the Dispatcher's office for orders.

The switch at Grape Creek bridge is considered a railroad crossing, and all engines and all trains must make a full stop before passing, and at a distance of not exceeding 400 feet, *and must not* proceed until the way is *known to be clear*, when two blasts of the whistle must be given at the moment of starting.

First Division—Leadville Section—Eastward Trains.

FIRST CLASS				LENGTH OF SIDINGS—FEET.	TIME TABLE No. 13. Nov. 13, 1881. STATIONS AND Passing Places.	DISTANCES BETWEEN STATIONS.	SECOND CLASS				
No. 50. Blue River Accom.	No. 72. Silver Cliff Passenger.	No. 4. Eastern Express.	No. 2. Denver Express.				No. 16.	No. 22.	No. 24.	No. 26.	No. 74. Silver Cliff.
		6 55 Am	8 00 Pm		Ar · Denver. Ar			4 45 Pm	12 35 Am	7 25 Am	
		12 40 Am	1 35 Pm		Ar South Pueblo. Ar	119.6		11 10 Pm	4 00 Am	10 15 Am	
		12 30	1 22		Dep Goodnight. Dep	4.6		10 43	3 37	9 50	
		12 17	1 08		" Meadows. "	5.2		10 16	3 10	9 22	
		12 06 Am	12 54		" Swallows. "	4.1		9 44 °	2 40	8 50	
		11 49 Pm	12 40		" Carlile Springs. "	6.4		9 17	2 14	8 22	
		11 40	12 34		" Beaver Creek. "	2.9		9 00	2 00	8 05	
		11 37	12 31		" Thompson. "	.4		8 55	1 55	8 00	
		11 13	12 09		" Labran. "	8.4		8 10•	1 10	7 05	
		11 10	12 06 Pm		" Florence. "	.4		8 05	1 06	7 00	
		10 45	11 45 Am		Dep Canon City. Dep			7 15	12 20 Am	6 00	
	11 25 Am	10 40	11 40		Ar Canon City. Ar	8.1	8 45 Pm	6 50	11 40 Pm	5 30	8 40 Pm
	11 15 Am	10 35	11 35		Dep Grape Creek Jun. Dep	1.8	8 34	6 38	11 30	5 20	8 30 Pm
		10 00	11 00		" Park Dale. "	8.2	7 43	5 50	10 25	4 30	
		9 43	10 45		" Spike Buck. "	5.6	7 09	5 15 Dep 4 57 Ar	9 43	4 00	
		9 17	10 23		" Texas Creek. "	9.2	6 10 Dep 5 25 Ar	3 58	8 48	2 57	
		8 56	10 05		" Cotopaxi. "	7.2	4 34	3 15	8 08	2 17	
		8 37	9 52		" Vallie. "	6.4	3 55	2 40	7 30	1 43	
		8 20	9 35		" Howards. "	5.3	3 24	2 12	6 42	1 13	
		8 14	9 30		" Badger. "	2.2	3 10	2 00	6 26	1 00	
		7 51	9 10		" Cleora. "	7.8	2 25	1 20	5 30	12 17	
		7 45	9 05		Dep Salida. Dep	1.9	2 15 Pm	1 10	5 15	12 05 Am	
		7 20	9 00		Ar Salida. Ar			12 30 Pm	4 45	11 45 Pm	
		7 01	8 42		Dep Brown's Canon. Dep	7.4		11 55 Am	4 10	11 05	
		6 55	8 35		" Hecla. "	2.1		11 46	3 59	10 52	
		6 33	8 12		" Nathrop. "	8.6		11 05	3 17	10 03	
		6 20	7 58		" Midway. "	4.8		10 45	2 53	9 35	
		6 10	7 50		Dep Buena Vista. Dep	2.7		10 30	2 40	9 20	
		6 05	7 30		Ar Buena Vista. Ar			10 10	2 30	8 15	
		6 02	7 25		Dep Boulder Siding. Dep	1.1		10 00	2 20	8 05	
		5 53	7 16		" Americus. "	2.7		9 39	2 05	7 50	
		5 43	7 03		" Riverside. "	3.9		9 10	1 45	7 25	
		5 25	6 45		" Pine Creek. "	5.8		8 25	1 16	6 50	
		5 15	6 33		" Granite. "	3.4		7 57	1 00	6 30	
		5 10	6 25		" Twin Lakes. "	2.2		7 40	12 45	6 17	
		5 00	6 15		" Haydens. "	3.7		7 12	12 20 Pm	5 55	
		4 45	6 00		" Crystal Lake. "	5.5		6 30	11 41 Am	5 13	
9 45 Am		4 40	5 55		" Malta. "	2.1		6 10	11 25	4 55	
9 30		4 25	5 45		" Eiler. "	2.4		5 55	10 45	4 35	
9 15 AM		4 15 Pm	5 35 Am		Dep Leadville. Dep	2.5		5 40 Am	10 30 Am	4 15 Pm	
(.30)	(.10)	(8.40)	(8.00)		(157-8)		(6.30)	(17.25)	(17.30)	(18.00)	(.10)

All trains leave terminal Stations daily.
No train or engine must leave Leadville, Buena Vista or Nathrop without the Conductor or Engineer inquiring at the Telegraph office for orders.
This Time Table is valid, and will be used by Train-men and Track-men between SOUTH PUEBLO and NATHROP only. Conductors and Engineers will provide themselves with the Joint Time Table of the D. & R. G. Ry. and the D., S. P. & P. Ry., before going west of Nathrop, and be governed by the Rules, Regulations and Time Table between Nathrop and Leadville.
Trains Nos. 71, 72, 73 and 74 of the Silver Cliff Branch will protect themselves against all regular trains on the main line between Grape Creek Junction and Canon City.

Second Division—Rio Grande Section—Southward Trains.

SECOND CLASS.					TELEGRAPH, WATER AND COALING STATIONS.	TIME TABLE. No. 13. Nov. 13, 1881. STATIONS AND Passing Places.		DISTANCES FROM DENVER.	FIRST CLASS.		
			No. 45. El Moro Freight.	No. 41. Through Freight.					No. 5. Passenger.		
					N W C	Dep	Denver. Dep		3 00 Pm		
			12 15 Pm	6 15 Am	N W C	Dep South Pueblo.	Dep	119.6	9 30		
			12 25	6 25		"	Bessemer. "	120.6	9 35		
			1 10	7 09	W	"	San Carlos. "	128.4	9 57		
			1 40	7 35	.	"	Greenhorn. "	133.1	10 10		
			2 22	8 17	W	"	Salt Creek. "	140.1	10 28		
			2 59	8 52	N	"	Graneros. "	146.1	10 45		
			4 00	9 51	W	"	Huerfano. "	156.1	11 20		
			4 38	10 27		"	Apache. "	162.1	11 39		
			5 20 Pm	11 10	N W C	Ar	Cuchara. Ar	169.1	11 59 PM		
				11 20 Am	N W C	Dep	Cuchara. Dep	169.1	12 01 Am		
				12 03 Pm	D W	"	Walsen's. "	175.8	12 17		
				12 45	W	"	Wahatoya. "	182.7	12 36		
				1 40	N W C	Ar	La Veta. Ar	190.9	1 00		
				2 00	N W C	Dep	La Veta. Dep	190.9	1 10		
				3 00	W	"	Ojo. "	198.9	1 40		
				3 30		"	Mule Shoe. "	201.7	2 00		
				4 05	D	Ar	Veta Pass. Ar	205.2	2 35		
				4 10	D	Dep	Veta Pass. Dep	205.2	2 40		
				4 30	W	"	Sangre de Cristo. "	207.1	2 53		
				5 10	D W C	Ar	Placer. Ar	212.2	3 23		
				5 30	D W C	Dep	Placer. Dep	212.2	3 25		
				6 06		"	Trinchera. "	218.7	3 38		
				6 40	D W	"	Fort Garland. "	225.7	4 02		
				7 40	W	"	Baldy. "	237.7	4 33		
				7 22		"	Hay Siding. "	246.2	4 55		
				8 40 Pm	N W C	Ar	Alamosa. Ar	249.7	5 05 Am		

(5.05)   (14.25)   (130.1)   (7.35)

All trains leave terminal Stations daily.

No train or engine must leave South Pueblo without the Conductor or Engineer inquiring at the Dispatcher's office for orders.

Under *no circumstances* will Trains or Engines exceed Schedule Time between La Veta and Placer.

Second Division—Rio Grande Section—Northward Trains.

FIRST CLASS.			LENGTH OF SIDINGS—FEET.	TIME TABLE No. 13. Nov. 13th, 1881.	DISTANCES BETWEEN STATIONS.	SECOND CLASS.				
		No. 6. Passenger.		STATIONS AND Passing Places.		No. 42. Through Freight.	No. 46. Denver Freight.			
		12 30 Pm		Ar Denver. Ar						
		5 55 Am		Ar South Pueblo. Ar	119.6	7 30 Pm	5 05 Am			
		5 50		Dep Bessemer. Dep	1.	7 20	4 55			
		5 28		" San Carlos. "	8.	6 40	4 09			
		5 15		" Greenhorn. "	4.5	6 14	3 46			
		4 54		" Salt Creek. "	7.	5 33	3 00			
		4 35		" Graneros. "	6.	4 58	2 22			
		4 00		" Huerfano. "	10.	4 00	1 21			
		3 42		" Apache. "	6.	3 20	12 45			
		3 23		Dep Cuchara. Dep	7.	2 30	12 01 Am			
		3 21		Ar Cuchara. Ar		2 15				
		3 05		Dep Walsen's. Dep	6.7	1 30				
		2 45		" Wahatoya. "	6.9	12 45 PM				
		2 20		Dep La Veta. Dep	8.2	11 45 Am				
		2 10		Ar La Veta. Ar		11 05				
		1 40		Dep Ojo. Dep	8.	10 15				
		1 15		" Mule Shoe. "	2.8	9 50				
		12 35		Dep Veta Pass. Dep	3.5	9 10				
		12 30		Ar Veta Pass. Ar		9 05				
		12 10 Am		Dep Sangre de Cristo. Dep	1.9	8 40				
		11 41 Pm		Dep Placer. Dep	5.1	8 05				
		11 39		Ar Placer. Ar		7 40				
		11 22		Dep Trinchera. Dep	6.5	7 08				
		11 03		" Fort Garland. "	7.	6 35				
		10 30		" Baldy. "	12.	5 37				
		10 08		" Hay Siding "	3.5	4 55				
		10 00 Pm		Dep Alamosa. Dep	8.5	4 30 Am				

(7.55)   (130-1)   (15.00)   (5.04)

All trains leave terminal Stations daily.

No train or engine must leave Alamosa without the Conductor or Engineer inquiring at the Telegraph office for orders.

Under *no circumstances* will trains or engines exceed schedule time between La Veta and Placer.

Second Division—New Mexico Section—Southward Trains.

SECOND CLASS.						No. 41. Freight.	TELEGRAPH, WATER AND COALING STATIONS.	TIME TABLE No. 13. Nov. 13th, 1881. STATIONS AND Passing Places.		DISTANCES FROM DENVER.	No. 5. Passenger.	FIRST CLASS.	
								Dep	Denver.	Dep		3 00 Pm	
						9 45 PM	N W C	"	Alamosa.	"	249.7	5 15 Am	
						10 53	W	"	La Jara.	"	264.4	5 54	
						11 59 Pm	N W C	Ar	Antonito.	Ar	278.4	6 30	
							N W C	Dep	Antonito.	Dep	278.4	7 05	
								"	Palmilla.	"	289.9	8 05	
								"	Volcano.	"	296.9	8 43	
								"	No Agua.	"	306.	9 30	
							N W	"	Tres Piedras.	"	313.1	10 07	
								"	Servilleta.	"	323.1	10 59 Am	
								"	Caliente.	"	336.	12 07 PM	
							D	Ar	Barranca.	Ar	343.	12 45	
							D	Dep	Barranca.	Dep	343.	1 10	
								"	Comanche.	"	346.	1 36	
							D W C	Ar	Embudo.	Ar	350.5	2 10	
							D W C	Dep	Embudo.	Dep	350.5	2 15	
								"	Alcalde.	"	358.5	2 58	
								"	Chamita.	"	364.8	3 33	
							D W C	Ar	Espanola.	Ar	369.6	4 00 PM	
						(2.14)			(119-1)			(10.45)	

All trains leave terminal Stations daily.
No train or engine must leave Alamosa without the Conductor or Engineer inquiring at the Telegraph office for orders.
Under *no circumstances* will trains or engines exceed schedule time between Barranca and Embudo.

Del Norte Branch—Westward Trains.

SECOND CLASS.						TELEGRAPH, WATER AND COALING STATIONS.	TIME TABLE No. 13, Nov. 13th, 1881. STATIONS AND Passing Places.		DISTANCES FROM DENVER.	No. 17 Accom.	FIRST CLASS.	
							Dep.	Denver,	Dep.		3 00 Pm	
						N W C	"	Alamosa,	"	249.7	9 00 AM	
						*	"	Siding No. 1	"	259.7	9 48	
							"	Lariat,	"	265.9	10 19	
						D W C	Ar	Del Norte,	Ar	280.2	11 30 AM	
							(30.5)			(2.30)		

All trains run daily.
No Train or Engine must leave Alamosa without the Conductor or Engineer inquiring at the telegraph office for orders.

Second Division—New Mexico Section—Northward Trains.

FIRST CLASS.		LENGTH OF SIDINGS—FEET.	TIME TABLE No. 13. Nov. 13th, 1881. STATIONS AND Passing Places.			DISTANCES BETWEEN STATIONS.	SECOND CLASS.				
No. 6. Passenger.							No. 42. Freight.				
12 30 Pm			Ar	Denver.	Ar						
9 45 Pm			Ar	Alamosa.	Ar	249.7	4 00 Am				
9 07			Dep	La Jara.	Dep	14.7	2 50				
8 30			Dep	Antonito.	Dep	14.	1 45 AM				
7 00			Ar	Antonito.	Ar						
5 58			Dep	Palmilla.	Dep	11.5					
5 20			"	Volcano.	"	7.					
4 32			"	No Agua.	"	•9.1					
3 55			"	Tres Piedras.	"	7.1					
3 00			"	Servilleta.	"	10.					
1 53			"	Caliente.	"	12.9					
1 15			Dep	Barranca.	Dep	7.					
12 50			Ar	Barranca.	Ar						
12 25 Pm			Dep	Comanche.	Dep	3.					
11 50 Am			Dep	Embudo.	Dep	4.5					
11 45			Ar	Embudo.	Ar						
11 13			Dep	Alcalde.	Dep	8.					
10 48			"	Chamita.	"	6.3					
10 30 AM			Dep	Espanola.	Dep	4.8					
(11.15)			(119-9)				(2.15)				

All trains leave terminal Stations daily.
No train or engine must leave Espanola without the Conductor or Engineer inquiring at the Telegraph office for orders.
Under no circumstances will trains or engines exceed Schedule Time between Embudo and Barranca.

Del Norte Branch—Eastward Trains.

FIRST CLASS.		LENGTH OF SIDINGS—FEET.	TIME TABLE No. 13. Nov. 13th, 1881. STATIONS AND Passing Places.			DISTANCES BETWEEN STATIONS.	SECOND CLASS.				
No. 18. Accom.											
12 30 PM			Ar	Denver.	Ar						
3 30 PM			Ar	Alamosa.	Ar	250.1					
2 40			Dep	Siding No. 1	Dep	10.					
2 10			"	Lariat.	"	6.2					
1 00 PM			Dep	Del Norte.	Dep	14.3					
(2.30)			(30.5)								

All trains run daily.
No Train or Engine must leave Del Norte without Conductor or Engineer inquiring at the Telegraph office for order.

San Juan Division—Westward Trains.

SECOND CLASS.				TELEGRAPH, WATER AND COALING STATIONS.	TIME TABLE No. 13. Nov. 13th, 1881. STATIONS AND Passing Places.		DISTANCES FROM DENVER.	FIRST CLASS.	
		No. 103. Freight.	No. 101. Freight.					No. 5. Passenger.	
				N W C	Dep	Denver. Dep		3 00 PM	
			8 00 Am	N W C	Dep	Antonito. Dep	278.4	7 00 Am	
			9 00	W	"	Lava. "	288.6	7 45	
			10 01		"	Bighorn. "	297.6	8 35	
			10 39	D W C	"	Sublette. "	303.2	9 05	
			11 15 Am		"	Toltec. "	308.5	9 35	
			12 31 Pm	D W C	"	Osier. "	316.5	10 15	
			1 05	W C	"	Los Pinos. "	320.3	10 37	
			2 17	D W C	"	Cumbres. "	328.6	11 31	
			2 31		"	Coxo. "	330.4	11 43 AM	
			2 55		"	Siding No. 9 "	333.6	12 02 PM	
			3 30		"	Lobato. "	338.1	12 35	
			4 00 PM	N W C	Arr	Chama. Arr	342.3	1 00	
		6 00 AM			Dep	Chama. Dep		1 30	
		6 25		W	"	Willow Creek. "	347.3	1 47	
		6 52			"	Azotea. "	352.1	2 05	
		7 45			Arr	Monero. Arr	361.3		
		8 15			Dep	Monero. Dep		2 42	
		8 50		N W C	"	Amargo. "	364.9	2 55	
		9 30			"	Dulce "	371.	3 20	
		10 00		W	"	Navajo "	375.8	3 37	
		10 55		D W	"	Juanita "	384.6	4 13	
		11 44 AM		W	"	Carracas "	393.1	4 46	
		12 30 Pm		N W C	"	Arboles "	401.6	5 19	
		12 52			"	Siding No. 22 "	405.	5 32	
		1 17			"	Vallejo "	409.	5 47	
		1 34			"	Solidad "	411.6	5 57	
		1 58			"	Serape "	415.2	6 11	
		2 12		W	"	La Boca "	417.4	6 20	
		2 56		N W C	"	Ignacio "	424.2	6 47	
		3 35			"	Silla "	430.	7 09	
		3 57			"	Colina "	433.6	7 23	
		4 15		W	"	Florida "	435 9	7 32	
		5 23			"	Bocea "	444.6	8 08	
		5 45			"	Carboneria "	447.5	8 18	
		6 00 PM		N W C	Arr	Durango Arr	450.	8 30 PM	
		(12.00)	(8.00)			(171-6)		(13.30)	

All trains will leave terminal Stations daily.

No Train or Engine must leave Antonito, Cumbres or Chama without Conductor or Engineer inquiring at the telegraph office for orders.

When approaching and passing ALL Switches, Engineers must have their Train and Engine under perfect control, READY AT ANY MOMENT to stop.

Trains must not, UNDER ANY CIRCUMSTANCES, exceed Schedule Time, without Special Orders.

San Juan Division—Eastward Trains.

FIRST CLASS.		LENGTH OF SIDINGS—FEET.	TIME TABLE No. 13. Nov. 13th, 1881. STATIONS AND Passing Places.		DISTANCES BETWEEN STATIONS.	SECOND CLASS.					
No. 6. Passenger.						No. 102. Freight.	No. 104. Freight.				
12 30 Pm			Ar	Denver.	Ar						
8 00 Pm			Ar	Antonito.	Ar	278.4	6 00 Pm				
7 15			Dep	Lava.	Dep	10.2	5 00				
6 25			"	Bighorn.	"	9.	3 58				
5 55			"	Sublette.	"	5.6	3 18				
5 25			"	Toltec.	"	5.3	2 40				
4 37			"	Osier.	"	8.	1 35				
4 15			"	Los Pinos.	"	3.8	1 05				
3 24			"	Cumbres.	"	8.3	12 01 PM				
3 14			"	Coxo.	"	1.8	11 43 Am				
2.55			"	Siding No. 9	"	3.2	11 17				
2 25			"	Lobato.	"	4.5	10 36				
2 00			Dep	Chama.	Dep	4.2	10 00 Am				
1 30			Arr	Chama.	Arr			6 35 Pm			
1 10			Dep	Willow Creek.	Dep	5.		6 09			
12 54			"	Azotea.	"	4.8		5 42			
12 20			Dep	Monero.	Dep	9.2		4 50			
			Arr	Monero.	Arr			4 20			
12 07 Pm			Dep	Amargo.	Dep	3.6		3 55			
11 45 Am			"	Dulce	"	6.1		3 20			
11 28			"	Navajo	"	4.8		2 51			
10 55			"	Juanita	"	8.8		2 03			
10 25			"	Carracas	"	8.5		1 16			
9 55			"	Arboles	"	8.5		12 30			
9 43			"	Siding No. 22	"	3.4		12 10 PM			
9 28			"	Vallejo	"	4.		11 45 AM			
9 18			"	Solidad	"	2.6		11 30			
9 05			"	Serape	"	3.6		11 07			
8 58			"	La Boca	"	2.2		10 54			
8 34			"	Ignacio	"	6.8		10 13			
8 12			"	Silla	"	5.8		9 37			
7 59			"	Colina	"	3.6		9 16			
7 50			"	Florida	"	2.3		9 00			
7 18			"	Bocea	"	8.7		7 52			
7 08			"	Carboneria	"	2.9		7 30			
7 00 Am			Dep	Durango	Dep	2.5		7 10 Am			
(13.00)			(171·6)			(8.00)	(11.45)				

All trains leave terminal Stations daily.

No train or engine must leave Durango, Chama or Cumbres without the Conductor or Engineer inquiring at the Telegraph office for orders.

When approaching and passing ALL Switches, Engineers must have their Train and Engine under perfect control, READY AT ANY MOMENT to stop. Trains must not, UNDER ANY CIRCUMSTANCES, exceed Schedule Time, without Special Orders.

Gunnison Division—Westward Trains.

SECOND CLASS.				TELEGRAPH, WATER AND COALING STATIONS.	TIME TABLE No. 13. Nov. 13th, 1881. STATIONS AND Passing Places.			DISTANCES FROM DENVER.	FIRST CLASS.	
			No. 85. Freight.						No. 91. Passenger.	No. 3. Passenger.
				N W	Dep	Denver.	Dep		8 00 Am	7 30 Pm
			6 00 Am	N W C	Dep	Salida	Dep	216.5	7 30 Pm	9 05 Am
			6 30	D W	"	Poncha	"	221.9	Ar 7 50 Pm	9 20
			7 04		"	Toll Gate	"	225.2		9 42
			7 28	D	"-	Mears	"	227.5		10 00
			7 51	D C	"	Shirley	"	229.7		10 15
			8 51		"	Gray's Siding	"	235.5		10 55
			9 59	D	"	Marshall Pass	"	242.1		11 41 AM
			10 31		"	Siding No. 7	"	245.2		12 02 PM
			11 04		"	Mill Switch	"	248.4		12 24
			11 21 Am		"	Siding No. 9	"	250.2		12 36
			12 05 Pm		"	Siding No. 10	"	254.4		1 05
			12 35	D C	"	Sargent	"	258.7		1 20 Ar 1 40 Dep
			1 31		"	Crooks	"	267.1		2 11
			1 57		"	Doyle	"	271.		2 25
			2 55	D	"	Parlins	"	278.9		2 55
			3 17		"	Cochetopa	"	281.9		3 07
			4 15 PM	D W C	Ar	Gunnison	Ar	290.2		3 40 PM
			(10.15)		(101.3)				(20)	(6.35)

Gunnison Division—Maysville Branch.

TRAINS WESTWARD.					DISTANCES FROM DENVER.	TIME TABLE No. 13. Nov. 13th, 1881. STATIONS AND Passing Places.			BETWEEN STATIONS.	TRAINS EASTWARD.		
Second Class.		First Class.								First Class.		2nd Class.
		No. 95. Freight.	No. 93. Passenger.	No. 91. Passenger.						No. 92. Passenger.	No. 94. Passenger.	No. 96. Freight.
			7 30 PM	8 00 Am		Dep	Denver.	Dep		8 00 Pm	6 55 Am	
		6 45 AM	9 25 Am	7 55 Pm	221.9	Dep	Poncha.	Dep	221.9	8 30 Am	6 40 Pm	9 35 Pm
		7 45 AM	10 05 AM	8 35 Pm	228.9	Ar	Maysville.	Ar	7.	7 55 Am	6 05 Pm	8 55 Pm
			(1.00)			(7)				(.40)	(.40)	

All Trains leave terminal stations daily.

No Train or Engine must leave Salida, Poncha Maysville or Gunnison without Conductor and Engineer inquiring at the telegraph office for orders.

When approaching and passing ALL Switches, Engineers must have their Train and Engine under perfect control, READY AT ANY MOMENT to stop.

Trains must not, UNDER ANY CIRCUMSTANCES exceed Schedule Time, without Special Orders.

J. A. MYERS, *Train Master.*

Gunnison Division—Eastward Trains.

FIRST CLASS.		LENGTH OF SIDING—FEET.	TIME TABLE No. 13. Nov. 13th, 1881. STATIONS AND Passing Places.	DISTANCES BETWEEN STATIONS.	SECOND CLASS.					
No. 4. Passenger.	No. 92. Passenger.				No. 86 Freight.					
6 55 Am	8 00 Pm		Ar Denver. Ar							
7 00 Pm	8 55 Am		Ar Salida. Ar	215.5	6 40 Pm					
6 45	8 35 Am		Dep Poncha. Dep	5.4	6 10					
6 23			" Toll Gate, "	3.3	5 40					
6 07			" Mears. "	2.3	5 16					
5 50			" Shirley. "	2.2	4 55					
5 10			" Gray's Siding, "	5.8	4 00					
4 24			" Marshall Pass, "	6.6	3 00					
4 02			" Siding No. 7, "	3.1	2 30					
3 40			" Mill Switch, "	3.2	2 00					
3 28			" Siding No. 9, "	1.7	1 43					
3 00			" Siding No. 10, "	4.3	1 05					
2 43			" Sargent, "	4.3	12 35 Pm					
2 11			" Crooks, "	8.4	11 36 Am					
1 57			" Doyle, "	3.9	11 10					
1 26			" Parlins, "	7.9	10 17					
1 16			" Cochetopa, "	3.0	9 57					
12 45 Pm			Dep Gunnison. Dep	8.3	9 00 Am					
(6.15)	(.20)		(101.2)		(9.15)					

Gunnison Division—Crested Butte Branch.

TRAINS NORTHWARD.		DISTANCE FROM DENVER.	TIME TABLE No. 13. Nov. 13th, 1881. STATIONS AND Passing Places.	DISTANCES BETWEEN STATIONS.	First Class.	TRAINS SOUTHWARD.				
First Class. No. 83. Accom.					No. 84 Accom.					
7 30 Pm			Dep Denver. Ar		6 55 Am					
4 35 Pm		290.2	Dep Gunnison. Ar	290.2	8 50 Am					
5 21		301.	" Taylor River. Dep	10.8	8 07					
5 43		306.	" Jack's Cabin. "	5.	7 46					
6 30 Pm		317.7	Ar Crested Butte. Dep	11.7	7 00 AM					
(1.55)			(27-7)		(1.50)					

All trains leave terminal stations daily.
No Train or Engine must leave Salida, Gunnison or Crested Butte without Conductor or Engineer inquiring at telegraph office for orders.
When approaching and passing ALL Switches, Engineers must have their Train and Engine under perfect control, READY AT ANY MOMENT to stop.
Trains must not, UNDER ANY CIRCUMSTANCES, exceed Schedule Time without Special Orders.
J. A. MYERS, Train Master.

Manitou Branch—Westward Trains.

SECOND CLASS.			TELEGRAPH, WATER AND COALING STATIONS.	TIME TABLE No. 13. Nov. 13th, 1881. STATIONS AND Passing Places.	DISTANCES FROM DENVER.	FIRST CLASS.			
		No. 61. Freight.				No. 63. Passenger.	No. 65. Passenger.	No. 67. Passenger.	
			N W	Dep Denver. Dep		8 00 Am			
		10 00 Am	N W C	Dep Colo. Springs. Dep	75.2	11 40	4 20 Pm	6 00 Pm	
		10 15		" Colorado City. "	77.9	11 50	4 30	6 15	
		10 25		" Quarry. "	79.6	11 56 Am	4 35	6 25	
		10 30 Am	D	Ar Manitou. Ar	80.5	12 00 M	4 40 Pm	6 30 Pm	
		(.30)		(5-3)		(.20)	(.20)	(.30)	

All trains leave terminal Stations daily.

No train or engine must leave Colorado Springs without the Conductor or Engineer inquiring at the telegraph office for orders.

On Theatre nights Train No. 69 will hold at Colorado Springs for parties attending.

Silver Cliff Branch—Westward Trains.

SECOND CLASS.			TELEGRAPH, WATER AND COALING STATIONS.	TIME TABLE No. 13, Nov. 13th, 1881. STATIONS AND Passing Places.	DISTANCES FROM DENVER.	FIRST CLASS.		
		No. 73. Freight.				No. 71. Passenger.		
		7 30 PM		Dep Denver. Dep		8 00 Am		
		6 00 Am		Dep Canon City. Dep	161.	4 10 Pm		
		6 10		" Grape Creek Junc. "	162.8	4 20		
		7 08		" Marsh. "	172.	5 17		
		7 37		" Soda Springs. "	176.8	5 48		
		7 46		" Benton "	178.3	5 58		
		8 19		" Blackburn. "	183.7	6 30		
		8 50		" Govetown. "	188.7	7 03		
		9 25 Am		Ar West Cliff. Ar	194.3	7 35 Pm		
		(3.25)		(33-3)		(3.25)		

All trains run daily.

All Silver Cliff branch trains must protect themselves against main line trains between Grape Creek Junction and Canon City.

First Division—Blue River Branch.

TRAINS WESTWARD.			TIME TABLE No. 13. Nov. 13, 1881. STATIONS AND Passing Places.			TRAINS EASTWARD.			
Second Class.	First Class.	LENGTH OF SIDINGS—FEET.		DISTANCES BETWEEN STATIONS.		First Class.	Second Class.		
No. 55. Freight.	No. 53. Passenger.					No. 54. Passenger.	No. 50. Freight.		
	7 30 Pm		Dep	Denver	Ar		6 55 Am		
4 00 Pm	10 00 Am	278.5	Dep	Leadville.	Ar		3 45 Pm	9 00 Am	
4 40	10 23	283.6	"	Bird's Eye.	Dep	5.1	3 25	8 27	
5 43	10 57	291.4	"	Summit.	"	7.8	2 54	7 37	
6 10 Arr 6 30 Dep	11 12	294.8	"	Robinson.	"	3.4	2 40 Dep 2 35 Arr	7 15	
6 45 Arr 7 00 Dep	11 20	296.5	"	Kokomo.	"	1.7	2 25	7 00 Dep 6 45 Arr	
8 00 Pm	11 55 Am	303.8	Ar	Wheeler's.	Dep	7.3	1 40 Pm	5 45 Am	
(4.00)	(1.55)			(25-3)			(3.30)	(3.15)	

All trains leave terminal Stations daily.

No train or engine must leave Leadville or Wheeler's without the Conductor or Engineer inquiring at the Telegraph office for orders.

COLE LYDON, Train Master.

First Division—Eagle River Branch.

TRAINS WESTWARD.				TIME TABLE No. 13. Nov. 13, 1881. STATIONS AND Passing Places.			TRAINS EASTWARD.			
Second Class.	First Class.	TELEGRAPH, WATER AND COALING STATIONS.	DISTANCE FROM DENVER.			DISTANCES BETWEEN STATIONS.	First Class.	Second Class.		
	No. 33. Passenger.						No. 34 Passenger.			
	7 30 PM			Ar	Denver	Ar		6 55 Am		
	9 15	N C W	277.4	"	Leadville,	"		3 00 Pm		
	9 45	N C W	272.4	"	Malta	"	272.4	2 30		
	9 54		275.1	"	Ryan's	"	2.7	2 20		
	10 09		278.6	"	Keeldar	"	3.5	1 05		
	10 20	D	281.2	"	Crane's Park	"	2.6	1 55		
	10 30		283.1	"	Tennessee Pass	"	1.9	1 45		
	10 50	D	287.1	"	Mitchell's	"	4.	1 25		
	11 15	D	293.8	"	Eagle Park	"	6.7	1 00		
	11 45 AM	D C W	299.1	Dep	Red Cliff	Dep	5.3	12 30 Pm		
	(2.00)				(26-7)			(2.00)		

Trains run daily.

No train or engine must leave Malta, Leadville or Red Cliff without the Conductor or Engineer inquiring at telegraph office for orders.

COLE LYDON, Train Master.

Alpine Branch—Westward Trains.

SECOND CLASS.						Telegraph, Water and Coaling Stations.	TIME TABLE No. 13. Nov. 13, 1881. STATIONS AND Passing Places.		Distances from Denver.	FIRST CLASS.	
										No. 75. Passenger.	No. 77. Passenger.
						N W	Dep	Denver. Dep		7 30 Pm	8 00 Am
						N W	Dep	Nathrop. Dep	235.	8 15 Am	8 20 Pm
						W C	"	Hortense. "	240.5	8 45	8 45
							"	Cascade. "	246.	9 20	9 15
						D W C	Ar	Alpine. Ar	248.5	9 45 Am	9 45 Pm
										(13.5)	(1.30) (1.25)

All trains leave terminal Stations daily.

No train or engine must leave Nathrop without the Conductor or Engineer inquiring at the Telegraph office for orders.

On this Branch Conductors and Engineers will be governed by the Rules, Regulations and Time of the Joint Time Table of the D. & R. G. Ry. and D., S. P. & P. R. R.

Alpine Branch—Eastward Trains.

FIRST CLASS.		LENGTH OF SIDINGS—FEET.	TIME TABLE No. 13. Nov. 13, 1881. STATIONS AND Passing Places.	DISTANCES BETWEEN STATIONS.	SECOND CLASS.				
No. 78. Passenger.	No. 76. Passenger.								
6 55 Am	8 00 Pm		Ar Denver. Ar						
6 35 Pm	6 50 Am		Ar Nathrop. Ar	235.					
6 15	6 30		Dep Hortense. Dep	5.5					
5 35	5 50		" Cascade. "	5.5					
5 20 Pm	5 30 Am		Dep Alpine. Dep	2.5					
(1.15)	(1.20)		(13·5)						

All trains leave terminal Stations daily.

No train or engine must leave Alpine without the Conductor or Engineer inquiring at the Telegraph office for orders.

On this Branch Conductors and Engineers will be governed by the Rules, Regulations and Time of the Joint Time Table of the D. & R. G. Ry. and D., S. P. & P. R. R.

Second Division—El Moro Branch.

TRAINS: SOUTHWARD.						TIME TABLE. No. 13. Nov. 13, 1881. STATIONS AND Passing Places.		TRAINS NORTHWARD.	
Second Class.			**First Class.**	TELEGRAPH, WATER AND COALING STATIONS.	DISTANCES FROM DENVER.		DISTANCES BETWEEN STATIONS.	**First Class.**	**Second Class.**
		No. 45. Freight.	No. 43. Accom.					No. 44. Accom.	No. 46. Freight.
						Dep Denver Ar			
		5 25 Pm	11 20 Am	N C W	169.1	Dep Cuchara Ar		2 10 Pm	11 05 Pm
		6 28	12 05 Pm		179.7	" Santa Clara "	10.6	1 25	10 07
		7 26	12 45	W	189.1	" Apishapa "	9.4	12 45	9 14
		7 55	1 10		194.6	" Barnes "	5.5	12 20 Pm	8 45
		8 20	1 31		198.5	" Chicosa "	3.9	11 58 Am	8 20
		9 00 Pm	2 10 Pm	D C W	205.8	Ar El Moro Dep	7.3	11 20 Am	7 35 Pm
		(3.35)	(2.50)			(36-7)		(2.50)	(3.30)

All trains leave terminal Stations daily.

No train or engine must leave Cuchara or El Moro without the Conductor or Engineer inquiring at the Telegraph office for orders.

Gunnison Division—San Luis Branch.

TRAINS SOUTHWARD.						TIME TABLE. No. 13. Nov. 13, 1881. STATIONS AND Passing Places.		TRAINS NORTHWARD.	
			First Class.	TELEGRAPH, WATER AND COALING STATIONS.	DISTANCES FROM DENVER.		DISTANCE BETWEEN STATIONS.	**First Class.**	
			No. 87. Accom.					No. 88. Accom.	
			7 30 Pm			Dep Denver Ar		6 55 Am	
			10 15 Am		227.5	" Mears, "		5 30 PM	
			10 55		230.8	" Poncha Pass, Dep	3.3	4 50	
			11 25		234.1	" Round Hill, "	3.3	4 20	
			12 35 Pm		246.7	" Villa Grove, "	12.6	3 10	
			1 30 PM		255.2	Ar Iron Mine, Dep	8.5	2 15 PM	
			(3.20)			(27.7)		(3.15)	

Trains run daily.

No train or engine must leave Mears, Villa Grove or Iron Mine without the Conductor or Engineer inquiring at telegraph office for orders.

J. A. MYERS, Train Master.

Manitou Branch—Eastward Trains.

FIRST CLASS.				LENGTH OF SIDINGS—FEET.	TIME TABLE No. 13. Nov. 13, 1881. STATIONS AND Passing Places.	DISTANCES BETWEEN STATIONS.	SECOND CLASS.			
	No. 68. Passenger.	No. 66. Passenger.	No. 64. Passenger.				No. 62. Freight.			
		8 00 Pm			Ar Denver. Ar					
	5 30 Pm	3 20 Pm	11 05 Am		Ar Colo. Springs. Ar	75.2	9 30 Am			
	5 20	3 10	10 55		Dep Colorado City. Dep	2.7	9 15			
	5 05	3 04	10 49		" Quarry. "	1.7	9 05			
	5 00 Pm	3 00 Pm	10 45 Am		Dep Manitou. Dep	.9	9 00 Am			
(.30)	(.20)	(.20)	(.30)	(.20)	(5-3)		(.30)			

All trains leave terminal Stations daily.

No train or engine must leave Manitou without the Conductor or Engineer inquiring at the Telegraph office for orders.

Silver Cliff Branch—Eastward Trains.

FIRST CLASS.		LENGTH OF SIDINGS—FEET.	TIME TABLE No. 13. Nov. 13, 1881. STATIONS AND Passing Places.	DISTANCES BETWEEN STATIONS.	SECOND CLASS.					
	No. 72. Passenger.				No. 74. Freight.					
	8.00 Pm		Ar Denver. Ar		6 55 Am					
	11 25 Am		" Canon City. "	161.	8 40 Pm					
	11 15		Dep Grape Cr'k Jun. Dep	1.8	8 30					
	10 24		" Marsh. "	9.2	7 37					
	9 59		" Soda Springs. "	4.8	7 10					
	9 50		" Benton "	1.5	7 02					
	9 20		" Blackburn. "	5.4	6 30					
	8 50		" Govetown. "	5.	5 59					
	8 15 Am		Dep West Cliff. Dep	5.6	5 25 Pm					
	(3.10)		(33.3)		(3.15)					

All trains run daily.

All Silver Cliff branch trains must protect themselves against main line trains between Grape Creek Junction and Canon City.

Locomotive Dispositions

NARROW-GAUGE STEAM LOCOMOTIVES

AMERICAN SMELTING & REFINING COMPANY

1	Arkansas Valley Smelting Co.	8	1899	2-4-0
2	Arkansas Valley Smelting Co.	103	1899	0-6-0T
3	Colorado & Kansas City Smelting & Refining Co.	?	1899	4-4-0
4	Colorado Eastern RR.	6	1916	2-4-0

ARKANSAS LUMBER COMPANY

?	Rio Grande Southern RR.	36	1900	4-4-0

ARKANSAS VALLEY SMELTING COMPANY

8	Denver & Rio Grande RR.	8	1888	2-4-0
19	Denver & Rio Grande RR.	19	1899	2-6-0
103	Denver & Rio Grande RR.	103	1896	0-6-0T

BERING MANUFACTURING COMPANY

?	Denver & Rio Grande RR.	35	1893	4-4-0

BLACKSOLER-MILLER LUMBER COMPANY

?	Rio Grande Western Ry.	6	1903	2-8-0

BOSTON COAL & FUEL COMPANY

1	Rio Grande Southern RR.	35	1901	2-8-0

BRADFORD, BORDELL & KINZUA RAILROAD

10	Denver & Rio Grande RR.	150	1892	2-6-0

CALUMET FUEL COMPANY

1	Boston Coal & Fuel Co.	1	1906	2-8-0

CAMERON LUMBER MILLS COMPANY

?	Denver & Rio Grande RR.	36	1893	4-4-0

CARMEN ISLAND SALT COMPANY

?	Denver & Rio Grande RR.	88	1892	4-4-0

CAROLINA & NORTHWESTERN RAILROAD

230	Rio Grande Southern RR.	27	1899	2-8-0

CITY OF ALAMOSA, COLORADO (For Preservation)

169	D & R G W RR.	169	1941	4-6-0

CITY OF ANTONITO (For Preservation)

463	Melody Ranch	463	1973	2-8-2

CITY OF BOULDER, COLORADO (For Preservation)

74	Rio Grande Southern RR.	74	1952	2-8-0

CITY OF CAÑON CITY, COLORADO (For Preservation)

486	D & R G W RR.	486	1962	2-8-2

CITY OF COLORADO SPRINGS, COLO. (For Preservation)

168	D & R G W RR.	168	1938	4-6-0

CITY OF DURANGO, COLORADO (For Preservation)

315	D & R G W RR.	315	1950	2-8-0

CITY OF GUNNISON, COLORADO (For Preservation)

268	D & R G W RR.	268	1955	2-8-0

CITY OF MONTROSE, COLORADO (For Preservation)

278	D & R G W RR.	278	1953	2-8-0

CITY OF SALT LAKE CITY, UTAH (For Preservation)

223	D & R G W RR.	223	1941	2-8-0

COLORADO EASTERN RAILROAD

6	Colorado Eastern Ry.	6	1890	2-4-0

COLORADO EASTERN RAILWAY

6	Denver & Scranton RR.	6	1886	2-4-0

COLORADO FUEL & IRON COMPANY

5	Denver & Rio Grande RR.	102	1893	0-6-0T

COLORADO & KANSAS CITY SMELTING & REFINING CO.

?	Denver & Rio Grande RR.	97	1893	4-4-0

COLORADO RAILROAD MUSEUM (For Preservation)

318	D & R G W RR.	318	1954	2-8-0
346	Montezuma Lumber Co.	346	1950	2-8-0

COLORADO & SOUTHWESTERN RAILROAD

1	D & R G W RR.	285	1926	2-8-0
3	D & R G W RR.	349	1926	2-8-0
4	D & R G W RR.	203	1926	2-8-0
5	D & R G W RR.	227	1926	2-8-0

CUMBRES & TOLTEC SCENIC RAILROAD

482	D & R G W RR.	482	1970	2-8-2
483	D & R G W RR.	483	1970	2-8-2
484	D & R G W RR.	484	1970	2-8-2
487	D & R G W RR.	487	1970	2-8-2
488	D & R G W RR.	488	1970	2-8-2
489	D & R G W RR.	489	1970	2-8-2
492	D & R G W RR.	492	1970	2-8-2
494	D & R G W RR.	494	1970	2-8-2
495	D & R G W RR.	495	1970	2-8-2

DENVER & SCRANTON RAILROAD

6	Denver & Rio Grande RR.	6	1886	2-4-0

DILLEY, G. M., & SONS (Dealer)

?	Denver & Rio Grande RR.	15	1891	2-6-0
?	Denver & Rio Grande RR.	11	1899	2-6-0
?	Denver & Rio Grande RR.	89	1893	4-4-0

ELMORE, MIKE (Dealer?)

?	Denver & Rio Grande RR.	20	1900	0-6-0T

FERROCARRIL NACIONALES DE MEXICO

400	D & R G W RR.	458	1941	2-8-2
401	D & R G W RR.	459	1941	2-8-2

FERROCARRIL TORRES & PRIETA

?	Denver & Rio Grande RR.	86	1896	4-4-0

FITZHUGH, LUTHER & COMPANY (Dealer)

?	Rio Grande Western Ry.	2	1903	2-8-0
?	Rio Grande Western Ry.	5	1903	2-8-0
?	Rio Grande Western Ry.	8	1903	2-8-0
?	Rio Grande Western Ry.	12	1904	2-8-0

GEORGE COUSIN LUMBER COMPANY

?	Rio Grande Western Ry.	10	1903	2-8-0

GHOST TOWN & CALICO RAILROAD

40	D & R G W RR.	340	1952	2-8-0
41	Rio Grande Southern RR.	41	1952	2-8-0
464	D & R G W RR.	464	1973	2-8-2

GURDON LUMBER COMPANY

?	Denver & Rio Grande RR.	85	1900	4-4-0

HALLACK & HOWARD LUMBER COMPANY

1	Rust, A. A.	56	1906	2-8-0
3	Denver & Rio Grande RR.	40	1917	2-8-0

JOSSERAND LUMBER COMPANY

?	Denver & Rio Grande RR.	14	1892	2-6-0

LA PLATA COAL COMPANY

23	Denver & Rio Grande RR.	23	1891	2-6-0

LAWS & BIGGS LUMBER COMPANY

28	Denver & Rio Grande RR.	28	1890	2-6-0

LESTER MILL COMPANY (Lumber)

?	Rio Grande Western Ry.	9	1903	2-8-0

LITTLE BOOK CLIFF RAILWAY

1	Denver & Rio Grande RR.	5	1889	0-6-0T

LIVINGSTON LUMBER COMPANY

?	Rio Grande Western Ry.	7	1903	2-8-0

MELODY RANCH (Amusement)

463	D & R G W RR.	463	1955	2-8-2

NARROW-GAUGE STEAM LOCOMOTIVE DISPOSITIONS Continued

MONTEZUMA LUMBER COMPANY

| 271 | D & R G W RR. | 271 | 1941 | 2-8-0 |
| 346 | D & R G W RR. | 346 | 1941 | 2-8-0 |

MORENCI SOUTHERN RAILROAD

10	Rio Grande Southern RR.	28	1900	2-8-0
11	Rio Grande Southern RR.	31	1900	2-8-0
12	Rio Grande Southern RR.	29	1900	2-8-0

NARROW GAUGE MOTEL (For Preservation)

| 42 | Rio Grande Southern RR. | 42 | 1953 | 2-8-0 |

NEVADA COUNTY NARROW GAUGE RAILROAD

| 283 | D & R G W RR. | 283 | 1933 | 2-8-0 |

NORTH SHORE RAILROAD

| 40 | Denver & Rio Grande RR. | 44 | 1903 | 2-8-0 |

RED CYPRESS LUMBER COMPANY

| ? | Rio Grande Western Ry. | 4 | 1903 | 2-8-0 |

RICE, S. S. & W. M. (Lumber)

| ? | Rio Grande Western Ry. | 24 | 1900 | 4-6-0 |

RIO GRANDE, PAGOSA & NORTHERN RAILROAD

2	Rio Grande & Pagosa Springs RR.	3	1912	2-6-0
37	Denver & Rio Grande RR.	37	1907	2-8-0
70	Denver & Rio Grande RR.	70	1907	2-8-0

RIO GRANDE & PAGOSA SPRINGS RAILROAD

1	Denver & Rio Grande RR.	153	1895	2-6-0
2	Denver & Rio Grande RR.	46	1903	2-8-0
3	Tierra Amarilla Southern RR.	2	1900	2-6-0

ROBINSON LAND & LUMBER COMPANY

| ? | Rio Grande Western Ry. | 14 | 1903 | 2-8-0 |

ROCKY MOUNTAIN RAILROAD CLUB (For Preservation)

| 20 | Rio Grande Southern RR. | 20 | 1952 | 4-6-0 |

RUST, A. A. (Lumber)

| 56 | Denver & Rio Grande RR. | 56 | 1902 | 2-8-0 |

SABINE TRAMWAY COMPANY

| ? | Denver & Rio Grande RR. | 27 | 1889 | 2-6-0 |

SANFORD & ST. PETERSBURG RAILROAD

?	Denver & Rio Grande RR.	99	1894	4-4-0
5	Denver & Rio Grande RR.	95	1894	4-4-0
?	Denver & Rio Grande RR.	92	1894	4-4-0
11	Denver & Rio Grande RR.	87	1894	4-4-0

SAN FRANCISCO CONTRACTING CO. (Construction)

| ? | Denver & Rio Grande RR. | 3 | 1888 | 0-6-0T |
| ? | Denver & Rio Grande RR. | 11 | 1888 | 0-6-0T |

SILVERTON RAILROAD

| 100 | Denver & Rio Grande RR. | 42 | 1887 | 2-8-0 |
| 101 | Rio Grande Southern RR. | 34 | 1892 | 2-8-0 |

SILVERTON, GLADSTONE & NORTHERLY RAILROAD

| 32 | Rio Grande Southern RR. | 32 | 1899 | 2-8-0 |
| 33 | Rio Grande Southern RR. | 33 | 1902 | 2-8-0 |

SILVERTON NORTHERN RAILROAD

| 1 | Silverton RR. | 101 | 1896 | 2-8-0 |

SISKIWIT & IRON RIVER RAILWAY

| ? | Rio Grande Southern RR. | 34 | 1899 | 0-4-4-0TG |

STEWART, R. W., & COMPANY (Lumber)

| ? | Denver & Rio Grande RR. | 17 | 1888 | 4-4-0 |

STREETER & KENNEFICK (Construction)

| ? | Denver & Rio Grande RR. | 21 | 1893 | 0-6-0T |
| ? | Denver & Rio Grande RR. | 98 | 1893 | 0-6-0T |

SULLENBERGER, A. T., & COMPANY (Lumber)

| Azotea | Denver & Rio Grande RR. | 2 | 1888 | 0-6-0T |
| 29 | Denver & Rio Grande RR. | 29 | 1888 | 2-6-0 |

SUMPTER VALLEY RAILROAD

| 6 | Rio Grande Western Ry. | 02 | 1900 | 2-8-0 |
| 7 | Rio Grande Western Ry. | 04 | 1900 | 2-8-0 |

TECHE RAILROAD & LUMBER COMPANY

| ? | Denver & Rio Grande RR. | 91 | 1893 | 4-4-0 |

TIERRA AMARILLA SOUTHERN RAILROAD

| 1 | Laws & Biggs Lumber Co. | 28 | 1895 | 2-6-0 |
| 2 | La Plata Coal Co. | 23 | 1895 | 2-6-0 |

TORBETT, A. C..(Dealer?)

| ? | Denver & Rio Grande RR. | 12 | 1899 | 0-6-0T |

UINTAH RAILWAY

| 11 | Denver & Rio Grande RR. | 55 | 1904 | 2-8-0 |

WHITE PASS & YUKON ROUTE

250	D & R G W RR.	470	1942	2-8-2
251	D & R G W RR.	471	1942	2-8-2
252	D & R G W RR.	472	1942	2-8-2
253	D & R G W RR.	474	1942	2-8-2
254	D & R G W RR.	475	1942	2-8-2
255	D & R G W RR.	477	1942	2-8-2
256	D & R G W RR.	479	1942	2-8-2

YELLOW PINE LUMBER COMPANY

| ? | Rio Grande Southern RR. | 14 | 1899 | 0-6-0T |

STANDARD-GAUGE STEAM LOCOMOTIVES

BARRY EQUIPMENT COMPANY (Dealer)

| ? | Denver & Rio Grande RR. | 941 | 1917 | 2-6-0 |

BROWN, J. E. (Lumber?)

| ? | Denver & Rio Grande RR. | 503 | 1906 | 4-6-0 |
| ? | Denver & Rio Grande RR. | 505 | 1906 | 4-6-0 |

COLORADO - KANSAS RAILROAD

| 2 | D & R G W RR. | 621 | 1921 | 2-8-0 |

COLORADO RAILROAD MUSEUM (For Preservation)

| 583 | Southern San Luis Valley | 106 | 1962 | 2-8-0 |

COLORADO & SOUTHEASTERN RAILROAD

| 1 | Denver & Rio Grande RR. | 581 | 1903 | 2-8-0 |
| 5 | D & R G W RR. | 605 | 1951 | 2-8-0 |

COLORADO & WYOMING RAILWAY

| 701 | Denver & Rio Grande RR. | 512 | 1903 | 4-6-0 |

COLUMBIA STEEL COMPANY

55	D & R G W RR.	55	1943	0-6-0
56	D & R G W RR.	56	1943	0-6-0
57	D & R G W RR.	57	1943	0-6-0

CRYSTAL RIVER & SAN JUAN RAILROAD

| 1 | Denver & Rio Grande RR. | 532 | 1915 | 4-6-0 |

DEEP CREEK RAILWAY

| 1 | Denver & Rio Grande RR. | 543 | 1916 | 4-6-0 |
| 2 | Denver & Rio Grande RR. | 597 | 1916 | 4-6-0 |

DENVER & INTERMOUNTAIN RAILROAD

| 1 | Denver & Rio Grande RR. | 823 | 1917 | 2-6-0 |
| 2 | Denver & Rio Grande RR. | 814 | 1917 | 2-6-0 |

DENVER, LAKEWOOD & GOLDEN RAILROAD

| 1 | Denver & Rio Grande RR. | 504 | 1899 | 4-6-0 |

ELK CREEK COAL COMPANY

1	Denver & Rio Grande RR.	809	1917	2-6-0

GENEVA STEEL DIVISION, U. S. STEEL CORPORATION

1143	D & R G W RR.	1143	1956	2-8-0
1180	D & R G W RR.	1180	1956	2-8-0

HAYDEN COAL COMPANY

61	D & R G W RR.	61	1944	0-6-0

INDIAN VALLEY RAILROAD

1	Denver & Rio Grande RR.	661	1916	2-8-0
2	Denver & Rio Grande RR.	668	1916	2-8-0

LIST CONSTRUCTION COMPANY

?	D & R G W RR.	603	1927	2-8-0
?	D & R G W RR.	656	1928	2-8-0

MORSE BROTHERS MACHINERY COMPANY

1	D & R G W RR.	1	1924	0-4-4-0TG
2	D & R G W RR.	2	1926	0-4-4-0TG
3	D & R G W RR.	3	1934	0-4-4-0TG
4	D & R G W RR.	4	1926	0-4-4-0TG
5	D & R G W RR.	5	1936	0-4-4-0TG

SAN LUIS VALLEY SOUTHERN RAILROAD

103	D & R G W RR.	657	1928	2-8-0
104	D & R G W RR.	633	1944	2-8-0
105	D & R G W RR.	688	1945	2-8-0
106	D & R G W RR.	683	1947	2-8-0

SOUTHERN SAN LUIS VALLEY RAILROAD

103	San Luis Valley Southern RR.	103	1955	2-8-0
104	San Luis Valley Southern RR.	104	1955	2-8-0
105	San Luis Valley Southern RR.	105	1955	2-8-0
106	San Luis Valley Southern RR.	106	1955	2-8-0

WESTERN PACIFIC RAILROAD

126	Denver & Rio Grande RR.	546	1917	4-6-0
127	Denver & Rio Grande RR.	549	1917	4-6-0

WHEELING & LAKE ERIE RAILWAY

6807	D & R G W RR.	1550	1948	4-8-2
6808	D & R G W RR.	1551	1948	4-8-2
6809	D & R G W RR.	1552	1948	4-8-2
6810	D & R G W RR.	1553	1948	4-8-2

WYOMING RAILWAY

1	Denver & Rio Grande RR.	943	1917	2-6-0

DIESEL-ELECTRIC LOCOMOTIVES

ALASKA RAILROAD

1517	D & R G W RR.	5552	1970	B-B
1524	D & R G W RR.	5571	1970	B-B
1525	D & R G W RR.	5653	1970	B-B
1530	D & R G W RR.	5654	1970	B-B
1532	D & R G W RR.	5664	1970	B-B
1520	D & R G W RR.	5711	1970	B-B
1528	D & R G W RR.	5714	1970	B-B
1526	D & R G W RR.	5724	1970	B-B
1519	D & R G W RR.	5732	1970	B-B
1521	D & R G W RR.	5743	1970	B-B
1522	D & R G W RR.	5744	1970	B-B
1523	D & R G W RR.	5753	1970	B-B

AMERICAN CRYSTAL SUGAR COMPANY

?	D & R G W RR.	5644	1969	B-B

COLORADO & WYOMING RAILWAY

1104	D & R G W RR.	115	1965	B-B
1105	D & R G W RR.	109	1965	B-B

GREAT LAKES CARBON COMPANY

?	D & R G W RR.	38	1964	B-B

GREAT WESTERN SUGAR COMPANY

40	D & R G W RR.	40	1954	B-B

KENTUCKY & TENNESSEE RAILWAY

101	D & R G W RR.	110	1963	B-B
102	D & R G W RR.	118	1963	B-B
103	D & R G W RR.	119	1963	B-B

MISSOURI PACIFIC RAILROAD

848	D & R G W RR.	5684	1967	B-B
848B	D & R G W RR.	5683	1967	B-B
849	D & R G W RR.	5694	1967	B-B
849B	D & R G W RR.	5693	1967	B-B

PENN CENTRAL TRANSPORTATION COMPANY

?	D & R G W RR.	5641	1970	B-B
?	D & R G W RR.	5642	1970	B-B
?	D & R G W RR.	5663	1970	B-B
?	D & R G W RR.	5664	1970	B-B
?	D & R G W RR.	5673	1970	B-B
?	D & R G W RR.	5691	1970	B-B
?	D & R G W RR.	5712	1970	B-B
?	D & R G W RR.	5721	1970	B-B
?	D & R G W RR.	5733	1970	B-B
?	D & R G W RR.	5754	1970	B-B

ROARING CAMP & BIG TREES RAILROAD

?	D & R G W RR.	50	1970	B

SANFORD & EASTERN RAILROAD

14	D & R G W RR.	39	1949	B-B
15	D & R G W RR.	43	1949	B-B

SOUTHERN PACIFIC COMPANY

9021	D & R G W RR.	4001	1964	C-C
9022	D & R G W RR.	4002	1964	C-C
9023	D & R G W RR.	4003	1964	C-C

UNITED ELECTRIC COAL COMPANIES

115	D & R G W RR.	115	1964	B-B

UTAH POWER & LIGHT COMPANY

41	D & R G W RR.	41	1954	B-B

WEIRTON STEEL CORPORATION

?	D & R G W RR.	108	1964	B-B

Bibliography

"American Railways As Investments," C. Snyder.

"America's Wonderlands," J. W. Buel.

"Annual Reports," D&RG Ry., D&RG RR., D&RGW Ry., D&RGW RR., RGS RR., RGW Ry.

"Baldwin Locomotives" (magazine), Baldwin Locomotive Works.

"Brand Books," The Westerners, Denver Posse.

"Brief Historical Sketch of the Rio Grande," D&RGW RR.

"Bulletin 77," Railway & Locomotive Historical Society.

"A Century of Passenger Trains," J. C. Thode.

"Chili Line," J. A. Gjevre.

"Colorado," F. Fossett.

"Colorado Eastern Railroad," C. S. Ryland.

"Colorado Magazine," State Historical Society of Colorado.

"Colorado Midland," W. M. Cafky.

"Colorado's Mountain Railroads," R. A. LeMassena.

"Colorado Rail Annuals," Colorado Railroad Museum.

"The Colorado Road," F. H. Wagner.

"Construction and Filing Map Records," D&RG Ry., D&RG RR., D&RGW Ry., D&RGW RR., RGS RR., RGW Ry.

"Crest of the Continent," R. Ingersoll.

"The Crystal River Pictorial," D. A. McCoy and R. Collman.

"Decisions," Public Utilities Commission of Colorado.

"Denver, Longmont & Northwestern Railroad," B. L. Boyles.

"Denver & Rio Grande Western Magazine," D&RGW RR.

"Denver, South Park & Pacific," M. C. Poor.

"Development of the Physical Property," A. C. Ridgway.

"Documentary History of the CB&Q Railroad," W. W. Baldwin.

"Early Financing of the D&RG Railway," H. O. Brayer.

"Earning Power of the Railroads," F. W. Mundy.

"Electrification Reports," D&RG RR., General Electric Co., Westinghouse Electric & Mfg. Co.

"Employees' Time Tables," D&RG Ry., D&RG RR., D&RGW Ry., D&RGW RR., RGS RR., RGW Ry.

"Equipment Folios and Rosters," D&RG RR., D&RGW Ry., D&RGW RR., RGS RR., RGW Ry.

"Feather River Route," Western Pacific RR.

"Fifty Candles for Western Pacific," G. H. Kneiss.

"First Five Years of the Railroad Era in Colorado," E. O. Davis.

"General William J. Palmer," G. L. Anderson.

"Green Light," employees' magazine, D&RGW RR.

"Guide to Colorado," G. A. Crofutt.

"Guide Books to the Western United States," U. S. Geological Survey.

"Gulf to Rockies," R. C. Overton.

"History of the Baldwin Locomotive Works," Baldwin Locomotive Works.

"History of Colorado," J. H. Baker and L. R. Hafen.

"History of Colorado," F. Hall.

"History of Denver," J. S. Smiley.

"Important Contracts," D&RG RR., RGS RR., RGW Ry.

"Intermountain Railroads," M. D. Beal.

"Locomotive Catalogs," Baldwin Locomotive Works.

"Locomotive Specifications," Baldwin Locomotive Works.

"Locomotives of the Western Pacific," G. L. Dunscomb.

"Logging Along the Denver & Rio Grande," G. S. Chappell.

"Manual of Investments — Railroads / Transportation," J. Moody.

"Manual of Railroads," H. V. Poor.

"Marvels of the New West," W. N. Thayer.

"Metal Magic," I. F. Marcosson.

"The Moffat Road," E. T. Bollinger and F. Bauer.

"Narrow Gauge in the Rockies," L. Beebe and C. Clegg.

"Narrow Gauge Locomotives," Baldwin Locomotive Works.

"New Mexico Railroader," New Mexico Railroad Club.

"New Overland Tourist," G. A. Crofutt.

"Official Guide to the Railways of the United States," National Railway Publication Co.

"Over the Range," S. Wood.

"Picture Maker of the Old West," C. S. Jackson.

"Profile Charts," D&RG Ry., D&RG RR., D&RGW Ry., D&RGW RR., RGS RR., RGW Ry.

"Railroad Development in the Colorado Region to 1880," S. D. Mock.

"Railroads and the Rockies," R. M. Ormes.

"Rails Around Gold Hill," W. M. Cafky.

"Railroad Red Book," D&RG RR., D&RGW RR.

"Rebel of the Rockies," R. G. Athearn.

"Records of Recent Construction," Baldwin Locomotive Works.

"Report of the Railroad Commissioner of Colorado, 1885," State of Colorado.

"Rio Grande, Mainline of the Rockies," L. Beebe and C. Clegg.

"The Rio Grande Pictorial," R. Collman and D. A. McCoy.

"Rio Grande Southern Story," J. M. Crum.

"Rocky Mountain Official Railway Guide," Rocky Mountain Official Guide Co.

"Santa Fe," J. Marshall

"Silver San Juan," M. H. Ferrell.

"Slopes of the Sangre de Cristo," D&RG RR.

"Steam in the Rockies," C. W. Hauck and R. W. Richardson.

"Titan of the Timber," M. Koch.

"Story of Western Railroads," R. E. Riegel.

"Union Pacific Country," R. G. Athearn.

"Valuation Reports for AT&SF, CB&Q, C&S, D&RG, UP Railroads," Interstate Commerce Commission.

"Wall Street 50 Years After Erie," E. Howard.

"Western Pacific," S. Crump.

"Western Pacific—Its First Forty Years," F. B. Whitman.

"Western Pacific Railroad Company," S. T. Borden.

INDEX

Index Continued

Index Continued

Index Continued

LIST OF ILLUSTRATIONS

Motive Power

Index Continued

DENVER & RIO GRANDE RAILWAY.

CONDENSED TIME CARD.

WESTWARD	SOUTHWARD		Distances bet. Stations.	NAMES —OF— STATIONS.	Distances from Denver.	NORTHWARD.		EASTWARD.
NO. 7.	NO. 5.	NO. 1.				NO. 2.	NO. 6.	NO. 8.
Accommodation.	Accommodation.	Express.				Express.	Accommodation.	Accommodation.
	Le. 3.55 p. m.	Le. 7.45 a. m.	.0	......DENVER......	.0	Ar. 5.25 p. m.	Ar. 11.10 a.m.	
	4.10 "	7.58 "	2.2	MACHINE SHOPS	2.2	5.15 "	10.55 "	
	4.35 "	8.15 "	5.8	...PETERSBURG...	8.0	4.58 "	10 32 "	
	4 50 "	8 23 "	2 6	...LITTLETON...	10 6	4.50 "	1 22 "	
	5.25 "	8.48 "	6 9	...ACEQUIA...	17 5	4.29 "	9.47 "	
	6.00 "	9 07 "	7 2	...PLUM...	24 7	4.02 "	9.07 "	
	6 22 "	9.25 "	4.4	...MILL NO. 2...	29 1	3.48 "	8.40 "	
	6.41 "	9.39 "	3.7	CASTLE ROCK..	32.8	3.38 "	8.10 "	
	7.10 "	10.00 "	5.8	...GLADE...	38 6	3.20 "	7.40 "	
	7.35 "	10.18 "	4.7	...LARKSPUR...	43 3	3 06 "	7.15 "	
	7.55 "	10 33 "	3.8	...GREENLAND...	47.1	2 55 "	Le. 6 55 "	*
							Ar. 6.35 "	*
	Ar. 8.20 "	Ar.10.55 " Le.11.00 "	5.3	...DIVIDE...	52 4	Le.2.40 " Ar.2.38 "	Le.6.10 a. m.	
		11 12 "	3.6	...MONUMENT...	56 0	2 22 "		
		11.32 "	6.	...HUSTED'S...	62.0	1 53 "		
		11.49 "	5 0	...EDGERTON...	67 0	1.35 "		
		*Ar.12.15 p.m Le. 12.50 "	8.2	...COL'O SPRINGS..	75.2	Le. 1.05 " Ar.12.30 "		*
		1.18 "	.8	...WIDEFIELD....	84.0	12 02 p. m.		
		1.33 "	4 6	...FOUNTAIN.....	88.6	11.49 a. m.		
		1 50 "	5.7	LITTLE BUTTES	94 3	11.30 "		
		2.55 "	23 2	NORTH PUEBLO	117 5	10.15 "		
Le. 6.30 a. m.	Ar. 3.05 " Le. 3.10 "	2.5	SOUTH PUEBLO	120.0	Le.10.05 " Ar. 9.58 "	Ar. 2 50 p. m.		
6.55 "		3 25 "	4 4	...GOODNIGHT...	124.4	9.48 "	2 25 "	
7.45 "		3 58 "	9.6	...SWALLOWS....	134 0	9.10 "	1.35 "	
8.20 "		4.25 "	6.5	CARLILE SPR'GS	140 5	8.48 "	1.00 "	
8.38 "		4.55 "	2 7	BEAVER CREEK	143 2	8.38 "	12.45 p. m.	
9.20 "		5 05 "	8 8	...LABRAN......	152 0	8.08 a. m.	12.00 m.	
			2.4	...COAL BANKS...	155.0		Le.11.40 a. m. Ar.11.20 "	
			.6	COAL JUNCTION	152 6		Le.11.05 "	
9.25 "		5.48 "	.6	COAL JUNCTION	152.6	8.05 "	Ar.11.05 "	
Ar. 10.05 "		Ar. 5 40 "	7.9	...CANON CITY...	160 5	Le. 7 35 a. m.	Le.10-25 a. m.	

*) STOP FOR MEALS.

Trains Nos. 1 and 2 Run Dally.
Trains Nos. 5, 7, and 8 Run Dally Except Sundays.
Train No. 6 Runs Dally Except Mondays.

ALL TRAINS RUN ON DENVER TIME.

CHICAGO - SAN FRANCISCO
VIA
OMAHA - DENVER - SALT LAKE CITY - OGDEN - RENO - SACRAMENTO

READ DOWN		ISSUED MARCH 23, 1970		READ UP
Leave CHICAGO Sunday Wednesday Friday	Miles From Chicago	TRI-WEEKLY SCHEDULE STATIONS		Arrive CHICAGO Wednesday Saturday Monday
NO. 11		BURLINGTON NORTHERN		NO. 12
11 59 AM CST	0	Lv CHICAGO, ILL. (Union Station)	Ar	8 40 PM CST
2 55 PM "	162	Lv Galesburg, Ill.	Ar	5 00 PM "
3 45 PM "	206	Lv Burlington, Ia.	Ar	4 05 PM "
9 10 PM "	501	Lv Omaha, Nebr.	Ar	9 45 AM "
10 25 PM "	556	Lv Lincoln, Nebr.	Ar	8 34 AM "
1 44 AM MST	784	Lv McCook, Nebr.	Ar	3 25 AM MST
6 00 AM "	1039	Ar DENVER, COLO.	Lv	11 30 PM "
Arrive and leave DENVER Monday Thursday Saturday		DENVER & RIO GRANDE WESTERN RIO GRANDE ZEPHYR		Arrive and leave DENVER Tuesday Friday Sunday
NO.17				NO. 18
6 30 AM MST	1039	Lv DENVER, COLO.	Ar	11 00 PM MST
9 05 AM "	1114	Lv Granby, Colo.	♦ Lv	8 35 PM "
10 30 AM "	1168	Lv Bond, Colo.	♦ Lv	7 00 PM "
12 05 PM "	1224	Lv Glenwood Springs, Colo.	Lv	5 20 PM "
12 40 PM "	1251	Lv Rifle, Colo.	♦ Lv	4 45 PM "
2 00 PM "	1313	Ar Grand Junction, Colo.	Ar	3 25 PM "
2 15 PM "	1313	Lv Grand Junction, Colo.	Lv	3 10 PM "
3 40 PM "	1392	Lv Thompson, Utah	♦ Lv	1 45 PM "
x4 05 PM "	1419	Lv Green River, Utah	♦ Lv	x1 15 PM "
5 20 PM "	1483	Lv Price, Utah	Lv	12 10 PM "
5 38 PM "	1490	Lv Helper, Utah	♦ Lv	11 55 AM "
7 35 PM "	1565	Lv Provo, Utah	♦ Lv	9 50 AM "
8 30 PM "	1609	Ar SALT LAKE CITY, UTAH	Lv	9 00 AM "
9 00 PM "	1609	Lv SALT LAKE CITY, UTAH	Note A Lv	8 30 AM "
10 15 PM "	1646	Ar Ogden, Utah	Note A Lv	7 15 AM "
NO. 101 Leave OGDEN Monday Thursday Saturday		(Train to train transfer) SOUTHERN PACIFIC CITY OF SAN FRANCISCO (Connecting Train)		NO. 102 Arrive OGDEN Tuesday Friday Sunday
10 30 PM MST	1646	Lv OGDEN, UTAH	Ar	7 00 AM MST
7 30 AM PST	2186	Lv Reno, Nev.	Lv	8 02 PM PST
12 30 PM "	2339	Ar Sacramento, Calif.	Lv	3 20 PM "
3 15 PM "	2426	Ar Oakland, Calif. (16th St.)	Lv	1 00 PM "
		(Via Bus over the Bay Bridge)		
3 45 PM "	2432	Ar San Francisco, Calif	Lv	12 30 PM "
		(S.P. 3rd St. Station)		
Arrive Tuesday Friday Sunday				Leave Monday Thursday Saturday

CST—Central Standard Time   MST—Mountain Standard Time
PST—Pacific Standard Time

EQUIPMENT
Vista Dome Chair Car (All Seats Reserved)—Chicago-Ogden.
Chair Car—(All Seats Reserved)—Ogden-Oakland.
Sleeping Cars—Chicago-Ogden and Ogden-Oakland (Roomettes and Bedrooms).
Chicago-Salt Lake City (Drawing-room and Bedrooms).
Meal and Lounge Service—Chicago-Salt Lake City; Ogden-Oakland.

REFERENCES
♦ No checked baggage handled at this station.
x Stops on flag to discharge revenue passengers, also to receive revenue passengers holding advance reservations made through Agent, Thompson, Price or Helper, Utah.

Note A—Utah intrastate passengers will not be handled between Salt Lake City and Ogden on Trains 17 and 18. As heretofore such passengers will be handled on Union Pacific trains between Salt Lake City and Ogden.

Pounding upgrade in the late afternoon sun, 2-8-8-2 Number 3610 was captured on film by the late, great railroad photographer, Otto Perry. As the dark clouds of a Rocky Mountain thunderstorm rolled over the hills at Tennessee Pass, this giant D&RGW articulated steam locomotive lifted a heavy freight train up the east slope of the Great Divide — heading toward the tunnel near the summit of the pass, 10,240 feet above sea level.

Eratum — The following items were inadvertently omitted from the text:
Page 195 — 1964 —
    3029-3038
    General Motors   DE B-B 62   GP 35

These diesel-electric locomotives were replacements for General Motors FT units which were retired.
Page 404 — Locomotive Dispositions —
    MAGIC MOUNTAIN RAILROAD
    42   Narrow Gauge Motel   42   1962   2-8-0

Twin Steel threads that vanish in the Setting sun

The Denver & Rio Grande Western main-line along the mystical Rio Colorado.

THE END